THE CASE FOR WOMEN
IN MEDIEVAL CULTURE

FOR
HANNAH AND SIMON

The Case for Women in Medieval Culture

ALCUIN BLAMIRES

CLARENDON PRESS · OXFORD
1997

Oxford University Press, Great Clarendon Street, Oxford OX2 6DP
Oxford New York
Athens Auckland Bangkok Bogota Bombay
Buenos Aires Calcutta Cape Town Dar es Salaam
Delhi Florence Hong Kong Istanbul Karachi
Kuala Lumpur Madras Madrid Melbourne
Mexico City Nairobi Paris Singapore
Taipei Tokyo Toronto
and associated companies in
Berlin Ibadan

Oxford is a trade mark of Oxford University Press

Published in the United States by
Oxford University Press Inc., New York

British Library Cataloguing in Publication Data
Data available

Library of Congress Cataloging in Publication Data
Data available

ISBN 0–19–818256–2

Typeset by Best-set Typesetter Ltd., Hong Kong
Printed in Great Britain
on acid-free paper by
Biddles Ltd.,
Guildford and King's Lynn

Acknowledgements

THE research for this project has been invigorated by opportunities to present its fledgeling ideas at several conferences. My thanks to Lesley Smith and Jane Taylor for the memorable stimulus of their medieval conference on women and the book; to Andrew Taylor and David Townsend for enabling me to explore Abelard for a medieval Latin conference; and to Kari Børresen, Sofia Gajano, and Anneke Mulder-Bakker for giving me the challenge of sharing ideas in a European context. It is also a pleasure to thank Gail Holian and her colleagues at Georgian Court College. For generous help with primary materials I am indebted to C. W. Marx, to Simon Tugwell, Oliver Pickering, and David D'Avray. Colleagues who have kindly answered queries or have supplied me with valuable offprints and drafts of their own work include Karen Pratt, Alastair Minnis, Felicity Riddy, Karen Winstead, Jocelyn Wogan-Browne, Roger Ellis, and Peter Biller. For various other kinds of encouragement, support, hints on reading, etc., I would like to thank especially Helen Cooper, Renate Blumenfeld-Kosinski, Nick Watson, Carolyn Muessig, Helen Phillips, Christine Jones, Linda Georgianna, and Rosalynn Voaden. Kathy Miles at University of Wales Lampeter cheerfully obtained recherché materials for me. But, much more than formal acknowledgement can ever express, I owe to Barbara Blamires my deepest debt for living with the writing of this book.

A.B.

Contents

Abbreviations   viii

Introduction   1

1. The Formal Case: The Corpus   19

2. The Formal Case: Origins, Procedures   50

3. Honouring Mothers   70

4. Eve and the Privileges of Women   96

5. The Stable Sex   126

6. Exemplifying Feminine Stability   153

7. Profeminine Role-Models   171

8. The Formal Case in Abelard, Chaucer, Christine de Pizan   199

Conclusion   231

Bibliography   245

Index   269

Abbreviations

CSEL   Corpus Scriptorum Ecclesiasticorum Latinorum
EETS   Early English Text Society
PG   *Patrologia Graeca*, ed. J.-P. Migne, 162 vols. (Paris, 1857–66), cited by volume and column
PL   *Patrologia Latina*, ed. J.-P. Migne, 221 vols. (Paris, 1844–64), cited by volume and column
SATF   Société des Anciens Textes Français

Introduction

'I HATE the way men are always talking about *women*. "*Women* do this," and "*Women* do that"—as though all women were exactly the same!' This protest by Rosemary in Orwell's *Keep the Aspidistra Flying* only incites her partner Gordon to generalize rampantly that every woman wants financial security, two babies, suburbia, and aspidistras: a diatribe of such 'palpable nonsense', according to Orwell, that Rosemary's exasperation gives way to merely routine and merry argument upon 'the eternal and idiotic question of Man versus Woman', an argument in which 'the moves . . . were always very much the same'.[1]

There is much about this scene that is reminiscent of medieval debate about women, including the suggestion that protest against misogyny is somehow foiled by misogyny's own high-spirited excess, which gets away with insult by producing a situation in which pursuit of protest would seem 'idiotic', or just a game. Particularly interesting (as this introduction will go on to show) is the perception that a classic starting-point for profeminine statement is simple reaction to generalization about women. Orwell also points us to the conventionality of gender polemic: the moves are always the same. Medievalists are very aware of 'the moves' in misogynous literature. They are less aware of the long-standing medieval tradition in defence of women. This book is about the roots of that tradition. Because it *was* a 'defence', generally presupposing that there were allegations to be answered (and indeed adopting strategies of judicial rhetoric), we may properly think of it as 'the case' for women. A moment's thought will suggest to the reader, accurately and revealingly, that Western cultural history discloses no matching 'case' for men: they have not hitherto needed one.

Of course there existed in the Middle Ages various laws purportedly in defence of women, for example against rape, and

[1] George Orwell, *Keep the Aspidistra Flying* (London: Secker & Warburg, 1954), 142–3.

there are records of judicial proceedings in which specific women were defended. These are major issues of feminist history but they are not explicit elements of the 'case' to be discussed here.[2] The nearest we shall come to proceedings affecting women's actual rights, as opposed to adoption of courtroom metaphors, is in the context of formal scholastic debate about categories of person who are or are not qualified to preach and to be ordained. In that context a mild 'case' is made for women, though it is usually one fabricated by someone whose objective is to establish the opposite.

Since what I mean by the case for women in medieval culture— a corpus of ideas about how to fashion a commendation of women explicitly or implicitly retaliating against misogyny—is a sufficiently capacious subject, it is important that readers distinguish it from several other sorts of discussion which might easily be confused with it. First, the 'case' to be heard is not a new feminist theory about medieval women; rather, it is a study of an aspect of medieval discourse on women (though, of course, such a study must necessarily be indebted to contemporary feminist debate). Second, I do not aspire to produce analysis of all possible ways in which an affirmative profile of women *was* produced in medieval culture; that would be a mind-boggling assignment. Third, this is not a 'case' which is presumed to have been made or championed fundamentally by medieval women. To the contrary (as will emerge), it may at many points have been a case which women would not eagerly have evolved for themselves, or even have wished to evolve, if they had exercised anything like the level of literary dominance which men generally had in the period. Some medieval women writers engaged specifically in the case for women; many did not, and although the ways in which their productions on quite other topics are 'proto-feminist' are of enormous interest to readers today, that is not the central subject of this book.

Before acknowledging other questions of definition, something should be said about why this book is needed. The answer is that while there have been several fine studies encompassing the case

---

[2] An excellent recent study is Kathryn Gravdal, *Ravishing Maidens: Writing Rape in Medieval French Literature and Law* (Philadelphia: University of Pennsylvania Press, 1991). See also Emilie Amt, *Women's Lives in Medieval Europe* (London: Routledge, 1993), 53–78.

for women in early modern literature,[3] analysis of medieval antecedents has largely been piecemeal, focused on particular late
medieval authors such as Boccaccio, Chaucer, and Christine de
Pizan, with Jean Le Fèvre as a recent addition.[4] The existence of
substantial antecedents, especially for Christine's arguments, has
not been adequately recognized. There is a tendency to think of
her as *sui generis*, as constituting in herself the roots of feminism.
'Christine's plea on behalf of women represents, of course, the
first literary "defense and illustration" of femininity', declares one
scholar: 'there existed before Christine no defense of women.'[5]
Without prejudice to the considerable milestone that her work
represents, we shall find that the roots of profeminine polemic
are longer. Blanche Dow brought a few of them to light in 1936.[6]
Since then scholars working on particular texts have excavated
more, but often understandably without being able to locate
them in the wider tradition. One characterizes as 'individual' a
thirteenth-century assertion that the substance from which
Eve was created was 'improved' from that used for Adam;
another thinks that Hildegard of Bingen is 'flying in the face of
every cherished cliché about women' in going 'as far as to claim
that the decline of the Church was the result of masculine
weakness, and could only be remedied by the work of

[3] Ruth Kelso, *Doctrine for the Lady of the Renaissance* (Urbana: University of
Illinois Press, 1956); Marc Angenot, *Les Champions des femmes: Examen du discours
sur la supériorité des femmes, 1400–1800* (Montreal: Les Presses de l'Université de
Québec, 1977); Linda Woodbridge, *Women and the English Renaissance: Literature
and the Nature of Womankind 1540–1620* (Urbana: University of Illinois Press, 1984);
Constance Jordan, *Renaissance Feminism: Literary Texts and Political Models* (Ithaca,
NY: Cornell University Press, 1990); Pamela Joseph Benson, *The Invention of the
Renaissance Woman: The Challenge of Female Independence in the Literature and
Thought of Italy and England* (Philadelphia: Pennsylvania State University Press,
1992).
[4] See Glenda McLeod, *Virtue and Venom: Catalogs of Women from Antiquity to the
Renaissance* (Ann Arbor: University of Michigan Press, 1991); Jill Mann, *Apologies
to Women*, inaugural lecture (Cambridge: Cambridge University Press, 1990), and
Geoffrey Chaucer (Hemel Hempstead: Harvester Wheatsheaf, 1991); Renate
Blumenfeld-Kosinski, 'Jean le Fèvre's *Livre de Leësce*: Praise or Blame of Women?',
Speculum, 69 (1994), 705–25. A start is made on defining the anti-misogynist tradition in *Woman Defamed and Woman Defended: An Anthology of Medieval Texts*, ed.
Alcuin Blamires, with Karen Pratt and C. W. Marx (Oxford: Clarendon Press,
1992), 223–302.
[5] Earl Jeffrey Richards, 'Christine de Pizan and the Question of Feminist Rhetoric', *Teaching Language through Literature*, 22 (1983), 15–24 (p. 15).
[6] *The Varying Attitude toward Women in French Literature of the Fifteenth Century*
(New York: Institute of French Studies, 1936).

women'.[7] The one is unaware of the medieval topos of the 'privileges' of women; the other, of the patristic and medieval topos
that women exceptionally appropriate powers in the Church as a
reproach to outbreaks of prelatical slackness or 'effeminacy'.

The fact is that the case for women has been slow to achieve
recognition because texts which incorporate it have remained
fairly inaccessible, and have not been studied extensively as a
group. This, in turn, has to do with certain elements of distrust
which, I suspect, have inhibited research of the materials even in
a feminist-oriented critical climate, and which I should like to
explore for a moment. The problem is that a major impulse in
medieval feminist studies has been to dismiss defence-of-women
writings (largely male-authored, and therefore suspect masculine
constructions of women, if not downright equivocal or facetious)
and concentrate instead on the voices of women themselves;
which means, on the whole, the voices of medieval female religious and mystical writers.

It is inevitable that, within such a patriarchal culture, many
medieval profeminine texts do indeed rehearse a male point of
view. Occasionally it is acknowledged, as when Marbod of
Rennes in the early twelfth century emphasizes the distinctive
solicitude (*femina cultus*) with which a woman sustains caring
responsibilities that 'our' rebellious male pride (*nostra superbia*)
disdains.[8] An affecting moment of honesty about his own sex?
Perhaps, but only within a context which lauds patriarchy's stereotype of long-suffering, nurturing, malleable femininity. Moreover, the use of the first-person plural pronoun really insinuates an
exclusive circle of male readers, momentarily chastened yet still

---

[7] Respectively Jeanette Beer, 'Richard de Fournival's Anonymous Lady: The
Character of the Response to the *Bestiaire d'amour*', *Romance Philology*, 42 (1988),
267–73 (p. 272); and Andrée Kahn Blumstein, *Misogyny and Idealization in the
Courtly Romance* (Bonn: Bouvier, 1977), 29.
[8] 'De matrona' (63–4), in *Marbodi liber decem capitulorum*, ed. Rosario Leotta
(Rome: Herder, 1984); tr. in Blamires, *Woman Defamed and Woman Defended*, 230.
For the use of the first-person masculine plural see also *Du bounté des femmes* (104–
5), ed. Paul Meyer in 'Les Manuscrits français de Cambridge, ii: Bibliothèque de
l'Université', *Romania*, 15 (1886), 236–357 (p. 318); and Giovanni Boccaccio, *De
mulieribus claris*, ed. Vittorio Zaccaria, in *Tutte le opere*, gen. ed. Vittore Branca, vol.
x (Verona: Mondadori, 1970), 378, tr. Guido A. Guarino, *Concerning Famous Women*
(New Brunswick, NJ: Rutgers University Press, 1963), 210–11. Where the author-
ship of a defence of women can be ascertained, it is usually male: e.g. Peter
Abelard, Étienne de Fougères, Robert de Blois, Albertanus of Brescia, Nicole
Bozon. Among rare exceptions, Hrotsvitha of Gandersheim and Christine de
Pizan are the most important for the present study.

comfortably contemplating the subdued stereotype of absent Woman.[9]

The masculine fantasy of the meek, compassionate, virtuous woman will haunt the pages of the present discussion, in corroboration of Kate Millett's observation that the Western stereotypes of both sexes are the construct of the dominant male, 'based on the needs and values of the dominant group and dictated by what its members cherish in themselves and find convenient in subordinates: aggression, intelligence, force, and efficacy in the male; passivity, ignorance, docility, "virtue", and ineffectuality in the female.'[10] It follows that even in the most nearly feminist medieval writings, those most affirmative of female autonomy, there will lurk a shadow of patriarchy, what Pamela Benson has identified in later texts as 'a subtext of restraint that results in the taming of the independent woman who is created in the explicit defence. It is the compromise by means of which authors seek to establish for themselves and their society a livable relationship with the threatening notion that women are equal to men.'[11]

As if such considerations were not enough to deter feminist scholarship from engaging substantially with medieval pro-feminine polemic, there is the further disadvantage that the defence smacks of facetious devil's advocacy. The suspicion arises not (as sometimes alleged) because some medieval writers wear two hats and defend today what they attacked yesterday: this, after all, is a consequence of the period's fascination with debate, though we shall see its real shortcomings later. Rather, the nub of the suspicion is that the defence hat appears sometimes deliberately cock-eyed. Parts of the case for women in Jean Le Fèvre's *Livre de Leësce* made by Leësce (Joy) herself seem to have impressed Christine de Pizan, but nevertheless Leësce has been thought to exude humorous signs of self-undermining—as though the poet 'laughed at women while pretending to defend them'.[12]

---

[9] Cf. 'Fame nos fait loer d'amors; | Fame nos fait porter les flors', etc., (67–72), in the *dit* edited by Wendy Pfeffer, 'La Louange des femmes: "Oez seignor, je n'otroi pas" (Berne, Bibliothèque de la Bourgeoisie no. 354)', *Neuphilologische Mitteilungen*, 93 (1992), 221–34 (p. 224).

[10] *Sexual Politics* (New York: Doubleday, 1970), 26.

[11] *Invention of the Renaissance Woman*, p. 47.

[12] Karen Pratt, 'Analogy or Logic; Authority or Experience? Rhetorical Strategies for and against Women', in Donald Maddox and Sara Sturm-Maddox (eds.), *Literary Aspects of Courtly Culture: Selected Papers from the Seventh Triennial Congress of the International Courtly Literature Society* (Cambridge: D. S. Brewer, 1994), 57–66 (p. 65).

For instance, after an earnest passage in which the efforts which industrious wives make to sustain their households are contrasted sharply with the dissoluteness of husbands who just drink or hunt their time away, Leësce goes on, most disconcertingly, to mention a woman called 'la Calabre' of Paris whose industrious application of herbal and other skills enabled her to shrink a vagina or a breast 'to be more pleasing to men'.[13] The poem's editor comments darkly on this historically elusive woman who 'put her shady art in the service of refined debauchery', but refinements of debauchery are probably not the point.[14] Le Fèvre's spokeswoman Leësce has been arguing that woman, created as 'helper' (*adjutoire*, 3735), has a natural and industrious bent to further her family and household in every way, above all to please men (*Afin qu'aux hommes puissent plaire*, 3757). Leësce has noted that childbearing costs mothers' bodies dear (3744): la Calabre's efforts therefore signify the lengths to which women changed by childbirth are prepared to go to 'please' husbands, even to appease the 'jalous'—the vindictive, sex-obsessed husband famously sketched in *Le Roman de la Rose*. This may instinctively strike some readers as such an outrageously un-feminist argument that it must be a joke. It is phallocentric. It proposes a role for women as voluntary domestic and sexual cushions for men; it implies that women *ought* to conform their bodies to the sexual pleasure of men; and it could be taken as symptomatic of masculine pornographic fantasies. Yet perhaps Le Fèvre does not have tongue in cheek here: he is deliberately shocking the reader with an extraordinary example of altruistic female behaviour in a context where the entire point has been to contrast that altruism (fulfilling the received function as 'helper') with egotistical male indolence and destructive male *fureur*. Le Fèvre is echoing the applause for the so-called *femina cultus*, the special caring capacity, ascribed by Marbod, where it is similarly polarized against

[13] 'J'en tray a tesmoing la Calabre | De Paris, qui d'erbes ou d'arbre, | Par mastic ou autre maistrie, | Dont elle scet bien l'industrie, | A fait maint con rapeticier | Et les mamelles estrecier, | Pour estre aux hommes plus plaisans, | Pour les jalous faire taisans' (3778–85); *Les Lamentations de Matheolus et le Livre de Leesce de Jehan le Fèvre, de Ressons*, ed. A.-G. Van Hamel, 2 vols. (Paris: Bouillon, 1892, 1905). Le Fèvre may have written both his translation of the late 13th-cent. *Liber lamentationum Matheoluli* and his *Livre de Leësce* in the 1380s, according to the dating in Geneviève Hasenohr-Esnos's edition of his *Respit de la mort* (Paris: Picard, 1969), p. liii.

[14] *Lamentations*, ed. Van Hamel, ii. 257.

ascribed male recalcitrance. Both writers are adopting one of the topoi of the medieval case for women, to which we shall return in a later chapter.

Nevertheless Jean Le Fèvre does have a facetious streak,[15] and it is undeniable that a rather hollow raillery occasionally infected the case for women, especially in the later Middle Ages when writers like Lydgate cultivated a tiresome habit of dropping heavy clangers amidst ostensibly profeminine discourse.[16] From this point of view, feminists are rightly wary of the defence literature. Yet, to suppose that because the tradition is largely male-constructed and tinged with prejudicial jest it has nothing to contribute to the project of rediscovering women's voices in the period is of course to overlook the degree to which those voices inevitably internalized precisely the case for their sex which patriarchy produced.

As an indication of this, the instance of Hildegard of Bingen's representation of her unusually public instructional role in the Church may be mentioned. In a famous passage near the beginning of the first vision of *Scivias*, she writes of a voice which bids her to pour out her own religious inspiration because those most qualified to do so are 'lukewarm and sluggish'.[17] Here she invokes a traditional ratification of the female right to take over the preaching role when male ecclesiasts fail to exercise it.[18] Barbara Newman shows how Hildegard's other writings echo the conviction that in the contemporary 'womanly age' (*muliebre tempus*) women had to assume the 'virile' prelatical roles abandoned by

[15] The epilogue to *Leësce* (3948–91) is ostensibly an appeal for mercy from women, but the passage is awash with *doubles entendres* which leave it unclear what sort of masculine efforts the narrator believes women reward, and which leave open whether the 'venality' which impedes the determination of their case is that of others or their own. I am very grateful to Karen Pratt for discussing this passage with me and for allowing me to see a draft paper, 'Voice, Gender, and Authority in Jean Le Fèvre's *Livre de Leësce*', which confirms and supplements my reading.

[16] A sample is: 'For as it longeth to men to be sturdy, | And sumwhat froward as off ther nature, | Riht so can women suffre paciently, | And alle wrongis humbli endure. | Men sholde attempte no maner creature, | And namli women, ther meeknesse for to preue, | Which may weel suffre whil no man doth hem greue'; *Lydgate's Fall of Princes*, ed. Henry Bergen, EETS ES 122 (London: Oxford University Press, 1924), bk. I, 4747–53.

[17] Hildegard of Bingen, *Scivias*, tr. Mother Columba Hart and Jane Bishop (New York: Paulist Press, 1990), 67.

[18] 'The visionary's gender is defiantly flaunted as a challenge to idle and "effeminate" clerics', observes Barbara Newman in her introduction to the translation of *Scivias*; tr. Hart and Bishop, 22.

men;[19] Newman compares Hildegard's disciple Elisabeth of Schönau, who invoked the Old Testament authority of Deborah and other prophetesses for female religious initiative.[20] Deborah, who was one of the model heroines of the profeminine case, is in fact the key to Hildegard and Elisabeth's self-validation. Both are remembering the type of exegesis found in Ambrose's treatise *On Widows*: 'When the Jews were being ruled under the leadership of the judges, because they could not govern them with manly justice, or defend them with manly strength, and so wars broke out on all sides, they chose Deborah, by whose judgement they might be ruled.'[21]

Tutored by this patristic argument, theologians of the Middle Ages repeated that it was as a reproach to men whose 'manliness' had lapsed that divine grace occasionally allowed women such as Deborah to assume positions of authority over men.[22] Clearly for a Hildegard or an Elisabeth, such a figure remained an enabling precedent even though (as they knew and ostensibly accepted) the inescapable patristic gloss introduced that 'subtext of restraint'[23] within profeminine discourse characterized by Benson as 'taming the independent woman'.

Deborah was tirelessly invoked in defences of women, and one can see why the medieval justification of her public role became part of the self-authorization of religious women aspiring to public roles themselves. As we have said, however, women's writing is not *per se* the subject of this book. There is a sense in which women writers from Hildegard to St Bridget and beyond 'speak for themselves' and for women in numerous subtle ways which scholars are beginning to elicit with increasing sophistication. But of medieval women writers, only Christine de Pizan and (to a lesser extent) Hrotsvitha will be discussed below, as participants in the specific defence of women.

How should we describe the 'case for women'? It is a mode of

[19] *Sister of Wisdom: St Hildegard's Theology of the Feminine* (Berkeley and Los Angeles: University of California Press, 1987), 3–4, 27–8.

[20] Ibid. 39.

[21] *De viduis*, VIII. 44, in *The Principal Works of St Ambrose*, tr. H. de Romestin, Select Library of Nicene and Post-Nicene Fathers, 2nd ser. 10 (Oxford: James Parker, 1896), 398; see *PL* 16. 248.

[22] Henry of Ghent, *Summa quaestionum ordinarium*, I. 11, q. 2. 11; text in Alcuin Blamires and C. W. Marx, 'Woman Not to Preach', *Journal of Medieval Latin*, 3 (1993), 34–63 (p. 54).

[23] Because the humiliation-of-men formula was a way of securing the power of a figure like Deborah to demonstrate *masculine* virtues.

discourse which aims to build a positive representation of women in response to either specified or implicit accusations. It can be thought of as a character reference, the obverse of a character assassination. It will characteristically take the form of direct oration, but forms such as debate, narrative, and even lyric can also accommodate it. Borrowing an idea from Linda Woodbridge, I shall adopt the expression 'the *formal* case' as a designation for systematic explorations of defence topoi.[24] The formal case has a quasi-judicial flavour and expressly sets out to promote women's cause and to exonerate them from slander. Its typical features are these: it questions the motives and morality of misogynists, who seem to forget that women brought them to life and that life without women would be difficult; it denounces antagonistic generalization; it asserts that God showed signs of special favour to women at creation and subsequently; it revises the culpability of Eve; it witnesses women's powerful interventions throughout history (from the Virgin Mary and scriptural heroines to Amazons and modern notables); and it argues that women's moral capacities expose the relative tawdriness of men's.

Several of these features can be traced, I shall later suggest, to one scriptural source. Some of them also had an independent prior existence, but they drew loosely together and stabilized during the twelfth and thirteenth centuries. (This was the period when misogynous literature ballooned, fuelled by manuscript compilations of misogynous extracts from Jerome's treatise defending virginity *Against Jovinian* and Walter Map's pseudo-Roman *Letter of Valerius to Ruffinus, against Marriage*. The boundary between the case for women and the case for marriage is, accordingly, sometimes difficult to draw; a section of Deschamps's *Miroir de mariage*, and Chaucer's *Wife of Bath's Prologue*, hover on that boundary.)

The formal case may be distinguished from the *incidental* case, by which I mean the appearance of one or more arguments or exemplifications characteristic of the formal case in a work not otherwise presented as a formal case. Incidental cases occur in patristic and medieval moral treatises or biblical commentary (on

[24] Woodbridge distinguishes between a 'formal controversy' carried on in Renaissance texts and a penumbra of 'noncontroversialist literature' in which the impact of argument from the formal debate is apparent; *Women and the English Renaissance*, 6–7, 13.

widowhood for instance, or on the female disciples' role during the Crucifixion and Resurrection). The *Lives* of female saints are a further major medium for incidental defence, whether in narrative or (in Hrotsvitha's innovative writings) dramatic form. Exemplary tales, represented in this book by Chaucer's *Clerk's Tale*, often provide an incidental case for women. Finally there are many romances which involve calumniation of the heroine—normally because she is accused of sexual betrayal—and yield an incidental case for women in rebutting the calumniation.

Clearly the survey in this book can only include a selective and perhaps uneven exploration of the wide range of writings which provide an incidental case. Even so, some readers may be surprised that the elevation of the courtly lady or *dompna* in medieval lyric as well as romance has not qualified for inclusion. Why not argue, in Diane Bornstein's words, that courtly love 'celebrated woman as an ennobling spiritual and moral force', expressing 'a new feminism that contradicted both the antifeminism of the ecclesiastical establishment and the sexual attitudes endorsed by the church'?[25] That view is increasingly open to doubt. First, because the courtly lady of lyric so often functions essentially as a mirror, projected by the male speaker, in which to explore not her feelings but his—to imagine the means to his own potential perfection (indeed, 'honouring ladies' came to be a proverbial definition of *male* honour).[26] Second, because the deification of woman in lyric or romance can be construed as an etherealizing misogyny which locates her virtue in her status as a virgin indefinitely deferred from human intercourse.[27] Third, because the pathos of the heroine presumed in romance to require chivalric protection

[25] *The Dictionary of the Middle Ages*, ed. Joseph R. Strayer (New York: Scribners, 1983), iii. 669. Compare Tony Hunt's formulation: 'it was inevitable that . . . the dissatisfaction generated by women's legal and economic dependence should be sublimated in an emotional hegemony whereby women were depicted as inspiring and directing reformed chivalric activity'; *Chrétien de Troyes: 'Yvain' ('Le Chevalier au lion')* (London: Grant & Cutler, 1986), 12.

[26] See Tilde Sankovitch, 'Lombarda's Reluctant Mirror', in William D. Paden (ed.), *The Voice of the Trobairitz: Perspectives on the Women Troubadours* (Philadelphia: University of Pennsylvania Press, 1989), 183–93 (p. 184), and Blumstein, *Misogyny and Idealization*, 13. The proverb 'Qui as femes honor ne porte | La seue honor doit estre morte' is noted in Angenot, *Champions des femmes*, 11, and in Pfeffer 'La Louange des femmes', 226–7.

[27] Woodbridge, *Women and the English Renaissance*, 58; R. Howard Bloch, *Medieval Misogyny and the Invention of Western Romantic Love* (Chicago: University of Chicago Press, 1991), 156–60.

trivializes her, incapacitates her as a decorative object of exchange, and hence reinforces masculine supremacy.[28] And finally
because the posture of the unrequited suitor aspiring to prove his
worthiness by sustained courtly service merely masks inter-male
competitiveness and ambition.[29]

On these grounds courtly 'exaltation' of women is skirted in the
present book, as a controversy requiring other books all to itself.[30]
But the first thing to acknowledge about even the formal medieval case for women is that strictly it, too, satisfies few feminist
criteria. Some readers may have been horrified by what they have
glimpsed of it so far. It is a very indirect ancestor of modern
feminism, precariously liable to collapse into what our culture
would describe on the contrary as misogynous modes of thought.
In the last part of this introduction its essentializing tendencies
will be considered, but if the adjective 'feminist' is going to be
problematic in this context, we must deal with this terminological
difficulty before going on.

Even where a medieval writer does fulfil some appropriate
criteria, there is a natural reluctance to designate her/him simply
as 'feminist', given the contemporary political connotations of
that word. For this reason Christine de Pizan has been described
as 'proto-feminist'.[31] As for the phenomenon of writing which
thinks it is positive about women but which does not reach the
condition of proto-feminism, no settled term seems to exist. 'Profeminist' is favoured by some critics.[32] One of them explains that

---

[28] Felicity Riddy, 'Engendering Pity in the *Franklin's Tale*', in Ruth Evans and
Lesley Johnson (eds.), *Feminist Readings in Middle English Literature* (London:
Routledge, 1994), 54–71 (p. 57); Roberta L. Krueger, 'Love, Honor, and the Exchange of Women in *Yvain*: Some Remarks on the Female Reader', *Romance Notes*,
25 (1985), 302–17.

[29] The suitor's self-abasement 'is not feminising' but rather 'a means of self-
definition in relation to other men; both pitying and being pitied are, for men,
positions of power', suggests Riddy, 'Engendering Pity', 57; and on the inter-male
rivalries involved, see further Christiane Marchello-Nizia, 'Amour courtois,
société masculine et figures du pouvoir', *Annales ESC* 36 (1981), 969–82.

[30] Apart from Blumstein, *Misogyny and Idealization*, see now Roberta L. Krueger,
Women Readers and the Ideology of Gender in Old French Verse Romance (Cambridge:
Cambridge University Press, 1993); Susan Crane, *Gender and Romance in Chaucer's
'Canterbury Tales'* (Princeton: Princeton University Press, 1994).

[31] Maureen Quilligan, *The Allegory of Female Authority: Christine de Pizan's 'Cité
des dames'* (Ithaca, NY: Cornell University Press, 1991), 12–13 n. 5. Quilligan sometimes uses variants such as 'pro-woman/anti-misogynist', 26.

[32] Benson, *Invention of the Renaissance Woman*, 2, gives 'reluctance to initiate
political reform' as her reason for using the term 'profeminist' rather than 'feminist' for Renaissance defences of women.

by this he means 'statements which *ostensibly* commend women, thereby functioning in accordance with the norms of the prevailing culture'.[33] However, since there is by now some consensus that 'feminine' and 'masculine' are best used to express cultural constructions of gender,[34] I believe that pre-modern texts which develop constructions of 'woman' which are positive according to the cultural ideology of their period ought logically to be called not 'profeminist' but *profeminine*.[35] That term will therefore be preferred in this book.

If we are to weigh the unfeminist quality of medieval profeminine discourse, it would be helpful to bear in mind two definitions of misogynous representation. Hope Phyllis Weissman describes as antifeminist 'any presentation of a woman's nature intended to conform her to male expectations of what she is or ought to be . . . indeed, the most insidious of antifeminist images are those which celebrate . . . the forms a woman's goodness is to take'.[36] R. Howard Bloch defines misogyny as 'a speech act in which woman is the subject of the sentence and the predicate a more general term'.[37]

Medieval writers were not totally unaware of the issues raised by these critics, as can be demonstrated by referring to a notorious moment in Chaucer's *Nun's Priest's Tale*. Here the cockerel Chauntecleer contrives a mischievous speech act in which woman is the subject and the predicate a more general term when he utters a mock-compliment to Pertelote the hen. Quoting the Latin *Mulier est hominis confusio* (woman is man's absolute ruin), he says that it means, 'Womman is mannes joye and al his blis.'[38]

---

[33] Alastair Minnis *et al.*, *Oxford Guides to Chaucer: The Shorter Poems* (Oxford: Clarendon Press, 1995), 429.

[34] Toril Moi, *Sexual/Textual Politics: Feminist Literary Theory* (New York: Methuen, 1985), 65; Caroline Walker Bynum, *Jesus as Mother: Studies in the Spirituality of the High Middle Ages* (Berkeley and Los Angeles: University of California Press, 1982), 167–8.

[35] *Feminine* and *femininity* are of course also nuanced, to the extent that attempts have been made to replace 'femininity' with 'femineity' as 'the noun signifying the quality or nature of the female sex'; McLeod, *Virtue and Venom*, 1 n. 1. But adjectival choices are limited, and *profeminine* surely poses fewer problems of nuance than *profeminist*.

[36] 'Antifeminism and Chaucer's Characterization of Women', in George D. Economou (ed.), *Geoffrey Chaucer: A Collection of Original Articles* (New York: McGraw-Hill, 1975), 93–110 (p. 94).

[37] *Medieval Misogyny*, 5.

[38] *The Riverside Chaucer*, ed. Larry D. Benson (Boston, Mass.: Houghton Mifflin, 1987), *The Canterbury Tales*, VII. 3163–6. All Chaucer quotations will be from this edition, citing line numbers in the body of the text.

There are all sorts of ways of taking this, including the possibility that the slippage from 'ruin' to 'blis' archly rehearses a traditional symmetry between Eve and the Virgin Mary. Whatever insinuations lurk in the jest,[39] they are compounded by an essentializing outburst later in the tale ('Wommenes conseils been ful ofte colde', VII. 3256) and by the narrator's blundering apologies for that. Evidently the speech acts isolated by Bloch are themselves under playful scrutiny in the tale: not only *Mulier est . . .*, and Woman is . . . , and Women's counsels are . . . , but also the converse where Pertelote generalizes flatly that 'We' (whether women or hens) 'alle desiren' husbands who are 'hardy, wise, and free' (VII. 2912–14). Of course the latter, in Weissman's terms, is interpretable as a conforming of women to a male narrator's stereotype of Woman's desire, which turns out to be desire for 'hardy' masculinity. Equally, the ostensibly eulogistic claim that 'womman is mannes joye' is a definition of woman which conforms her to a masculine idea—as Chauntecleer goes on to make clear—that she exists to provide sexual *solas* for the male.

Formal defences of women before Chaucer's time rarely match this witty self-aware encapsulation of the problematics of misogynizing generalization.[40] More often, exasperatingly and in Bloch's terms self-underminingly, they launch into generalizing defence of women. This is especially so in some of the short Old French poems (*dits*) of the thirteenth century, which are prone to the worst excesses of *fame est . . .* ('woman is') and other categorical assertions. One ninety-eight-line example, 'Oez seignor, je n'otroi pas', makes a *tour de force* of such constructions. Woman is worthy, courteous, wise, does not care for uncivilized men, is without crudeness (*vilenie*) herself, makes 'us' bring her flowers and talk of love, is 'worth' more than silver, gold, castles, horses:

---

[39] Mann detects 'a comic reflection of the comfortable cohabitation of . . . polarised views of women in conventional male ideology'; *Geoffrey Chaucer*, 190–1. For other suggestions about Chaucer's wider concern with the strategy of reversal involved, see Alcuin Blamires, 'Questions of Gender in Chaucer, from *Anelida* to *Troilus*', *Leeds Studies in English*, NS 25 (1994), 83–110 (pp. 101–2); and Priscilla Martin, *Chaucer's Women: Nuns, Wives and Amazons* (Basingstoke: Macmillan, 1990), 1–4.

[40] For a good account of the complications surrounding the issue of essentialism, see Diana Fuss, *Essentially Speaking: Feminism, Nature, and Difference* (London: Routledge, 1989).

Fame est preuz, et cortoise, et saje;
Fame n'a soin d'ome salvaje;
Fame est la flors de cortoisie;
Fame n'a point de vilenie. (59–62)[41]

At about the same time, in the English bird-debate *The Thrush and the Nightingale* on the pros and cons of women, the Nightingale also insists on their courtesy ('Hit is shome to blame leuedy, | For hy beth hende of corteisy', 25–6) and objects to the Thrush's vilification of 'wimmen' because the greatest 'murthe that mon haueth here' is when a woman is in his arms (73–81).[42] Woman is therefore man's joy and all his bliss, again. In fact generalizations are pointedly exchanged by the antagonists in the poem, prosecution claiming that Sir Gawain rode far and wide without finding a single 'trewe' woman (88–92) but defence holding that if a thousand ladies are lined up, not one will be found 'wickede' (52–4).[43]

This might not be a matter for so much comment if indignation, not to say outrage, against misogynous generalization were not a prominent feature of the literature of defence. The complaint goes back at least to Ovid who (notwithstanding that he was a prime offender) protested against the habit of pinning the evil repute of one girl on all.[44] This observation was widely dispersed in debate on women during the thirteenth century.[45] Defenders took Ovid's point most to heart with regard to accusations of female promiscuity. The writer of an English verse account (before 1290) of the

[41] Pfeffer, 'La Louange des femmes', 224; and see 'Fame nos fait loer d'amors', etc. (67–70), and 'Fame valt mialz que nul tresor', etc. (81–6). Monotonous initial repetition of 'femina . . .' is evidenced in 12th-cent. misogynous poems quoted by Susan L. Smith, *The Power of Women: A Topos in Medieval Art and Literature* (Philadelphia: University of Pennsylvania Press, 1995), 32, and by Carolyn Dinshaw, *Chaucer's Sexual Poetics* (Madison: University of Wisconsin Press, 1989), 6.

[42] The poem is in *Early Middle English Texts*, ed. Bruce Dickins and R. M. Wilson (London: Bowes & Bowes, 1951), 71–6; tr. Blamires in *Woman Defamed and Woman Defended*, 224–8.

[43] Tacitly defying Eccles. 7: 29: 'one man among a thousand I have found, a woman among them all I have not found.'

[44] *Ars amatoria*, III. 9–10, in *Ovid: The Art of Love and Other Poems*, ed. and tr. J. H. Mozley, 2nd edn. rev. G. P. Goold (Cambridge, Mass.: Harvard University Press, 1979).

[45] Thus Albertanus of Brescia's female personification Prudence reproves her husband for despising women in general terms, 'non deberes ita generaliter despicere mulieres', *Liber consolationis et consilii*, ch. iv, ed. Thor Sundby (London: Trubner, 1873), 14; *Book of Consolation and Advice*, tr. C. W. Marx in Blamires, *Woman Defamed and Woman Defended*, 237–42 (p. 238); but muted to 'certes ye despisen alle wommen in this wyse' in Chaucer's version, *Tale of Melibee*, VII. 1069.

Passion argues strenuously; 'should a woman importuned by a lecher do wrong, don't thrust forward your half-baked logic claiming that all women . . . deserve disgrace'.[46] As Jean Le Fèvre puts it, a personal failing (*mal particuler*) is not to be visited on a whole sex, male or female.[47] One of many interconnections between Le Fèvre and Christine de Pizan is that they both suggest that women should no more be censured *en masse* for the shortcomings of a few than all the angels should be censured for the defection of a few who fell with Lucifer.[48]

The objection to generalization is commendably sensible. Yet the medieval writers adopting it to defend women do not often sense how it must logically limit their scope for broad counterclaims. One could suggest two reasons why this happens. One is that the objection to generalization about people was ineradicably an objection to *negative* generalization. Nobody minded benign generalization; it was preferable to the sin of detraction. Another explanation would be that while on the one hand the principle of non-generalization derived support from the presumption that evil was a matter of individual will, on the other hand it clashed with a supposition that certain 'natural' properties were proper to each sex.[49]

The difficulty which the formal case experienced in negotiating between these contradictory principles is highlighted just where a resolution might have been hoped for, in Christine de Pizan's *Epistre au dieu d'amours*. In this poem she is eager to endorse the kind of polemic seen above in *The Southern Passion*, for she devotes a whole passage (185–204) to the error of generalized

---

[46] 'þey a woman þorwȝ bysokne of a foul man mysdo, | þyne balled resoun ne polt nouȝt forþ anon | . . . þat hy weren alle worþe to habben chame inouȝ' (132–5), ed. O. S. Pickering, 'The "Defence of Women" from the *Southern Passion*: A New Edition', in *The South English Legendary: A Critical Assessment*, ed. Klaus P. Jankovsky (Tübingen: Stauffenburg, 1992), 154–76; tr. Blamires, *Woman Defamed and Woman Defended*, 247. For an almost identical point, see Nicole Bozon, *De la bonté des femmes*, in *Les Contes moralisés de Nicole Bozon*, ed. Lucy Toulmin Smith and Paul Meyer, SATF (Paris: Firmin Didot, 1889), pp. xxxiii–xli: 'Donks la gent q'escryent | Totes les autres que bones sunt | Pur une sote, | Malement avisez sunt, | Qu les bones medlez sunt | Ove la male rote' (115–20).

[47] *Leësce*, 1409–18, and see further criticism of generalization at 800–9.

[48] *Leësce*, 1112–29: cf. Christine, *L'Epistre au dieu d'amours*, 193–200, ed. Thelma S. Fenster and Mary Carpenter Erler in *Poems of Cupid, God of Love* (Leiden: Brill, 1990), 42–3.

[49] There was also the difficulty that the medieval understanding of how one consolidated an argument of any sort was deeply dependent on the cumulative evidence of precedent; a factor to be considered later.

slander. She returns near the end of the poem to the ignominy of
being a *mesdisant*, a slanderer, above all 'when women as a group
[*communement*] are criticized' (735–8). It is consistent with this that
she has taken care to avoid generalizing against men, many of
whom she says are not misogynists (217–22), and to avoid generalizing in women's defence: she claims only to champion *femmes
honorables* (289) and the common run (*le commun cours*) of women
(655); and argues for example that 'most' women are loyal (472).
At the same time she is strongly attracted to the view that woman
has certain 'natural' dispositions or *condicions* (676), characterized
by trustingness (101), compassion towards men (169–78), and a
gentleness entirely alien to brutality and violence (668–76). An
individual woman who by chance lacks these *condicions* 'dena-
tures' herself (677–8)—exceptions prove the rule. Accordingly,
even Christine with her acute awareness of the problem of generalization cannot altogether evade it. In fact just before her rejection of criticism which lumps women together *communement*, she
identifies woman as that which man properly loves best by 'natural law', and as she who 'affords each man the greatest joy' so that
'natural man has no joy without woman' (723–8).[50]

The context as a whole makes it clear that there is here a nexus
of reactions to misogyny as rudeness, ingratitude, 'unnatural-
ness', and above all disgraceful slander. In slandering women
communement, misogynists carry the morally and socially unpal-
atable sin of detraction to its furthest extreme, but compound it
with ingratitude, returning evil for good (722) and failing to reciprocate all those altruistic feminine traits ascribed by Christine, as
well as failing to abide by 'natural' law. In sum, the framework of
thought runs in a direction which resists generalized or
essentializing misogyny precisely because that amounts to a failure to abide by another generality, according to which woman is
by nature man's joy and all his bliss.

Both Christine de Pizan and Chaucer intervened in the inherited arguments about women, but it should not surprise us that
they could not transcend essentializing impulses that were to
survive for centuries. Chaucer, who seems to ironize gender stereotyping in *The Nun's Priest's Tale*, assents quietly to it in other

---

[50] 'Car c'est la riens ou monde par droiture I Que homme aime mieulx et de
droite nature. I Si est moult lait et grant honte a blasmer I La riens qui soit que l'en
doit plus amer I Et qui plus fait a tout homme de joye. I Homs naturel sans femme
ne s'esjoye.'

texts.[51] Later in this book I shall ask how both writers situated themselves within the tradition of defence, while the extent to which that tradition was able to acknowledge the constructedness of the 'natural' qualities which culture assigned to women is discussed in the Conclusion.

After first surveying a corpus of texts articulating the formal case for women and investigating origins and procedures, the core of the book will present and evaluate key areas of the defence portfolio: women's nutritional and peacemaking functions; creation privileges and the exoneration of Eve; feminine stability; and role-models of autonomous women. Two chapters will track explorations of defence traditions in writings by Hrotsvitha, Abelard, Chrétien de Troyes, Chaucer, and Christine de Pizan. Since the whole study is driven in part by a perception that the defence has been underestimated because its intellectual foundations and its affiliations with other medieval discourses have escaped notice, a decision has been taken to pursue its topoi backwards and sideways. The drawbacks of this are two. First, my analysis does not proceed into the fifteenth century. (Gender polemic continues apace in that century but does not, I would argue, substantially affect the lineaments of the case for women which emerge from this book.) The second drawback is that in order to satisfy my objectives, space for historicizing the materials has been severely curtailed. This is not a curtailment lightly allowed, but historicization over the timespan covered here would, I believe, risk superficiality.

Admittedly there is precedent in books such as those by Dyan Elliott, and Katharina Wilson and Elizabeth Makowski, for historicizing even such a capacious chronology of writings as this.[52] Moreover recent scholarship should make it possible to locate, say, profeminine pieces by Marbod of Rennes and Peter Abelard, who wrote in the early twelfth century, within the 'gender crisis' increasingly ascribed to that very period, when the campaign for religious celibacy coupled with a 'crescendo' in clerical misogyny released ideologically unlooked-for pressures

---

[51] For instance, *The Squire's Tale* commends its heroine for being 'ful mesurable, as wommen be' (V. 362): it is perhaps doubtful whether this generalization could be ascribed to the persona of the Squire.

[52] Dyan Elliott, *Spiritual Marriage: Sexual Abstinence in Medieval Wedlock* (Princeton: Princeton University Press, 1993); Katharina M. Wilson and Elizabeth M. Makowski, *Wykked Wyves and The Woes of Marriage: Misogamous Literature from Juvenal to Chaucer* (Albany: State University of New York Press, 1990).

18 INTRODUCTION

into the gender system, whose impact it became necessary to limit by measures and writings 'designed to reconstitute the separation of the sexes'.[53]

Yet it seems to me that the historicization of discourses on women from late antiquity to the Middle Ages is as yet so tentative that comment remains at best precarious. These are realms of intellectual reconnaissance where further consolidation is really required before the case for women can be confidently mapped onto them. Besides, there is so much to be learned first about the configurations and the longevity of that case. Hence the decision to put the emphasis on establishing key profeminine conventions in the chapters that follow. In a situation where even the first article of defence—that men, including misogynists, owe their existence to mothers—is capable of being mistaken (in Christine de Pizan's case) as a strategy for 'establishing the authority of the woman poet on the female's capacity to give birth', one may perhaps be forgiven for putting description and analysis of the conventional topoi at the top of the agenda.[54]

In the mean time it is hoped that this introduction has made a start on key issues and texts in such a way as to clarify how in the light of contemporary understandings of feminism(s), the medieval case for women requires (at least) the insertion of cautionary inverted commas: it is only a case 'for' women. And yet, there was more of it, and it was more robust and more influential, than the reputation of the Middle Ages as an epoch of misogyny might lead people to expect.

[53] Jo Ann McNamara, 'The *Herrenfrage*: The Restructuring of the Gender System, 1050–1150', in Clare A. Lees, with Thelma Fenster and Jo Ann McNamara (eds.), *Medieval Masculinities: Regarding Men in the Middle Ages* (Minneapolis: University of Minnesota Press, 1994), 3–29 (esp. pp. 6, 19). McNamara's is the most brilliant analysis to date of a much-studied phenomenon. She briefly locates Abelard and Marbod within it on pp. 13 and 16.

[54] Lori Walters, 'The Woman Writer and Literary History: Christine de Pizan's Redefinition of the Poetic *Translatio* in the *Epistre au dieu d'amours*', *French Literature Series*, 16 (1989), 1–16 (pp. 11–12). Walters fruitfully discusses the relation of the *Epistre au dieu d'amours* to the *Roman de la Rose*, but perceives no traditional topoi underpinning Christine's defensive arguments. That Christine imbues motherhood with subtle meanings in the poem is not impossible, but would require a demonstration taking account of the overriding importance of motherhood in the genre she is adapting.

1

The Formal Case: The Corpus

THE medieval defence of women is liable to strike readers new to it as a glorious cocktail: common-sense observations about respect for mothers mixed up with bits of biblical discussion, encomia on the Virgin Mary, *exempla* of Amazon and other antique heroines jostling with those of women saints, bizarre claims about the creation of woman, blunt assertions of female virtue driven home with moral indignation against detractors, and a spicy dash of psychological speculation on the sexual or other frustrations of misogynists. In order to become attuned to ways in which these elements were harnessed together it will be useful to survey the relevant corpus of texts, up to a cut-off date around 1405. Equipped thereby with the basis for a generic description, we shall be in a better position to embark on discussion of origins and evaluation of the chief lines of defence.

Although what I have called the incidental case for women is quite pervasive in medieval culture, the available pool of formal defences with which I am so far conversant is much less extensive and cannot easily be pursued further back than the end of the eleventh century.[1] Around this time Marbod of Rennes, a teacher and bishop whose career spanned the eleventh and twelfth centuries, wrote an undated poem of 125 lines in praise of women, known variously as 'De matrona' or 'De muliere bona', as the fourth of the rhetorical set-pieces in his *Book with Ten Chapters*. Its juxtaposition with a preceding poem attacking women ('De meretrice', or alternatively 'De muliere mala') may imply an already solid tradition;[2] along with the topic of old age in the ensuing poem, it may have been related to student assignments at the cathedral schools of Angers where Marbod had taught. Debate about womankind very likely already was in these schools,

---

[1] Encomia in praise of specific women constitute of course a different, though allied, genre having a more continuous history.

[2] The variant titles are those, respectively, in the editions of the *Liber decem capitulorum* by Walther Hulst (Heidelberg: Carl Winter, 1947) and Rosario Leotta (Rome: Herder, 1984).

and (as others have suggested) continued to be in the medieval universities which succeeded them, a 'prescribed exercise . . . , a vehicle for acquiring and demonstrating logical and rhetorical skill'.[3] Marbod begins with a scientific assertion of gender equality within the first tier of nature, proving that women along with men are more worthy than animals, plants, and silver, gold, and jewels (18–36); then commends women's biological and social functions, gives cameos of courageous biblical women, saints, and pagan wives (Alcestis and Arria), and concludes that gender is irrelevant to woman's moral status.

Peter Abelard's contribution to the genre in the 1130s, *The Authority and Dignity of Nuns*, is perhaps a borderline instance as its title would imply, but an extraordinarily interesting and substantial one.[4] Abelard dwells almost lyrically on the 'dignity' accorded specifically to women by Christ, especially to the woman who anointed him, to the Samaritan woman who conversed with him and who summoned her fellow citizens, and to the women who showed their loyalty during the Crucifixion. Abelard highlights women's prominence in the realm of prophecy, and elucidates the female diaconate and the history of chastity. As a demonstration of female authority, precedence, and exclusivity in religious life this piece, written in answer to a request by Heloise, is unsurpassed in the Middle Ages.

Rather less ambitious is another twelfth-century exercise which reverts to Marbod's Good versus Disgraceful Woman paradigm. This occurs in an 'estates' poem of the 1170s about sections of society, the *Livre des manières* by Étienne de Fougères. The section on the *bonté* of women warrants mention because it is clearly conceived as a unit, touching briefly on a string of profeminine

[3] Woodbridge, *Women and the English Renaissance*, 5; and R. Warwick Bond, in the introduction to his edition of William Bercher, *The Nobility of Women* (London: Roxburghe Club, 1904), 56. On woman as a topic for master–pupil instruction, see Helen Solterer, *The Master and Minerva: Disputing Women in French Medieval Culture* (Berkeley and Los Angeles: University of California Press, 1995), ch. 1.

[4] Numbered Letter 6 in the Abelard/Heloise correspondence and given the not necessarily authorial manuscript title 'De auctoritate vel dignitate ordinis sanctimonialium' in the edition by J. T. Muckle, 'The Letter of Heloise on Religious Life and Abelard's First Reply', *Mediaeval Studies*, 17 (1955), 240–81 (pp. 253–81); but numbered Letter 7 in *The Letters of Abelard and Heloise*, tr. C. K. Scott Moncrieff (New York: Cooper Square, Inc., 1974), 131–75, and by others who take the *Historia calamitatum* as Letter 1. There is only a summary of the letter in *The Letters of Abelard and Heloise*, tr. Betty Radice (Harmondsworth: Penguin, 1974), 180–2. See further Ch. 8, below.

topoi.[5] Étienne names 'wise' women (Thecla, Margaret), suggests
that it is boorish to insult women, emphasizes the Virgin Mary's
triumph, recollects that nuns, but not monks, require bishops to
consecrate them, lauds the happiness of wives and their pleasure
in children (despite their cost and their mortality), and concludes
with an encomium on the Countess of Hereford who lost *her*
children but is a model of cheerful charitable behaviour. (Here is
the phenomenon of the 'modern instance', whereby the method
of authenticating an argument through appeal to celebrated example is sharpened by being brought up to date.)

Praise-of-women texts become more numerous in the thirteenth century. Several vernacular examples take the form of *dits*,
short and at this period generally non-narrative poems, associated with public recitation.[6] One, on the virtues of women (*Le Bien
des fames*), warns that maligning women is not *cortois*; they are to
be honoured by men as a tribute to the Virgin Mary and because
all men are born of women. Love of women is morally sanctioned
and it is ennobling, for they have a marvellous power to improve,
soften, change, and inspire men to great exploits and to song:
besides, it is their work which enables men to look good in
clothes.[7]

Another *dit*, mentioned in the Introduction and known by its
first line as 'Oez seignor, je n'otroi pas', again champions respect
and love for women on the grounds that this is courteous and
natural and that men are joyless without women's love. Not
merely poetry and a culturally civilizing impetus, but birdsong
itself (a conventional feature of courtly lyric) is romantically ascribed to woman's influence. In her power to transform men she
exceeds all conventional valuables.[8] There is an interesting overlap with the probably contemporary English debate poem *The*

[5] Étienne de Fougères, *Le Livre des manières*, ed. R. Anthony Lodge (Geneva:
Droz, 1979), lines 1125–253. For some discussion, see Jeri S. Guthrie, 'La Femme
dans *Le Livre des manières*: Surplus économique, surplus érotique', *Romanic Review*,
79 (1988), 251–61.
[6] *Three Medieval Views of Women*, tr. and ed. Gloria K. Fiero, Wendy Pfeffer, and
Mathé Allain (New Haven: Yale University Press, 1989), 2.
[7] Text and translation ibid. 106–13.
[8] Text in Pfeffer, 'La Louange des femmes', 223–5. Pfeffer dates the poem to the
late 13th or possibly the beginning of the 14th cent. (p. 230) because in envisaging
detractors as banned from the fountain of love (line 48) it seems to respond to a
central image in the *Roman de la Rose*. Two further extant *dits* in praise of women
are the *Dit des femmes* (see Paul Meyer, 'Mélanges de poésie française, iv: Plaidoyer
en faveur des femmes', *Romania*, 6 (1877), 499–503), and *Du bounté des femmes*, in
Meyer, 'Manuscrits français de Cambridge', 315–20.

Thrush and the Nightingale, in the incidental but bold contention that without women, the world would be worthless,[9] 'This world nere nout ȝif wimen nere', as the Nightingale puts it.[10] The line provokes laconic comment on the latter poem from Derek Pearsall—'the standard of debate is not high'[11]—but for present purposes it is not literary ambition but compilations and continuities of argument that concern us.

In any case, the procedures in *Thrush and Nightingale* show to somewhat better advantage when the piece is inserted within the praise/blame tradition. Although Thrush rehearses formulaic *exempla* of the high and mighty (Samson, Alexander) 'brought low' by women, he also plays precisely the part of sly gossiping detractor whose psychology Christine de Pizan was to subject to penetrating criticism. Dismissing women as fickle betrayers of men's trust (4–6), he insinuates that his knowledge of their fickleness derives from personal bedroom experience of their willingness to exchange sexual favours for profit (60–3). The female Nightingale defends, in more genteel register, the courtesy of 'ladies' (25–6, 77–8) and—not to be outdone—claims to possess inside information gained in orchards where the ladies commune with her (97–103). She asserts their calming ability to mediate in disputes and their welcoming/soothing/curative faculties (28–33, 151–3), and enthuses over the delight of embracing them, but only in the context of insisting on their principled aversion to the sort of impropriety alleged by Thrush. Nightingale wins the day not with these arguments nor with the bland romantic clichés she cultivates (woman is brighter than the summer's dawn) but by triumphantly producing the example of the Virgin Mary to counter what Thrush cynically estimates as a 5 per cent chance of female chastity.

The Virgin Mary transcends not only statistics but most other misogynous polemic in the case for women, so it is not surprising that she appears also in the more erudite context of another debate, dated 1246, by the Italian judge Albertanus of Brescia.[12] His

---

[9] 'Se fame n'estoit, jo di bien, | Toz li mondes ne valdroit rien' (33–4).

[10] Ed. Dickins and Wilson, line 34.

[11] *Old English and Middle English Poetry* (London: Routledge, 1977), 98.

[12] Latin text ed. Thor Sundby; English translation of the profeminine chapters by C. W. Marx in Blamires, *Woman Defamed and Woman Defended*, 237–42. An interesting historicizing study is James M. Powell, *Albertanus of Brescia: The Pursuit of Happiness in the Early Thirteenth Century* (Philadelphia: University of Pennsylvania Press, 1992).

debate is really an ethical treatise written for one of his sons. It stages a discussion in which Prudentia or Prudence (performing, let it be noted, precisely the calming role ascribed to women by Nightingale) seeks to displace the retaliatory attitude of her husband Melibeus, a representative nobleman, when their home is raided and their daughter is injured. Ostensibly this text offers an instance of an incidental case made within a structure having another purpose—to assert the ethical value of prudence, especially over the aggressive instinct—but arguably the consequence is that the *Liber consolationis* as a whole is actually structured to elevate a 'feminine' view of violence over a 'masculine' one.[13]

Albertanus is distinctive for the density of his gnomic quotations, sometimes from quite recherché sources. In his professional capacity he must have been able to swamp a courtroom with them. Yet together with the moral thoughtfulness of the debate, they gave the work such cachet that it circulated in translation all over Europe, reaching Chaucer for instance through a French adaptation.[14] I have no doubt that the gender implications attracted Chaucer's notice. In the narrative, the brutal raid on Melibeus' home by known enemies leaves him in a rage: he is *furiosus*, and *fureur* would be the Old French misandronist word for it, though that signal is confused by a contrary hint that he is being cast in the role of mourning mother.[15] He accepts Pru-

[13] On the implicit critique of aggressive 'manhod' in Chaucer's *Tale of Melibee*, translated from a French adaptation of Albertanus' treatise, see Alcuin Blamires, 'Chaucer's Revaluation of Chivalric Honor', *Mediaevalia*, 5 (1979), 245–69. Celia R. Daileader urges the underlying narrative's feminist basis, in that its critique of male violence 'indicts patriarchy as institutionalized aggression' and in that it culminates in 'the transformation of a misguided male character through the medium of a woman', 'The *Thopas-Melibee* Sequence and the Defeat of Antifeminism', *Chaucer Review*, 29 (1994), 26–39 (pp. 31, 38).

[14] Chaucer used a French abridgement by Renaud de Louens dating from after 1336. Powell estimates the number of MSS of Albertanus' works at around 500, making him 'among the most popular medieval authors'; *Albertanus of Brescia*, 14 n. 22.

[15] Seeing Melibeus tear his own clothes in his tearful anger, Prudence thinks of him in an Ovidian simile as a distraught mother who must be left a while to grieve the death of a child: a configuration which, Daileader suggests, reverses gender stereotypes because 'the husband is acting "womanish"—impassioned and irrational—while the wife maintains a "manly", calm demeanor', '*Thopas-Melibee* Sequence', 33: see Sundby edn., 2 for 'Melibeus ... coepit ... vestes suas quasi more furiosi dilacerare' and Prudence's allusion to Ovid's *Remedia amoris*, 127–30. The Ovidian context, however, authorizes the reversed stereotype, because it concerns the impracticality of trying to counsel a jilted *male* lover while he is still too much in the grip of emotion: 'Dum furor in cursu est, currenti cede furori,' *Remedia*, 119, ed. Mozley, *Art of Love and Other Poems*.

dence's suggestion of a meeting with friends and advisers to discuss what to do; but when the meeting favours vengeful action he is displeased with Prudence's respectful warning against a too precipitous course. This is the point at which a case for women is prompted, because to begin with, Melibeus pompously rejects advice from her, trotting out some misogynous prejudices; that no good woman is to be found, that women babble indiscreetly, and subdue men through evil advice. Prudence is therefore able to offer the kind of bipartite response which is found in much late medieval profeminine literature—first (Albertanus' chapter 4) undermining the opposition's allegations, and second (chapter 5) replacing them with a positive view of women.[16] In a way, the context makes this a more highly charged and 'political' defence than usual. The abstractness of the 'good versus bad' debate is absorbed into a more pragmatic question: whether women's voices can be taken seriously in deciding grave issues affecting a whole kin.

Melibeus' dismissive quotation from Ecclesiastes 7: 28 that no good woman is to be found begs contrary examples. Those firmly offered by Prudence are Christ's choice of a woman both for his Incarnation and for the first news of the Resurrection. However, she makes accompanying moves which go beyond the crossfire of scriptural citation. She perceives that Melibeus' culpably general contempt for women is also a general allegation of their *imprudentia* and quotes Seneca to the effect that one should 'not despise the *imprudentia* of anyone'.[17] Medieval translators tended to lose sight of this witty punning on her own name, 'Prudentia'.[18] It is as though somebody named Faith ironically referred to herself as faithless; but the deeper implication is that Melibeus' attitude casually negates his wife's particular identity, within his negation of women's capacities generally. At the same time the Senecan maxim she quotes about not despising anyone's

---

[16] Ed. Sundby, 12–19; Blamires, *Woman Defamed and Woman Defended*, 237–42.

[17] Ed. Sundby, 14; Blamires, *Woman Defamed and Woman Defended*, 238.

[18] The pun is obscured in Chaucer's *Melibee* by use of the term *sapience*, VII. 1070. The Chaucerian text also omits a passage (ed. Sundby, 19–20, immediately after this section of their debate) in which the pun is actually discussed, and in a sense undermined. Prudentia says that to live prudently Melibeus must 'have prudence'. Of course he 'has' prudence, he replies, because he 'has' her, and that's her name. She replies that she 'is not' prudence, but just 'the words of prudence' (*prudentiae verba*) and proceeds to give a scholastic analysis of *prudentia* itself.

'imprudence' is calculatedly gender-neutral. Melibeus is challenged to abide by principles applicable to human, not gender-specific, behaviour. Her other move is to subject the Solomonic *dictum* from Ecclesiastes to a process of textual analysis: what did Solomon *mean* by 'not finding a good woman'? Both this process and the implications of the Senecan quotation are germane to the evolution of profeminine discourse in Chaucer and Christine de Pizan.

Enough has been said to suggest the breadth of Albertanus' approach and the interest of a ventriloquizing strategy whereby, assigning what counted in his day as a 'feminine' set of peace-making attitudes to Prudence, he gave her the argumentative faculties of a judge. In her further rebuttal of allegations she invites Melibeus to consider the gap between 'babbling women' and his actual experience of her identity, then cuts through prejudice against female advice by declaring that people ought indeed to be 'subdued' by any good advice and are free to reject any bad advice.

Prudence now switches from defence (*excusatio*) to proof: specifically, proof that women are good and that their advice should be listened to.[19] Anticipating Christine de Pizan, she eschews generalization for a moment and diplomatically concedes that the *consilium* of certain women may well be worthless before citing Rebecca, Judith, Abigail, and Esther as exemplars of women's excellent counsel, and suggesting that woman's created role as man's 'helper' presupposes her helpful counsel.[20] The thought prompts Prudence to totalizing remarks very similar to those in the *Thrush* and the *dits*, contending that the world would not endure without women's counsel and that the one sex can hardly exist without the other. Still pursuing *dit*-like territory, she ad-

---

[19] Ch. 5, ed. Sundby, 16; tr. in Blamires, *Woman Defamed and Woman Defended*, 240.

[20] Albertanus' 'malum auxilium Deus homini dedisset, si ab eis consilium petere minime deberet' (ed. Sundby, 18), i.e. 'it would have been a very poor help-mate which God had given to man if man was obliged to seek counsel from women only as a last resort' (tr. in Blamires, *Woman Defamed and Woman Defended*, 241), emerges in Chaucer's translation from Renaud's French version as: 'if that wommen were nat goode, and hir conseils goode and profitable, | oure Lord God of hevene wolde nevere han wroght hem, ne called hem help of man, *but rather confusioun of man*' (VII. 1104–5, my italics). This speculation about alternative epithets for Eve is possibly the source of the jest involving 'mulier hominis confusio est' and its antithetical translation in the *Nun's Priest's Tale* (VII. 3164–6), though the note to VII. 3164 in *The Riverside Chaucer* connects it with a definition attributed to Secundus instead.

duces a jingle which holds woman to be 'better than gold or jewels'. She concludes with a flurry of *sententiae* approving a wife's benignity, tongue, and obedience—only she conceives this as a kind of obedience through which, it is suggested, a woman may paradoxically exercise power. If Melibeus will proceed 'prudently' (*prudenter*; as Prudentia dictates) she promises to 'heal' his wounded daughter and to bring him out of the crisis with honour. In the light of her 'sweet words' and his recognition of her loyalty and discretion, he declares that he has now changed his mind: but it is left to our imagination whether this change is really triggered by the case for women's *consilium* and the exhortation to prudent action, or whether Prudentia has simply touched his vulnerable spot: his 'honour' and his affection for his daughter.[21]

What is refreshing about the case for women in Albertanus' treatise is that an attempt is made to imagine a woman as subject, speaking out against blanket misogyny with assurance and self-knowledge. Prudentia dismisses the scriptural adage that ill-tempered wives hound men from their own homes by declaring simply (in Chaucer's version), 'by youre leve, that am nat I' (VII. 1087),[22] thus exposing the silliness of *dicta* which prove so absolutely irrelevant to personal lives. It became increasingly the norm to lodge anti-misogynist protest in a female persona. However, further examples of the discourse in the thirteenth century return to explicitly male-conducted defence, indeed in the case of *L'Honneur des dames* by Robert of Blois there is a return to the clubbishness of the first-person plural generalization: 'we' have no joy or pleasure without women.[23] Robert's placement of this 150-line poem, which identifies itself as an autonomous 'book' named 'L'onor es dames' (458), is elusive. In the manuscripts it occurs once near the beginning of a longer poem about the proper behaviour of the noble male, once as the prologue of the same poem, and twice as the prologue of a companion poem advising

[21] The narrative sustains a stereotype of feminine healing, even in Chaucer's version where the daughter is allegorized as 'Sophie' (i.e. *sophia*, Melibeus' 'wisdom').

[22] Albertanus: 'Me autem non invenisti talem,' ed. Sundby, 15.

[23] *L'Honneur* is edited as lines 315–464 of *L'Enseignement des princes*, a poem of social and political instruction for men; *Die didactischen und religiösen Dichtungen Robert's von Blois*, ed. Jacob Ulrich (Berlin: Mayer & Müller, 1895); my reference is to 'Et vos resavez bien trestuit, | Que joie, solaz ne deduit | N'avons entierement sanz eles' (353–5). All further quotations are from Ulrich's edition.

on women's behaviour, the *Chastoiement des dames*. Perhaps as
Roberta Krueger observes it befits either context,[24] though the
implicitly male audience that it constructs ('you' as well as 'we')
makes most sense to me in the context of the former.

L'Honneur begins with a now familiar emphasis on the dis-
gracefulness (*vilonie*) of maligning women, which in fact dishon-
ours the person who perpetrates it (315–22). Since the womb is
man's first 'lodging', and flesh and blood a gift so painfully and
tenderly nurtured by women, misogyny is tantamount to the
vileness of a bird which fouls its own nest (323–40)—a type of
subrational behaviour on which God is likely to take vengeance.
The ensuing argument that man's joy cannot be complete without
woman then yields an afterthought (not often explicitly considered in the formal case) that some men's 'disloyalty' to women
might arise from homosexuality. The vengeance implausibly invoked in that eventuality is that males acting 'against nature'
should be struck with deformity leading to mutual indifference in
order to silence their misogyny (359–74).

Women are now praised for their transformative impact on
men, using the 'they make X become its opposite' formula.
Women inspire daring exploits and are peacemakers, and can
tame the arrogant. The reflection that Robert derives from this
(evidently connecting it with the 'taming' effect ascribed to
courtly love) is that God demonstrated great love for women in
establishing that men should be *en lor dongier*. It seems an unusual
proposition, since the god of love, not God, is more often credited
with this arrangement. But it allows Robert to make a transition to
other definitive proofs of God's greater love for woman, namely
her creation inside paradise; the birth of Christ from woman
without male co-operation; and the sign of priority whereby
Christ appeared first to women after the Resurrection (395–446).
The honour paid to Christ's mother by all the saints and archan-
gels establishes, with finality, the honour which is all women's by
right. Needless to say, there is not the slightest indication how all
this 'honour' is going to affect women's lives. Women remain
implicitly the inactive focus of a superior divine benevolence
which justifies an aristocratically proper male deference: in the
'proofs' offered by Robert woman *does* nothing—is merely created in a privileged location, is that from which Christ is born, is

[24] 'Constructing Sexual Identities in the High Middle Ages: The Didactic Poetry
of Robert de Blois', *Paragraph*, 13 (1990), 105–31 (pp. 114–15).

that to which he reveals himself risen. One can see how much more can be achieved when the case is energized, as by Albertanus, so that the reaction of a woman to repression can be explored rather than God's putatively wrathful reaction to hypothetically ungallant males.

Nevertheless *L'Honneur des dames* represents the main directions of thirteenth-century defence, which are again quite zestfully transmitted in an Anglo-Norman poem *Du bounté des femmes*, extant in a manuscript miscellany from the end of the century.[25] The poem's speaker, announcing himself as women's 'champion', lays down the gauntlet by lauding the honour of the Virgin Mary as means to salvation, and the honour implicit in woman's creation from fine bone rather than from mud. After arguing that women's sexual resolve far exceeds men's, the speaker then spurns stories of Solomon's 'betrayal' by women as lying 'fable'. Misogyny is condemned because it amounts to rejection of one's origin and nurture (as though fruit sought to damage the tree on which it grew). Christ needed no father but he did need a mother, who therefore has maternal rights over the almighty. The poem culminates in an elaborate, legalistic exoneration of Eve: the strategy is to insist on Adam's responsibility both for his own folly and also (because apparently he failed to instruct her sufficiently) for Eve's as well. We shall return to equivocal acquittals of this kind in Chapter 4.

So far we have not seen much recourse to female exemplars for the defence, but one route was to deduce the case for women entirely from witnesses, that is, from legendary 'good women'— as Jerome in the fourth century had fashioned a paean to virginity and chaste wifehood from a catalogue of 'good' examples.[26] An unedited late thirteenth-century French prose text of this kind entitled the *Miroir des bonnes femmes* was described in two articles in *Romania* in 1961–2.[27] It was written by a Franciscan, conforming in some ways to 'the current of didactic works written for the ruling classes' in the period, yet possibly qualifying as a sermon

[25] Cambridge Univ. Lib. MS Gg. I. 1, fos. 390ᵛ–392ᵛ, ed. Meyer, 'Manuscrits français de Cambridge', 315–20. The poem is localized by allusions to Westminster and the Tower of London.
[26] *Adversus Iovinianum (PL* 23. 221–352), I. 41–6; tr. W. H. Fremantle, *The Principal Works of St Jerome*, Select Library of Nicene and Post-Nicene Fathers, 2nd ser. 6 (Oxford: James Parker, 1893), 379–83.
[27] J. L. Grigsby, '*Miroir des bonnes femmes*', pt. i, *Romania*, 82 (1961), 458–81, and pt. ii, *Romania*, 83 (1962), 30–51.

resource.[28] It echoes the oppositional sequence illustrated in Marbod's Bad Woman/Good Woman, by devising two series of *exempla*, first on 'Mauvaises femmes' and then on 'Bonnes femmes'. The method is to trawl scriptures fairly systematically under each heading, the biblical examples being intermittently supplemented with animal lore, history, hagiography, and anecdote. The pedagogical point of the polarization, the author declares, is to encourage readers to shun evil models and emulate good.[29] The whole is therefore to be a 'mirror' of behaviour—taking a cue from a reference to the mirrors of the women outside the temple in Exodus. It will be a mirror very different from the salacious material to be found in 'les romanz'.[30]

The questions we might have in mind are, whether the author can break interesting ground in the examples presented in his second section, and particularly whether he can derive from biblical narrative a genuinely positive construction of women's capacities. Since the section on evil women discovers (apart from predictable figures such as Eve, Lot's wife, Potiphar's wife, Delilah) several obscure candidates not usually shortlisted for infamy elsewhere (e.g. Penninah, the nurse of Miphiboseth, Michal), the reader turns to the complementary section with some sense of anticipation. In the catalogue of the good are Sara, Rebecca, Leah, Rachel, Pharaoh's daughter (because she saved infant Moses), Rahab (helped men of God), Samson's mother (received angelic prophecy), Deborah, Ruth, Hannah mother of Samuel, Abigail, Abisag, Tobias's wife, Esther, Judith, Susanna, and a courageous mother in Maccabees—whom Abelard also noticed. However the commentary both on these, and on the sprinkling of rarer figures like a maidservant who assisted Naaman to be cured of leprosy, is never stirring. Esther's entry is expansive, but only because she is supposed such a beacon of obedience. The author's rather pallid approach continues into the New Testament series, which covers the Virgin, Anna the prophetess, Mary Magdalene and Martha, the women who supported Christ's preaching, women who wept at the Crucifixion, and the Maries who anointed Christ's body.

The fact is that a catalogue such as this, conceived as a behavioural and ideological mirror, is governed by admonitory inten-

---

[28] Ibid., pt. i, pp. 464–5.
[29] Ibid. 469.
[30] Exod. 38: 8; Grigsby, '*Miroir*', pt. ii, pp. 30–1.

tions that prove to be divergent from genuine defensive strategies. More elaborately than most other writers by this date, the
author is prepared to notice roles women play in the Bible, and
this in itself is of some consequence. But those roles are comprehensively interpreted in support of a husband-centred ideology.
Thus, whereas for Abelard the women whom St Luke identified
as participants in Christ's preaching tours—including a certain
Joanna who was the wife of Herod's steward—are a powerful
demonstration of the absolute importance of women in Christ's
ministry,[31] in the *Miroir* the emphasis falls on their status *as wives*.
For this author it is not a matter of appreciating the women's
closeness to Christ and their role alongside the male disciples but
of using the example to define the special circumstances under
which a wife might legitimately remove herself (like Joanna) from
her husband:

> Women, who were wives of non-believers, ministered to Jesus. This
> shows that a woman should do good works even if her husband is an evil
> man. Isidore says that that there are two kinds of magnets: placed to-
> gether they attract iron more quickly than they do alone, but when
> separated after contact one magnet attracts and the other repels. So it is
> with a woman and her husband in regard to God. When a husband
> is with God a wife should obey her husband in all things. When he is
> dissevered from God, she should not leave God. . . . Prudent wives often
> bring salvation to their husbands.[32]

What is clarified by this excursion into the realms of the 'Good
Woman' in the *exemplum* tradition, therefore, is that while the
growth and refinement of the *exempla* themselves were to be of
real significance in the evolution of the case for women, the models presented were likely to be 'false friends' to the profeminine
argument wherever socializing propaganda commandeered exemplification. One can see in the sample of the *Miroir* just given

---

[31] Luke 8: 1–3 tells how Christ travelled preaching with the twelve and with
women who had been healed, and Mary Magdalene, 'And Joanna the wife of
Chusa Herod's steward, . . . and many others who ministered unto him of their
substance.' See Abelard, *Authority and Dignity of Nuns*, ed. Muckle, 259, tr. Scott
Moncrieff, 141.

[32] *Bonnes femmes*, in Grigsby, '*Miroir*', pt. ii, pp. 49–50. The important Augustinian argument that wives should, as it were, obey God direct over the head of errant
husbands is reproduced in *Dives and Pauper*, ed. Priscilla H. Barnum, vol. i, pt. ii,
EETS os 280 (Oxford: Oxford University Press, 1980), 70, 'in þat he doth omys leet
hym nout ben þin hefd to ledyn þe but let þin God ben þin hefd': on this, see my
article 'Paradox in the Medieval Gender Doctrine of Head and Body', forthcoming
in P. Biller and A. J. Minnis (eds.), *Medieval Theology and the Natural Body* (York:
York Medieval Press, 1997).

how carefully patriarchy licenses any deviation from gender hierarchy when the latter is threatened by biblical precedent. Of
course, *exempla* were always liable to articulate socializing propaganda, even if covertly. Yet at least they could (as we shall note in
Chapter 7) provide a hospitable site for inspection and revision of
assumptions in that propaganda.

Meanwhile, the threads of polemic present in the *dits* and in
L'Honneur des dames can be seen developing in a short Anglo-
Norman poem known from its first line as *De la bonté des femmes*
by Nicole Bozon, a friar writing in the north of England around
1325–50.[33] It is again a piece which participates in the Blame/
Praise convention, to which, however, it gives a tweak of dramatization by offering itself as an atonement for aspersions on
women detected by an unnamed woman reader in Bozon's earlier
work, the *Char d'Orgueil*. On this basis Jill Mann situates the *Bonté*
within an 'apologies to women' convention which encompasses
other fourteenth-century poems such as Le Fèvre's *Livre de Leësce*,
Machaut's *Judgement of the King of Navarre*, and Chaucer's *Legend
of Good Women*. Perhaps Mann is right to suggest that 'writing
against women and then apologising for it' was frequently 'just a
convenient way of manufacturing a literary subject; neither activity is evidence of a seriously held view of women'.[34] Yet a distinction should be made between the seriousness with which the
views are held by the writers (the old intractable question of
'sincerity' in literature) and the seriousness which a reader is able
to find in the views constructed. This is not quite the same, I think,
as Mann's own rider 'this is not to say, of course, that such works
didn't have serious *consequences*'—for consequences imply some
kind of radical effect on people's lives. One might be better off
envisaging the gradual consolidation of a profeminine stance,
whose consequences trickle slowly over centuries, despite the
determined efforts of individuals like Christine de Pizan to speed
up the process.

Bozon reshuffles and freshens some of the topoi we have already met. Announcing that Truth (*verité*) could properly accuse
him if he did not declare woman's goodness, he makes the usual
point that man has an obligation to esteem a good woman (4–6,
16–18). He suggests that antifeminist accusation arises as unfair
generalization against the sex on the basis of a few individual

---

[33] Ed. Smith and Meyer, *Contes moralisés de Nicole Bozon*, pp. xxxii–xli.
[34] *Apologies to Women*, 25.

lapses—a claim keenly pursued in this poem by protesting the illogicality of blaming a strong-growing plant if another identical one nearby happens to wither, and by complaining that men's indiscretions are shrugged aside while women's are subjected to public inflation (19–36, 109–20): moreover, women are under such scrutiny that their every move is liable to be misconstrued (79–96). The front-line weapon of misogyny, the Fall, is disarmed through the thesis (to which we shall return) that Adam sinned more by his acceptance than Eve sinned by her offer of the apple because she understood the situation less fully (37–54).

Bozon's development of profeminine positions is strident. To the commonplace that men owe gratitude to women as mothers and nurturers he adds the provocative thought that no man can calm a squealing infant like a woman (55–72). Inscribing a series of feminine virtues, he introduces woman's superior steadfastness or *estableté* with a horticultural variant of the conventional argument that she is handicapped with less 'strength' than man by nature; she is a tender shoot whose resistance to life's gales therefore highlights by contrast the pathetic collapse of man, likened to a stout but uprooted pear-tree.[35] Her 'stability' is reinforced anecdotally by appealing to readers' recollections. Do 'jousters'—the designation is doubtless phallic—waste their time hanging around households where wives' affection for husbands is obvious? *De la bonté des femmes* is curtailed in the manuscript after commendations of women's humility, their generosity or *franchise*, and their *naturesce*—which seems to mean the 'worth' of a daughter as against a son and indeed woman's worth generally, considered more precious than any precious stone (217–34, and see 73–5). If this last value-judgement seems to us misconceived, a reinforcement in fact of the commodification of women into objects of exchange and signs of masculine status, rather than a recognition of 'worth' in any intrinsic sense,[36] it was nevertheless a standard topos of this discourse in the Middle Ages. It also

[35] That great trees are uprooted sooner than reeds was an admonition against pride (Newman, *Sister of Wisdom*, 1); but readers of Chaucer's *Troilus and Criseyde* will also recall how Pandarus tries to inscribe Criseyde as a sturdy tree that may be felled rather than as a flexible reed, II. 1380–9.

[36] For examples of discussion of commodification, see Krueger, 'Love, Honor, and the Exchange of Women', 302–17; and David Aers's comments on Chaucer's Emelye in *Chaucer* (Brighton: Harvester, 1986), 77–82. A classic discussion is Gayle Rubin, 'The Traffic in Women: Notes on the "Political Economy" of Sex', in Rayna Reiter (ed.), *Toward an Anthropology of Women* (New York: Monthly Review, 1975), 171–7.

provides, as will become apparent, a trace of the origins of the discourse.

Besides, Bozon makes a credible effort to achieve empathy for women. He adopts something like a subject position, projecting the pain of being 'given' in marriage to 'please' husbands, and understanding the dignified social mask which (in a culture inimical to female displays of desire and emotion) hides both the anguish of knowing about husbands' infidelities and the power of women's own love (169–98). Doubtless there is a fine line between empathy for women's stoic endurance of a state of affairs which blatantly advantages males, and patriarchal commendation of women for a long-suffering which actually makes them accomplices in their own victimization—especially when all this is voiced by a male. But at least Bozon's method of sketching miniature scenes from household life has the effect of taking him closer to the energizing mode of Albertanus's work, in which underlying issues rather than mere compliments to women begin to surface.

By the last decades of the fourteenth century there was something like a vogue for structuring both misogynous and profeminine discourse into a dramatized situation, and for complicating its effect by problematizing the nature of the persona who utters it. Howard Bloch has seen the entire literary tradition of misogyny as an essentially citational mode, endlessly deferring responsibility for its allegations to an absent source (Theophrastus), but one can particularly apply to the period of Deschamps and Chaucer Bloch's suggestion that in confronting misogyny 'one is to some degree always dealing with a problem of voice, the questions of who speaks and of localizing such speech'.[37] The evasive complexities and ruses of the voicing of misogyny in Chaucer (or *for* Chaucer, by reader inference) have been finely analysed.[38] But of course defence could be couched in equally destabilizing contexts, as Deschamps demonstrates in *Le Miroir de mariage*.[39]

The *Miroir* is an unfinished 'whether-to-marry' debate belonging to the 1380s, but which may not have been in circulation until

---

[37] 'Medieval Misogyny', *Representations*, 20 (1987), 1–14 (p. 7).

[38] Mann, *Geoffrey Chaucer*, esp. the section on *The Merchant's Tale* (pp. 58–65) and on *The Nun's Priest's Tale* (pp. 193–4).

[39] *Œuvres complètes de Eustache Deschamps*, ix, ed. G. Raynaud, SATF (Paris: Firmin-Didot, 1894). All further references are to this edition.

after 1400.[40] In it Franc Vouloirs (Free Will) is urged not to marry in a massive and deeply misogynous letter from his friend Repertoire de Science ('Collective Wisdom').[41] The case for marriage—simultaneously the case for women—is assigned primarily to the female character Folie, head of a gang of three seeming undesirables: Desir, Servitute, and Faintise. What we want to know is, which way does the irony cut? Is Free Will being counselled by Four Cardinal Errors? Is an argument for marriage and wisdom going to be an argument of *folie* because Collective Wisdom is right, or is Folie's profeminine stance a self-mockingly 'foolish' argument in the eyes of 'wise' detractors only, recalling the biblical maxim that 'the foolishness of God is wiser than men'?[42]

Deschamps plays hard to find. Obliged to try to demolish all Wisdom's Theophrastan chestnuts, Folie risks ambivalence. For instance, she shows a suspicious amount of enthusiasm for St Bernard's *dictum* that a man of noble spirit does not seek to know too much about his wife's activities (8957–80).[43] Moreover it is clear that Deschamps means to tease us with the implications of the speaker's name, because Folie is interrupted by Desir with a speech of mock-compliment on her magnificent *rethorique* (9892–924). Yet Desir's raillery nevertheless acknowledges that Folie has proved not to be foolish (9895). There is some kind of double bluff; a game releasing Free Will, Deschamps, and the reader from taking seriously positions on marriage and women which run counter to urbane currents of wisdom and wit, and insinuating that woman equals folly, while sneaking in the contrary thought that the world's wisdom is folly, its folly wisdom.[44]

Nor is it clear how far Deschamps ventriloquizes a woman's voice in Folie's. Unlike the Wife of Bath, she does not use the

[40] In the *Œuvres complètes*, xi. 105, Raynaud suggests that Deschamps was writing the *Miroir* between around 1381 and 1389 and that it did not circulate until his death in 1406. However, its circulation before 1403 is implied in a letter Deschamps wrote that year; see *Les Quinze Joies de mariage*, ed. Jean Rychner (Geneva: Droz, 1963), pp. xvi–xviii.

[41] Helen Cooper's felicitous translation of the name, in *Oxford Guides to Chaucer: The Canterbury Tales* (Oxford: Clarendon Press, 1989), 204.

[42] 1 Cor. 1: 25.

[43] 'le noble cuer hault et sain | Les euvres des femmes n'enquiert, | Mais ignorance en leurs faiz quiert' (8966–8); cf. 'De feminis tuis suspectis quid agant, ignorantiam, non scientiam quaeras', St Bernard, Letter 456, *PL* 182. 649, and *Wife of Bath's Prologue*, III. 316–22.

[44] A negative attitude to Folie certainly characterizes the poem's last surviving section, in which Deschamps enumerates evils attributable to Folie through the course of human history.

partisan 'we'—except in one case where she slips by mistake into the men's team, appealing to men to honour women 'lest we dishonour ourselves'.[45] She signals her gender occasionally by projecting herself in the wifely role explicitly,[46] or more often implicitly. There seems to be an element of professional pride in women's home-warming skills when she satirizes the 'chilly' welcome offered by the households of clerks and other bachelors. Punning on the abbey of Fontevrault she dubs them 'Froitvaulx' houses, and expresses rhetorical dismay at men's ideas of looking after a home.[47] (It is a reminder that much medieval 'profeminine' argument would now count as covert misogyny, congratulating women on running a domestic prison so well.)

On the whole Deschamps does not push the possibilities of the female respondent so as to dramatize the case for women as far as he might. The speaker's gender, however, lends a certain frisson to the traditional preamble that it is unnatural to malign women and amazing that anyone would dare to utter or write misogynous insults, which should be burned (8512–14, 8584–9). There is certainly a keen edge in Folie's objection to the way men shuffle their sexual guilt onto women and typically blame Bathsheba for the sin which David—her king—instigated (8637–70).[48] Some hint of 'female' perspective and solidarity perhaps enters the speaker's diagnosis of a vicious circle whereby male oppression and miserliness and wife-beating cause angry remonstrations which then give *women* a bad name; but this objectivity collapses rather readily into endorsement of the patience with which women 'rightly' bear a husband's oppressions, capped with a confusingly different assumption that a woman is 'good' or 'bad' according to her husband's own disposition (8981–9004).

What is above all conspicuous in Deschamps is the increasing confidence of the defence position. Sarcastic counter-attack is becoming more frequent. Women martyrs like St Catherine and St Agatha are not only found to be resolute, but more resolute than men, who so harp on women's *grant fragilité* (9063–70). As in

[45] 'Tuit hommes, femmes honourons, | Ou nous tous nous deshonourons' (9095–6).

[46] 'Se je a mon mari ne plaisoie' (8679).

[47] 'Puis qu'il y a seigneur sanz dame, | L'en treuve hostel de Froitvaulx' (8864–5); 'Par ma foy, esbahie suy | Comment homs scet tenir mesnage' (8874–5).

[48] The case of David and Bathsheba was often raised in debate about women: see Blamires, *Woman Defamed and Woman Defended*, 8, 15, 32–3, 75, 95–6, 101, 105–6, 116, 267.

L'Honneur des dames we are told that maligning women from whom all men come is 'fouling one's own home'—the home occupied during gestation. But when Folie proceeds to the familiar proposition that she can field a thousand 'good' women against every one of the prosecution's 'bad' examples, she puts a sting in her wager by adding that *her* witnesses will not come from mere legends (*histoire trouvée*) of Hercules and Troy (9081–105). While misogynists, she says, use *fables* to allege women's 'instability', she therefore pointedly appeals instead to modern chronicle to argue the opposite, citing the resolve of Blanche of Castile, who brought factious barons to heel during the minority of her son St Louis, the French boy-king (9387–511). Folie finishes (inconsistently, but never mind) by wishing upon Collective Wisdom the fabled nemesis meted out to Orpheus by the 'Ciconian women' he had scorned: stoning to death.[49] It is a rare invocation of violent female solidarity, which will merit attention later in this study. It raises the same problem as Chaucer raises in the Wife of Bath's vision of masses of women writing infinite retaliatory stories of the 'wikkednesse' of men (III. 693–6): how is the defence to avoid perpetuating the belligerence which it is opposing? Deschamps himself is a writer whom Chaucer surely read—and whom Chaucer somewhat unfairly overshadows, for us, by outmatching him in his own experiments with ironizing intricacies of 'voice'.

As we have seen, ironizing has also been suspected (somewhat less justifiably) in the case of Jean Le Fèvre's spokeswoman in the *Livre de Leësce*, a key late fourteenth-century case for women written as a refutation of Le Fèvre's own translation of the misogynous *Liber lamentationum Matheoluli*.[50] Christine de Pizan was to find useful ideas in this refutation. Intertextuality links Le Fèvre's case for women with the *Roman de la Rose*: Leësce's name ('Joy') is precedented in Leësce the partner of Pleasure (*Deduit*) in the *Roman de la Rose*, suited to Le Fèvre's purposes because she is defined as an antithesis of hate.[51] The name is also

[49] Ovid, *Metamorphoses*, X. 1–67, tr. Mary M. Innes (Harmondsworth: Penguin, 1955), 246–7.

[50] In *Lamentations*, ed. Van Hamel. I would not go so far as to state categorically, with Jill Mann, that 'there are no indications that the defence of women in the *Livre de Leësce* is to be read ironically'; *Geoffrey Chaucer*, 34.

[51] 'Savés vous qui estoit s'amie? | Leesce qui nel haoit mie, | L'envoisie, la bien chantans, | Qui, des lors qu'el n'ot que set ans, | De s'amor li donna l'otroi', Guillaume de Lorris and Jean de Meun, *Le Roman de la Rose*, ed. Daniel Poirion

reminiscent of some lines near the conclusion of the *Lamentations,* where marriage is alleged to close the path of joy and open that of sorrow.[52] Although irony can be interpreted in both these literary echoes,[53] each can be read more straightforwardly in terms of the antithetical function which Le Fèvre himself envisages for this book as an atonement reversing (*par argument de sens contraire*) his regrettable translation of a work on the miseries of marriage (1–40). As indicated in the previous chapter, the *Livre de Leësce* is not assumed to be pervasively facetious in the present study.

Like Deschamps, Le Fèvre entangles a case for women within a point-by-point refutation of specific misogynous allegations, themselves entangled within a dissuasion (of males) from marriage. Since the *Lamentations* is a sprawling text and its course is meticulously rehearsed in *Leësce,* the latter inevitably sprawls too. Of its 3,991 lines, 3,467 mix *reprise* of allegations with explicit responses and with digressions into further lines of defence. Le Fèvre keeps promising to organize the defensive effort more comprehensively. His last section launches, at last independent of the *Lamentations,* into a profeminine statement marshalled under three broad headings: Courage (*Prouesce*), Knowledge (*Science*), and Stability or Chastity. This is quite reminiscent of Bozon, whose case leads into a sequence of qualities held to be superior in women: 'stability', 'humility', and *franchise.* Leësce herself meanwhile remains a very shadowy presence. The book is ostensibly entitled after her because written out of love of her, but she is an offstage dramatis persona—a cursory tutelary figure fitfully invoked for the direction of the narrator's argument ('Leësce says . . .', 981, 'Leësce puts this defence . . .', 1112, 'my mistress Leësce proposes . . .', 3529) in an arrangement which preserves the fiction of presenting a woman's case without energizing her voice.

(Paris: Garnier-Flammarion, 1974), lines 831–5; 'And do you know the name of his sweetheart? It was Joy, with her gaiety and sweet voice, who did not hate him in the least, but had given him her love when she was no more than seven years old,' Guillaume de Lorris and Jean de Meun, *The Romance of the Rose,* tr. Frances Horgan (Oxford: Oxford University Press, 1994), 14. All further references will be to Poirion's edition and Horgan's translation. Blumenfeld-Kosinski connects Leësce with Deduit's *amie,* but thinks that Le Fèvre's interest was in following the implications of Guillaume's description of Leësce (line 840) as a 'new rose'; 'Jean le Fèvre's *Livre de Leesce*', 714.

[52] 'De leesce luy clos la sente | Et luy doins les cles de tristesce', *Lamentations,* IV. 812–13.   [53] Pratt, 'Analogy or Logic', 64.

Several familiar topoi surface, in some cases repeatedly, in the poem. It is four times noted that every misogynist owes existence to a mother, and that to condemn what one comes from is self-undermining.[54] Generalization is ubiquitously denounced. The 'benefits' women bring to men are elaborated. In response to the jocular idea that women are noisy because originally created from bone, 'privileges' of women are catalogued (1203–310): not just that woman was created of better stuff than man, and created inside Paradise, but more eruditely that her being taken from the middle of Adam's sleeping body signifies human companionship and is a figure of the sacraments of the Church, issuing from Christ's side on the cross.[55]

Le Fèvre also pursues—only more incisively than precursors—a reconstruction of gender stereotyping when he argues that pro-miscuity characterizes men more than women (1532–4): behind the misogynous caricature of the old bawd is detected male lust and instigation which leads to the existence of prostitutes and go-betweens in the first place, (2327–55). The poem's closing passages firmly insist on male instigation of lechery. Leësce asserts that fickleness cannot rightly be gendered feminine because it is masculine pressure, deceit, and inconstancy which are exerted to subvert the sexual loyalty of women (3832–73, 3894–905). Men submerge themselves in lust: they allow their excess (*fureur*, but we might now say their testosterone) to run riot (3894–905).

It is doubtful whether we should worry about the fact that Leësce has lapsed into reverse generalization against men here. The logic that *is* at work is a logic that yields promising—albeit rudimentary—sociological and psychological observations. Le Fèvre is confronting questions of responsibility which also loom in Deschamps's roughly contemporary *Miroir de mariage*. The re-sult of trying to perceive misogynous allegation as a conduit for unacknowledged male failings is that routine *exempla* such as that of David and Bathsheba (the sight of whom was alleged to have 'caused' David's sins of adultery and homicide) are exposed in both texts to more bracingly logical scrutiny, so that responsibility is more equitably assigned.[56] Admittedly the scrutiny is some-times applied by Le Fèvre in a sophistical way. The *exemplum* of

---

[54] 517–18, 1017–36, 2775–7, 3013–14.
[55] Discussed below in Ch. 4.
[56] *Leësce*, 248–66 and 1539–41: cf. *Miroir*, 8637–70.

Lot's wife, archetype of disobedience because she looked back at the destruction of Sodom, provokes an uneasy defence attempt to shift responsibility to God on the grounds that God's foreknowledge of Lot's procreation of tribes by intercourse with his own daughters obliged the Almighty to terminate her (2167–88).

Elsewhere, however, Le Fèvre's scrutiny produces fleeting penetrations of encompassing masculine ideology that one might not have expected in that culture. This is especially the case when he considers the obstacle to women's intellectual potential posed by a certain Calphurnia, whose legendary immodesty while pleading a case was held by Matheolus to epitomize a female indiscipline of speech and action that disqualified all subsequent women from public speaking.[57] Two counter-*exempla* are introduced: first Heloise, described as wise in law and custom and, interestingly, as *philosofesse*, and second the daughter of 'maistre Jehan Andrieu' who studied law and demonstrated woman's equality with man in a public all-day lecture with more than seventy watertight propositions (1130–54). It would be interesting to know more about the forms in which this report was circulating, for behind Le Fèvre's account is a certain Novella, born in 1312, daughter of Giovanni Andrea who lectured on law at Bologna until 1348. Giovanni dedicated one of his commentaries to her by entitling it *Novella in Decretales*.[58] Primed (perhaps) by Le Fèvre, Christine de Pizan also adduces Novella in her *Cité des dames*, only Christine's report focuses on Novella's ability to stand in for her father in his absence, when she lectured behind a curtain lest her beauty 'distract' the students.[59] Christine's account incidentally testifies to the residual power of medieval patriarchy's supposition that women would constitute a sexual tempta-

[57] Le Fèvre, *Lamentations*, II. 177–200: tr. Karen Pratt in Blamires, *Woman Defamed and Woman Defended*, 183–4.

[58] *Lamentations*, ed. Van Hamel, ii. 241, n. to *Leësce*, 1140–54.

[59] Maureen Cheney Curnow, 'The *Livre de la cité des dames* of Christine de Pisan: A Critical Edition', Ph.D. dissertation, Vanderbilt University (1975), 874–5; tr. Earl Jeffrey Richards (New York: Persea Books, 1982), II. 36. 3, p. 154. All further references will cite Curnow's edition and Richards's translation. Andrea's reputation was doubtless known to Christine's father who himself studied and taught at Bologna; see Maureen Cheney Curnow, ' "La Pioche d'inquisicion": Legal-Judicial Content and Style in Christine de Pizan's *Livre de la cité des dames*', in Earl Jeffrey Richards *et al.* (eds.), *Reinterpreting Christine de Pizan* (Athens, Ga.: University of Georgia Press, 1992), 157–72 (p. 169). Christine's account is somewhat sceptically discussed in Paul O. Kristeller, 'Learned Women of Early Modern Italy: Humanists and University Scholars', in P. H. Labalme (ed.), *Beyond their Sex: Learned Women of the European Past* (New York: New York University Press, 1984), 102–14.

tion if they spoke in public,[60] but more important is the fact that Le Fèvre anticipates the kind of deduction about male ideological control which Christine derives from Novella's example. In *Leësce* there is a brief but incisive suggestion that since women evidently have abundant and sophisticated intellectual talent one can only conclude that men's exclusion of them from pleading at law arises from fear.[61] Christine confronts the possibility of this shabby motivation more elaborately, through the specious justification under which men hide it—the claim that they oppose the education of women 'because [women's] mores would be ruined as a result', a claim offered by 'foolish men' (Rectitude tells Christine) 'because it displeased them that women knew more than they did'.[62]

Christine skirts generalization here, with its attendant ideological questions, by diagnosing a problem among 'foolish men' rather than joining Le Fèvre in diagnosing (momentarily anyway) an inbred male conspiracy. Neither writer is prepared to take the step of championing a female right to enter the legal profession. Yet both writers are productively probing motivation. They are willing to ask what is the status of misogynous utterances and *exempla*, and to ask what could have caused such utterances. In the evolution of the case for women, in fact, attempts to expose the motivation of detractors can be seen as part of the same phenomenon as the increasingly critical attitude to the authority of 'proofs' the detractors use. Although the discussion of motivation is not particularly ambitious, and although it tends to return issues to a personal level rather than to the institutional or socio-

[60] See Blamires and Marx, 'Woman Not to Preach', 40–1, 44, 52.

[61] 'Femmes sont de noble matere, | L'engin et la science ont clere, | Plaine de grant subtilité. | Si puis conclure, en vérité, | Que les hommes moult les doubterent; | Pour ce toutes les debouterent | De l'office d'avocacie' (1155–61).

[62] *Cité*, II. 36. 1 and II. 36. 4, ed. Curnow, 872–5, tr. Richards, 153–4. Christine claims in *L'Avision Christine* to have met a man who said that it was not right for a woman to have learning when he had little; her retort was that it was less appropriate for a man to have ignorance, which he had much of; see Diane Bornstein, 'Self-Consciousness and Self Concepts in the Work of Christine de Pisan', in Diane Bornstein (ed.), *Ideals for Women in the Works of Christine de Pizan* (Detroit: Michigan Consortium for Medieval and Early Modern Studies, 1981), 11–28 (p. 15), and *L'Avision Christine*, ed. Sr. Mary Louise Towner (Washington: Catholic University Press, 1932), 162. Christine refers earlier in the *Cité* to the *exemplum* of Calphurnia, whom she refuses to dignify with a name: men say, she tells Reason, that women are excluded from judicial functions 'because of some woman (whom I don't know) who governed unwisely from the seat of justice'; I. 2. 1, ed. Curnow, 664, tr. Richards, 31.

logical spheres occasionally visible in *Leësce*, it does significantly demystify the authority of misogynous tradition. Le Fèvre hypothesizes at one point a psychological sequence whereby the author of the *Lamentations* stopped 'paying the sexual debt' to his wife as a result of impotence, lost some of her affection by his sexual indifference, and revenged himself on her reaction by maligning her (900–30). Leësce then represents this as a cardinal principle of misogyny near the poem's conclusion: women know, she declares, whence male attacks on women derive. No man maligns the sex—rather, they sue for peace and grace—so long as 'Master Sucker' is serviceable.[63]

The formula is engagingly simple. A positive attitude to women is in proportion to a capacity for erection. This can partly be seen as a corollary of the axiom, found in the *dits*, that a man's attraction to a woman makes him *cortois*, but it seems also to derive from increasingly lurid medieval biographical speculation about an authority who was particularly associated with misogyny, namely Ovid. Christine de Pizan presents an Ovid (deduced from his love-poetry) who lives a dissolute life of promiscuity in youth: eventually, castrated ('diffourmez de ses membres') as well as exiled for being dissolute, this Ovid attacks women out of impotent frustration and envy of other men.[64] It is tempting to argue, as does Maureen Quilligan, that Christine here and elsewhere in the *Cité* 'goes straight to the heart of a castration anxiety that may be said to be the originary moment for the misogyny' in texts such as the *Roman de la Rose*, in anticipation of modern feminist critiques of Freudian theory.[65] Yet the castration anxiety ascribed to the 'Ovidian' misogynist in the medieval texts is an anxiety that others are enjoying sexual satisfactions no longer available to himself: we are not in the realms of a male fear of or revulsion from the 'otherness' of the female, construed as 'lack' or castration. The psychology projected is a psychology of jealous reaction to one's own actual castration or impotence, not a fear of potential castration. Le Fèvre anticipates Christine. Ovid's testicles were cut off: thence, he presumes, the animus Ovid di-

---

[63] 'Femmes scevent bien que ce monte; | Car nuls homs ne blasme leur gendre | Tant que maistre jobart puist tendre. | On n'en mesdit en nulle place, | Mais veult bien que la paiz se face' (3879–83).

[64] *Cité*, I. 9. 2, ed. Curnow, 648, tr. Richards, 21; see also I. 8. 5 and I. 8. 7, ed. Curnow, 643–5, tr. Richards, 18–19.

[65] *Allegory of Female Authority*, 42.

rected against women, whom he never afterwards loved (2709–22).[66]

What is instructive about this probing of motivation in *Leësce* is that Ovid's authority is being undermined precisely in the context of the wider question of reliability in received *exempla*. The point is not just that Ovid's misogyny is a misrepresentation bred of personal spite but that all the illustrative stories about women handed down by Homer and others (like Ovid) who wrote of gods and metamorphoses lack reliability too, for they are trifles and 'fables', heresies even, written under pagan law and therefore devoid of truth (2674–706). The *Livre de Leësce* makes the criterion of credibility a crux. 'Modern' witnesses like Heloise and Novella, or witnesses from 'true' Scripture, are preferred to 'pagan' witnesses. Admittedly the distinctions are neither absolutely clear nor firmly adhered to. Lucretia and Penelope are unquestioningly presented as exemplars of marital loyalty. A catalogue of strong women names the Nine Female Worthies (Semirimis, Thamiris, Penthesilea, etc.) alongside saints and a contemporary abbess, Jeanne de Neuville (2795–958). In the section in praise of women's *science* which lists Carmentis (legendary inventor of the Latin alphabet) alongside Medea, Sappho, the goddess Pallas, the Sibyl, and Cassandra of Troy (3618–87), one might have thought that some of these were queasy candidates in the light of the stated antipathy to pagan deities and the repeated spurning of *fable*.[67] Anyway misogynist authorities are seen as purveyors of jests and figments of the poetic imagination, *fable controuvée*, lies (1517–18), based on untruths such as the notion in the story of Eurydice that someone might come back from the dead (2089–100). Pasiphaë's reported intercourse with a bull is an implausible literary jape, to be contrasted with 'true' examples of self-sacrificial female chastity like Jephtha's daughter and Virginia (2467–530).

If we begin to wonder whether Le Fèvre is mischievously construing versions of women 'true' if they are nice versions, there are two factors to be considered. One is the earnestness with which he pursues the truth-criterion. Against the literary opposition of Juvenal and company he appeals to God as Truth, guard-

---

[66] Van Hamel's note, ii. 249, finds no known source for this legend.

[67] Le Fèvre does not clarify boundaries between 'fable' and 'true' history. After many heroines from antique story have been identified in the eulogies on female *prouesce* and *science*, as though an inconsistency has been discovered too late, it is stated that Leësce has named those rather than modern French heroines in order to eschew flattery (3786–93).

ian of Right and Equity, and to Reason 'our judge' (760–4, that is, to verité, droiture, equité, and raison, who might benefit from capitalization since that would draw attention to a possible source for the presiding figures Raison, Droitture, Justice in Christine's Cité). Le Fèvre's whole poem, indeed, is explicitly founded on a desire to sustain 'truth', which, he points out, is proved in Scripture to be stronger even than woman (herself stronger than kings or wine),[68] and which the shepherdess Alithie ('Truth') championed against a proponent of pagan mythology called Pseustis of Athens (43–80).[69] The second factor is that the notion of *grading* the credibility of *exempla* is not a ruse dreamed up by Le Fèvre but an engagement with a literary development of considerable relevance to the bandying of proofs in discourse about women. As we saw, Deschamps is aware of it in his distinction between *histoire trouvée* and *escripture*,[70] but it is present—indeed fundamental—earlier on in the preamble to the 'good women' section of the prose *Miroir des bonnes femmes*. There the writer contrasts the 'mirror' of biblical *essample* with the deceiving mirror of *les romanz*. By the latter is probably meant epic or Ovidian narrative, since the preamble goes on to recall a famous dream of Jerome in which that erudite saint was rebuked for preferring pagan books to Christian ones.[71] Hence the writer's decision to give precedence to biblical women.

What all this discloses is that suitable reinforcement for the case for women was available, for those who wished to use it, in the shape of suspicions levelled at 'pagan' poetry. Typical of these suspicions, as A. J. Minnis has shown, was a contrast between the eye-witness veracity of *historia* and the poetic artifice of *fabula* which, indeed, dealt in 'events which are neither true nor probable'.[72] Homer was criticized for muddling fables of gods with the history of Troy.[73] As for Ovid, learned medieval disciples such as

[68] Discussed below in Ch. 2.
[69] Le Fèvre had translated the *Theoduli ecloga*, which presents the Alithie/Pseustis dialogue.
[70] *Miroir de mariage*, 9099–103.
[71] Grigsby, 'Miroir', pt. ii, p. 31; with reference to Jerome, Letter 22 to Eustochium. The dream reached a wide readership through its mention in the *Legenda aurea*; see Jacobus de Voragine, *The Golden Legend: Readings on the Saints*, tr. William Granger Ryan, 2 vols. (Princeton: Princeton University Press, 1993), ii. 212.
[72] A. J. Minnis, *Chaucer and Pagan Antiquity* (Cambridge: D. S. Brewer, 1982), 22–3, drawing on 13th-cent. definitions and earlier rhetorical handbooks.
[73] Ibid. 23–5.

the compiler of the Old French *Ovide moralisé* (1316–28) sought to justify their translations of his *fables* into French (*en romans*) on the basis that truth could be extracted from them allegorically.[74] Chaucer shows a comically oblique awareness of such responses when in *The Book of the Duchess* (44–59) his narrator refers airily to Ovidian material as bedtime reading, 'fables' of bygone times, queens, kings, and other such trifles or 'thinges smale'. By applying the allegation of triviality unexpectedly to kings and queens, Chaucer seems to unhinge it. We should not expect, and shall not find, that fable-bashing is a profeminine tactic congenial to Chaucer.

This discussion should help the reader to sense what is distinctive about the contribution of Le Fèvre and to sense where he does (as well as does not) share interests with Chaucer. The profeminine impetus of the logical critique which Le Fèvre applies to misogynous allegations and of his resistance to the essentializing use of *exempla* and other forms of 'analogical thought' have been interestingly discussed by Karen Pratt. She detects limitations in his profeminine stance: his generalization against men, his indulgence in one or two potentially subversive literary jokes, and his readiness to incorporate large slabs of the opposition's arguments.[75] Although it is easy to trip Le Fèvre up, his analytical pressure remains notable. Where once it was enough to jam the airspace by matching assertion with counter-assertion and example with counter-example, it is now a matter of querying the credentials of all statements and illustrative examples. In this respect *Leësce* partially realizes what Chaucer was to realize more fully: that misogyny and anti-misogyny provided superbly fertile ground for debate about the authority and validity of speakers, utterances, and received 'proofs'.

Although Christine de Pizan absorbed ideas from *Leësce* and was a keen investigator of motivation, she differed somewhat in her appetite for validity puzzles of this kind. We shall round off this chapter's survey of the formal case for women by looking at her first formal profeminine text, reserving the *Cité des dames* for later discussion.

Christine de Pizan wrote *L'Epistre au dieu d'amours* in 1399. Like Le Fèvre, she deploys a fictional mouthpiece—in this case a male,

---

[74] Minnis, *Chaucer and Pagan Antiquity*, p. 18.
[75] Pratt, 'Analogy or Logic', 63–5; a view severely pursued by Solterer, *The Master and Minerva*, 131–50.

the God of Love, though he in turn is represented as making an official declaration, penned by Christine herself as clerk, on behalf of all kinds of women whose protests against men he has received.[76] It would be interesting to know whether Christine thus intended to amalgamate, as it were, female and male voices in one 'androgynous narrative voice',[77] or whether she wanted to embed female protest in a masculine authority-figure. If *Leësce* was envisaged to some extent as a 'rewrite' of the *Roman de la Rose*, the selection of the God of Love here invokes the *Rose* even more pointedly. Amours now speaks up for women where formerly he was instructor of the young male and commander of the siege of female virginity. Christine makes him the scourge of two manifestations of slander of women: the egotistical insinuations of the unscrupulous 'modern' courtly predator, and the malignity of clerkish misogyny.[78]

The first section decries the modern gallant as mostly fake, operating 'by false seeming' (*par faulx semblans*, (50), i.e. by the unscrupulous code of Faux Semblant in the *Rose*) and flattering his ego by dishonouring women with exaggerated gossip and insinuation about sexual conquests, in order to preserve esteem in the masculine peer-group. This not only betrays a lover's proper courtesy, it 'disnatures' the proper tenderness of a man towards the sex which has mothered and nurtured him (165–84). The follies which may be detected in some women are neither to be personally attacked nor imputed to all women by confusing fallen angels with unfallen. Two modern instances of ideal men identified for emulation are Hutin de Vermeille and Oton de Grandson: like Le Fèvre, Christine says she refrains from the flattery involved in naming others (223–58), but the naming of profeminine men, rather than 'good' modern women, is a new development.

Familiarity with the formal case enables one to see that the next

---

[76] Ed. and tr. Fenster and Erler in *Poems of Cupid*; for another translation of most of the poem by Karen Pratt, see Blamires, *Woman Defamed and Woman Defended*, 279–86.

[77] A phrase used by Walters, 'The Woman Writer and Literary History', 4.

[78] Kevin Brownlee, who states that Christine 'speaks "through" the mouth of a corrected version of the *Rose*'s structurally central authority character, Cupid', sees the two categories of offender as representing the 'courtly and clerkly registers' of the *Rose*—respectively the 'deceptive courtly lover' who is tutored in the *Rose*, and the misogynistic learned clerk who authorizes that deception; 'Discourses of the Self: Christine de Pizan and the *Rose*', *Romanic Review*, 78 (1988), 199–221 (esp. pp. 200–2).

part of the *Epistre* (259–556) amounts to a further enormous expansion of the usual preliminary aspersions on the motives of detractors, as Christine now investigates 'written' (as opposed to putatively 'oral') detraction. There are significant similarities with and divergences from the critique in *Leësce*. Ovid is again picked out as malignant source—particularly for advising how not to love women in the *Remedia amoris*—and is taken to epitomize the womanizing clerk who associates with women as freewheeling and immoral as himself for half a lifetime and then spends the impotence of age masking his guilt by attacking women's freewheeling immorality (321–40).[79] Chaucer's Wife of Bath encapsulates this unforgettably:

> The clerk, whan he is oold, and may noght do
> Of Venus werkes worth his olde sho,
> Thanne sit he doun, and writ in his dotage
> That wommen kan nat kepe hir mariage! (III. 707–10)

Christine herself probably owes this line of thought to Le Fèvre, and aims like him to qualify the prestige of writings presumed so authoritative. She has no intention, however, of emulating his campaign against the 'implausibility' of Ovidian *fable*. Le Fèvre's strictures against pagan stories of gods and goddesses were incompatible with her quasi-humanist interest in classical story and in the gods and goddesses—many of whom she names at the end of the *Epistre*. Since her 'predilection for the inhabitants of Mount Olympus undoubtedly came to her by way of Ovid',[80] it is inevitable that her attitude to Ovid is somewhat schizophrenic: 'for Christine, there are two Ovids, the good one, her *auctor* and source (most often via the *Ovide moralisé*) for much mythological material, and the bad one, the misogynist.'[81]

Instead of *fable*, Christine targets the twin problems of male

---

[79] Misogyny's origin in male association with the 'wrong' sort of women is alleged against Jean de Meun by Christine a couple of years later in the *Débat* on the *Rose*: 'by having resort to many dissolute women of evil life . . . he thought, or feigned to know, that all women were of that kind; for he had known no others'; tr. Joseph L. Baird and John R. Kane, *La Querelle de la Rose: Letters and Documents* (Chapel Hill: University of North Carolina Press, 1978), 52; French text in *Le Débat sur le 'Roman de la Rose'*, ed. Eric Hicks (Paris: Champion, 1977), 18.

[80] Charity Cannon Willard, 'A New Look at Christine de Pizan's *Epistre au dieu d'amours*', in Franco Simone *et al.* (eds.), *Seconda miscellanea di studi e ricerche sul quattrocento francese* (Chambéry: Centre d'Études Franco-Italien, 1981), 74–91 (p. 78).

[81] Renate Blumenfeld-Kosinski, 'Christine de Pizan and the Misogynistic Tradition', *Romanic Review*, 81 (1990), 279–92 (p. 283).

monopoly of writing and of education. That there are so many tales of 'deceitful' women in such books as Ovid's is a mark, not of the implausibility of the tales but of the masculine subjectivity which dominates books. Men write on and 'plead their case' unopposed. They are envisaged as bullies dealing confidently with unresisting opponents. Christine seems to mean that women are voluntarily non-combative rather than vulnerable or even 'illiterate'; they do not defend themselves (*ne se deffendent*, 416) rather than cannot. She goes on to add that 'If women, though, had written all those books, I know that they would read quite differently.'[82] We should notice that rider. If women are silent, they nevertheless *know*—as if in silent judgement—that blame is wrongly allocated. In a dining metaphor devastatingly adjusted to shatter masculine self-concepts of dignity, of fair play, and of the hospitality of a paterfamilias, she shows men what they are really doing: cutting the biggest slices of everything for themselves (419–22). The speculation about what might happen if women wrote instead (though not the accompanying metaphor) is famously paralleled by the Wife of Bath. It is in *The Wife of Bath's Prologue* that Chaucer comes closest to combining an interest in the relativities of 'authority' broached by Deschamps and Le Fèvre with an interest in the subjectivity of misogyny signalled by Christine.

For Christine, masculine subjectivity perniciously perpetuates misogyny through indoctrination of the young at school, where grammar classes trot out verses against women. Momentarily there is the prospect of an alternative educational agenda—a prospect once again glimpsed in the *Cité*[83]—which Christine nevertheless relinquishes in favour of attending to what seems to have been a more urgent anxiety for her at this period, the scandalous dissemination of misogyny through the popularity of the *Roman de la Rose*. The critique she mounts is a brilliant adaptation of an existing component of the formal case. Building on a configuration implicit in Nicole Bozon and explicit in medieval commentary on sexual mores, Le Fèvre had championed women's

---

[82] 'Mais se femmes eussent li livre fait, | Je sçay de vray qu'aultrement fust du fait' (417–18). Christine asserts the 'truth' that female experience can tell about women in the *Débat* (ed. Hicks, 19, and tr. Baird and Kane, 53) and in the *Cité*, *passim*.

[83] I. 27. 1, ed. Curnow, 721–2, tr. Richards, 63–4. Although the emphasis there is on women's access to education, rather than its content, the two issues are of course not unconnected.

sexual loyalty by contrasting it with the frenetic predatory behaviour of wheedling, manœuvring, and deceiving men. Men 'pervert' women's morality, according to the *Livre de Leësce*: but you do not see women begging *folies* from males (3834–54). Christine adopts this paradigm, based on a simple gendering of active male, passive female, to deride a self-contradiction which she perceives both in Ovid's position and in that of the *Roman de la Rose*. They accuse women of sexual deceit, her mouthpiece Amours observes, (a) without acknowledging that all the agency, pursuit, knocking on doors in sexual matters (which indeed Amours rehearsed from Ovid at length in Guillaume de Lorris's poem), is done by males who stretch every sinew to beguile their prey; and (b) without acknowledging that all the elaborate 'art' prescribed for 'lovers' in the sexual siege actually presupposes not the flexible loyalties of the victim, but her stern resistance.

Into these distinctive arguments are inserted vignettes of Medea's love for Jason, Dido's for Aeneas, and Penelope's for Ulysses; standard *exempla* of female loyalty, in fact (431–66). Christine has one more surprise in store before broaching other familiar elements of the case for women. She suggests that where disloyalty does occur in women, it is precipitated by a context saturated with male treachery (482–92). The betrayal of Troy (perhaps by implication the central myth of masculine epic) stands as an emblem of the spectacular extent of male perjury and therefore of the power which it can exert on—as Christine mockingly puts it—a poor little woman (535–48).[84]

There remains one-third of the poem which develops the topoi of the formal case more briskly. Christine begins where Abelard begins, with the Gospels' warm account of women and their loyalty to Christ. She goes on to argue that every woman shares in the honour Christ accorded the Virgin Mary. The 'privileges' of woman's creation (material and place) are recalled. Eve is defended, on grounds comparable with Nicole Bozon's, because she trusted the serpent and had no intention to deceive Adam. Preferring to hold a consistent position and praise rather than detract,

[84] 'Une ignorant petite femmellette' (548): Nadia Margolis has shown how the diminutive acts here as an ironizing device, miming the vulnerability ascribed by patriarchy; 'Elegant Closures: The Use of the Diminutive in Christine de Pizan and Jean de Meun', in Richards *et al.* (eds.), *Reinterpreting Christine de Pizan*, 111–25 (p. 117). The self-assurance with which Christine can neutralize the 'sexist feminine diminutive' is also discussed in Richards, 'Christine de Pizan and the Question of Feminist Rhetoric', 23.

the speaker makes a point of cataloguing major crimes *not* committed by the majority of women, rather than stating outright that
men commit them.[85]

Confronting a logical consequence of this, that women are perhaps not to be praised for a 'natural' disposition against major
crime, Christine is happy to endorse and dwell on the 'mildness'
of that disposition, which she sees as a mark of God's courtesy to
women; but she resists the assumption that active exercise of
virtue deserves no merit. Finally, men are exhorted to value
women as their 'natural' partners who bring them joy and are
indeed the very mothers whose likeness men bear. The poem
ends with the pronouncement of formal penalties against persistent offenders.

It is clear that by 1399 all sorts of issues latent in the formal case
for women—questions about motivation, authority, consistency,
subjectivity, and masculine hypocrisy—were clamouring for attention, and that Christine de Pizan was ready to rise to them. At
the same time, the *Epistre* clearly sustains many topoi developed
by precursors. This chapter will have achieved its aim most surely
if the reader has begun to sense that certain strong conventions
affect the kind of profeminine discourse which even a Christine
develops. Having surveyed a corpus of writings which participate in the formal case for women, the next step is to summarize
generic features of this discourse and ponder their sources and
rhetorical affiliations.

---

[85] In the *Cité*, Christine abandoned the cautious stance of the *Epistre*; Droitture
declares that 'you will never find such perversion in women as you encounter in
a great number of men', II. 49. 5, ed. Curnow, 899, tr. Richards, 170. Droitture's
examples are Judas, Julian the Apostate, and Denis of Sicily, the latter being one of
those named in a list of men 'never mentioned' by misogynists according to *Leësce*,
3811–19. Le Fèvre asserted that he *could* make counter-charges of grievous male
crimes—which he listed—if this tactic were any use against the 'ire' of Matheolus
(1177–97).

2

The Formal Case: Origins, Procedures

SINCE the medieval case for women has hardly begun to be studied, the fact that its sources have not really been investigated is not surprising.[1] Attention has generally been confined to rhetorical antecedent, specifically the concept of judicial oratory, which will require consideration in a moment. Yet, for all its relevance, rhetorical prescription for arguing legal cases gives only recommendations about how to organize materials; it does not provide the kind of authoritative palpable demonstration which medieval writers liked to chew on. In the history of misogyny, for instance, the long quotation ascribed to Theophrastus in St Jerome's *Adversus Iovinianum* became, in this sense, the core precedent for the Middle Ages. To point to judicial oratory as the complementary core of defence would be a kind of sidestep. Where do we turn for a core text for the defensive tradition? Had Plato's formulations concerning the sexes and the parallel education of women and men been available, profeminine discourse in the period might have been quite different. As it is, the knowledge of Plato among humanists after about 1500 is a significant factor in differentiating Renaissance from medieval discourse on the subject.[2]

The single most cogent source and paradigm for the medieval case for women is located, I believe, in one of the Old Testament apocrypha, namely the third book of Esdras, and its analogues. Esdras books 3 and 4 belonged to the Greek tradition of the Old

---

[1] Contributory traditions are beginning to be explored, for example in McLeod, *Virtue and Venom*. Scholarship on what I am calling the 'core' materials seems largely to have stalled since Meyer's 'Mélanges de poésie française, iv', though there are new beginnings in Fiero *et al.*, *Three Medieval Views of Women*, and Fenster and Erler, *Poems of Cupid*.

[2] The Italian humanist Marsilio Ficino (d. 1499) translated Plato into Latin. Agostino Strozzi's *Defensio mulierum* (c.1501) draws attention to Plato's argument in *The Republic* for dividing all work between the sexes; Benson, *Invention of the Renaissance Woman*, 50. Thereafter, citations were frequent in defence literature, including influential texts such as Agrippa's *De nobilitate et praecellentia foeminei sexus* and Castiglione's *Il cortegiano*.

Testament corpus (the 'Septuagint') which was influential among the earliest Christian writers. However, the two books were not accepted by St Jerome when he made his inaugural rendition of the Vulgate Bible, based on Hebrew texts.[3] His rendering of the Hebrew Ezra and Nehemiah became, in the medieval Vulgate, '1 and 2 Esdras', but despite his rejection of the further Esdras books, they were still frequently included in vulgates as '3 and 4 Esdras' until the Council of Trent in 1546, after which they were relegated to an appendix. The situation thenceforth is rather confusing in that usually 1 and 2 Esdras are renamed 'Ezra' and 'Nehemiah', so that medieval Vulgate '3 and 4 Esdras' are renumbered as apocryphal '1 and 2 Esdras'.[4] For present purposes '3 Esdras' will be the preferred designation rather than (apocryphal) '1 Esdras'.

The portion of 3 Esdras which concerns us is a self-contained narrative occupying the whole of chapter 3 and most of chapter 4. Here, following a banquet given by King Darius, three of his bodyguards engage in a competition whereby each is to identify in writing—as if in a secret ballot—whatever 'one thing' he considers to be 'strongest', with the intention that the one whose opinion on this is subsequently adjudged wisest by a panel of experts (the king and his princes) may gain particular reward and favour from Darius. One of the young men nominates wine as strongest; the second nominates kings as strongest; and the third (in the version of the story channelled through the Vulgate) hedges his bets by writing that 'women are strongest: but above all things Truth beareth away the victory' (3 Esdras 3: 10–12).

When the bodyguards are duly summoned to defend their choices, the first champions the power of wine because it can make anyone err, level the minds of king and peasant, transform misery into mirth, induce eloquence, and also provoke sudden hostility among friends or kin. We can immediately see that strength (*fortitudo*) is here being located especially in transformative agency, in a power to overturn normative hierarchies

[3] *Oxford Dictionary of the Christian Church*, 2nd edn., ed. F. L. Cross and E. A. Livingstone (Oxford: Oxford University Press, 1974), 470.

[4] For discussion and translation see *The Apocrypha and Pseudepigraphia of the Old Testament in English*, ed. R. H. Charles, 2 vols., i: *Apocrypha* (Oxford: Clarendon Press, 1913). All translations below are from Charles, 29–32. For the Latin text I have used a 16th-cent. printing of the Vulgate: *Biblia breves in eadem annotationes . . .* (Paris: Robertus Stephanus, 1532).

and mores. The second retainer adopts a cruder mode in setting out to prove the power of kings. Men seem generally to exercise power over sea and land and whatever is in them, he begins: but a king exercises dominion over all men, such that if he bids subjects fight against each other, they do so; if he bids them overcome mountains, they do so. Whatever is won in war or harvested from land is paid in tribute to the king; but above all his every command—whether to kill or spare, to build or cut down— is obeyed, and his subjects must put his comfort and will before their own (3 Esdras 4: 1–12).

The third speaker who has nominated women as strongest is named as Zorobabel. He aims to outmatch both his rivals by urging women's power both to exercise dominion and to effect transformations in their subjects. Since the text is not widely known, it is perhaps worth rehearsing in some detail.

Zorobabel's first argument establishes female priority through maternity, reducing men, winemakers, and kings to women's offspring: 'Women have borne the king and all the people that bear rule by sea and land. Even of them came they: and [women] nourished them up that planted the vineyards, from whence the wine cometh' (4: 15–16). His second argument is somewhat ellip-tical. It can be interpreted to mean either that women make clothes for men and that they [the clothes] bring 'glory' to men, or that women make clothes for men and they [women] bring glory to men. Whether as a corollary or as a separate totalizing hypoth-esis, it is asserted that men cannot live separately from women: 'These [women] also make garments for men; these bring glory unto men; and without women cannot men be' (4: 17).[5] The next proof envisages women as objects of desire easily eliminating rival desiderata such as material wealth:

Yea, and if men have gathered together gold and silver and every other goodly thing, and see a woman which is comely in favour and beauty, they let all those things go, and gape after her, and even with open mouth fix their eyes fast on her; and have all more desire unto her than unto gold or silver, or any goodly thing whatsoever. (4: 18–19)

This is reinforced by a claim that it is for women that men leave parents and birthplace behind: 'A man leaveth his own father that

[5] Vulgate: 'Et ipsae faciunt stolas omnium hominum, & ipsae faciunt gloriam hominibus, & non possunt homines seperari a mulieribus.' There is perhaps a connection with 1 Cor. 11: 7 and 11, which state that woman is the glory of man ('mulier autem gloria viri est') as well as asserting indivisibility of man and woman. However, evidence in some profeminine texts indicates that some readers took the Esdras verse to mean that women provided clothes to the glory of men.

brought him up, and his own country, and cleaveth unto his wife. And with his wife he endeth his days, and remembereth neither father, nor mother, nor country' (4: 20–1). Zorobabel goes on to squash both his rivals. First he instates woman, rather than monarch, as the being for whom men scale mountains in order to bring tribute to her:

By this also ye must know that women have dominion over you: do ye not labour and toil, and give and bring all to women? Yea, a man taketh his sword, and goeth forth to make outroads, and to rob and to steal, and to sail upon the sea and upon rivers; and looketh upon a lion, and walketh in the darkness; and when he hath stolen, spoiled, and robbed, he bringeth it to his love. Wherefore a man loveth his wife better than father or mother. (4: 22–5)

Second, he implicitly matches the claims made for wine's transformative power by suggesting that for better or worse, men abandon their identities for women: 'Yea, many there be that have run out of their wits for women, and become bondmen for their sakes. Many also have perished, have stumbled, and sinned, for women' (4: 26–7). The demonstration requires only a final tactical exemplification to round it off, and this is forthcoming in Zorobabel's mocking first-hand account of the king's own pliancy in the hands of a concubine, whose whims he accepts and whose moods he flatters:

And now do ye not believe me? Is not the king great in his power? Do not all regions fear to touch him? Yet did I see him and Apame the king's concubine, the daughter of the illustrious Bartacus, sitting at the right hand of the king, and taking the crown from the king's head, and setting it upon her own head; yea, she struck the king with her left hand: and therewithal the king gaped and gazed upon her with open mouth: if she laughed upon him, he laughed also: but if she took any displeasure at him, he was fain to flatter, that she might be reconciled to him again. O sirs, how can it be but women should be strong, seeing they do thus? (4: 28–31)

This vignette of Apame's self-conscious mischievousness and Darius' monarchal dotage concludes the debate on a curiously pantomimic or even sardonic note. According to 3 Esdras, Zorobabel goes on to raise the tone of the proceedings by praising truth instead, as that which is stronger and more abiding than wine, king, or woman—all of which are 'unrighteous' (*iniquus*) and perishable. One of two conjectures about the transmission of this Esdras material which warrant brief mention here, however, is that the supplementary nomination of truth could represent an early addition to a debate whose symmetry it appears to confuse,[6] and whose internal logic it does not crown. Another conjecture is that the order of the first two contenders in the biblical debate has perhaps suffered transposition, since it might seem more predictable for the king to be nominated as 'strongest' first, thence to be successively displaced by wine then woman.[7]

Some variation is found in a rendering by the first-century Jewish historian Josephus in his *Jewish Antiquities*, which constituted a second avenue of transmission for the story, outside the Vulgate.[8] Here it is King Darius, suffering from insomnia, who himself challenges his three chamberlains to say what thing is strongest on earth. Here also, an important variation in Zorobabel's speech is that the negative implications of Esdras 4: 23–7 (that men fight and steal to bring plunder to women, and lose their wits and sin for women) are muted:

We even leave our fathers and mothers and the land which nourished us, and often become forgetful of our best friends for the sake of women, and we have the courage to lose our lives by their side. But you may most clearly perceive the strength of women from the fact that when, after labouring and enduring all kinds of hardship both by land and by sea, we have gained something from these labours, we bring it to women.[9]

It is also interesting that rather than coupling women's clothes-making and male dignity (*gloria*), Josephus less enigmatically couples it with domestic skill: 'it is they who weave our clothes for us, and it is through them that the affairs of the household receive due care and attention.'

One piece of evidence for medieval circulation of the story in a form indebted to Josephus, but also with the contenders in a different order *and* minus the truth-sequel, can be seen in one of Nicole Bozon's *Contes moralisés* on the theme of 'The Strength of

---

[6] 'The fine Praise of Truth seems to be an early addition: it is loosely appended to the paean of women', Charles (ed.), *Apocrypha*, 29.

[7] That transposition has occurred is even implied within 3 Esdras by the order in which Zorobabel lists the rival claimants: 'O sirs, is not the king great, and men are many, and wine is strong? Who is it then that ruleth them, or hath the lordship over them? are they not women?' (4: 14).

[8] *Josephus*, ed. and trans. H. St J. Thackeray and Ralph Marcus, 9 vols., vi: *Jewish Antiquities, Books IX–XI* (London: Heinemann, 1937), XI. 2–7, pp. 329–41. For Darius' question see p. 331, and for Zorobabel's speech on women, pp. 337–8. The text, written in Greek, was known to the Middle Ages largely through a Latin translation, of which the relevant portion is not yet available in a modern edition.

[9] *Jewish Antiquities*, 337–9.

Woman'.[10] Bozon uses the story to suggest that women have power in excess of their physical strength. After summarizing the (transposed) arguments of the first two speakers, he paraphrases Zorobabel's verdict, sharpening up the implication in Josephus that women (for whom men forget friends; have the courage to lose lives) exert a transformative impact on men.[11] The *conte* is close to the Josephus version in arguing next that a woman remains in the house 'at ease' while her lord 'labours by sea or land' and hastens to please her on his return.[12] One manuscript of the *conte* concludes here ('so it is true that woman is more powerful than any other creature') while another offers the *exemplum* of Darius and his concubine as conclusion. The Esdras sequel on truth is either deliberately deleted by Bozon, or not available in the account he is following.

A cross-check on this tradition is furnished by two further recapitulations late in the fourteenth century: one in John Gower's *Confessio Amantis*, the other (much abbreviated) in Jean Le Fèvre's *Livre de Leësce*.[13] Both reinstate truth as the competition winner. However, both (unlike Esdras but like Josephus and Bozon) make Darius rather than the bodyguards the instigator of the question. In both, the order of nominations is king; wine; woman. Le Fèvre is aberrant in that—either because he misremembers salient detail, or because he wishes to insist pedantically on the ostensible rule of the competition (one nomination per player)—he makes Zorobabel a *fourth* speaker, championing truth after the other three nominations have been aired by three preceding speakers.

Gower's fuller account, though, is the more interesting. Admittedly he, too, abbreviates Zorobabel's key arguments. Women are 'myhtieste' because kings and winemakers are born of them, and because (Gower condenses like mad, relative to Esdras) men are

---

[10] *Contes moralisés de Nicole Bozon*, ed. Smith and Meyer, no. 54, 'De fortitudine mulieris', 75–6.

[11] 'Femme fet homme guerpir piere et miere, e femme fet ly leaus devenir leere. Femme fet coward hardi, e quant ke l'en purchace deporter a ly,' ibid. 76.

[12] 'Femme demort a meison e se fet a eese, tant qe son baron travaille par mier ou par terre, e a son revenir mout est heité a sa femme pleere,' ibid. 76.

[13] Respectively in *The English Works of John Gower*, ed. G. C. Macaulay, 2 vols., EETS es 81–2 (London: Oxford University Press, 1900–1), ii (VII. 1783–975); and *Livre de Leësce*, 55–68, in *Lamentations*, ed. Van Hamel. Gower refers vaguely to 'the Cronique' as his source, and furnishes names (Arpaghes and Manachaz) not found in Esdras for Zorobabel's two companions.

driven to 'obeie' willy-nilly by the strength of their love for 'wommanhede'.[14] The control of the concubine Apemen (as Gower names her) over the king is recalled 'to schewe of wommen the maistrie' (VII. 1881), but with an adjustment to the spectacle of royal thraldom in the suggestion that an affectionate look from his concubine could render the tyrannical king 'debonaire and meke' when his wrath was most aroused against imperial opponents (VII. 1884–91). This hint of a benign power to subdue irascibility has to coexist, however, with the *exemplum*'s otherwise indelibly sarcastic depiction of Darius swung by her caprice like a weathervane.[15]

The case does not rest with Apemen. Gower proceeds to try to remould Zorobabel's speech idealistically, in terms of men's dependence on women for 'solas', and in terms of women's instigation of knighthood, honour, and love.[16] He even goes so far as to insert here (still seeking, perhaps, to counterpoise the mockery inherent in the concubine's triumph?) a second *exemplum*, of Alceste sacrificing her own life to save that of her sick husband Ametus (VII. 1917–43). Hers is a self-obliterating rather than self-assertive exercise of *fortitudo*, so it enables Gower to finish the proof of feminine strength on a more decorous (more stereotypically laudatory) note than the concubinage anecdote allowed. More important, it enables him to bridge the awkward gap between Zorobabel's claim for Woman and his claim for Truth. Alceste's altruism demonstrates that 'the trouthe of wommen and the love' is, excepting only God himself, 'myhtiest upon this grounde' (VII. 1946–8). Woman's strength is not as in the apocrypha a hollow victory, instantly demeaned by being *displaced* by the superior claims of truth. Rather, woman's power is alleged to reside in her special capacity for participating in

---

[14] 'And ek he seide hou that manhede | Thurgh strengthe unto the wommanhede | Of love, wher he wole or non, | Obeie schal', VII. 1877–80.

[15] 'And be the chyn and be the cheke | Sche luggeth him riht as hir liste, | ... Whan that sche loureth, thanne he siketh, | And whan sche gladeth, he is glad: | And thus this king was ouerlad | With hire which his lemman was,' VII. 1892–9. Kurt Olsson comments that 'the devotion of this subjected "king" merely provokes "game", a sheer wantonness in Apemen's exercise of power'; *John Gower and the Structures of Conversion: A Reading of the 'Confessio Amantis'* (Woodbridge: Boydell & Brewer, 1992), 207.

[16] This involves some strain, for, as Olsson notes, the 'inverted tribute to the power of woman' in the concubine *exemplum* 'hardly supports Zorobabel's following statement, that woman is man's "solas" and "worldes joie"', ibid. 207.

truth: to laud truth is therefore merely to laud that which is found mightiest *in her*.[17]

The attempt to enhance woman's victory in this revision of the competition story in the *Confessio* is the more remarkable in that Gower's subject here is not woman but really *is* truth, identified as the sovereign virtue of royal government within the seventh book's syllabus for the education of a king. What may have happened is that in deciding to use the Zorobabel material, Gower found himself recalling the larger profeminine discourse woven around that material in the culture which he inherited. His generalizations are reminiscent of those in the *dits*. The assertions that among men 'is no solas, | If that ther be no womman there', and that without women 'This worldes joie were aweie', and that women 'make a man to drede schame' (VII. 1900–6), echo sentiments we have found in earlier poems. It is therefore time to gather some thoughts on the character of the episode in 3 Esdras, and on how it fuelled the medieval case for women.

It has to be admitted that in the Vulgate version, Zorobabel's 'praise' of woman's power could be interpreted as an exercise in bathos. One could argue that it plunges from incontrovertible and ethically neutral claims about the power of women to *deliver* future kings and about the interdependence of the sexes, through increasingly worrying emphases on women's power to make men 'gape' so that they stop at nothing 'for women' (including robbery and madness), to a concluding farce in which a king's concubine openly flaunts her power by slapping her lover and playing games with his crown. On top of that we might protest that women, as usual, constitute the absent object in a competitive masculine discussion, and that the terms in which their strength is defined are stereotypes of procreation, nourishment, commodity, and sexual captivation. The claim that women dominate through sexual attraction actually differs hardly at all from the medieval misogynous cliché of woman's power to 'destroy' the greatest men through infatuation. The nearest a woman gets to active rulership here, as opposed to being the passive recipient of trib-

<hr />

[17] In the light of Gower's introduction of the transitional Alceste *exemplum*, Olsson's formulation, that Zorobabel 'modulates his argument' to celebrate truth 'without cancelling' his prior praise of woman's power, seems more apt than Russell Peck's emphasis on the 'unexpectedness' of truth's victory in *Kingship and Common Profit in Gower's 'Confessio Amantis'* (Carbondale: Southern Illinois University Press, 1978), 143.

utes and stares, is as a mistress toying with the symbolism of power.

Perhaps because competing versions of the story such as Josephus' softened it somewhat, this is not how it struck those who saw its bearing on the case for women. Indeed, in the language of Zorobabel's claim that it is woman who has dominion over wine or kings (*qui dominatur eorum*, 4: 14) and over the very lords he is addressing (*mulieres dominantur vestri*, 4: 22), there lay interesting authority for questioning the famous words of the punishment pronounced by God upon Eve—that her husband would have dominion over her (*ipse dominabitur tui*).[18] Above all, what was available here was a structure of ideas for defending women, a selection of cues. It may be useful at this point to codify these in order of appearance:

1. those who claim superiority were born of, and nourished by, women;
2. women make the garments which dignify men;
3. men 'cannot be separated from' women;
4. women transcend all valuables, gold and silver, in the estimate of their admirers;
5. a man leaves parents and country to live out his life with a woman;
6. a man toils, fights [Josephus: is courageous], travels far, to bring things to the woman he loves;
7. men have lost wits or freedom, sinned, died, for women [omitted in Josephus];
8. even a king conforms himself to the will of a mistress.

As is demonstrated in Josephus and medieval successors, this structure of ideas required only mild tinkering and modernization to generate a more unequivocally positive statement than it yielded in 3 Esdras. Take, for example, 'The Virtues of Women' (*Le Bien des fames*).[19] It begins with an argument that men should honour women on account of the Virgin Mary (1–18). This is an interpolation, inserted prior to Zorobabel's starting-point: but the French poem's second argument on behalf of women is, sure enough, that all are born of them (19–33). Both arguments come with lashings of *cortois* sentiment, which then develops into a separate point: i.e. woman's transformative, educative, effect on

[18] Gen. 3: 16.
[19] Ed. and tr. Fiero *et al.*, *Three Medieval Views of Women*, 106–13.

coarse males, her ability to 'make the coward brave', to make the miserly generous, to prompt acts of prowess. These are modernizations of the Esdras material. The transforming of the miserly is seen in Zorobabel's observation that a man no longer hoards silver and gold when he falls in love with a woman. The access of bravery ascribed in the French is a chivalric reflex of Zorobabel's depiction of man taking on the world for woman with his sword (*accipit homo gladium suum*, Esdras) or of men finding the courage to die for women (Josephus). Although courtly expectations necessitate elaboration of other kinds of service performed for women (floral chaplets, songs, dances) in *Le Bien*, the French writer also includes another of the proofs used in Esdras, namely women's exercise of implicit power by clothing men.[20]

The hypothesis of the influence of the Zorobabel paradigm is not an *idée fixe* of this book. It is more a question of saying that it represents the nearest discoverable counterpart to Theophrastus/Jerome's influence on medieval misogyny. Admittedly some of its emphases filtered more widely than others. Admittedly, again, some of its emphases might alternatively be thought ubiquitous commonplaces. Furthermore in its restriction to the question of 'dominion' and by virtue of its very antiquity, the Zorobabel model leaves untouched other topics which were to preoccupy medieval proponents of the case for women, such as the problem of the Fall, the status of women in the Gospels, and the example of female saints.

Nevertheless there is room to argue that some of the emphases in the defence literature—among them those which might seem most 'obvious'—derive, however indirectly, from the Contest of Darius. When Nicole Bozon himself writes his poem in praise of women (*De la bonté des femmes*) he moves from a discussion of Eve to the topos that we are all born of women and nourished by them, and thence to an assertion that a good woman outmatches any 'treasure'.[21] More than two hundred years before Bozon's time, Marbod of Rennes opens his profeminine poem with an erudite analysis of women's equality with men in the order of nature,

[20] 'Fame fet fere les bliaus, | Si fet fere les hommes biaus | Et acesmés et gens et cointes' (63–5), 'To her we owe the robes we wear | That flatter men so we appear | Attractive and refined', and see further 83–8.

[21] Ed. in *Contes moralisés de Nicole Bozon*, lines 61–6 and 73–5; see also 'Ja n'est trovee en tere ou en mer | Piere preciouse nule si chere | Qe vayle a femme', 229–31.

where both are held to be situated in the fourth tier above animals, plants, and precious metals. 'Therefore', Marbod continues,
'since woman is more worthy than all these, more beautiful
than silver, more precious than yellow gold, more radiant than
jewels . . . she ought to be admired, or rather loved, more than
they.'[22] For the elaboration of human participation in a fourfold
chain of being Marbod had to go probably to St Gregory's
homilies,[23] but the underlying prompt is the topos, shared with
3 Esdras (4: 19), that men 'have all more desire unto [woman]
than unto gold or silver, or any goodly thing whatsoever'. The
'De matrona' then proceeds with other now familiar topoi: no
father would exist without woman's childbearing; it is women
who nourish; it is women who weave cloth 'for our [men's?]
benefit'.[24]

In order to ascertain what heirlooms other than the Darius
Contest there might be in the discourse of anti-misogyny, the
logical next step is to identify generic features which typically
constructed such discourse, say, around the beginning of the fourteenth century. For convenience I give a kind of catalogue in the
same format as adopted above for Zorobabel's case, but of course
with the proviso that this is a summary not of an existing text but
of a hypothetical and madly eclectic one:

1. attacking women constitutes discourteous, self-dishonouring
   slander;
2. men who slander women are vilifying those who gave
   them birth and brought them up, often with much personal
   suffering;
3. God gave several 'privileges' to women;
4. misogynists blame Eve, but Eve's culpability has been exaggerated and/or without Eve there would have been no
   Virgin Mary and/or the Virgin Mary cancelled Eve's guilt;
5. the Virgin Mary occupies a sublime position in heaven and
   every woman is to be honoured for her sake;
6. besides childbearing, women excel in further functions

---

[22] Leotta (ed.), 'De matrona' (34–8), tr. in Blamires, *Woman Defamed and Woman Defended*, 229.

[23] *Hom. in Evang.* 2. 39; *PL* 76. 1214.

[24] *Woman Defamed and Woman Defended*, 230. Thereafter, Marbod switches to a topic of commendation—woman's 'submissiveness'—which is antithetical to the context of the Esdras passage.

(nursing, healing, running households) which the world cannot do without;

7. women bring men joy and repose more than can any treasure, and can transform men's behaviour;

8. if physically weak, women are thereby the more praiseworthy for their moral strength, being conspicuous—more than men, who on the contrary commit very serious crimes—for chastity, resolution, loyalty, wisdom, piety;

9. their loyalty during the Crucifixion pleased Christ, who chose a woman (Mary Magdalene) to be the first to spread the news of the Resurrection;

10. generalized criticism of women is unfair and can be countered by all sorts of shining examples to the contrary, of prophetesses and female saints, heroines from antiquity, and modern instances.

The advantage of extrapolating generic features in this way is that the chief modes of argument become clearly distinguishable. Thus, it can quickly be deduced (for instance) that in comparison with the limited framework of the case by Zorobabel, the whole phenomenon of misogynous slander is problematized in the typical medieval defence. Then, the topos of maternity shows expansion to introduce an element of *debt* incurred by the pains of pregnancy and delivery. Then there is misogyny's star witness, Eve, to be dealt with. The generally positive role of women in the New Testament also comes into focus, either separately or in alliance with one of two further strategies. These strategies are, first, an offensive declaring the 'virtues' of women (often expressly rebutting customary allegations about their vices, and sometimes laced with disdain for the immorality of men); and second, the fertile phenomenon of demonstration by example— the use of the extendible catalogue of women of the past to disprove criticisms, give celebrated narrative proof of particular virtues, and generally overthrow opposition by sheer weight of 'good women'.

We have already glanced at some generic elements of the formal case, such as its concern with slander and generalization: others will be explored in subsequent chapters. For the moment, it is the implicitly symbiotic relation between defence and misogyny—the recognition that the case *for* is being conducted in response to habitual accusations—that calls for comment, in the context of its possible formal affiliations. 'Woman' in this arena is not a visibly secure category but an obscured and threatened one, requiring legal aid: for, as Christine de Pizan wittily put it, there was a great clutter of muck and debris to remove before she could even begin to see how to build up her confidence. The case for woman inevitably had the character of judicial defence, and presupposed that woman was in trouble, in the dock. The question arises, should her defence therefore be described and analysed specifically in terms of the judicial oration and of the rhetorical *causa* whose conventions had been passed down to the Middle Ages from classical times?

Christine's *Cité* is actually one example of a text which, it has been claimed, is systematically organized according to forensic formula. Glenda McLeod suggests that Christine observes the sixfold structure commended for arguing legal cases by Cicero in his *De inventione*: *exordium* (introduction, employing devices to secure a sympathetic hearing); *narratio* (statement of facts); *partitio* (division of arguments to be proved); *confirmatio* (proof); *refutatio* (exposure of flaws in the opponent's allegations); and *peroratio* (summing up, exciting *indignatio* against the opponent and reinforcing sympathy for the client). The detection of *exordium* and *peroratio* at beginning and end of the *Cité* is not implausible. But the strain involved in maintaining the rhetorical fit otherwise becomes apparent when one notices that McLeod has to represent *refutatio* as occurring in book II, duly following a *confirmatio* that is assumed to begin book I: but where does this leave the conspicuous refutation which actually occupies most of Christine's first book, exposing (for instance) the inadequacy of misogynist allegation that women are lecherous and gluttonous?[25]

Certainly there is no need to doubt either Christine's rhetorical learning or her familiarity with legal language and procedure. Left a widow at quite an early age, she found herself embroiled in lawsuits for many years. The traces of this, in terms of her extensive and witty use of legal terminology, have been studied by Maureen Curnow.[26] Whether it is necessary to go beyond that kind of observation to propose that conventions of judicial oratory provide a precise structural foundation for her case for

[25] McLeod, *Virtue and Venom*, 114–15.
[26] ' "La Pioche d'inquisicion" ', in Richards *et al.* (ed.), *Reinterpreting Christine de Pizan*, 157–72.

women and those which preceded hers, I am inclined to doubt. There is some discouragement in the fact that scholars who urge the basis for profeminine discourse in ancient rhetoric tend to apply the theory rather loosely and guardedly. Angenot carefully tries to locate defence writings within the six-point prescription mentioned by McLeod, but he suggests that the defining model is the epideictic (praise-and-blame) rhetorical mode rather than the judicial (defence-and-accusation) mode.[27] He also warns that rhetorical considerations are not the be-all and end-all of the discourse, which in reality is a 'discursive system' representing a kind of intersection of heterogeneous fragments of discourse pulled from their normal contexts.[28] And although Linda Woodbridge is confident that Tudor misogyny uses the ancient formulae of judicial oratory, when she comes to defence-of-women literature she has to admit that 'rhetoricians were undecided' as to the 'proper use' of the *narratio* in defence. Whereas in an attack, the *narratio* should comprise the facts surrounding the accusation, a defence denial of accusation did not itself constitute a *narratio*, though the querying of the 'facts' might. Woodbridge shows how the defensive *narratio* resorted to the epideictic mode (which Quintilian called 'panegyric or laudatory') when it accommodated praise of women's virtues.[29] That this insertion of one mode within another might be necessary, Cicero conceded when he wrote that 'in judicial and deliberative causes extensive sections are often devoted to praise or censure'.[30]

The tendency of rhetorical categories to collapse into one another in practice is also noted by Pamela Benson in her account of Renaissance 'profeminist' works. These works, she states,

participate in two large generic categories: panegyric (laud, encomium) and defense. The defense is contentious. It employs, at least to some extent, the places of forensic rhetoric: it attacks the character of the accuser, and it defends the accused on the grounds of place of birth, character, and so forth. The panegyric is less controversial. It demonstrates the positive attributes of women, whereas defenses alternate positive assertions about women with negative assertions about their detractors. . . . This separation of the genres is artificial, however; most works combine the two.[31]

[27] *Champions des Femmes*, 152–3.
[28] Ibid. 160–1.
[29] *Women and the English Renaissance*, 33.
[30] Marcus Tullius Cicero (attrib.), *Rhetorica ad Herennium*, tr. Harry Caplan (London: Heinemann, 1954), 183–5.
[31] *Invention of the Renaissance Woman*, 45–6.

In the case of medieval works it is necessary to acknowledge not only what Woodbridge and Benson acknowledge for Renaissance ones—that there is much toing and froing between 'defence' and 'panegyric'—but also that the very attempt to distinguish components such as *narratio* and *refutatio* from each other is only intermittently viable. Medieval writers, that is, showed less devotion to the subcategories of rhetorical procedure than modern scholars, lacking clues to what else their discourse springs from, sometimes think they should show.

This is not to belittle the broad influence of (especially judicial) rhetorical models on the case for women. The defence tradition does pervasively cultivate a courtroom ambience. The *Livre de Leësce* characterizes itself as presented to sustain women's 'cause' (3950), and it promotes the litigious flavour by adopting, for example, legalistic techniques of hair-splitting: thus Leësce protests at one point, 'this article [clause of the indictment] is not strictly pertinent to the claim which Matheolus [her opponent] wants it to sustain' (1925–7). A refinement, already present in *Leësce*, of the underlying courtroom drama thus projected is the hypothesis that the speaker who defends, defends not only women against calumny, but himself against women's suspicion that he has himself been one of the calumniators. (The speaker therefore adopts the stance of defending women in order to defend himself from their detestation.)

While few of the writers are as self-consciously legalistic as Le Fèvre, who was probably trained in canon law, the case for women is deeply permeated by an *implicit* orientation against specific allegations. In the end this is what probably matters more than the rhetorical strategies putatively informing the texts. It matters because it constricts the potential of this discourse in two fundamental ways. First, it threatens always to limit discussion to themes laid down by the prosecution—those defined by misogynous complaint—however frivolous they might be. Second, the implied judicial context prevents the case for women from being constructed affirmatively, in a way that is not everywhere shadowed by negatives: and this in turn is an impediment to positive thinking on what roles women *might* play in society. This disadvantage still hampers the case in the Renaissance, according to Linda Woodbridge:

The position of Woman as 'the accused' placed severe limitations on constructive discussion of women and their role in society. The formal controversy was prevented by its own rhetoric from becoming more than a literary pastime. How could the sincerest advocate discuss the economic deprivations or social disadvantages of a client who stands accused of high crimes and misdemeanors? Little wonder that defenders defined their task primarily as clearing the client of charges against her.[32]

While it is part of the point of this book to modify the dispiriting impression given by such claims, it cannot be denied that defences of women were usually caught in the reactive bind Woodbridge envisages. For example, given the 'secondariness' often attributed to woman in the chronology of creation, it was a natural defence to look for contrasting areas of female 'priority'; so the medieval case lays stress on the fact that Christ's first appearance after the Resurrection was to a woman, Mary Magdalene. As we shall see, this was among the more seriously pondered profeminine arguments in the Middle Ages, yet even so it provoked return fire from snipers on the other side. Of course Christ appeared first to a woman, they said: he relied on female garrulity to spread the news quickly.[33] (A later sarcastic variant was that Christ also appeared first, at the Nativity, to an ox and an ass.[34])

Even in the realms of the appeal to example, the defence clearly risks becoming embroiled in vicious circles of misogyny. Yet the *exemplum* was an important category of *confirmatio* in judicial oratory. I shall conclude this chapter with a glance at interconnected problems associated with the *exemplum* by the rhetoricians and by modern commentators.

Quintilian claimed that 'the most efficacious' of methods of proof (*confirmatio*) was that which is termed 'example'. To mention an example was to lend cogency to persuasion by adducing historical fact, or supposed fact, or famous narrative incident from the poets.[35] Medieval writers understood the use of the *exemplum* to be the essence of 'proof', as is clear when Le Fèvre tells us that Leësce will offer proof in this way,[36] and as is then demonstrated when she proceeds to 'prove' women's wisdom by

---

[32] *Women and the English Renaissance*, 38.

[33] On Christine de Pizan's indignation about the 'garrulity' joke, see below, Ch. 4.

[34] Angenot, *Champions des Femmes*, 107 (source not cited).

[35] *The Institutio oratoria of Quintilian*, V. 11. 5–21, tr. H. E. Butler, 4 vols. (London: Heinemann, 1960), ii. 275–83.

[36] 'Leesce seule parlera | Et ses fais prouvés monstrera | Par exemples et par figures | Des ystoires des escriptures' (3490–3).

citing Carmentis (legendary inventor of the Latin alphabet), the Nine Muses, Medea, Sappho, and others (3618–79). In my earlier discussion of attitudes to *exempla* found in Deschamps and Le Fèvre, it became clear that *gradations* of credibility were being applied so as to query the validity of pagan 'fable'. Now, with judicial oratory in mind, it is possible to identify a significant (possibly the most significant) source for the idea of grading *exempla*. For, when Quintilian had commended the cogency of historical example, he went on: 'a similar method is to be pursued in quoting from the fictions of the poets, though we must remember that they will be of less force as proofs.'[37] Here was an interesting suggestion of relativity. It clearly never crossed the minds of some medieval writers, who threw *exempla* around like confetti. But those writing in defence of women were subject to two impulses tending to problematize the *exemplum*. One lay in the hint (bland though it was) in received formulation of judicial rhetoric, that 'force' might be a subjective matter, distributable according to a reader's sliding scale of historicity. The other problematization arose from the sheer accumulation of *exempla* on either side of the woman question (implying that truth was on both sides, or neither), and also from the bewildering capacity of some *exempla* to score for both sides.

A further way in which the medieval case reveals its concern for the historicity of example is in its adoption of the Modern Example. The modern instance could be used in any polemical field of course,[38] but seems to have been unusually prominent in profeminine contexts. As often, a cue was given by patristic precedent, especially by St Jerome and St Ambrose. Among Jerome's well-known letters is one addressed to Furia after she was widowed. Jerome regales her with role-models for widowhood: two from the New Testament (Anna, and the widow who offered two mites) sandwiching four from the Old (the widow of Zarephath; Judith; Deborah; Naomi). But the list is strategically brought up to date by referring to one of his own acquaintances in Rome; 'why should I recall instances from history and bring from books types of saintly women, when in your own city you have many before your eyes whose example you may well imitate? I shall not re-

---

[37] 'nisi quod iis minus adfirmationis adhibetur', *Institutio*, V. 11. 17, tr. Butler, 280–1.

[38] Chaucer uses modern instances among other *exempla* of adverse fortune in *The Monk's Tale*.

count their merits here lest I should seem to flatter them. It will suffice to mention the saintly Marcella.'[39] Although the probability of the writer's obligation here to a wealthy named patroness complicates the effect,[40] it does not invalidate the clear expectation of a peculiar cogency deriving from reference to a contemporary witness. This caught on. Something like the same blend of personal admiration with appeal to 'real-life' witness probably explains the encomium to the Countess of Hereford in the 'good woman' section of Étienne de Fougères's *Livre des manières*. Étienne, writing probably in the 1170s, is assumed to refer to Cécile, widow of Count Roger of Hereford (died 1155). He represents her as a model of cheerful piety and decorum, hospitable to male ecclesiasts and a great provider of church vestments: a fine *essample* of behaviour for younger women.[41]

Writing two centuries later Le Fèvre mounts on behalf of Leësce (Joy) a roll-call ('une annexe', 2803) of examples of valiant women old and new. Most are 'old'; St Ursula and the 11,000 virgins, St Catherine of Alexandria, nine virgin saints and sainted nuns celebrated in the *Golden Legend*. Separating these *exempla* from those of courageous antique and biblical heroines is the thirty-five-line example (2853–88) of 'Sister Jeanne de Neuville', a woman of Le Fèvre's own locality, whose name is recorded as abbess at Longchamp in 1375.[42] He salutes her as a 'second St Clare' for combining humility with efficacy as pastoress to her nuns.

The question is, though, what are the implications of this splicing-in of modern example? Is Jeanne meant to stand out as specially effective 'proof' of woman's strength by virtue of modernity? It may well strike us, as it strikes one scholar, that 'the vivid evocation of the lives of competent and pious women in a contemporary convent does more for [Le Fèvre's] cause than the

[39] Letter 54. 16–17; *Selected Letters of St Jerome*, tr. F. A. Wright (Cambridge, Mass.: Harvard University Press, 1963), 262–3. Le Fèvre echoes the 'reluctance to flatter' topos in *Leësce*, 3786–90. Somewhat like Jerome, Ambrose anticipates that his audience may object that they prefer a recent example rather than the Virgin Mary and Thecla (disciple of St Paul according to her legend) whom he furnishes as role-models for virginity: so he cites a virgin 'lately at Antioch'; *De virginibus*, II. iii. 21–II. iv. 22, *PL* 16. 212–13, *Principal Works of St Ambrose*, tr. de Romestin, 376.

[40] On Jerome and Marcella, see Peter Brown. *The Body and Society: Men, Women and Sexual Renunciation in Early Christianity* (London: Faber, 1989), 367–9.

[41] Lodge (ed.), *Livre des manières*, 1205–28; 'En lei poent essample prendre | celes qui bien volent entendre', 1225–6.

[42] See n. to 2853–88 in *Lamentations*, ed. Van Hamel, ii. 251. Van Hamel speculates that this reference to Jeanne in *Leësce* amounts to a kind of personal congratulation to Le Fèvre's 'illustrious compatriot' on her 'recent promotion'.

repetitive use of exempla like Dido'.[43] This implies that Jeanne de Neuville is consciously imported to freshen the proof which tired examples are less capable of providing. The same scholar also suggests that the modern instance functions as 'true' example capable of *reinforcing* traditional *exempla* surrounding it. For instance, Le Fèvre seeks to demonstrate feminine loyalty by mentioning a married woman burned at the stake as a result of false allegations by the Chevalier de Bailleul when she rejected his advances:[44] 'This tragic story then serves to head a series of classical exempla of such figures as Lucretia and Penelope. Through their association with the contemporary event . . . they now belong to the category of true exemplars and are by implication removed from the realm of fable and thus of falsehood.'[45] This gets closer to the tantalizing complexities which lurk in the medieval writers' equivocal recognitions of historicity. Modern instances can be included as a kind of insurance, insisting on temporal difference, to counter the over-familiarity *or* the fictitiousness latent in standard antique examples. But alternatively they can be included, insisting on continuity, to crown a proof by bringing it—like a chronicle—to the present; or they can be included, insisting on continuity again, as an implied admonition urging that the venerable standards of antiquity *can* prevail among contemporary women.

The crux of all this, which has been brilliantly elucidated by Elizabeth Clark in relation to the Church Fathers' use of the past, is the inherited tendency of exemplification to *erase* history.[46] Clark argues that, because the point of harping on women from the Bible (Rebecca, Sarah, Mary and Martha) and women from the Roman past (Lucretia, Dido) was to promote the 'moral uplift' of women, their stories 'acquired a certain timelessness, . . . they took on features of myth'. Subjected to habitual repetition, they became extracted from history: 'history is (paradoxically) erased on the very occasion that it is appealed to.'[47] Le Fèvre is uncomfortably located at a juncture where the problems of historicity are just beginning to be perceived. They are largely articulated in terms of the 'truth' (i.e. credibility) of received story, and they are

[43] Blumenfeld-Kosinski, 'Jean le Fèvre's *Livre de Leësce*', 719–20.
[44] *Leësce*, 1429–58, alluding to events of c.1350.
[45] Blumenfeld-Kosinski, 'Jean le Fèvre's *Livre de Leësce*', 718.
[46] 'Ideology, History, and the Construction of "Woman" in Late Ancient Christianity', *Journal of Early Christian Studies*, 2 (1994), 155–84 (pp. 169–70).
[47] Ibid. 170.

incipiently engaged with by paying particular attention to recent example. But the underlying paradox of the exemplifying custom, that history is erased on the very occasion that it is appealed to, has not gone away.

Of course proof by example was too ingrained in the medieval consciousness to be lightly dethroned from its customary rhetorical eminence. Some of the important role-models it contributed to the case for women will be discussed in Chapter 7. In the mean time I investigate in more detail some of the favourite means of defence, beginning where many of the texts begin, with motherhood.

3

Honouring Mothers

FROM 1355 until about 1359, Giovanni Boccaccio worked on a collection that was to become highly influential in discourse about women: the *De mulieribus claris* (*Concerning Famous Women*). It is sharply equivocal in its representations of women—often inanely disdainful in the stereotypical assumptions it incidentally discloses about 'womanly weakness', and yet attentive to evidence in received story of the possibility of feminine transcendence of such stereotype. Characteristic of this doublethink is a passage in which women's capacity for *parity* of attainment with men is forcefully asserted, in order to lift the horizons of those who have a low self-concept, but only at the cost of simultaneously appearing to denigrate the then traditional female functions of motherhood and nurture. Contemplating the legendary poetic talent of a certain Cornificia, Boccaccio reflects that

> She brought honour to womankind, for she scorned womanly concerns and turned her mind to the study of the great poets. Let slothful women be ashamed, and those who wretchedly have no confidence in themselves, who, as if they were born for idleness and the marriage bed, convince themselves that they are good only for the embraces of men, giving birth, and raising children, while they have in common with men the ability to do those things which make men famous, if only they are willing to work with perseverance.[1]

This is challenging and provocative in equal measure: challenging, because it recognizes reservoirs of untapped talent in women; provocative, because masculine endeavour is held up as the only benchmark of achievement to which women should aspire. In its disparagement of the nurturing role, it is also completely at odds with the received case for women.[2]

Medieval defence of women often begins with (or soon turns to)

---

[1] *De mulieribus claris*, ed. Zaccaria, 338, tr. Guarino, 188.
[2] Moreover in the chapter on Niobe, Boccaccio resentfully denies women any pride in childbearing: having children is 'a work of Nature' so a mother should not behave as if producing them 'had been her own accomplishment'; ed. Zaccaria, 80, tr. Guarino, 32.

an archetypal argument about origins: simply an argument that people—including misogynists—are brought into the world by mothers. It may seem elementary (something 'known far and wide' as one writer puts it) to assert that women ought to be respected and not denounced by those, of whatever status, who are necessarily born of them.[3] And indeed this *was* elementary, a matter not owing its perpetuation to the Esdras tradition alone but to the dissemination of an ethical commonplace in and beyond the Bible. Although being nice to women out of respect for mothers is only the most blatant aspect of an admiration for women as nurturers whose wider scope this chapter will go on to develop, it will be worthwhile to remind ourselves initially of the emphasis given in Scripture to the 'honouring' concept in particular.

One of the Commandments bids, 'Honour thy father and thy mother', though rather as a prudential requirement for a successful life than as an ethical requirement.[4] Medieval commentary on the Commandments makes use of supplementary scriptural quotations to redress the ethical balance; for example,

Honour thy father, and forget not the groanings of thy mother: Remember that thou hadst not been born but through them: and make a return to them as they have done for thee. (Ecclus. 7: 29–30)

The eye that mocketh at his father, and that despiseth the labour of his mother in bearing him, let the ravens of the brooks pick it out, and the young eagles eat it. (Prov. 30: 17)[5]

The second of these is actually remarkable for its immediate context in the Bible, for it follows after and therefore implicitly modifies a *locus classicus* for misogyny—the claim that 'the mouth of the womb' is one of 'three things' which 'are never satisfied'.[6] Criticism and defence are tantalizingly juxtaposed with each other, as so often they were to be in the Middle Ages.

In relation to mothers, both passages quoted above appeal to a concept of reciprocation; they aim to rebuke human indifference to the pains of pregnancy and parturition, pains which give life

---

[3] The writer of *Le Bien des fames*, ed. and tr. Fiero *et al.*, declares it to be widely known ('Que l'en set bien et loing et prés') that women are to be honoured because everyone ('tuit, grant et menor | Et un et autre, haut et bas') is born of woman (19–24).

[4] 'that thou mayst be long-lived upon the land which the Lord thy God will give thee', Exod. 20: 12.

[5] *Dives and Pauper*, ed. Barnum, vol. i, pt. i, p. 306.

[6] Prov. 30: 15–16: much quoted after St Jerome included it in his *Adversus Iovinianum*, I. 28, PL 23. 250; tr. Fremantle, 367.

even to that indifference. This is again the thrust of another Old Testament snippet, where Tobit is found admonishing his son to look after his mother: 'When God shall take my soul, thou shalt bury my body: and thou shalt honour thy mother all the days of her life: For thou must be mindful what and how great perils she suffered for thee in her womb' (Tobit 4: 3–4). This struck Wyclif, for one, as a significant profeminine text. He worked round to it in one of his sermons, in the course of a rambling discourse on women prompted by reflections on their drastic role in Herod's life. The proper riposte to misogynous male talk of woman as 'vessel of dung', he surmised, was the consideration that she is a 'precious' vessel because 'she nourishes every male except Adam in her womb', hence 'thou shalt honour thy mother' etc., as Tobit bids.[7]

From the cumulative weight of these biblical texts and indeed from others like them such as a Psalm verse quoted in *Leësce*,[8] it is easy to see why proponents of the case for women were so keen on invoking obligation-to-your-mother's-womb. Obligation was not the only emphasis available, it is true. One could stress instead a gender *exclusivity* whereby woman's role as what Genesis called 'helper' was construed specifically to mean the sex's capacity to deliver children. In this view God 'made woman's help indispensable [*inseparabile*] to man' because He 'decreed that all virile flesh begin in feminine bodies'.[9] The same factual note is struck in Marbod of Rennes's observation that without woman's biological function (her *propria causa*) the human race ceases.[10] That there were no exceptions was important, because Christ's birth seemed to confirm the rule even while it suspended the necessity for a human father: 'none can be born without woman, but Scripture tells how a man was born from woman without man.'[11] A more assertive refinement of this, aimed against mi-

[7] *Johannis Wyclif, Sermones*, ed. J. Loserth, 4 vols., ii (London: Wyclif Society, 1888), Sermon 22, pp. 159–65 (pp. 161–3). Wyclif accommodates some misogynous topoi and then seems to dismiss them.

[8] 'The wicked are alienated from the womb, they have gone astray from the womb, they have spoken false things' (Ps. 57: 4), *Leësce*, 1022–5.

[9] *Life* of the 9th-cent. nun Glodesind, in *Sainted Women of the Dark Ages*, ed. Jo Ann McNamara and John E. Halborg, with E. Gordon Whatley (Durham, NC: Duke University Press, 1992), 141.

[10] Leotta (ed.), 'De matrona', 44–5; tr. in Blamires, *Woman Defamed and Woman Defended*, 229. Marbod is perhaps constructing an argument on the basis of efficient and material causality—immediate and instrumental origins.

[11] 'Sanz femme ne put nul neestre, | Mès sanz home, come dit l'escrit, | De femme un home nasquist'; *Du bounté des femmes*, 163–5, ed. Meyer, 'Manuscrits français de Cambridge', 319.

sogamy, was to observe that there would be no such thing as privileged clerical celibacy or female virginity if there were not the procreative capacity of women to *produce* celibates or virgins in the first place. This is the observation epigrammatically recapitulated by the Wife of Bath ('And certes, if ther were no seed ysowe, | Virginitee, thanne wherof sholde it growe?' III. 71–2) from the 'heretical' argument of Jerome's opponent in *Adversus Iovinianum* (where it was noticed by other medieval writers besides Chaucer).[12]

Most defences nevertheless concentrated on the perspective of obligation, which enabled defenders to rebuke misogynists in a way that drew pointedly upon behavioural ideals associated with *cortoisie*. Only an uncivilized lout (*rusticus*) would malign woman, from whom we all come, ran a proverbial-sounding maxim in the Latin *Facetus*.[13] A line or two was frequently enough to invoke the topos. In a more developed example, an objection may be made to the element of perversity in criticizing a sex which has provided one's own 'home' (the womb), never mind flesh and blood, during gestation. Robert de Blois writes that to deride the suffering source and nurture of one's being is to act like the worst of creatures—a bird fouling its own nest.[14] A second analogy is added to this in *Du bounté des femmes*: since men are grown by women like fruit on a tree, isn't it totally unnatural for the fruit to attack the source of its nourishment?[15]

Near the end of the fourteenth century the possibilities in the topos are proliferating, especially in terms of interpreting self-undermining flaws in the opponent's position. Le Fèvre suggests that those who slander women, erring against nature, forgetting whence they come, and defaming the place where they were born, exemplify the proverb about disfiguring one's face while cutting one's nose (1022–36); and he notes with acid logic that the more the slanderers allege universal female fickleness or lust, the more they unwittingly commit self-disparagement—implying that they

[12] *Adv. Iov.* I. 12, *PL* 23. 227: 'If the Lord had commanded virginity He would have seemed to . . . do away with the seed-plot of mankind, of which virginity itself is a growth,' tr. Fremantle, 355. Deschamps's Folie expands the same argument, *Miroir de mariage*, 9036–47.

[13] 'Rusticus est vere qui turpia de muliere | Dicit, nam vere sumus omnes de muliere,' quoted in Meyer, 'Mélanges de poésie française, iv', 500, and in Dow, *Varying Attitude toward Women*, 92.

[14] Ulrich (ed.), *L'Honneur des dames* (327–44). Deschamps, *Miroir de mariage*, insisting that misogyny is *villains* (i.e. *rusticus*), repeats the analogy of defiling the 'house' where one has lived for nine months (9084–94).

[15] Lines 146–63; ed. Meyer, 'Manuscrits français de Cambridge', 318–19.

are 'sons of whores'.[16] Christine de Pizan shows how she is
schooled in such possibilities as this when she introduces a discreet variation in her *Epistre au dieu d'amours*. Given that man
derives physically from woman, then if she is defined as an evil,
so must he be: 'good fruit doesn't come from rotten trees', and
sons take after mothers (750–4).[17] Hoccleve, who rendered the
Epistre into English, repeats Christine's 'tree/fruit' metaphor, but
adds the nest-fouling analogy which had for him, as for Robert de
Blois, both proverbial force and, perhaps, a traditional connection
with respect for mothers.[18]

These apt logical extensions apart, the underlying model here,
and one which Christine wholeheartedly accepts, is that defamation of women reverses a 'natural' order of gratitude which ought
to be felt by men towards women for their ministrations in carrying, delivering, and then constantly 'nourishing' them throughout life (168–84). The pertinent verb is indeed *nourrir*. The model
has been internalized by Christine (who encapsulates it in her line
'Let none return them evil for their good')[19] though it may be
suspected of being a model which, under the guise of teaching
males due respect for mothers, actually constructs the feminine all
the more rigidly into the childbearing/nourishing role. A credible
dramatization of how the model might be seriously invoked by an
exasperated mother is even available in the French epic *Raoul de
Cambrai*, for when Raoul sharply rejects the advice of his mother

---

[16] 'Qui dit mal sa bouche putains; | si seroient filz de putains | Tous ceulx qui
sont de mere nés!' (2775–7). Solterer rather elaborately proposes that the description of misogyny as rebounding on the speaker is an androcentric manœuvre
disguising masculine 'hatred of alterity' as 'a form of self-loathing . . . in a self that
is inflected in masculine terms'; *The Master and Minerva*, 56.

[17] Fenster and Erler (eds.), *Poems of Cupid*. On the face of it, Christine is making
a quasi-scientific claim here for a decisive transmission of maternal influence to a
son, somewhat conflicting with the tendency of medieval scientific opinion to exalt
the paternal influence.

[18] 'For swich the fruyt is as þat is the tree | Take heede of whom thow took thy
begynnynge . . . | An old prouerbe seid is in englissh | Men seyn þat brid or foul
is deshonest | What so it be | and holden ful cherlissh | þat wont is to deffoule his
owne nest' (176–86), *Letter of Cupid*, in Fenster and Erler (ed.), *Poems of Cupid*.
Diane Bornstein comments adversely on these proverbial elements in the poem
without realizing their centrality as defence topoi; 'Anti-Feminism in Thomas
Hoccleve's Translation of Christine de Pizan's *Epistre au dieu d'amours*', *English
Language Notes*, 19 (1981), 7–14 (pp. 10–11).

[19] 'Nor should they [reasonable men] have a mind to deprecate | The female
sex, from which each man is born. | Let none return them evil for their good'; 'Et
ne doivent avoir cuer de blamer | Elles de qui tout homme est descendu. | Ne leur
soit pas mal pour le bien rendu' (720–2).

Aalais, she reproaches him for filial ingratitude: 'Dear son, I nourished thee with the milk of my own breast, and why dost thou
give me such a pain now beneath my heart?'[20] At the margins of
the ethically 'normative' model of obligation is a glimpse of a
counter-model—a stereotype of masculinity sweeping women
and all their 'nourishment' aside in peremptory gestures of egotistical restlessness. The ethically normative medieval model exists partly in order to restrain that counter-model of self-indulgent
masculinity but also no doubt to console women with the supposition that any frustrations they may feel with their own lives as
endless 'nourishers' are reflections not on masculine society's
arrangement of their destinies but on the inadequate *cortoisie* of
those they nourish.

Just how traditional the vocabulary of obligation was, can be
seen from St Jerome's recourse to it in one of his letters. This time
the topos is used to lecture a daughter who cannot get on with her
mother:

Do you think that her house is too small for you whose womb was not too
small? · · · She carried you long, and she nursed you for many months;
her gentle love bore with the peevish ways of your infancy. She washed
your soiled napkins and often dirtied her hands with their nastiness. She
sat by your bed when you were ill and was patient with your sickness,
even as she had before endured the sickness of maternity which you
caused.[21]

Here, however, the general debt to mothers is being enhanced by
laying particular stress on the mother's deprivations; suffering
maternity sickness, and putting up subsequently with the child's
troublesomeness. The Middle Ages owed much of its insistence
on the motherhood debt to the powerful late antique and early
Christian topos of the Troubles of Marriage (*molestiae nuptiarum*),
from which Jerome is himself borrowing in this letter.[22] The

---

[20] Penny Schine Gold cites this passage (*Raoul*, 1001–11) in a discussion of the
poem's repetitive concern with woman's 'nurturing' role; *The Lady and the Virgin:
Image, Attitude, and Experience in Twelfth-Century France* (Chicago: University of
Chicago Press, 1985), 13.

[21] Letter 117, 'To a Mother and Daughter Living in Gaul'; *Letters*, tr. Wright,
374–9.

[22] The one context which, as Jerome and others agreed, might exceptionally
justify filial disdain rather than obligation was where parents tried to prevent
offspring from opting for religious life. In this case it is 'piety' to be 'cruel' to a
mother and ignore her pleas even if she should 'bare her breasts, the breasts that
gave you suck'; Bynum, *Jesus as Mother*, 145–6, quoting St Bernard, Letter 322
(which itself is quoting Jerome), *PL* 182. 527.

connection of the Troubles with the case for women is interesting and requires discussion, because it introduces some complicating paradoxes into the defence strategy.

In the *molestiae nuptiarum*, a rhetorician could deploy alternative sets of deeply conventional arguments appropriate to dissuading either a man or a woman from marriage.[23] They became so familiar in the writings of the Fathers (Jerome even gives a bibliography of them[24]) that they could be summoned up for readers by the barest abbreviation. So Jerome, commending virginity to Eustochium, writes that he will not bother to 'reckon up the disadvantages of marriage, such as pregnancy, a crying baby, the tortures of jealousy, the cares of household management, and the cutting short by death of all [marriage's] fancied blessings'.[25]

To the subdivisions itemized here, each generating its own subtopoi, might be added the Troubles of Eligibility (*molestiae eligendae*, to coin a phrase). St Ambrose projects these in his *De virginibus*, with what appears to be some real insight into female subjectivity. The marriageable girl is, he suggests, in the wretched position of being 'in a species of sale put up as it were to auction to be bid for'. Ambrose expertly identifies encompassing social traps. If she presumes to *choose* a fiancé 'it is an offence'; if she does not choose 'it is an insult'. Should she make efforts to be 'seen' by potential suitors, or is that indecorous? A turmoil of wishes and anxieties is imagined as to the varieties of victimization which are to be anticipated from the spectrum of possible husbands: a poor one may trick her, a rich one ignore her, a handsome one mock her, an aristocratic one despise her.[26] What is refreshing about this is that it keenly reverses the incessantly repeated male-centred view (found in the 'Theophrastus' passage in Jerome) of a man's no-win situation when choosing a wife.

[23] Sources and traditions are described in *Grégoire de Nysse: Traité de la virginité*, ed. Michel Aubineau (Paris: Éditions du Cerf, 1966), 87–96. The Fathers' use of the convention is discussed in Elizabeth Castelli, 'Virginity and its Meaning for Women's Sexuality in Early Christianity', *Journal of Feminist Studies in Religion*, 2 (1982), 61–88 (esp. pp. 68–71).

[24] Letter 22. 22, 'To Eustochium', tr. Wright, 102–3.

[25] 'nec enumeratorum molestias nuptiarum, quomodo uterus intumescat, infans vagiat, cruciet paelex, domus cura sollicitet, et omnia, quae putatur bona, mors extrema praeciat', Letter 22. 2, tr. Wright, 56–7

[26] *De virginibus*, I. 9. 56, *PL* 16. 203–4, tr. de Romestin, 372. Pre-betrothal anxieties for a girl are also described by St John Chrysostom; see *On Virginity, against Remarriage*, tr. Sally Rieger Shore (Lewiston, NY: Edwin Mellen Press, 1983), 91–2.

Thus the suggestion that the girl's volition is paralysed as she is reduced to an item of sale parries the Theophrastan satire that is recalled by the Wife of Bath, namely the suggestion that men can test the quality of livestock and utensils before purchase, 'But folk of wyves maken noon assay' before marriage, 'And thanne, seistow, we wol oure vices shewe' (III. 285–92). Moreover the probability that variant potential husbands merely signify varieties of oppression is an equally pointed reversal of the Theophrastan nightmare of choice, that a poor wife will be expensive, a rich one full of 'pride and . . . malencolie', a beautiful one will be constantly 'assailled' by other men, yet an ugly one 'coveiteth every man that she may se' (III. 248–68).

If these reversals of Theophrastan misogyny are at first sight welcome, should we have misgivings about the tactic of reversibility itself? 'Reversible topoi', it has been observed, end up being 'bounced back and forth like a tennis ball between misogynist and feminist courts'.[27] The imputation of futile ricochet would not be appropriate in this instance, however. Critical analysis of marriage from a female (even an imaginary female) point of view was a necessary and educative antidote to the virulence of masculine invective against wives. Chaucer hints that he understands an educative function in reversibility when he forces upon the objectionable rapist knight of the *Wife of Bath's Tale* (III. 1219–27) the kind of unwanted 'choice' of evils which is anticipated by the bride-to-be in Ambrose. The distinction is that the Chaucerian knight is, finally, allowed to choose *between* evils: for the Ambrosian bride, and for many women still in the Middle Ages, the very concept of even that miserable degree of marital choice was a mockery.

This concentration on the Troubles of Eligibility has diverted us from the more central concern of the *molestiae*, which was with pains within marriage. Chrysostom catalogues these as follows: the woman's fear of childlessness *or* fear of having too many children; her fear of miscarriage during pregnancy; her anxieties in case a baby will be malformed; at delivery, labour pains which 'rend and tear' her womb (almost every year, he adds); perennial worries over the child's health; and the constant threat of bereave-

[27] Barbara Newman, 'Renaissance Feminism and Esoteric Theology: The Case of Cornelius Agrippa', in Barbara Newman, *From Virile Woman to Woman Christ: Studies in Medieval Religion and Literature* (Philadelphia: University of Pennsylvania Press, 1995), 224–43 (p. 242).

ment.[28] The topoi were zealously reproduced by twelfth-century writers such as Hildebert of Lavardin and Peter of Blois (whose characterization of wives was that they 'bear in sorrow, suckle in fear, are constantly anxious about the living and inconsolably grieved for the dying').[29]

In the early thirteenth century, the same pessimistic sketches of the downside of wifehood and motherhood reached a vernacular English audience—probably of young women considering consecration as novice nuns or recluses—in the prose piece associated with the West Midlands known as *Hali Meiðhad* or *A Letter on Virginity*.[30] Here again there is the litany of suffering and anxiety attributed to childbearing and childrearing, with additional comment on the problems of an infant's all-night crying and of the mess it makes in cradle or lap.[31] Here too, produced with quasi-medical precision, is a sort of 'worst case' for the adverse effect pregnancy might have on a woman's body; pallor, darkened eyes, dizziness, bulging womb, aching bowels, stitches, backache, gravid breasts, vomiting.[32] Here also, partly reminiscent of ser-

[28] *On Virginity*, lvi and lxv, tr. Shore, 91–5 and 101. Among others, St Gregory of Nyssa also catalogues *molestiae*, emphasizing the constant threat of sudden death (husband's or children's); discomfort of pregnancy, pains of childbirth, and mothers' death *in partu*; the particular distress which a mother may experience through her children's own troubles because 'she experiences in her own being whatever happens to them'; *On Virginity* (before AD 371), in *Saint Gregory of Nyssa: Ascetical Works*, tr. Virginia Woods Callahan, Fathers of the Church, no. 58 (Washington: Catholic University of America Press, 1967), 13–21.

[29] 'in dolore pariunt, in timore nutriunt, de viventibus semper sollicitae sunt, de morientibus inconsolabiliter affliguntur', Letter 55, *PL* 207. 167, tr. Barbara Newman in her discussion of the *molestiae* in 'Flaws in the Golden Bowl: Gender and Spiritual Formation in the Twelfth Century', in *From Virile Woman to Woman Christ*, 19–45 (p. 32). On 12th-cent. texts see also *Hali Meiðhad*, ed. Bella Millett, EETS os 284 (London: Oxford University Press, 1982), p. xxxvii.

[30] Ed. and tr. Bella Millett and Jocelyn Wogan-Browne in *Medieval English Prose for Women from the Katherine Group and 'Ancrene Wisse'*, rev. edn. (Oxford: Clarendon Press, 1992), 1–43 (esp. pp. 23–33).

[31] 'in carrying it there is heaviness and constant discomfort; in giving birth to it, the cruellest of all pains, and sometimes death; in bringing it up, many weary hours. As soon as it comes into this life, it brings more anxiety with it than joy, especially to the mother. For if it is born handicapped · · · it is a grief to her · · · If it is born healthy and seems to promise well, fear of its loss is born along with it, for she is never without anxiety lest it should come to harm until one of the two of them first loses the other'; tr. Millett and Wogan-Browne, 30–1. For the crying and the 'filth in the cradle', see pp. 32–3.

[32] Many of these symptoms are paralleled in other pro-virginity writings such as Letter 20, to Cecilia, and 40, to Ida, by Osbert of Clare (12th cent.); *The Letters of Osbert of Clare, Prior of Westminster*, ed. E. W. Williamson (London: Oxford University Press, 1929), 92–3 and 136. See further Millett and Wogan-Browne, *Medieval English Prose for Women*, pp. xix–xx.

mons on marriage, is a powerful sympathetic projection of an abused wife: for the writer asks, what if a woman finds her partner loathsome, or angry? Chrysostom had glanced at the violence and tyranny a wife might have to endure,[33] and the possibilities are quite luridly developed in an anti-matrimonial poem by Serlo of Bayeux.[34] In the same vein *Hali Meiðhad* unforgettably etches a woman's dread when her loud-mouthed husband comes home: 'He rails at you and scolds you and abuses you shamefully, treats you disgracefully as a lecher does his whore, beats you and thrashes you like his bought slave and his born serf. Your bones ache and your flesh smarts, your heart within you swells with violent rage'—but she is tied in the 'knot' of marriage and, far from being able to articulate her anger, finds herself confronted with yet more distastefulness in bed where 'all his indecencies and improper games' are to be put up with.[35]

The *molestiae* tradition clearly generates concern and alarm at the plight of women experiencing social, biological, and psychological disadvantages of marriage and procreation. In the process the tradition provides a large reservoir of empathy on which the case for women can draw to reinforce its cardinal emphasis on a universal debt to mothers. Marbod of Rennes gives rhetorical force to the debt in a classic *occupatio* or refusal to describe;

I shall not dwell on the hard and prolonged labours of pregnancy or the anxious moments of one suffering the pains of giving birth. This is the

[33] 'What if she is discreet and gentle . . . but he is rash, contemptuous, irascible, putting on airs either because of his wealth or his power? What if he treats her as a slave, though she is free, and considers her no better than the maids-in-waiting? How will she endure such duress and violence?', *On Virginity*, xxix, tr. Shore, p. 60.

[34] In the pro-virginity poem 'Ad Muriel sanctimonialem' (to Muriel the nun) Serlo projects the 'iron regime' (*ferrea jura*, 58) a husband may impose, treating his wife more harshly than a servant, tormenting her with a whip, locking her up, taking mistresses, cutting down her food, explosively angry if he imagines himself crossed by her: text in *Anglo-Latin Satirical Poets and Epigrammatists of the Twelfth Century*, ed. Thomas Wright, Rolls Ser., 2 vols., ii. 233–40 (London: Longman, 1872); translations are mine.

[35] 'Chit te ant cheoweð þe ant scheomeliche schent te, tukeð þe to bismere as huler his hore, beateð þe ant busteð þe as his ibohte þrel and his eðele þeowe. þine banes akeð þe ant ti flesch smeorteð þe, þin heorte wiðinne þe sqwelleð of sar grome · · · ; alle his fulitoheschipes ant his unhende gomenes, ne beon ha neauer swa wið fulðe bifunden, nomeliche i bedde ha schal, wulle ha, nulle ha, þolien ham alle,' ed. Millett and Wogan-Browne, 28–9.

price of bearing a child which the careworn mother pays in bringing us into the light, but she soon forgets such sorrows. Who, I ask, makes up for such kindness with love to match?[36]

Nevertheless it would be naïve to enthuse unreservedly over the *molestiae* and the 'suffering mothers' topoi as profeminine phenomena. For one thing, they self-consciously offer a fiercely selective view of female experience. The *molestiae* constitute virginity-propaganda. If they manage to include an idea of the pain inflicted on some women by primitive gynaecological, post-natal, and paediatric knowledge,[37] this arises from a calculated intention to scare girls who might be recruits for the religious life away from expectations of secular marriage. In the most cynical view it might be claimed that the treatises existed to divert dowries from bridegrooms to convents.[38] They certainly did not aspire to an objective view of motherhood. 'By the simple method of describing only the disadvantages of every possible contingency', Millett observes, 'marriage is presented as a series of equally unattractive alternatives.'[39] In *Hali Meiðhad* the unattractiveness is consciously opposed to an inscribed reader's rosy-hued stereotype of wedded prosperity replete with 'a brood of fine children who give much happiness to their parents'.[40] Undermining this with an aggressively negative view, the *molestiae* texts not infrequently collapse from postures of sympathy for wives and mothers into a near-revulsion from the circumstances of pregnancy and childbirth. The misandronist nuances (describing tyrannous, abusive husbands) should not be allowed to blind us to the subtle point of convergence between misogyny and the *molestiae* tradition, namely their common representation of childbearing as oppressive: 'the satirist who feels aggrieved by the caprices of a pregnant wife, and the monk who looks with pitying condescen-

[36] Leotta (ed.) 'De matrona', 48–52; tr. in Blamires, *Woman Defamed and Woman Defended*, 229–30.

[37] Peter Brown perceives in the early Christian *molestiae* texts 'a glimpse of the huge pain that any underdeveloped society places on the bodies of its fertile women', *Body and Society*, 25.

[38] 'Legitimated by a spiritual patriarchy and institutionalised in an ecclesiastical one, the virgin's freedom perhaps amounts to no more than the contribution (kin permitting) of dowry to a convent rather than to a family'; Jocelyn Wogan-Browne, 'The Virgin's Tale', in Evans and Johnson (eds.), *Feminist Readings in Middle English Literature*, 165–94 (p. 171).

[39] Millett (ed.), *Hali Meiðhad*, introduction, p. xxxv.

[40] 'Of wif ant weres gederunge worldes weole awakeneð, ant streon of feire children þe gladieð muchel þe ealdren'; ed. Millett and Wogan-Browne, 22–5.

sion on her sufferings, are brothers under the skin.'[41] We might add that defender and attacker alike betray signs of squeamishness about, or revulsion from, female biological processes, imply an inability to discuss parturition as a positive, let alone neutral phenomenon.[42] (Moreover there always lurked a denigratory connection between the 'woes' of childbirth and the Fall, because Genesis insinuated that God instituted labour pains as Eve's punishment.[43])

Reservations can be set against this critical verdict on the *molestiae* topos, not so much because fragments of evidence suggest that women sometimes viewed their own biological processes precisely as the tradition viewed them (a factor which would merely confirm masculine control of female habits of thought),[44] as because reflections on daily chores and bodily experiences seem a more promising place to begin a defence of women than hypotheses (say) about their piety and constancy. As Linda Woodbridge puts it, 'a discussion of dirty diapers brings us closer to the universal female condition than do pronouncements on Ceres and Minerva or debates about the relative culpability of Adam and Eve'.[45] Woodbridge makes this point only to challenge it, believing that all the attention to pregnancy and childrearing

[41] Newman, 'Flaws in the Golden Bowl', 33–4.

[42] By contrast Hildegard of Bingen thinks of childbirth as a focus of great energy, an 'explosive bursting-out', and conveys a positive sense of the power of giving birth; Clarissa Atkinson, *The Oldest Vocation: Christian Motherhood in the Middle Ages* (Ithaca, NY: Cornell University Press, 1991), 52–4.

[43] Chrysostom, *On Virginity*, lxv; tr. Shore, 101. St Augustine elaborated the pains of parturition as a post-Fall phenomenon (*Opus imperfectum contra Julianum*, 6. 25–30), though his opponent Julian of Eclanum thought it 'insane' to attribute such pains to sin rather than to 'the condition of the sexes'—and even thought that labour pains might be variable according to circumstances such as class and culture; Elaine Pagels, *Adam, Eve, and the Serpent* (Harmondsworth: Penguin, 1990), 133–6.

[44] One example is Melania the Younger, who was in charge of a female community near Jerusalem in the early 5th cent. 'Among those healed by her powers was a young woman afflicted with a dead fetus which she could not deliver. Melania visited her in the company of her nuns and cured her, but not before making the case an object lesson for her virgins on the curses of childbearing from which chastity had delivered them'; Rosemary Ruether, 'Mothers of the Church: Ascetic Women in the Late Patristic Age', in Rosemary Ruether and Eleanor McLaughlin (eds.), *Women of Spirit: Female Leadership in the Jewish and Christian Traditions* (New York: Simon & Schuster, 1979), 72–98 (p. 92), citing Gerontius, *Vie de Sainte Mélanie*, tr. and ed. Denys Gorce, Sources Chrétiennes 90 (Paris: Éditions du Cerf, 1962), s. 61. One cannot be certain that Melania's actual views are presented, however.

[45] *Women and the English Renaissance*, 34, commenting on an exhibition of the *molestiae* topoi (though unrecognized as such by Woodbridge) in Gosynhyll's *The Prayse of All Women, Called Mulierum Pean* (c.1542).

merely promotes the 'stereotype of woman's innate nurturing qualities' and envisages nothing more than male *gratitude* as a redress to the sufferings represented.[46] As already hinted, I would interpret a more positive educative and corrective efficacy in the tradition, but in any case it would be somewhat anachronistic to look in the Middle Ages for any discourse in which innate nurturing qualities were *not* an axiomatic part of the defence of women. The complement of an emphasis on the sufferings of maternity was an essentializing emphasis on women's caring capacity, to which it is time to turn our attention.

There are several factors to be considered here: women's sympathetic, caring profile; their ability to 'soften' men, bring them to 'repose'; their perceived facility in 'peacemaking'; and their ascribed skill in running households. All these factors were underpinned by a universalizing etymology, to an extent that was perhaps so utterly pervasive in medieval consciousness as to be capable of catching us by surprise even when we know it in theory.

'Woman' was normatively associated with 'softness' by standard medieval etymological compendia such as Isidore of Seville's in the seventh century: 'Woman [*mulier*] gets her name from "softness" [*mollities*], or as it were "softer" [*mollier*], with a letter taken away or changed.'[47] Isidore goes on with a phallocentric gloss, claiming that woman's 'softness' renders her submissive to male strength in order that male sexual desires will not be rebuffed, lest there be a mass defection of male sexual activity along some other route.

The alleged connection with 'softness' was ubiquitously accepted, together with the frequent assumption that softness defines women in relation to men (though not usually in relation to the 'risk' of diverted male desire evoked by Isidore). Softness could be understood passively as a sort of malleability; hence Marbod of Rennes's formulation, that woman is co-operative, responsive, can be moulded 'into the pattern of goodness like soft wax' (an idea that Chaucer's old lecher January has got hold of in

---

[46] *Women and the English Renaissance*, 35.

[47] *Isidori Hispalensis Episcopi: Etymologiarum sive originum libri xx*, ed. W. M. Lindsay, 2 vols. (Oxford: Oxford University Press, 1911), XI. ii. 17, tr. in Blamires, *Woman Defamed and Woman Defended*, 43. The 'favourable' etymology was balanced by an unfavourable one for the alternative word *femina* linking her with lust, through derivation from a word for 'thighs' or a word for 'burning'; Isidore, XI. ii. 23, and Blamires, *Woman Defamed and Woman Defended*, 43.

The Merchant's Tale, reckoning that 'a yong thyng may men gye, | Right as men may warm wex with handes plye', IV. 1429–30).[48] More generally woman's softness was hailed as an active capacity. Le Fèvre flourishes the old etymology in *Livre de Leësce* amidst positive arguments about woman's creation: she is called *mulier* in Latin, he remarks, because she 'assuages' or 'softens' (*amolie*) man.[49] He has already invoked the stereotype of sweet/softening femininity earlier in the poem, to refute the misogynous allegation that a man can have no peace (*repos*) with a wife. Woman 'assuages' a man, Le Fèvre argues; she brings him towards peace and sweetness (*doulceur*) and contentment (365–8).[50]

Here it is useful to distinguish in turn two ways in which feminine softness (*mollitia* or *mollities*) could define woman actively: first, actively in relation to positive complementary masculine 'strength' (*virtus*); and second, actively in relation to antithetical masculine 'hardness' (*durities*). The first involves a supposition that women supply men with what I shall call (after Bonaventure) 'quietude' (*quietatio*), while men reciprocally supply women with a sustaining/protective power. Bonaventure codified these concepts in a discussion of the interdependence he inferred from the fact that Eve was created from Adam's side, specifically in light of the detail that Eve was produced while Adam slept (signifying woman's ability to give quietude) and that his bone supplied the substance for her creation (signifying the sustaining strength which man gives woman).[51]

[48] Leotta (ed.), 'De matrona', 67–8: 'Plus amat et citius valet ad praecepta moveri | Inque boni formam ceu mollis cera reflecti.'

[49] '*Mulier* en latin langage | Est dite, car l'omme assouage, | Ou *moulier*, l'omme amolie' (1241–3); perhaps slightly garbling the Isidorian use of *mollier*.

[50] Le Fèvre confirms the utterly androcentric tenor of this tribute by adding that woman is the sweetest thing that God ever created for man. 'Sweetness' (*douceur*) is emphatically ascribed to women in a prose dialogue which overlaps with the formal case; 'Li Houneurs et li vertus des dames par Jehan Petit d'Arras', ed. Rudolf Zimmermann in *Archiv für das Studium der Neueren Sprachen und Literaturen*, 108 (1902), 380–8.

[51] 'Vir enim et mulier secundum suorum sexuum proprietatem et naturam sic facti sunt, ut invicem coniungerentur, et ex hoc unus in altero quietaretur et unus ab altero sustentaretur. ... Quia vero illa coniunctio dat viro quietationem, ideo producta est de viro dormiente. Rursus, quia vir dat mulieri fortitudinem et sustentationem, hinc est, quod mulier dicitur esse facta de osse,' Bonaventure, II *Sentences*, dist. 18, a. 1, q. 1, in *Doctoris seraphici S. Bonaventure ... opera omnia* (Quaracchi: Collegium S. Bonaventurae, 1882–1902), ii. 432b; and see John Hilary Martin, OP, 'The Ordination of Women and the Theologians in the Middle Ages', *Escritos del Vedat*, 16 (1986), 115–77 (pp. 154–5); Joan M. Ferrante, *Woman as Image in Medieval Literature* (New York: Columbia University Press, 1975), 105–7.

The proposition that woman has a generic role as man's *quietatio* (in which, presumably, her sexual satisfaction of the male is a tacit element) is mostly diffused in defence writings within commendations of gentleness or of a power to bring joy.[52] Defenders felt that the most arresting way of highlighting women's perceived calmative qualities was to exploit the contrast not with masculine 'strength' but with masculine 'hardness', taking account of the intimations of harshness, rigour, and oppressiveness present in the Latin noun. Marbod stereotyped masculinity in terms of the 'stubborn' (*durus*) mentality of 'stiff-necked' men who are defiant of any curb.[53] Much later, beyond the Middle Ages, the hardness or *durities* of the masculine heart is identified by a profeminine Renaissance writer as an ancient mechanism of men's 'usurpation' of authority, to the disadvantage of women.[54] But the classic medieval configuration was, of course, one in which the archetypal female 'softness' worked upon archetypal, undesirable male 'hardness' with beneficial results.

This configuration was well noticed in an influential article by Sharon Farmer on medieval preachers' recommendations that wives might soften husbands' hearts by a sort of domestic preaching.[55] She quotes a confessional manual (*c*.1215) by Thomas of Chobham which suggests that women should be pressed 'to be preachers to their husbands, because no priest is able to soften [*emollire*] the heart of a man the way his wife can', since a wife can use intimate persuasions if, for instance, her husband is a harsh (*durus*) and a merciless oppressor of the poor.[56] There is biblical

---

[52] See Christine, *Epistre*, ed. and tr. Fenster and Erler: woman 'is pleasant, gentle, sweet; | When he's in need, she understands and helps. | She's done and does so many services | For him; how right her ministrations are | Gently to serve the creature needs of man'; 'souëve, doulce, et amiable, | A son besoing piteuse et secourable, | Qui tant lui a fait et fait de services, | Et de qui tant les œuvres sont propices | A corps d'omme souëvement nourrir' (171–5).

[53] Leotta (ed.), 'De matrona', 70–1: 'At mens dura viri rigida cervice repugnat | Vixque iugum patitur, dum se negat inferiorem', tr. in Blamires, *Woman Defamed and Woman Defended*, 230.

[54] 'many things were permitted to men because of their hard-heartedness against women [*propter duritiem cordis eorum in mulieres*] . . . but these things in no way prejudice the dignity of women'; *De nobilitate et praecellentia foeminei sexus*, tr. Newman, in 'Renaissance Feminism and Esoteric Theology', *From Virile Woman to Woman Christ*, 240.

[55] Sharon Farmer, 'Persuasive Voices: Clerical Images of Medieval Wives', *Speculum*, 61 (1986), 517–43.

[56] Ibid. 517, citing *Summa confessorum*, 7. 2. 15, ed. F. Broomfield, Analecta Mediaevalia Namurcensia 25 (Louvain, 1968), 375.

analogy for this sort of wifely persuasion in the chaste behaviour (*conversatio*) by which it is suggested in the first Epistle of St Peter that wives may 'win' husbands towards faith.[57] Farmer seeks to locate within the period's economic and theological currents both Chobham's formulation and an example in a *Life* of Ermengard, which tells how this woman of the eleventh century 'softened' (*mitigabat*) her husband's 'ferocity' on behalf of religious foundations;[58] but there is a strong case for inserting the vocabulary of softening within the long-standing stereotype of emollient femininity.

What we are dealing with here is in fact part of a perennial configuration whereby the masculine is constructed as 'harsh', 'cruel', 'irascible', and the feminine is constructed as 'soft', 'merciful', and 'pacific'. The presence of the irascible/pacific polarity in this configuration has been noticed in the later Middle Ages by Felicity Riddy:

Anger in late-medieval aristocratic culture is part of the construction of masculinity. . . . Peaceableness, on the other hand, is a feminine attribute in which women were trained. In the fifteenth-century courtesy text, *The Good Wife Taught Her Daughter*, the daughter is taught to answer her husband meekly and thus 'slake his mood', since 'A faire worde and a meeke I dooth wraþþe slake'.[59]

The point is amusingly reinforced by Riddy's evidence from correspondence among the Pastons in the 1480s, when a proposal was made that Paston women should approach the Duchess of Norfolk to help settle a family dispute over land, on the grounds that one word from a woman would do more than the words of

---

[57] 1 Pet. 3: 1–2: 'In like manner also let wives be subject to their husbands: that if any believe not the word, they may be won without the word, by the conversation of the wives: considering your chaste conversation with fear'; but the Douai–Rheims translation 'conversation' is probably misleading: *conversatio* generally meant 'manner of living' in medieval Latin.

[58] Farmer, 'Persuasive Voices', 535–6.

[59] ' "Women talking about the things of God": A Late Medieval Sub-culture', in Carol M. Meale (ed.), *Women and Literature in Britain, 1150–1500* (Cambridge: Cambridge University Press, 1993), 104–27 (p. 116). The vocabulary is very reminiscent of *The Knight's Tale*, where the impact of the ladies who kneel and plead to Theseus for Arcite and Palamon is that 'at the laste aslaked was his mood' (I. 1760). In a classic expression of the stereotype, Gottfried von Strassburg represents Isolde as torn between 'sweet womanhood' and anger when she wonders whether to attack Tristan as her enemy: *Tristan* (10261–84), ed. Karl Morold and Werner Schröder (Berlin: de Gruyter, 1969); tr. A. T. Hatto (Harmondsworth: Penguin, 1960), 176–7.

twenty men.[60] But, as with many of the gender constructions pertinent to this book, the ascribed (and hence, through acculturation, sometimes actual) feminine pacifying seems to go far back in Western culture.

In its outwardly more attractive guise (that is, calmative mediation amidst hostilities), the role is everywhere performed. Prudence performs it in Albertanus' treatise, preventing the outbreak of full-scale vendetta between her husband and his enemies.[61] Queen Philippa of England performs it in Froissart's account of the war with France, kneeling to dissuade Edward III from angry retaliation against the citizens of Calais. Blanche, mother of the French king St Louis, performs it when she brings factious barons together to acknowledge the rule of the boy-king: 'Elle appaisa la grant discorde', as Deschamps admiringly puts it.[62] In *The Knight's Tale* Theseus' wife and her sister Emelye kneel with other women, weeping, to mediate on behalf of his enemies Arcite and Palamon (the one banished, the other an escaped prisoner) when he has pronounced a death sentence against them (I. 1748–59). But centuries before, the *Lives* of female European saints were already representing this 'softening' power of women. Of Queen Clothild it is stated that 'her sweetness softened the hearts of a pagan and ferocious people' through a programme of conversion.[63] In the *Life* of the sixth-century royal St Radegund, by Venantius Fortunatus (d. 609), her busy canvassing among the King's advisers to mitigate his severity against condemned men is rhetorically underlined.[64] Anglo-Saxon culture yields similar examples. A famous instance is the 'peace-weaving' of Queen Wealhtheow in *Beowulf*, whose words calm

[60] Riddy, ' "Women talking about the things of God" ', 126 n. 85; *Paston Letters and Papers of the Fifteenth Century*, ed. Norman Davis, 2 vols. (Oxford: Clarendon Press, 1971, 1976), i. 664–6.

[61] Jean Leclercq summarizes an analogous narrative by a Cistercian abbot in the 12th cent., concerning a wilful and violent man whose wife uses 'gentle rebuke', 'tears', and 'exhortation' against his conviction that he is bound to retaliate against enemies, until he is 'overcome by her persistent kindness' and 'softened' (*delinitus*) by her charity. The softening is at first short-lived: he beheads a priest. See *Monks on Marriage: A Twelfth-Century View* (New York: The Seabury Press, 1982), 57–8.

[62] *Miroir de mariage*, 9411.

[63] McNamara *et al.* (eds.), *Sainted Women of the Dark Ages*, 47.

[64] Ibid. 74: 'And if the king, according to custom, condemned a guilty criminal to death, wasn't the most holy queen near dead with torment lest the culprit perish by the sword? How would she rush about among his trusty men, ministers and nobles, whose blandishments might soothe the prince's temper until the king's anger ceased . . .!'

the emotions stirred by a hostile interchange between Beowulf and Unferth.[65]

Medieval writers readily champion women as peacemakers. For the profeminine Nightingale in the late thirteenth-century Middle English bird-debate *The Thrush and the Nightingale*, it is a first line of defence that there is no conflict women cannot ease, with their ability to turn men's wrath to gladness.[66] Hoccleve emphasized the same when he reworked Christine de Pizan's *Epistre au dieu d'amours*, asserting that 'wel [women] can a mannes ire asswage | With softe wordes discreet and benigne'.[67] And yet we may wish to ask, for all its ethical attractiveness, how far does this rancour-softening role imply any empowerment of the women who are commended for exercising it?

No doubt women were lauded as peaceweavers because this suited masculine ideology first, etymology second, and women third. The ideological constraints are actually disclosed in an episode within Chrétien de Troyes's romance of *Cligés*. Here, a potential conciliatory role for Queen Guinevere is anticipated when, after a successful siege, one of the story's heroes, Alexander, presents defeated rebel knights to her, rather than to Arthur who 'would quickly have them hanged'.[68] It transpires, however, that this is a serious error of tact which Arthur 'does not find amusing'. (He insists the traitors be handed over to him, and subjects them to horrific punishment.) The point surely is precisely a difference between the acceptability of female *supplication* to try to mitigate the severity of lordly action, and the unacceptability of

---

[65] *Beowulf*, 612–41, ed. C. L. Wrenn, rev. W. F. Bolton (London: Harrap, 1973); see Bernice W. Kliman, 'Women in Early English Literature: *Beowulf* to the *Ancrene Wisse*', *Nottingham Medieval Studies*, 21 (1977), 32–49 (pp. 33–4), and Larry H. Sklute, 'Freothuwebbe in Old English Poetry', *Neuphilologische Mitteilungen*, 71 (1970), 534–41.

[66] 'Ne wes neuere bruche so strong, | I-broke wiþ riȝte ne wiþ wrong, | þat wimmon ne miȝte bete' (28–30); in *Early Middle English Texts*, ed. Bruce Dickins and R. M. Wilson (London: Bowes & Bowes, 1951), 71–6; tr. in Blamires, *Woman Defamed and Woman Defended*, 225. Cf. Fiero *et al.* (eds.), *Le Bien des fames*, 49–51.

[67] Fenster and Erler (eds.), *Letter of Cupid* (341–2), in *Poems of Cupid*, and see the same editors' n. to *Epistre*, line 673. It is interesting that Gower equally feels the need to attribute a pacifying agency to the king's concubine, Apemen, in his summary of the Zorobabel speech: 'When he was hotest in his ire | Toward the grete of his empire, | Cirus the king tirant sche tok, | And only with hire goodly lok | Sche made him debonaire and meke'; Macaulay (ed.), *Confessio Amantis*, VII. 1887–91.

[68] *Cligés*, 1349–65, ed. Claude Luttrell and Stewart Gregory (Cambridge: D. S. Brewer, 1993); *Chrétien de Troyes: Arthurian Romances*, tr. D. D. R. Owen (London: Dent, 1987), 111.

female *pre-empting* of such mitigation: while a lord might elect
conciliatory judgement after female supplications have been presented—or even hand judgement to a woman, as does Arthur in
The Wife of Bath's Tale in the case of a rapist knight[69]—the choice of
judgement is initially a male prerogative. Women are confined to
a ritual begging function. Theirs is a 'diplomacy which is born of
impotence',[70] indeed a diplomacy which is *ceded* to them by an
ideology which thereby sustains a profile of masculine rigour
cherished by the male ego. Jo Ann McNamara encapsulates such
a reading in relation to Dark Age structures: 'The intervention of
women on behalf of prisoners may indicate an aspect of the division of labor whereby the harsh military face of kingship could be
softened through the merciful quality of queenship without making the king appear weak or indecisive.'[71] Generalizing this
mechanism across the Middle Ages, one can see how it protects a
male 'right' to wrath; enables men to perceive the control of
vengeful instincts as something which it may be women's job to
beg them for;[72] and thereby *makes women responsible* for tempering
masculine aggression.[73] This element of responsibility emerges
clearly (though it is dressed up as God-given privilege) in a florid
description of Queen Anne as intercessor at the ceremonial recon-
ciliation in 1392 between Richard II and the city of London. 'Let
the queen soften royal severity', writes a Carmelite commentator,
'that the king may be forbearing to his people. A woman mellows

[69] Even this instance is presented initially as a response to female supplication:
'the queene and other ladyes mo | So long preyeden the kyng of grace | Til he his
lyf hym graunted in the place, | And yaf hym to the queene, al at hir wille, | To
chese wheither she wolde hym save or spille' (III. 894–8). The women's 'actualiza-
tion of feminine power . . . requires masculine permission', as noted by Lynne
Dickson, 'Deflection in the Mirror: Feminine Discourse in *The Wife of Bath's Prologue* and *Tale*', *Studies in the Age of Chaucer*, 15 (1993), 61–90 (p. 86).

[70] Kliman, 'Women in Early English Literature', 34.

[71] *Sainted Women of the Dark Ages*, 74 n. 47.

[72] The *pitee* called forth by female entreaty is in a sense not even the male
authority's pity for the (usually male) defendant, but rather for the distress of the
begging women themselves: hence the revealing articulation of the ladies' plea to
Theseus in *The Knight's Tale*, ' "Have mercy, Lord, upon [not Palamon and Arcite,
but] us wommen alle!" ' (I. 1757).

[73] In a probing discussion of the feminine intercessory role, Paul Strohm speculates that men eagerly endorsed it because it consigned women to a domain
where, non-competitively, they could 'supply a male "lack" '; because it facilitated
royal changes of mind; and because the spectacle of the abject, emotional female
intercessor helps to 'affirm "maleness" '; 'Queens as Intercessors', in Paul Strohm,
Hochon's Arrow: The Social Imagination of Fourteenth-Century Texts (Princeton:
Princeton University Press, 1992), 95–119 (pp. 103–4).

a man with love: for this God gave her; for this, O blessed woman, may your sweet love aspire.'[74]

Locked inside that ideology, people could barely be expected to puncture it. Christine de Pizan accepts peacemaking as a 'proper duty' of queen or princess. She argues that it is women's business because 'men are by nature more courageous and more hot-headed, and the great desire they have to avenge themselves prevents their considering either the perils or the evils that can result from war', whereas women's 'sweeter' disposition renders them (given the wisdom and the inclination) 'the best means of pacifying men'.[75] There is an interesting hint here of scorn for masculine short-sightedness and recklessness: but Christine takes a certain pride in the beneficent impact that women can make through the 'duty' of peacemaking.[76] And whether it empowered or ultimately disempowered them, one can understand how women could have felt that this 'softening' exercise was worthwhile, and worth being complimented on.

Rather less comprehensible now is the notion that women should be commended for adopting the same 'softening' stance in response to abusive husbands; but the medieval case for women propounds that notion nevertheless. Women were praised, that is, for making a virtue of necessity. The 'necessity' was the assumed imperative of putting up with marital duress for which, according to inherited doctrine, a woman had only two solutions: 'either take great pains and train him or, if this is impossible, endure

[74] 'Flectere regales poterit regina rigores, | Mitis ut in gentem rex velit esse suam. | Mollit amore virum mulier: Deus huic dedit illam; | Tendat ad hoc vester, O pia, dulcis amor'; Strohm, 'Queens as Intercessors', 108, citing Richard Maidstone, *Concordia: Facta inter Regem Riccardum II et civitatem Londinie*, ed. Charles Roger Smith (Ann Arbor: University Microfilms, 1972).

[75] *Le Livre des trois vertus*, ed. Charity Cannon Willard and Eric Hicks (Paris: Champion, 1989), I. 8; tr. Sarah Lawson, *The Treasure of the City of Ladies, or the Book of the Three Virtues* (Harmondsworth: Penguin, 1985), 51. Christine's somewhat deterministic view of gender difference here finds a parallel in ch. ci of the book of instruction for the daughters of the Chevalier de la Tour-Landry (later 14th cent.) which holds that 'a woman of her nature oughte to be more swete and pyteous than the man | For the man oughte to be more hard and of more hyghe courage | And therfore they that haue the herte nother meke nor pyteous maye be called mannysshe'; *The Book of the Knight of the Tower Translated by William Caxton*, ed. M. Y. Offord, EETS ss 2 (London: Oxford University Press, 1971), 135.

[76] 'O God, how many great blessings in the world have often been caused by queens and princesses making peace between enemies, between princes and barons and between the rebellious people and their lords! The Scriptures are full of such examples'; tr. Lawson, *Treasure*, 51.

nobly this unproclaimed war, this battle without a truce.'[77] What
was most held up for admiration was a wife's continuing gentleness in the face of infidelity, a refined version of the self-sacrifice
that was always latent in the 'softening' role. Nicole Bozon congratulates the *humble femme* who conceals her husband's errancy,
and exerts only tenderness to draw him from it.[78] A later chapter
will consider Chaucer's Griselda, whose 'pacient benyngnytee'
under marital duress prompts the Clerk to complain that clerks
fail to realize how far women's *humblesse* exceeds men's.[79]

The praiseworthiness of wifely tolerance, of seeking to 'mollify'
husbands (if a last flick of the etymology may be pardoned), was
therefore part of the case for women. Yet the relentless cultural
reinforcement of mollification need not be assumed to have stran-
gled women's critical faculties on the matter altogether. Christine
de Pizan follows best practice in other instructional books in her
Treasure of the City of Ladies by commending humble compliancy
in a wife as well as clear demonstrations of love through conspicuous attention to the husband's well-being. But Christine also
anticipates a backlash of scepticism from readers who think this is
'nonsense' because it fails to acknowledge 'certain defects' which
raise the question whether some husbands 'deserve to be treated
so well'. Her answer is that prudence and honour still dictate—
we might whisper, ideology dictates—'pleasant and kind' responses rather than remonstrations. If these do not work, the wife
should resign the problem to God.[80] That is, even when woman's
etymologically defined power of 'softening' meets with an impervious masculinity, no self-assertion is warranted and there is no
social redress; the problem is simply kicked upstairs. And yet,
amidst this endorsement of the 'caring' role which the period's
profeminine (as well as instructional) discourse supports,
Christine has managed to gesture patronizingly towards a bunch
of husbands entirely undeserving of tolerance: she makes clear
that a powerful current of female opinion would consider it 'non-

---

[77] Chrysostom, *On Virginity*, xxix, tr. Shore, 60.

[78] Smith and Meyer (ed.), *De la bonté des femmes*, 169–80. The same concept of
conquering by toleration is systematically upheld in the *Book of the Knight of the
Tower*: with 'softe and swete wordes' and 'by grete curtosye and obeysaunce a
woman may best ouercome . . . hir lord and husbond . . . sonner than by rudesse',
man's temperament being so inflammable (ed. Offord, ch. xvi); see further chs.
xvii, lxiii, lxv, and lxxi.

[79] 'Though clerkes preise wommen but a lite, | Ther kan no man in humblesse
hym acquite | As womman kan' (IV. 935–7).

[80] *Treasure*, I. 12, tr. Lawson, 62–4.

sense' to sweet-talk such errant husbands. She therefore contextualizes wifely benignity (a policy which effectively countenances the double standard) as a policy that is sustained *voluntarily*, in the interests of honourable criteria of feminine loyalty and love: the policy is not urged primarily as a doctrine of submission, and it is expressly only sustained slenderly against a legitimate background of female scepticism and anger.[81]

Two further facets of the defence of women as nurturers should be identified before moving on: these are respectively healing, and running households. Curative skills are among those acclaimed in *The Thrush and the Nightingale*, where woman 'with her sensitive mind and solicitude' is reckoned 'hard to match for healing men's wounds'.[82] Marbod of Rennes equally ascribes a special feminine facility for attending to the sick.[83] Christine de Pizan suggests that comforting the sick and taking care of hospitals are women's specialities, among the works of mercy enjoined on all Christians.[84]

This praise of feminine healing capacity assumes particular importance in relation to the articulation of love-relationships, as may be seen in a moment. But for the defenders, it is just one aspect of the nurturing 'gift' which women have, and which is held to extend to domestic organization generally. The underlying rationale is inherited and passed on in the fourth century by Chrysostom in a treatise *Against Remarrying* when he comes to the ticklish question whether women *need* to remarry, to avoid having to 'take up men's affairs'. Chrysostom courts equivocation: plenty of widows have managed their affairs independently and 'added to their possessions', he urges—but at the same time as strategically enhancing widows' management skills he wants to retain an absolute division of labour between public and private spheres, so falls back on the formula that 'household matters depend upon womanly skills and in this area a woman is much better suited than a man'. Accruing wealth outside the home is a

---

[81] *Treasure*, I. 12, tr. Lawson, 62–5.

[82] 'In þe worlde nis non so goed leche, | So milde of þoute, so feir of speche, | To hele monnes sore' (151–3); in Dickins and Wilson (eds.), *Early Middle English Texts*.

[83] 'Mollius aegrotos tractat, plus sedula lecto | Assistit'; 'She treats the sick more gently [than a man], is more painstakingly attentive at the bedside': Leotta (ed.), 'De matrona', 65–6, tr. in Blamires, *Woman Defamed and Woman Defended*, 230. See also Le Fèvre, *Leësce*, 3758–61.

[84] *Cité*, I. 10. 1; ed. Curnow, 656, tr. Richards, 26.

man's duty: woman's is to protect and conserve that wealth at home.[85]

The medieval consciousness elicited clear profeminine cues from this emphasis on women's 'conserving' skills in late antique culture. One topos noted by defenders was that women's industrious domestic management showed up the contrasting profligacies and inadequacies of husbands. St Jerome takes this thought to surprising lengths when he debates whether the verb *timeat* in Ephesians 5: 33, 'let the wife fear her husband' ('uxor autem timeat virum suum'), really should be interpreted to mean something other than 'fear'. From mere semantic quibble Jerome's commentary launches eye-catchingly into the idea of a matriarchy that might be justified by superior female commitment, organization, and morality, because

wives are often found much better than husbands and rule them, and rule the house, and raise children, and see to the direction of the servants, while husbands are busy with debauchery and with running after prostitutes. I leave to the reader's judgement whether these wives ought to govern [*regnare*] their husbands or 'fear' them.[86]

Profeminine writings usually rehearse conventional home-making skills without inviting such interesting judgements about hierarchy,[87] but in Le Fèvre's *Livre de Leësce* the model rhetorical

---

[85] *On Virginity, against Remarriage*, tr. Shore, 136–7. That 'conserving' remained normative is demonstrated by its mention in (*a*) the negative context of Serlo of Bayeux's 'Ad Muriel', where the tyrannical imagined husband criticizes his wife for an innocent theatre visit and demands that she attend to household matters: 'conserve what we have accumulated' ('Congestam serva', 121), ed. Wright, 236; (*b*) Boccaccio's *De mulieribus claris*: 'Frugality is proper for women, and within the house it is up to them faithfully to save what is acquired by their husbands', ed. Zaccaria, 318, tr. Guarino, 174; and (*c*) the gnomic force of the sarcastic line 'A wyf is kepere of thyn housbondrye', *Merchant's Tale*, IV. 1380. That woman was 'naturally the custodian of children, household goods and the acquisitions of her husband' was an idea received from Aristotle's *Economics*, I. 3. 4; see Ian Maclean, *The Renaissance Notion of Woman: A Study in the Fortunes of Scholasticism and Medical Science in European Intellectual Life* (Cambridge: Cambridge University Press, 1980), 57.

[86] 'Cum frequenter multo meliores maritis inveniantur uxores et eis imperent, et domum regnent, et educunt liberos, et familiae teneant disciplinam: illis luxuriantibus et per scorta currentibus. Hae viros suos utrum regnare debeant an timere, lectoris arbitrio derelinquo,' *In Eph.* 3. 5. 33 (*PL* 26. 536), my translation. I owe this reference to Antti Arjava, 'Jerome and Women', *Arctos: Acta philologica Fennica*, 23 (1989), 5–18 (p. 15).

[87] Marbod of Rennes, ed. Leotta, 'De matrona', 62–3: 'woman accomplishes more efficiently with special female care very many things which looking after a household requires', tr. in Blamires, *Woman Defamed and Woman Defended*, 230. In Deschamps, there is a contrast between the embarrassingly draughty emptiness of a single man's residence (not much more than a stable) and the commodious warm reception women know how to furnish; *Miroir de mariage*, 8862–86.

contrast between abstinent female diligence and indolent male dissipation comes through loud and clear: women sustain households, are busy with thread, food, plants, furniture, and they drink water, while if men go off to work their motive is only greed, and they are usually found boozing in taverns cultivating idleness.[88]

Such a commendation of the good wife at home amounts to the direst provocation from a feminist perspective, despite its countervailing verdict on male complacency. Impatient with this way of promoting women we may be: but there is little to be gained for a reader of medieval texts by ignoring the ingrained idea that women were to be honoured as childbearers, mothers, nourishers, healers, nest-providers. Recognition of the power of these topoi can clarify deep structures within the period's articulation of male–female relationships. Take Chaucer's formulation of that relationship in *Troilus and Criseyde*. David Aers has drawn attention to the way in which Troilus—abetted by Pandarus— thinks obsessively of Criseyde as his healer.[89] The poem makes us massively aware of Troilus' single-tracked *need* of her, whereas her need of him tends to be displaced in her mind by self-effacing expressions of empathy for his distress.[90] Her instincts are for how he (not she) will sustain their parting.[91] Aers is so struck by Troilus' contrasting construction of Criseyde as 'only physician, a person whose sole existence is in relation to his own demands', that he feels the phenomenon needs explanation as a 'psychodrama' of male 'infantilization' whereby 'the female lover is represented as the nourishing, encompassing mother and physician, the adult male as the nurtured, protected infant', for whom loss of the woman signifies withdrawal of a life-source.[92] Aers turns to psychoanalysis because for him Troilus' anxieties of dep-

---

[88] 3694–724, 3734–77.

[89] Samples of this quoted by Aers are, that at the prospect of losing Criseyde, Troilus exclaims 'Who shal now yeven comfort to my peyne?' (IV. 319); and that Pandarus bids her 'shapeth yow his sorwe for t'abregge' (IV. 925); see also V. 1415–20; 'Masculine Identity in the Courtly Community: The Self Loving in *Troilus and Criseyde*', in David Aers, *Community, Gender, and Individual Identity: English Writing 1360–1430* (London: Routledge, 1988), 117–52 (esp. pp. 132–43).

[90] Aers (p. 133) quotes IV. 757–60, Criseyde's reaction when she hears that she must leave Troy: 'She seyde, "How shal he don, and ich also? | How sholde I lyve, if that I from hym twynne? | O deere herte eke, that I love so, | Who shal that sorwe slen that ye ben inne?"'

[91] See further IV. 792–5, 897–900.

[92] There is interesting supporting evidence in vocabulary which projects a mother–infant relation at III. 1169 and 1180. Aers draws on the work of Melanie Klein and Herbert Moller.

rivation go far beyond traditional courtly medieval imaging of mistress as lover's healer (pp. 139–40), *and* beyond social gender construction. For me, the latter seems nevertheless a sufficient explanation. That the contrastive roles of the lovers are locatable in 'the social making of "masculine" and "feminine" roles, ones that she, as much as Troilus, has internalized', and that 'her identity is bound up with being "needed" by a male as his "healer", with being a nurturer of men' (as Aers himself puts it, p. 134), is utterly consistent with the structure of thought disclosed within the present chapter. And small wonder, given the altruistic quality of Criseyde's love (on which I absolutely agree), that the whole nurturing and softening stereotype was rounded off with a suggestion that women exerted a *civilizing* influence over men.[93] As Sharon Farmer noticed, habits of diction made women 'agents of the civilizing process: they harnessed and brought under cultivation wild, savage men'.[94] This was what the case for women said, too, for (one of the French *dits* claimed) '*cortoisie* is rarely seen to occur except under the influence of women'.[95]

As this chapter has earlier shown, gestures such as that are sometimes less profeminine than they ostensibly seem. Why couldn't men be responsible for their own courtesy? In concluding the discussion of nurturing topoi, a cautionary note might be further registered by noting both their contextualization and their fictiveness. They need to be contextualized in relation to a sometimes competing stress on other female potential—whether in favour of intellectual or virginal goals, or in favour of the rather contrary profile of the tough Amazon (to be considered later). Then, the fictiveness of the topoi can be glimpsed by situating them in relation to the maternal or filial perceptions of actual women who used them. Here I am thinking of Heloise as mother, and Christine de Pizan as daughter. In neither case, so far as can be deduced, was unqualified enthusiasm shown for nurturing as a feminine ideal. In the first case, the couple's correspondence implies that Heloise construes the arrival of their baby son Astralabe as an impediment to intellectual pursuits, and never once does she invoke her motherhood of Astralabe as any part of

[93] Seen in *Troilus and Criseyde* at, for instance, III. 1723–5, 1786–92.
[94] 'Persuasive Voices', 541.
[95] My translation of 'Quar nous veons poi avenir | Cortoisie se n'est par fames', *Le Bien des fames*, 39–40, in Fiero *et al.* (eds.), *Three Medieval Views of Women*, where the translation 'For it's woman who interjects | The rules of *courtoisie*' is somewhat loose.

the debt of love which she feels Abelard owes her.[96] In Christine's case, the topos of debt to the nurturing mother is expressed occasionally, but in the *Cité des dames* it has to compete with hints of reproach for a mother whose only ambitions for Christine were 'girlish', as against her father's encouragement of her intellectual aspirations.[97] Near the beginning of the same text, the narrator's mother actually *functions* as a kind of impediment: she interrupts her daughter's reading, calling her to supper.[98] Renate Blumenfeld-Kosinski's insight is that 'the mother's role is emblematic of the difficulties Christine perceived in her own career: how to combine a serious literary intent with being a woman in a society that valued nurturing, piety and passivity in women above all else.'[99]

We are back to a paradox of medieval profeminine discourse with which the chapter began: the difficulty of asserting women's capacities to fulfil talents in parity with men, without potentially undermining the status of the nurturing role. Nevertheless the case for women in the Middle Ages generally privileged that role. The role has been redefined thus by Hélène Cixous: 'In women there is always more or less of the mother who makes everything all right, who nourishes, and who stands up against separation; a force that will not be cut off but will knock the wind out of the codes.'[100] It was the first part of this formulation that prevailed in medieval culture.

---

[96] Her arguments about the impediment children constitute are reported (though probably embroidered) by Abelard in the *Historia calamitatum*: ed. J. T. Muckle, 'Abelard's Letter of Consolation to a Friend (*Historia calamitatum*)', *Mediaeval Studies*, 12 (1950), 161–213 (p. 186); tr. Radice, *The Letters of Abelard and Heloise*, 71. On the significance of the 'debt' urged by Heloise, see Alcuin Blamires, '*Caput a femina, membra a viris*: Gender Polemic in Abelard's Letter "On the Authority and Dignity of the Nun's Profession"', forthcoming in Andrew Taylor and David Townsend (eds.), *Gender in the Tongue of the Fathers*.

[97] 'L'oppinion femenine de ta mere, qui te vouloit occupper en fillasses selonc l'usaige commun des femmes, fu cause de l'empeschement que ne fus en ton enffance plus avant boutee es sciences et plus en parfont'; 'The feminine opinion of your mother, however, who wished to keep you busy with spinning and silly girlishness, following the common custom of women, was the major obstacle to your being involved in the sciences'; II. 36. 4, ed. Curnow, 875, tr. Richards, 154–5.

[98] *Cité*, I. 1. 1, ed. Curnow, 617, tr. Richards, 3.

[99] Blumenfeld-Kosinski's 'Christine de Pizan and Misogynistic Tradition' includes an excellent discussion of symbolic functions of the mother role in Christine's works, 285–92.

[100] 'The Laugh of the Medusa', in Elaine Marks and Isabelle de Courtivron (eds.), *New French Feminisms* (Hemel Hempstead: Harvester, 1981), 245–64 (p. 252).

4

Eve and the Privileges of Women

On the basis of a selective reading of the Book of Genesis, patriarchy in the medieval West constructed woman to be *secondary* in creation, and *primary* in guilt.[1] Nevertheless, this construction was neither universal nor inevitable. As early commentators already saw, woman's role in foundational myth emerged more positively if alternative emphases were selected. During the Middle Ages there grew up an argument that woman actually occupied a privileged position in creation, and this was consolidated by identifying complementary privileges in post-creation history. Meanwhile (as this chapter will go on to show) on the one hand the distribution of guilt for the Fall was kept open for revaluation, and on the other, defenders of women always sought to close down the propaganda against Eve by appealing to her transcendent and necessary heir, the Virgin Mary.

The 'privileges of women' constitute one of those conventions which seem to appear from nowhere and quickly assume categorical, almost proverbial, status. In their fully developed form they identified six (optionally seven) cardinal points of feminine superiority, deduced in even proportions from woman's relation to Adam and her relation to Christ.[2] In relation to Adam, her first privilege is to be created from his bone, a better substance (*materia*) than the muck used to create him; her second privilege (of place or *locus*) is to be created within paradise whereas Adam

---

[1] It was, as Kate Millett observed, an enduring construction: 'this mythic version of the female as the cause of human suffering, knowledge, and sin is still the foundation of sexual attitudes'; *Sexual Politics*, 52.

[2] The 'privileges' were noted by Paul Meyer, 'Mélanges de poésie française, iv', 500, quoting from a Cambridge MS five proofs that woman is to be preferred to man: 'Materia: quia Adam factus de limo terre, Eve de costa Ade. Loco: quia Adam factus extra paradisum, Eve in paradiso. In conceptione: quia mulier concepit Deum quod homo non potuit. Apparicione: quia Christus primo apparuit mulieri post resurrectionem, scilicet Magdalene. Exaltacione: quia mulier exaltaba [*sic*] est super choros angelorum, scilicet beata Maria.' These are cited again in Blanche Dow, *Varying Attitude toward Women*, 92; see also McLean, *Renaissance Notion of Woman*, 91. The dissemination of the privileges receives some attention in Fenster and Erler, *Poems of Cupid*, 13–14, but they deserve fuller study.

had been introduced to paradise only after his creation; and her third is of sequence (*ordo*), to be created not so much 'after' him as *last*, that is as the crowning triumph or *chef d'œuvre* of God's handiwork. An optional extra here was to dwell on the definition of Eve's name as 'life', and to revere her as mother of all the living (a strategy which converges with the debt to mothers already discussed).[3] Then in relation to Christ, woman's privilege is of *conceptio* as his mother; afterwards to take priority over men in being given first sight of him after the Resurrection (the *apparitio*). Finally, in the person of the Virgin Mary she outranks angels—let alone men—in the lofty position (*exaltatio*) she has attained in the celestial hierarchy.

Where did this schema come from? Doubtless at some point in the thirteenth century it acquired its aura of scholastic rigour, identifying and matching auspicious beginnings and ends: the what, where, and when of woman's origin complemented by her delivery of whom, her selection for whose first risen appearance, and her eventual glorious whither. The convention owes much to scholastic habits of interrogation: why was Eve made of bone? why in paradise? and so forth.[4] But of course the 'privileges' were not conjured, fully shaped, from nowhere. From the available evidence (albeit fragmentary) I think it most credible to suggest that they were the result of incremental growth, as writers opportunistically picked up cues in patristic debate. A further

---

[3] Having earlier named her *isha* (like man; *ish*), Adam subsequently names her 'Eve', which is immediately glossed 'because she was the mother of all the living' (Gen. 3: 20). The interpretation *vita* ('life') was repeated by Isidore of Seville, *Etymologiarum*, VII. vi. 5, and by Peter Comestor, *Historia scholastica, liber Gen.*, ch. xviii (*PL* 198. 1071) among others—though both also rehearse more pejorative possibilities, on which see Blamires, *Woman Defamed and Woman Defended*, 44–5, and John M. Fyler, 'St Augustine, Genesis, and the Origin of Language', in *Saint Augustine and his Influence in the Middle Ages*, ed. Edward B. King and Jacqueline T. Schaefer (Sewanee, Tenn.: The Press of the University of the South, 1988), 69–78 (pp. 73–4). This topos is not characteristic of medieval defences of women but, as Barbara Newman points out, it is eagerly adopted by Agrippa (1529) who remarks that Adam's name only means 'earth', and who then 'transforms the common-place by adding that, "according to the mystic symbols of the cabalists, the wo-man's name has a greater affinity than the man's with the ineffable name of the divine omnipotence, the Tetragrammaton"'; 'Renaissance Feminism and Esoteric Theology', in *From Virile Woman to Woman Christ*, 230.

[4] Angenot senses the influence of Aristotelian method and category in the plan of showing woman superior in 'ordre, lieu, matière, finalité'; *Champions des femmes*, 155. I would add that commentaries on the *Sentences* of Peter Lombard diversified the interrogation of details of the creation of Adam and Eve that had begun in the Fathers.

argument to be pursued here is that even if they often are, in reductive form, unsophisticated clichés of the medieval case for women, some at least of the 'privileges' derive from an Augustinian 'theology of the feminine' whose subtler shape continued to be available for sophisticated renewal—as it was, for example, by the celebrated visionary women writers of the twelfth century.

Of all the privileges, Eve's creation from the 'superior' substance of bone particularly caught people's imagination.[5] It is one of those remembered by the sermon writer Jacques de Vitry (d. 1240) when he argues that God 'did not want woman to be despised, because he especially gave her three privileges: one, that woman was created inside paradise but man outside it; another, in that man was created just from dirt, woman from his excellent side (*pulcra costa*); and the third, that God wished to have a woman as mother but not a man as a father'.[6] Another thirteenth-century writer, probably a woman, underlines the idea that because God used Adam's bone 'we are created of nobler stuff than you were': women represent in fact what advertisers call a new improved formula.[7] Having briefly asserted this cause for celebration of female perfection and seniority, she graciously and disappointingly resigns it in deference to the hierarchical principle of *derivation*—the doctrine of a created being's obedience to that from which it derives.[8] No such resignation

[5] In *Du bounté des femmes* it is characteristically identified as a sign of the greater honour and love reserved for women by God, bone being pure, dry, clean, and tough as opposed to the putrid dirt of which Adam was made (56–76); ed. Meyer, 'Manuscrits français de Cambridge', 317.

[6] 'Noluit igitur deus feminam homine conculcari, quam tribus privilegiis specialiter exornavit: unum quia mulier facta est in paradiso, vir autem factus est extra. Aliud, quia homo factus est de limo, femina de pulcra costa. Tercium quod deus voluit habere feminam matrem, et non hominem patrem'; *Sermones vulgares*, Sermon 66, from a transcription of MS BN Lat. 17509 (fo. 135ᵛ) generously supplied to me by David D'Avray.

[7] This argument is reinvented as part of a modern feminist discussion of Genesis: 'to claim that the rib means inferiority or subordination is to assign the man qualities over the woman which are not in the narrative itself. Superiority, strength, aggressiveness, dominance, and power do not characterize the man in Genesis 2. By contrast he is formed from dirt', etc.; Phyllis Trible, 'Depatriarchalizing in Biblical Interpretation', in Elizabeth Koltun (ed.), *The Jewish Woman: New Perspectives* (New York: Schocken, 1976), 217–40 (p. 223).

[8] 'we are created of nobler stuff than you were, fair master, but must nevertheless obey you . . . for it is fitting that this thing that derives from the other should be obeisant to it. Thus woman must obey man, and man the earth, and the earth God'; the *Response* to Richard de Fournival's *Li Bestiaire d'amour* (*c.*1250), tr. Jeanette Beer, *Master Richard's Bestiary of Love and Response* (Berkeley and Los Angeles: University of California Press, 1986), 42–3. The resignation is to be balanced against the speaker's self-confidence ('I who am a woman in conformity

disturbs the assurance derived by Christine de Pizan from contemplation of the noble material of woman's creation, drawn
from man's body which was itself, she writes, the noblest thing
yet created.[9]

Among competing explanations about why God created Eve
from Adam, hypotheses about derivation or indivisibility (as will
be seen in a moment) could sustain Adam's dignity, whereas the
hypothesis about product improvement threatened it. We have
already seen Bonaventure countering that threat by interpreting
the rib as the 'strength' which Adam 'supplied' to Eve. Yet in St
Augustine, to whom I would tentatively trace the profeminine
'improvement' topos, a symbolic reading of the creation story
specifically contrasts the relative weakness of Adam with the
relative strength of Eve.

One instance of this symbolic reading occurs when Augustine
decides to reconcile his classic interpretation of Eve's creation
out of Adam's side as a prefigurement of the creation of the
Church from the wound in Christ's side,[10] with a pronouncement
made at the beginning of the Gospel narrative of Christ's meeting
with the Samaritan woman: 'Jesus therefore being wearied with
his journey, sat thus on the well' (John, 4: 6). That Jesus is
'weary' is a 'mystery' requiring meditation. Augustine supposes
him weak and weary because 'in the flesh'. But his weakness
supplies strength to humanity. By analogy, suggests Augustine,
the Church's strength was produced from the side of a Christ
made weak, 'sleeping' on the cross, and this in turn is anticipated

with Our Lord's good pleasure, Who did not want to make me of less
good substance than He made you') and against her drastic allegation that
Adam murdered a woman created prior to Eve. The allied principles of
precedence and derivation are exemplified in (for example) the Middle
English treatise *Dives and Pauper* which states that one meaning of Eve's derivation
from Adam is that woman ought to 'takyn gret materie of lownesse & þynkyn
þat man is hir perfeccioun & hyr begynnynge & han man in reuerence as
hyr perfeccioun, as hyr principal, as hyr begynnyng & hyr firste in ordre of
kende'; ed. Barnum, vol. i, pt. ii, 67, and tr. Blamires, *Woman Defamed and
Woman Defended*, 261. Aquinas had endorsed the argument that 'woman is rightly
formed from the man, as her origin and chief' (*sicut ex suo principio*), *Summa
theologiae*, Ia. 92, art. 2, in *St. Thomas Aquinas, Summa theologiae*, gen. ed.
Thomas Gilby, OP, 60 vols. (London: Blackfriars, 1963–   ), xiii, tr. Edmund Hill,
OP, 40–1.

[9] 'Si lui donna forme moult noblement | Et fu faite de moult noble matere, |
Car ne fu pas du limon de la tere, | Mais seulement de la coste de l'omme, |
Lequel corps ja estoit, s'en est la somme, | Le plus noble des choses terriennes';
Fenster and Erler (eds.), *Epistre*, 594–9.
[10] Best known from *City of God*, XXII. 17, *PL* 41. 778–9, tr. Henry Bettenson
(Harmondsworth: Penguin, 1984), 1057.

by Eve's 'strength' produced from the side of a 'weakened' Adam:

It is the weakness of Christ that makes us strong. A remarkable figure of this went before in the case of Adam. God could have taken flesh from the man to make of it a woman, and it seems that this might have been the more suitable. For it was the weaker sex that was being made, and weakness ought to have been made of flesh rather than of bone; for the bones are the stronger parts in the flesh. . . . He could have taken, not a rib, but flesh, for the making of the woman. What, then did this signify? Woman was made, as it were, strong, from the rib; Adam was made, as it were, weak, from the flesh. It is Christ and the Church; His weakness is our strength.[11]

Augustine has predecided that women are 'the weaker sex', but is conspicuously struggling to reconcile that with their origin in strong bone, in an act which leaves man 'weak'. Exegetical wizardry makes the problem disappear as Eve's strength becomes that of the Church. But what the reader's mind most likely retains is that woman was 'made strong from the rib' in a manufacturing choice which is assumed deeply significant and in a configuration which enfeebles Adam.

Since this model does not specify (though it implies) a contrast between the rib and the dirt previously used for Adam, it is not a perfect match with the 'privilege'.[12] Nevertheless it represents the kind of patristic curiosity about details which underlies the trenchant simplicity of the 'privilege'. Moreover it pushes Augustine—despite his commitment to gender hierarchy—momentarily towards what might be called a 'theology of the feminine'. This expression is applied by Barbara Newman to the celebrated twelfth-century German visionaries Elisabeth of Schönau and

[11] 'Infirmitas Christi nos facit fortes. Magna ibi imago praecessit. Potuit Deus carnem detrahere homini unde faceret feminam, et magis videtur quasi congruere potuisse. Fiebat enim sexus infirmior, et magis de carne infirmitas fieri debuit quam de osse: ossa enim in carne firmiora sunt. . . . Poterat ad faciendam mulierem non costam, sed carnem detrahere. Quid igitur significavit? Facta est mulier in costa tanquam fortis: factus est Adam in carne tanquam infirmus. Christus est et Ecclesia, illius infirmitas nostra est fortitudo'; *In Johannis evangelium*, Tractatus XV. 8, PL 35. 1513; tr. in *St Augustin: Homilies on the Gospel of John, Homilies on the First Epistle of John*, in Philip Schaff (ed.), A Select Library of Nicene and Post-Nicene Fathers 7 (Grand Rapids, Mich.: Eerdmans, 1956), 101.

[12] This is clearer in the briefer statement of the same creation doctrine in Augustine's *Literal Meaning of Genesis*, IX. 18. 34, PL 34. 407: 'he was made weak for her sake because in place of his rib it was flesh, not another rib, that was substituted,' *The Literal Meaning of Genesis*, tr. John Hammond Taylor, 2 vols., ii. 94, Ancient Christian Writers, no. 42 (New York: Newman Press, 1982).

Hildegard of Bingen. Elisabeth's understanding of feminine weakness and feminine strength came, writes Newman, from elucidation of Christ's humanity, epitomized in what is said in one of her visions:

All the virtue and strength of the Church grew out of the Savior's weakness, which he incurred through the flesh. The weakness of God is stronger than men. This was well demonstrated by a figure in the first parents, when the vigor of bone was taken from Adam that Eve might be made; that the woman might be confirmed whence the man was made infirm [*inde firmaretur mulier, unde infirmatus est vir*].[13]

Elisabeth is tracking Augustinian paradox here, and so does her mentor Hildegard.[14] But these are refinements which are generally beyond the horizon of the formal case for women in its simplified rehearsal of women's 'privileges'. Jean Le Fèvre is an exception when, flourishing his erudition, he goes so far as to recall part of the doctrine when he connects Eve's production with the inception of the Church from Christ's side.[15] But Augustine's *City of God* is his guide here, and it guides him to an alternative, more muted way of locating defence of women in the rib myth, into which we shall digress for a moment.

In the *City of God* Augustine suggests that woman's creation out of man 'emphasizes the idea of the unity between them'.[16] A similar line was taken by St Ambrose. He thought that Eve was made out of Adam rather than out of a separate bit of earth in order to show that their 'physical nature . . . is identical' and to establish the unity of human nature.[17] As this passed into the Middle Ages it became polemically charged. The suggestion of unity, mutuality, and love interpreted in Eve's mode of creation from Adam's *side* was understood as a strategy whereby God meant to rule out absolute gender hierarchy: for her creation from

[13] Elisabeth, *Liber visionum*, III. 31, in F. W. E. Roth (ed.), *Die Visionen der heiligen Elisabeth und die Schriften de Abte Ekbert und Emecho von Schönau* (Brünn, 1884), 87; quoted by Barbara Newman, *Sister of Wisdom*, 41. Newman's splendid book perhaps makes Elisabeth sound more novel than she is at this point.

[14] Newman, *Sister of Wisdom*, 182, compares a passage in Hildegard's *Book of Life's Merits*, IV. 32, which alludes to the 'weakness' of Christ in the flesh.

[15] *Leësce*, 1271–1310.

[16] XXII. 17, *PL* 41. 778–9, tr. Bettenson, 1057; see also: 'the fact that a woman was made for the first man from his own side shows us clearly how affectionate should be the union of man and wife,' XII. 28, *PL* 41. 376, Bettenson, 508.

[17] *De Paradiso*, X. 47, *PL* 14. 298; *Saint Ambrose: Hexameron, Paradise, and Cain and Abel*, tr. John J. Savage, Fathers of the Church 42 (New York: Fathers of the Church, Inc., 1961), 327. Augustine converges with this view in *City of God*, XII. 22, *PL* 41. 372–3, tr. Bettenson, 502–3.

(say) man's head or foot could have implied either her tyranny over him or his over her. This interpretation appears in one seminal work by Hugh of St Victor (d. 1142), the *De sacramentis*, and then in another even more seminal, Peter Lombard's *Sentences* (1155–8).[18] So far as God's imputed intentions were concerned, the interpretation was a huge blow on behalf of gender equality. In the words of the early fifteenth-century discussion in *Dives and Pauper*, 'God did not make woman out of the foot, as if to be man's slave, nor out of the head, as if to be his superior, but out of his side and his rib, so as to be his companion in love and his helper in difficulty.' However there was usually, as in this text, a rider which retrieved gender hierarchy while simultaneously and awkwardly insisting on the lesson of mutuality:

But, when Eve sinned, woman was made subject to man, so that the wife should be ruled by her husband and be in awe of him and serve him—as companion in love, helper in difficulty, and closest comfort in distress: not as slave and serf in base subjection, for the husband ought to respect and esteem his wife in that they are one flesh and blood.[19]

The muddle of misogynous and profeminine impulses here is palpable. The rib myth 'means' that men and women are equal

[18] Ferrante notes the topos in *De sacramentis*, I. 6. 35; *Woman as Image*, 31–2. See also Lombard's *Sentences*, II, dist. XVIII, ch. 2, entitled 'Quare de latere viri et non de alia parte corporis formata sit', in *Magistri Petri Lombardi Sententiae in IV libris distinctae*, 3rd edn. (Rome: Editiones Collegii S. Bonaventurae ad Claras Aquas, 1971), i. 416–17. Relationships between these texts and a passage in the *Summa* of Aquinas have recently been considered by Earl Jeffrey Richards, 'In Search of a Feminist Patrology: Christine de Pizan and "Les Glorieux Dotteurs"', in Liliane Dulac and Bernard Ribémont (eds.), *Une femme de lettres au Moyen Âge: Études autour de Christine de Pizan* (Orléans: Paradigme, 1995), 281–95 (pp. 289–92). Ian Maclean seems to imply, erroneously, that assertions about companionship between men and women belong to a 'shift in emphasis' concerning marriage relations 'from scholastic to Renaissance writing'; *Renaissance Notion of Woman*, 19.

[19] 'God made nout woman of þe foot to ben mannys þral ne he made hyr nout of þe hefd to ben hys maystir but of his syde & of his rybbe to ben his felawe in loue & helper at nede. But whan Eue synnyd, þan was woman maad soget to man, þat þe wyf schulde ben rewlyd be hyr housebonde & dredyn hym & seruyn hym as felaw in loue & helper at nede & as nest solas in sorwe, nout as þral & bonde in vyleyn seruage, for þe housebonde owyth to han his wyf in reuerence & worchepe in þat þey ben boþin on flesch & on blood'; *Dives and Pauper*, VI. 4, ed. Barnum, vol. i, pt. ii, pp. 66–7. Readers of Chaucer will find the first sentence echoed in *The Parson's Tale*, where, however, misogynous innuendo wrecks the profeminine possibilities: Christ 'ne made [woman] nat of the heved of Adam, for she sholde nat clayme to greet lordshipe. | For ther as the womman hath the maistrie, she maketh to muche desray. Ther neden none ensamples of this; the experience of day by day oghte suffise. | Also, certes, God ne made nat womman of the foot of Adam, for she ne sholde nat been holden to lowe; for she kan nat paciently suffre. | But God made

companions; the Fall myth 'cancels' that equality. There are symptoms of what Maclean called 'a desire to improve the status of woman in theology without tampering with the conceptual structure or with the notion of her inferiority to man'.[20] Yet the Middle English writer tampers. The rib myth is anxiously reinvoked to *guarantee* wives against 'base subjection'—it comes back, as it were, to haunt and query the level of female 'subjection' ascribed to the Fall. The whole thing becomes a matter of emphasis. Le Fèvre throws more outright emphasis on fellowship in his formulation.[21] So does Christine de Pizan, in her reflections on woman's creation in the *Cité des dames*. The formation signified 'that she should stand at his side as a companion and never lie at his feet like a slave, and also that he should love her as his own flesh'.[22]

By contrast the privileges proper were enunciated in a more propagandist profeminine spirit, as signs of women's superiority. So the early fourteenth-century Italian poet and jurist Francesco da Barberino cited the exalted ingredient of Eve's creation as a sign of woman's superior nobility.[23] This is particularly true of the other two privileges detected in woman's creation—place and time of creation—which aim to up-end standard reflexes by giving Eve both priority and a climactic status in paradise.

Curiously, the prompt for a positive interpretation of her creation within paradise may have come from the *negative* attention

---

womman of the ryb of Adam, for womman sholde be felawe unto man' (X. 925–8). The earnest but uneasy compromise formulation in *Dives* is the more typical, being anticipated in, for instance, John Gower, *Mirour de l'omme*, 17, 521–44, tr. William Burton Wilson (East Lansing, Mich.: Colleagues Press, 1992), 240–1.

[20] *Renaissance Notion of Woman*, 15.

[21] See *Leësce*, 1245–70, and esp. 'Et ne fu pas faite du chief, | Pour segnourir; et de rechief, | Dieu ne la voult pas asservir | Ne faire des piés, pour servir, | Mais du moyen, par la maniere | Que dame ne que chamberiere | Avecques l'omme ne feüst, | Et qu'elle seist et geüst | Delés luy, pour son plaisir faire, | Comme sa compaigne et sa paire' (1255–64).

[22] *Cité*, I. 9. 2, ed. Curnow, 651, tr. Richards, 23.

[23] 'La fenmina è più degna d'onor che l'uomo, ché l'uomo fu fatto di fango, cioè del limo terre, e la fenmina della gentil costa fatta prima da Dio'; Francesco da Berberino, *Reggimento e costumi di donna* (dated 1307–15), ed. Giuseppe Sansone (Turin: Loescher-Chiantore, 1957), p. 253, introducing a brief debate in section 19 on the relative superiority of men and women. The topos was developed ever more ingeniously. Thomas Hoccleve wrote at the start of the 15th cent. that the rib of Eve's creation participated in a property of roundedness which characterized all supreme phenomena such as the sun, the moon, and heaven; *Regement of Princes* (5104–94), ed. F. J. Furnivall, EETS es 72 (London: Oxford University Press, 1897), 184–7.

directed to this point in Ambrose. He saw the potential blot on the status of Adam (created outside paradise), and attempted to erase it by making the relative locations an object lesson in the irrelevance of background circumstances to personal virtue: 'although created . . . in an inferior place, man is found to be superior, whereas woman was created in a better place . . . yet is found to be inferior.'[24] It was left to Peter Abelard in the twelfth century to reinstate the sign of 'native dignity' which Ambrose had cleverly belittled:

If we seek out afresh from the very beginning of the world the favours or honour shown by divine grace to women, we shall immediately discover a certain dignity enhancing woman's creation, since she was made in paradise, but man outside it. Consequently women are warned to take special note that paradise is their native country and that they are more amply suited to follow the celibate life of paradise.[25]

It is instructive to see how deftly one could convert Ambrose's emphasis on the moral degeneracy of women from aristocratic backgrounds into an exhortation on the suitability of women to their transcendent birthplace. Whether or not Abelard was the first theologian to extol the 'honour' of woman's place of creation,[26] it soon entered the 'privilege' collection; for we have seen it used by Jacques de Vitry as one of three, and it is one of a variant set of three in the formal case offered by Robert of Blois to prove that God loves woman more than man (i.e. creation in paradise; Christ's incarnation in woman without a human father; and his appearance first to women when risen).[27] After this it is no surprise to find that Le Fèvre launches his catalogue of women's prerogatives with the combined privileges (woman made in paradise from noble matter, Adam outside from a bit of muck[28]), and

---

[24] *De Paradiso*, IV. 24, *PL* 14. 284. The passage from which this comes is translated in Blamires, *Woman Defamed and Woman Defended*, 61.

[25] Tr. in Blamires, *Woman Defamed and Woman Defended*, 236–7; see also *Letters of Abelard and Heloise*, tr. Scott Moncrieff, 156. The passage is from *The Authority and Dignity of Nuns*, ed. Muckle, 'The Letter of Heloise on Religious Life and Abelard's First Reply', 268. Abelard goes on to quote Ambrose verbatim, as though in total agreement with him.

[26] Peter Dronke suggests this in 'Peter Abelard: *Planctus* and Satire', in his *Poetic Individuality in the Middle Ages* (Oxford: Clarendon Press, 1970), 137. That the letter here quoted may not have been in circulation until the 13th cent. makes no difference, because the point is repeated elsewhere in Abelard, e.g. in a sermon on the day of the Assumption of the Virgin Mary, *PL* 178. 542.

[27] Ulrich (ed.), *L'Honneur des dames*, 395–446.

[28] *Leësce*, 1203–21; esp. 'L'os est plus noble et si vault mieulx; | Et pour ce l'en voult faire Dieux | dedens le paradis terrestre. . . . L'omme fu fait d'un pou

that Christine de Pizan followed suit in the *Cité des dames* as well as noting in her *Epistre* that woman, not man, was the first creation occurring within paradise.[29]

The argument from Eve's place in the *sequence* of creation may have been a late entrant among the privileges. In the Middle Ages it remains largely implicit, latent within the claims that her production bettered Adam's in terms of location and substance— because hers supersedes even his, which is the best yet created.[30] What Barbara Newman refers to as the 'daring exegetical move' of the Renaissance polemicist Agrippa who identifies woman as 'the last of creatures and the goal, the most perfect completion of all the works of God', was perhaps merely the logical fulfilment of these emphases.[31] The medieval case for women had certainly prepared the ground for the interpretation of Eve as the crown of creation, an interpretation which was unwittingly resurrected by one feminist theologian in the 1970s and questioned by another in the 1980s.[32]

It would be easy to disdain the profeminine potential of the 'privileges' of woman's creation. The reader will have noticed how they obsessively situate the female in relation to the male, and how indeed they move to enhance her worth precisely on the basis of her production out of the male. Moreover, in seeking to convert possible disadvantages of sequence into advantages, they reinforce the concept of sequence itself—something introduced by the Yahwist Genesis writer but not present in the first Genesis

d'ordure, | Du limon de la terre dure, | Ou val d'Ebron, enmi les champs' (1215–21).

[29] 'Now, to turn to the question of the creation of the body, woman was made by the supreme craftsman. In what place was she created? In the terrestrial Paradise. From what substance? Was it vile matter? No, it was the noblest substance which had ever been created: it was the body of man from which God made woman'; *Cité*, I. 9. 2, ed. Curnow, 651–2, tr. Richards, 23–4; and see Fenster and Erler (eds.), *Epistre*, 601–4.

[30] Christine de Pizan, *Epistre*, 594–604; and *Response* to Richard de Fournival's *Bestiaire d'amour*, tr. Beer, 42. The concept of a progression towards Eve can be seen in the *Miroir des bonnes femmes*, where the 'second honour' of Eve is that whereas angels were created from the void, and man was created from mud, she was created from man; Grigsby, 'Miroir', pt. ii, 32.

[31] 'Renaissance Feminism and Esoteric Theology', 230–1.

[32] Phyllis Trible suggests that 'the Yahwist account moves to its climax, not its decline, in the creation of woman. She is not an afterthought, she is the culmination', 'Depatriarchalizing in Biblical Interpretation', 222. John A. Phillips maintains against this that the Yahwist writer of Genesis means to subordinate Eve to androcentric dogma, *Eve: The History of an Idea* (New York: Harper & Row, 1984), 33–4 and 110.

account of human creation.[33] Yet their latent benefit would be to expose the androcentric view of creation to competition, and thereby to solidify the *possibility* of a gynocentric view of creation. Here was a profeminine growth point, from which further challenge could stem. Christine de Pizan prefaced the privileges in the *Epistre* with an outright statement that God 'created [woman] resembling him' (*la forma a sa digne semblance*, 591), and subsequently when introducing a further passage on the privileges in the *Cité* she underlined her opposition to any claims that the 'image of God' in humankind is gender asymmetrical.[34] It would be quite amiss to set Christine's usage—or, I think, to set any of the other medieval examples of the topos we have seen—in the context of rhetorical paradox, jest, and 'flippancy' which Ian Maclean applies to Renaissance use of the 'privileges'.[35]

Less need be said about the privileges associated with women through the New Testament. Albertanus' Prudence draws on two of them, first when she dismisses an old misogynous chestnut from Ecclesiastes by declaring that if no good woman could be found, 'Jesus Christ would have refused to take life within a woman', and second when she argues that it was in view of the goodness of women that the newly risen Christ considered it apt to show himself to Mary Magdalene before the apostles.[36] Divine reason (*divina ratio*) is therefore held to be profeminine to this extent already in 1246.

As often, a text of Augustine probably hovers in the background of the privilege through *conceptio*, for he had represented Christ as intent on 'honouring' each sex by his birth. Christ's decision to be mothered is represented *as* a decision (for the creator who had produced a male without mother or father could arguably have taken flesh without a mother). Since he decided to

---

[33] Respectively Gen. 2: 7–23, and 1: 27.

[34] 'She was created in the image of God. . . . But some men are foolish enough to think, when they hear that God made man in His image, that this refers to the material body. . . . The soul is meant, the intellectual spirit which lasts eternally just like the deity. God created the soul and placed wholly similar souls, equally good and noble, in the feminine and in the masculine bodies'; *Cité*, I. 9. 2, ed. Curnow, 651–2, tr. Richards, 23.

[35] *Renaissance Notion of Woman*, 90–1.

[36] 'si nulla bona mulier inveniretur, Jhesus Christus in muliere venire dedignatus fuisset. . . . Et etiam Dominus noster, Jhesus Christus, propter bonitatem mulierum, post resurrectionem suam prius dignatus est se manifestare mulieribus quam viris, quia prius se ostendit Mariae Magdalenae quam apostolis'; *Liber consolationis*, ch. iv, ed. Sundby, 14; tr. in Blamires, *Woman Defamed and Woman Defended*, 239.

honour both sexes when he came to liberate them, 'we have no right to attribute any gender prejudice to the Creator'. The honour of the male sex is in the body of Christ; the honour of the female sex is in the mother of Christ.[37] The latter 'honour', sometimes reinforced by noting Christ's refusal to have a human father, is routinely presented in some texts,[38] but more pointedly developed in others.[39] Abelard not only hails woman's glory in conceiving Christ but also unexpectedly interprets Christ's delivery as a 'consecration' of female genitals, one moreover which exceeds his consecration of male genitals at his circumcision.[40]

However, the most revisionist development, available by 1405, was a double-barrelled approach, on the one hand playing out the logic of Christ's conception solely from woman (implying that woman must have been less corrupted in the first instance, or that only woman's offspring could heal humankind), and on the other hand teasing out possible logic in the conception as male (implying that male sin must be more serious, requiring atonement in male form). These claims, partly predicated on a diminished assessment of Eve's responsibility for the Fall, are rehearsed by Pauper to the astonishment of Dives in the Middle English treatise *Dives and Pauper*.[41] As often, there is a tendency to assume that

[37] 'Dominus veniens quaerere quod perierat, utrumque voluit honorando commendare. . . . In nullo igitur sexu debemus injuriam facere Creatori: utrumque ad sperandam salutem commendavit Nativitas Domini. Honor masculini sexus est in carne Christi: honor feminini est in matre Christi'; Sermon 190, *Nativitates Christi duae: Cur nasci ex femina voluit*, PL 38. 1008 (my tr.).

[38] Robert de Blois, *L'Honneur des dames*, 407–10; *Leësce*, 1232–8.

[39] *Du bounté des femmes*, 163–73, ed. Meyer, 'Manuscrits français de Cambridge', 319. It has been an enduring topos. See e.g. Thomas Adams, 'Though Christ honoured our sex in that he was a man, not a woman: yet he was born of a woman and was not begot of a man,' *Meditations upon the Creed* (published 1629), in Kate Aughterson (ed.), *Renaissance Woman. A Sourcebook: Constructions of Femininity in England* (London: Routledge, 1995), 30; and Sojourner Truth, who, when a Protestant clergyman queried her campaign for women's suffrage in 1851 by arguing that Christ was a man, retorted: 'Where did your Christ come from? From God and a woman! Man had nothing to do with him!'; quoted in Clark, 'Ideology, History, and the Construction of "Woman"', 184.

[40] *The Authority and Dignity of Nuns*, ed. Muckle, 'Letter of Heloise on Religious Life and Abelard's First Reply', 271; tr. in Blamires, *Woman Defamed and Woman Defended*, 236; and see *Letters of Abelard and Heloise*, tr. Scott Moncrieff, 160. Abelard rather spoils his point by simultaneously referring to the female pudenda as 'most vile' (*vilissima*). The context presupposed by his discussion would appear to be controversy (keenest in the 9th cent.) about the worthiness of female sexual organs to deliver Christ: see Hilda Graef, *Mary: A History of Doctrine and Devotion*, 2 vols., i (New York: Sheed & Ward, 1963), 176–9.

[41] *Dives*, VI. 10, ed. Barnum, 84; tr. in Blamires, *Woman Defamed and Woman Defended*, 266.

when these radical arguments appear in Renaissance polemic they are new: for instance, in Cornelius Agrippa's sixteenth-century discourse 'it is, refreshingly, the Savior's maleness that needs explanation'.[42] They are probably not very fresh even in *Dives*, nor are they to be discounted as facetious: Pauper holds all the winning cards in this treatise and his stance is throughout morally rigorous.

Awe of the Virgin contains Dives' astonishment, and awe informs assertions generally about both Mary's privilege of conception and her privilege of exaltation. Christine de Pizan contemplates the Virgin's *grant honneur* in a rhetorical passage combining both privileges by suggesting that women should delight in sharing her 'form' because only Jesus incarnate outmatched her in created perfection, and because she occupies her celestial seat at the Father's right—a sign of status of course—to the honour of 'maternal womankind' (*Epistre*, 572–88). Mary's celestial elevation above saints and angels alike elsewhere attracts routine profeminine notice,[43] and can be seen as a facet of a tendency from the twelfth century onwards to assign her a co-regnant status in heaven.[44]

The more the Virgin's exceptional status was underlined, of course, the more the 'privilege' of sharing the Virgin's sex was attenuated, as will be noted in the last part of this chapter. By contrast there was perhaps more to be gained through sisterhood with Mary Magdalene, a more ordinary heroine in being a 'sinner', who was nevertheless recipient of Christ's first post-Resurrection appearance.[45] Albertanus' Prudence interprets this as a deliberate choice by Christ, giving women priority because of their 'goodness'.[46] Frequently it was interpreted as a kind of re-

[42] Barbara Newman, commenting on Agrippa's argument that Christ was born male because the male sex more urgently needed redemption and because (which *was* new, and a piece of bravado) this was the 'humbler' sex; 'Renaissance Feminism and Esoteric Theology', 235.

[43] Robert de Blois, *L'Honneur des dames*, 447–54; *Le Bien des fames*, 15–16 and n. (*Three Medieval Views of Women*, ed. Fiero *et al.*, 115).

[44] Graef notes an impulse 'to assimilate Mary . . . to the transcendence of God himself', leading to a view of her (e.g. in Engelbert of Admont, 14th cent.) as constituting a unique hierarchy next only to the divine; *Mary: A History of Doctrine*, 241 and 298.

[45] 'Quant deus de mort resuscita, | Es femmes premiers se mostra', Robert de Blois, *L'Honneur des dames*, ed. Ulrich, 445–6.

[46] 'And even our Lord Jesus Christ, because of the goodness of women, regarded it as fitting after His Resurrection to show Himself to women before men, because He showed Himself to Mary Magdalene before the Apostles'; 'Et etiam

ward for the conspicuous devotion shown to Christ during the
Passion by Mary Magdalene particularly, and/or by a group of
women followers generally. Alternatively, Mary's priority in seeing the risen Christ could be coupled with her consequent prerogative of announcing his Resurrection to the disciples. In the
Cité des dames Christine de Pizan bases a defence of female speech
on the pivotal role here assigned to a woman by Christ, and
shows herself particularly incensed with the flippant misogynous
suggestion that Christ picked on a woman because he anticipated
that so-called feminine garrulity would ensure wide dissemination of his news.[47]

And well might Christine be incensed. The 'jest' complacently
deflates the dignity of a woman whose centrality in the Resurrection drama had piqued the androcentric instincts of many a
commentator. Strategies of deflation are already in place in St
Ambrose. He interprets Christ's injunction that Mary Magdalene
shall not touch him who 'has not yet ascended' to mean that he
has not ascended for those, like her, who seek him in an
uncomprehending physical way. Then in being sent to disclose
the news, she is reduced by Ambrose to mere messenger to the
male apostles who have greater 'strength' to preach the Resurrection, and although she is the first to tell, she is 'compensating' for
the evil that issued first from Eve's mouth.[48] St Augustine similarly (but less carpingly) supposed that Mary could not 'touch'
Christ because she still related to him as man not God, and that
she announced the Resurrection, as the Virgin bore Christ, to

Dominus noster, Jhesus Christus, propter bonitatem mulierum, post resurrectionem suam prius dignatus est se manifestare mulieribus quam viris, quia
prius se ostendit Mariae Magdalenae quam apostolis'; tr. in Blamires, *Woman
Defamed and Woman Defended*, 239, and ed. Sundby, *Liber consolationis*, 14.

[47] If women's language had been as lacking in authority as some men argue,
observes Lady Reason, Christ 'would never have deigned to wish that so worthy
a mystery as His most gracious Resurrection be first announced by a woman'; the
claim that he appeared first to a woman because 'she did not know how to keep
quiet' is little less than 'blasphemy'; *Cité*, I. 10. 5, ed. Curnow, 660–1, tr. Richards,
28–9. Christine probably noticed this 'blasphemy' in the *Lamentations of Matheolus*,
II. 2309–22, ed. Van Hamel; cf. William Langland, *The Vision of Piers Plowman*, ed.
A. V. C. Schmidt (London: Dent, 1978), XIX. 161–2.

[48] *Expositio evangelii secundum Lucam*, in Ambrose, *Opera*, ed. M. Adriaen, CCSL
xiv, pt. iv (Turnhout: Brepols, 1957), X. 155–60, pp. 390–2; tr. in Blamires, *Woman
Defamed and Woman Defended*, 63. The argument that Mary Magdalene cannot
transcend 'mortal' understanding (and hence touch Christ) is anticipated in
Eusebius of Caesarea, *To Marinus*, III; *Ante-Nicene Exegesis of the Gospels*, tr. Harold
Smith, 6 vols. (London: SPCK, 1926), vi. 124–5.

reverse woman's primal sin.[49] The shadows clinging to Mary Magdalene's role produce a classic instance of gender prejudice when St Bernard manages to decry her in one sermon for being rooted in earthly touch and sense-perception, then to congratulate Thomas a few sermons further on because his demand to touch Christ's wound was a 'superb consequence of his greatness of soul'.[50] (Even Tertullian articulated this contrast more credibly, reflecting on Christ's appearance to 'so faithful a woman coming to touch Him from love, not from curiosity or from the unbelief of Thomas'.[51])

In any case the privilege of the *apparitio* to Mary survived all varieties of exegetical deflation.[52] In particular, the 'apostolic' privilege of announcing the Resurrection *to the apostles* became strongly associated with her.[53] In the tenth century Odo of Cluny was pressing home the logic: 'If the disciples were called "apostles" because they were sent by the Lord to preach the gospel to everyone, no less was the blessed Mary Magdalene dispatched by him to the apostles, in order that any doubt or incredulity about his Resurrection might be removed from their hearts.'[54] Others simply designated her without more ado 'apostle to the apostles',[55] and as her cult began to take off, they expressed ever more

[49] *In Joannis evangelium*, 121. 3; Sermons 232, 244, 245, *PL* 38. 1108, 1147–51, 1152–3. The influence of Ambrose and Augustine is strong in Odo of Cluny's seminal (10th-cent.) homily on Mary Magdalene, *PL* 133. 713–21.

[50] Bernard of Clairvaux, *On the Song of Songs II*, tr. Kilian Walsh, Cistercian Fathers series 7 (Kalamazoo, Mich.: Cistercian Publications, 1976), Sermons 28 (esp. pp. 94–6) and 32 (esp. pp. 140–1).

[51] *Praxeas*, 25, in *Ante-Nicene Exegesis*, tr. Smith, vi. 126.

[52] St Bernard himself saw it as a preferential sign; see Leclercq, *Monks on Marriage*, 99, citing *In Dominica VI post Pentecosten*, II. 4.

[53] Occasionally, however, it was associated with the women—however identified—who were given instructions at the tomb (Mark 16: 7; Matt. 28: 1), from the 3rd-cent. theologian Hippolytus who said they 'became apostles of the apostles, sent by Christ', to St Bernard who said that 'sent by an angel they did the work of an evangelist, and became the apostles of the apostles' (Matt. 28: 1–10); see respectively *Ante-Nicene Exegesis*, tr. Smith, vi. 114 and *The Life of Saint Mary Magdalene and of her Sister Saint Martha*, tr. David Mycoff, Cistercian Studies series 108 (Kalamazoo, Mich.: Cistercian Publications, 1989), n. to 1457–9, p. 143.

[54] 'Et si discipuli ideo apostoli vocati, quia missi sunt ab ipso ad praedicandum Evangelium omni creaturae, nec minus beata Maria Magdalene ab ipso Domino destinata est ad apostolos, quatenus dubietatem et incredulitatem suae Resurrectionis, ab illorum cordibus removeret'; *In veneratione Sanctae Mariae Magdalenae*, *PL* 133. 721 (my tr.).

[55] For her loyal attentiveness at Christ's tomb, writes Honorius, she deserved to see the angel, and the Lord appeared first to her, 'eamque apostolam apostolis suis misit'; *De Sancta Maria Magdalena*, *PL* 172. 981.

rhapsodically the remarkable 'honour' and elevation implicit both in being present at Christ's 'first and most privileged' appearance and in exercising her 'apostolate'.[56] Later, the *Meditations on the Life of Christ* reports an uncanonical oral tradition that Christ first appeared to his mother (a sort of reflex of 'obligation to mothers'?) but nevertheless acknowledges the canonical priority of Mary Magdalene's conversation—and mitigates the misogynous insinuations woven by the Fathers around Christ's bidding *Noli me tangere* even to the extent of declaring that Christ must, after all, have let her touch him.[57]

These details have seemed worth pursuing because they restore to us the sense of contentious frisson and awe which the Middle Ages associated with the episode which supplied this particular 'privilege' of woman. Moreover the exemplary status ascribed to Mary's privilege is certainly not a contrived piece of profeminine casuistry: it is a natural component of Gospel paraphrase, incorporated for instance in the Cotton manuscript of the Middle English *Cursor mundi* ('A grete honour to wymmen | did he in that cas'; and, 'Here may we see ensaumple | That wymmen mony are gode'), and capable of triggering, in the case of the thirteenth-century *Southern Passion*, an indignant defence of women's moral reliability.[58] When people thought of Mary Magdalene with Christ in the garden, no amount of patristic fuss about the prohibited 'touch' could stop them thinking of strong female loyalty, of

---

[56] 'ascensionis suae eam ad apostolos instituit apostolam, digna mercede gratiae et gloriae, primoque et praecipue honoris privilegio,' etc., *De vita beatae Mariae Magdalenae* (late 12th cent.), xxvii, *PL* 112. 1474; 'he made her the apostle of his ascension to the apostles—a worthy recompense of grace and glory, the first and greatest honor . . . Mary, seeing herself elevated . . . to such a high position of honor and grace; seeing herself favored with the first and the most privileged of his appearances . . . could not do otherwise than exercise the apostolate with which she had been honored', *The Life of Saint Mary Magdalene*, tr. Mycoff, 73.

[57] 'Although it seemed at first that the Lord held back from her, I can hardly believe that she did not touch Him familiarly before He departed. . . . One can piously believe that He visited her thus lovingly and singularly, before all the others that are referred to in writing, for her pleasure, and not to distress her. Mysteriously, therefore, not pertinaciously, He spoke those words'; *Meditations on the Life of Christ*, tr. Isa Ragusa and ed. Rosalie B. Green (Princeton: Princeton University Press, 1961), lxxxvii, p. 363. The novel appearance to the Virgin is narrated in lxxxvi, pp. 359–60, and defended in xcvi, p. 373: 'how He appeared to His mother is not mentioned anywhere, but is piously believed.'

[58] *Cursor mundi: Four Versions*, ed. Richard Morris, pt. iii, EETS os 62 (London: Oxford University Press, 1876), 988; and Pickering, 'The "Defence of Women" from the *Southern Passion*', also in *The Southern Passion*, ed. Beatrice Brown, EETS os 169 (London: Oxford University Press, 1927), lines 1899–990.

a sign of female *distinction* in her seeing Christ thus, and of a further sign of female authority in her apostolic mission to the doubting disciples. Here indeed was a growth point for female religious authority. Early Christianity had worked to dethrone Mary Magdalene.[59] But her 'apostolate' reverberated in the Middle Ages, as will be seen in a later chapter.

Mary's apologists were happy to repeat and embroider the Church Fathers' idea that she figured as an anti-Eve. 'Just as Eve in Paradise had once given her husband a poisoned draught to drink', as her twelfth-century *Vita* put it, 'so now the Magdalen presented to the apostles the chalice of eternal life.'[60] Yet this strategy complimented woman in one department only by accepting and even underlining her alleged guilt in another department. For Mary Magdalene—or the Virgin Mary—to be seen to cancel Eve's 'sin' was in fact a strategy which levelled the score against women only at the cost of leaving presumptions about originary guilt intact. Turning from the 'privileges', therefore, we shall ask what further arguments were available to defend Eve, and how far the formal case in the Middle Ages developed them.

Views of Eve's role occasionally crop up which clearly aggrandize her. One underlying question was why the serpent/Satan chose to tempt Eve, not Adam. The rarer answer was that there was something paramount in her, a glory or beauty, as well as a procreative capacity to replace Satan's own angels in heaven, which induced profound and malicious envy in him, and drew him to attack humanity through her. This line of thought appears to be confined to the incidental case for women in the Middle Ages, appearing variously in Hildegard of Bingen and in St Bernard. It gains ground in the formal case during the Renaissance.[61] But the more commonplace (indeed nearly universal) explanation for Eve's selection for temptation was one intended

---

[59] For a summary of gnostic and other texts which ascribe authority to Mary Magdalene and disclose its repression, see Elizabeth Fiorenza, *In Memory of Her: A Feminist Reconstruction of Christian Origins* (New York: Crossroad, 1983), 305–7; and Marjorie Malvern, *Venus in Sackcloth: The Magdalen's Origins and Metamorphoses* (Carbondale: Southern Illinois University Press, 1975), ch. 3.

[60] The symmetries are protracted through twelve more lines: *The Life of Saint Mary Magdalene*, tr. Mycoff, 73–4; *PL* 112. 1475–6.

[61] For Hildegard of Bingen on Satan's envy, see Newman, *Sister of Wisdom*, 112–13. For Renaissance polemic, building on St Bernard, see Angenot, *Champions des femmes*, 19, discussing Rodrigue de la Cámara's *Triunfo de las doñas* (1440; tr. into French c.1490); and Newman, 'Renaissance Feminism and Esoteric Theology', 234–5, on Agrippa's 16th-cent. argument 'that Satan tempted Eve out of envy, recognizing that her angelic beauty made her Adam's superior'.

by patristic initiators to denigrate her, but which could also be interpreted in her favour.

The broad consensus of received commentary was that Satan tempted Eve as the more vulnerable party, in some sense 'weaker'. Augustine claimed that the serpent dared not speak to the man but used the woman to topple him, gaining the stronger through the weaker.[62] In other formulations Eve's 'weakness' might be further defined in terms of her being more guileless (*simplicius*), or in terms of 'softness' (*mollities*), or as short-sightedness and uncertainty (she is *minus provida et certa*).[63] Augustine most influentially glossed the 'weakness' as a type of intellectual inferiority—her mind, he alleged, was the more credulous and in some sense more material, as well as incipiently presumptuous. When St Paul wrote that 'it was not Adam, but Eve, who was seduced' (1 Tim. 2: 14) he meant (according to Augustine) that Eve was taken in by the serpent's persuasions whereas Adam would not have believed them, and joined her in sin out of solidarity.[64]

The Augustinian thesis (deriving from Philo) that Eve somehow lacked intellectual vision or 'represented' the senses was developed further in subsequent thinkers such as John Scotus Erigena (ninth century), as has been well observed by Susan Burchmore.[65] It was familiar in the type of simple paradigm used by Pope Gregory; 'The Serpent suggested the first sin, and Eve, as

[62] Sermon 190; *PL* 38. 1008.

[63] Respectively Chrysostom, who states that when the serpent spoke to her 'eo quasi instrumento quodam usus est, per quod mulierem, utpote simplicius et infirmius vas, illius familiaritate in errorem et deceptionem provocaret', *Homily 14 on Genesis*, 2, *PG* 53. 127; pseudo-Bede, who asserts that the serpent tempted woman and not man 'id propter mollitiem vel infirmitatem mulieris', *De sex dierum creatione*, *PL* 93. 231; and Peter Comestor, who characterizes Satan as afraid of being seen through (or captured) by the man but hopeful that woman, more vulnerable, can be brought to err, 'timens vero deprehendi a viro, mulierem minus providam et certam, in vitium flecti aggressus est', *Historia scholastica*, *PL* 198. 1072.

[64] 'a parte scilicet inferiore illius humanae copulae incipiens, ut gradatim perveniret ad totum; non existimans virum facile credulum, nec errando posse decepi,' *De civitate Dei*, XIV. 11, *PL* 41. 419; 'no doubt starting with the inferior of the human pair so as to arrive at the whole by stages, supposing that the man would not be so easily gullible, and could not be trapped by a false move on his own part,' tr. Bettenson, 570. Cf. *Literal Meaning of Genesis*, XI. 41. 58, *PL* 34. 452–3, esp. the rhetorical question 'was it because the man would not have been able to believe [the serpent's claims about God's motives] that the woman was employed on the supposition that she had limited understanding, and also perhaps that she was living according to the spirit of the flesh?', tr. Taylor, 175.

[65] 'Traditional Exegesis and the Question of Guilt in the Old English "Genesis B"', *Traditio*, 41 (1985), 117–44 (pp. 127–8). Bibliography on culpability for the Fall

flesh, took physical pleasure in it, while Adam, as spirit, con-sented.'[66] However, while all this may have seemed to chime in perfectly well with a gender hierarchy that harped on feminine inferiority, an important corollary of the notion that Eve was restricted to credulous corporeal perception was, as Burchmore remarks, that 'the senses by themselves cannot separate good from evil and consequently are deceived by malice in the disguise of virtue'; in fact 'Eve, as the senses, cannot, as Augustine points out, be expected to perceive spiritual truth'.[67] In other words, the more Eve's *lack* of strong intelligence or rationality was alleged, and the more she was condescendingly referred to as a soft target for Satan, the less guilt she might logically seem to attract. That is something which is most nearly articulated among patristic texts in commentary on the 'excuse' of Adam to God ('The woman, whom thou gavest me . . . gave me of the tree, and I did eat', Gen. 3: 12). Chrysostom condemns Adam with notable sarcasm on the grounds that as 'head' of his partner (woman being the 'body') it was his place to point out the enormity of her sin, not to give in to her suggestion.[68] This underlines the potential for mitigation of Eve's responsibility. If so little was—by definition—to be ex-pected of her and so much of Adam, as even Aquinas acknow-ledged,[69] was this not a cogent argument (albeit a patronizing one) for the medieval case for women?

In fact, it was slow to catch on. The impression is that Eve was

is potentially massive, and there is no aspiration to cover the intricacies of the subject here: besides Burchmore's interesting discussion I have particularly benefited from: Phillips, *Eve: The History of an Idea*, ch. 5; and Ferrante, *Woman as Image*, esp. 30–5. Philo's argument that the senses are deluded more easily than the mind, and that 'woman is of a nature to be deceived rather than to reflect greatly', is in his *Questions and Answers on Genesis*, tr. Ralph Marcus in *Philo* (London: Heinemann, 1953).

[66] From Gregory's answer to Augustine of Canterbury's 9th question, in *Bede's Ecclesiastical History of the English People*, ed. Bertram Colgrave and R. A. B. Mynors (Oxford: Clarendon Press, 1969), I. 27, pp. 100–1.

[67] 'Traditional Exegesis', 128.

[68] *Homily 12 on Genesis*, 4; PG 53. 139.

[69] Aquinas recalls from an Augustinian sermon the principle that if man is the 'head' of woman, he should 'live better' than his wife and lead her in good deeds; therefore, Aquinas concedes, Adam who ought to have done better than Eve because he was 'more perfect', sinned more gravely. St Thomas feels that this argument limited to the 'condition of the persons' is outweighed by other argu-ments concerning the definition of their respective transgressions, especially the extent of Eve's alleged pride which was not to be 'excused' by her 'ignorance'; *Summa theologiae*, IIa IIae. 163, 4, vol. xliv, tr. Gilby, 158–63, esp. *ad primum* 2, and *responsio*.

thought too risky a witness for the formal defence since it was a premiss of misogyny, as the Wife of Bath hears at the start of her fifth husband's book of wicked wives, that 'expres of womman may ye fynde | That womman was the los of al mankynde' (III. 719–20). Most defenders were content to mute Eve's 'sin' by making perfunctory reference to the commonplace of the *felix culpa* or Fortunate Fall: 'what Eve lost, the mother of Christ regained'. This is found in the Old French *dits*, in *Le Livre des manières*, and in Deschamps's *Miroir de mariage*, for instance.[70] The solidity of this unadventurous tradition is the more interesting in light of an indication that the exonerative possibilities discussed above did have profeminine appeal as early as the twelfth century, at least to Hildegard of Bingen. In her *Scivias* she concluded that Satan 'knew that the susceptibility of the woman would be more easily conquered than the strength of the man', and that Adam's love for Eve would do the rest.[71] Elsewhere Hildegard further suggested that the fact that the first transgression was by the 'weaker' party rendered it the more easily undone.[72]

Elsewhere in the twelfth century, in the eighth dialogue of the *De amore*, Andreas Capellanus assigns a bold statement about Eve's trustingness to a noblewoman during an argument about the eligibility of clerics as lovers. The noblewoman has alleged that because clerics eschew the physical exertion of warfare and live idly as slaves to their bellies, they cut an embarrassing figure as lovers.[73] Her debating opponent retorts that if clerics have greedy bellies so do many others—women especially, in that they live (allegedly) more sedentary lives, and in that it was Eve who first displayed gluttony and urged it on man. Andreas's noblewoman dismisses the charge of gluttony. Eve ate because she believed the devil's deceitful words and desired not food but the knowledge of good and evil. Undeterred, the noblewoman's opponent suggests that the reason why the devil tempted woman— the lesser antagonist—first was that he supposed the female more 'inclined to yield to her belly's appetite'. The noblewoman retorts: 'It happened as it did because women naturally believe things more easily than men, known as they are to be innocent and naive

---

[70] 'Oez seignor', in 'La Louange des femmes', ed. Pfeffer, 23–4; *Livre des manières*, ed. Lodge, 1143–8; *Miroir de mariage*, ed. Raynaud, 8596–607.

[71] *Scivias*, I. 2. 10, tr. Hart and Bishop, 77.

[72] Newman, *Sister of Wisdom*, 114–15, citing Hildegard's *Causae et curae*, 47.

[73] *De amore*, I. 490; *Andreas Capellanus on Love*, ed. P. G. Walsh (London: Duckworth, 1982), 187.

[*simplices*], and so they believe all they are told.'[74] It is interesting that her 'clerical' opponent gives up the topic at this point on the scholar's pretext that it is potentially too enormous and digressive. The noblewoman is allowed to 'win' this sensitive point, not only destroying the charge of female gluttony but also locating Eve's reactions in 'natural' female qualities; women are 'innocent' and 'guileless' (to adopt for *simplices* a less prejudicial translation than Walsh's 'naive'). Like so much else in Andreas's wily treatise the exchange is hard to gauge, not least because a woman who clearly believes hardly any of the male's arguments in this dialogue is arguing that women always believe what they are told. What nevertheless remains striking is that a considered pro-Eve position is already ascribable to a confident female voice in the twelfth century.

Analysis of Eve's position is pushed in a quasi-judicial direction in the anonymous thirteenth-century *Du bounté des femmes*. This condemns Adam on the basis of the rationale already located in Chrysostom. Adam should have acted with the wisdom proper to his station: first, by ordering Eve (as his 'subject') not to eat the fruit; and second, by not 'childishly' accepting the fruit himself, without the slightest coercion by her. Eve cannot be blamed for well-meaningly (*saunz malice*) taking the fruit, in the absence of effective instruction by Adam. As for his attempt to blame her for 'tempting' him to eat, this is about as convincing as if a murderer pleaded 'not guilty' to homicide on the pretext that a friend tempted him to it.[75]

By the time of Nicole Bozon in the fourteenth century, exoneration of Eve's part in the Fall was becoming a regular feature of the case for women. It was not woman, he declares, but man who really put humanity in jeopardy. Although the woman enticed Adam to take the apple, she was 'of tender age' and meant no harm in her words to him; he was 'wiser' and comprehended the grave implications, so sinned more by assenting.[76] In stressing

---

[74] 'Hoc ideo contigit, quia mulieres omnia facilius credunt ex ipsa nature quam masculi. Innocentes enim inveniuntur et simplices et ideo credunt omni verbo,' *De amore*, I. 502; ed. Walsh, 188–91. The noblewoman adds that, had the devil made a first unsuccessful attempt on the man, he would have got nowhere with the woman, whose resolve would have been strengthened by the (hypothetical) male example.

[75] Meyer (ed.), *Du bounté des femmes*, 212–84, 'Manuscrits français de Cambridge', 319–20.

[76] Smith and Meyer (eds.), *De la bonté des femmes*, 'La famme ne fist for purparla | Et son baron entisza | A la pomme, | Meis son baron plus pecha | Qaunt a la

that Adam was 'wise' and 'knew' the gravity of what he was doing, both the *Du bounté* author and Bozon are exploiting the question of intentionality raised by Augustine's admission that one cannot describe Adam as 'less guilty', because he 'sinned knowingly and deliberately' (*sciens prudensque peccavit*).[77]

Of course, this argument comes with the notable disadvantage that it risks acquitting Eve by reducing her to the state of diminished responsibility characteristic of a *naif*.[78] Tactically, it is too close for comfort to the sell-out of John Lydgate's flippantly cynical protest on behalf of women like Criseyde, that they are not blameworthy if they are 'naturally' deceitful.[79] It cannot match the insouciance of an idea revived from ancient gnostic sources in the Renaissance, namely that knowledge was deliberately *permitted* to Eve, and that she liberated the human intellect.[80] Nevertheless it is a crucial starting-point enabling a pro-Eve perspective to be developed by foregrounding some aspects of exegesis and rejecting others. Christine de Pizan welcomes and significantly sharpens that perspective in the *Epistre*. She argues that Eve did not 'deceive' Adam: rather, since Eve innocently (*simplement*) accepted and believed Satan's words as truth and went to communicate them in that spirit to Adam, this cannot be counted as deceit. Deceit requires hidden malice and intent to deceive, which is not compatible with 'guilelessness' (*simplece*).[81] Thelma Fenster has pointed out the power of this defence—one which represents Eve's attitude as transparent trust rather than as either credulity

folye s'acorda, ǀ Com sage home. ǀ La femme qe fu de tendre aage ǀ N'entendi pas tel damage ǀ En son dit, ǀ Mes li home qe fu plus sage ǀ Ben savoit le graunt hountage ǀ Qe il enprist' (43–54).

[77] *City of God*, XIV. 11; *PL* 41. 419, tr. Bettenson, 570.

[78] Noting that the 15th-cent. Florentine humanist Vespasiano da Bisticci excuses Eve 'on the grounds that Adam was supposed to be her head because she had less reason', Pamela Benson comments: 'while this does absolve woman of responsibility, it does not gain respect for her,' *Invention of the Renaissance Woman*, 37.

[79] *Troy Book*, III. 4407–8; an example I owe to Mann, 'Apologies to Women', 19.

[80] Respectively, the interpretations of Cornelius Agrippa, discussed by Newman, 'Renaissance Feminism and Esoteric Theology', 234–5, and of Bartolomeo Goggio, discussed by Benson, *Invention of the Renaissance Woman*, 62. Pagels explains how the early Christian gnostics (2nd cent. AD) 'often depicted Eve—or the feminine spiritual power she represented—as the source of spiritual awakening'; *Adam, Eve, and the Serpent*, 68.

[81] 'Je di pour vray qu'onque Adam ne deceut ǀ Et simplement de l'ennemi conceut ǀ Le parole qu'il la donna a croire. ǀ Si la cuida estre loyale et voire. ǀ En celle foy de lui dire s'avance, ǀ Si ne fu donq fraude ne decevance, ǀ Car simplece, sans malice celee, ǀ Ne doit estre decevance appellee. ǀ Nul ne deçoit sans cuider decevoir' (609–15), ed. Fenster and Erler, 62–4.

or deficient intellect, and one which rests on a quality of guilelessness directly commended in the Gospels.[82] Although Christine's
emphasis could hardly have developed *without* the precedents in
Augustine (and recyclings of them such as Bozon's), Fenster is
partially right to see it as innovative. Credulity sinks almost out of
sight,[83] the alleged contrasting 'wisdom' of Adam is deleted, and
only the sincerity of Eve is left in bold relief: a more decisive
reorienting of her situation than Bozon had imagined when he
complimented the benignity of her 'tender age'. Christine's English translator Hoccleve takes her point, dwells on it, and uses a
Chaucerian idiom to drive it home ('willyngly the feend
deceyued Eeue | So dide shee nat Adam, by your leeue'), but also
manages to muddle things up by reinserting categorical remind-
ers of Eve's 'disobedience' along with earnest but woolly assur-
ances that this is 'excusable' because most men disobey God's
commands too.[84]

The distinctiveness of Christine's position can be further confirmed by comparing it with the more congested justification
adopted in *Dives and Pauper* just a few years afterwards. There a
discussion of guilt for the Fall is sparked, interestingly, by the
suggestion that it is a typical masculine ploy for men to 'blame'
sins of their own doing on the 'deceit' of women. Pauper considers that the 'fals excusacioun' of pinning blame on 'the malyce of
woman' originates in Adam, who tried to blame his sin on

---

[82] Thelma Fenster, '*Simplece* et *Sagesse*: Christine de Pizan et Isotta Nogarola sur
la culpabilité d'Eve', in Dulac and Ribémont (eds.), *Une femme de lettres*, 481–93
(pp. 482–4). Fenster notes that the Bible advocates such an attitude: e.g. Jesus
commending one 'in whom there is no guile' (John 1: 47) and urging the disciples
to be prudent but also 'simple (Vulg. *simplices*) as doves' (Matt. 10: 16). *Simplece*
was a quality of directness and transparency admired in the medieval English
heroine: it is associated with Blanche in Chaucer's *The Book of the Duchess* (918 and
934–6). But *simplicitas*, trustingness, meant vulnerability too, as used of Ovid's
heroines in the *Heroides*, II. 64, XII. 90, and XXI. 104.

[83] Except for a hint in Eve's interpreting 'simplement' the words which Satan
gave her to believe ('lui donna a croire', 609). Roger Ellis suggests that 'in arguing
for Eve's innocence' Christine 'very nearly turns her into a type of the gullible
woman' but *conceals* that difficulty by rendering the temptation as 'a kind of
antetype of the Annunciation' (if lines 608–9 can be read to mean that Eve 'simply
conceived from the enemy the word he gave her to believe'); 'Chaucer, Christine
de Pisan, and Hoccleve: The "Letter of Cupid" ', in C. Batt (ed.), *Essays on Thomas
Hoccleve*, Westfield Publications in Medieval Studies 10 (London: Centre for Medieval and Renaissance Studies, Queen Mary and Westfield College, 1996), 29–54. I
am grateful to Roger Ellis for allowing me to read a draft of this article.

[84] *Letter of Cupid*, in *Poems of Cupid*, ed. and tr. Fenster and Erler, 351–92. The 'by
your leeue' couplet (cf. *Wife of Bath's Prologue*, III. 112) is at 391–2 and the comment
on disobedience is at 354–6 and 378–85.

woman even though her guilt was less. His greater 'defaute' is confidently alleged on several counts. First, the prohibition was issued by God 'pryncipaly' to Adam, Eve knowing it only second-hand (as indeed St Ambrose insisted);[85] second, she was exposed to powerful temptation by the disguised fiend; third, Adam had no external temptation, just the 'symple' (interesting choice of adjective) word of Eve offering the apple—nor do we find that she said anything 'deceyuable' to him; fourth, he tried to pass the blame whereas she admitted to God that the serpent deceived her; and finally, there is the familiar claim that as the 'wiser' party, Adam committed the greater sin.[86] Although the cumulative re-allocation of blame here is purposeful and important and yields a hearty sense of redress, it entails a policy of wrangling and reversal which is not what Christine wants. Buried in Pauper's speech is Christine's guileless Eve, innocent of deceit; but in ac-cordance with her distaste for the negatively slanderous effect of misogyny Christine wants to rewrite Eve without lapsing into a contrary vilification of men, so she presents only the positive point and trenchantly leaves us to draw our own conclusions about Adam.

Defence of Eve was clearly maturing by the beginning of the fifteenth century. One could fill a book on the topic, and in touch-ing on the main emergent threads here I have omitted some rather eye-catching variants such as an allegation that Adam murdered his first wife before Eve's creation; a protestation that Eve cannot be blamed for the Fall if God foreknew it; and Julian of Norwich's inventive strategy in narrating the Fall without any reference to Eve at all.[87]

---

[85] *De Paradiso*, XII, esp. chs. 54 and 56, *PL* 14. 301–3, tr. Savage, 333, 336. Agrippa eventually built upon it the notorious speculation that God's prohibition *did not apply* to Eve; see Newman, 'Renaissance Feminism', 234–5, and Woodbridge, *Women and the English Renaissance*, 40.

[86] *Dives and Pauper*, VI. 10, ed. Barnum,vol. i, pt. ii, 81–3.

[87] For the first, see the *Response* to *Master Richard's Bestiary*, tr. Jeanette Beer, 42, offering a theory of dual creation of woman based on Jewish theories about Gen. 2: 23 (cf. ch. 18 of Peter Comestor's section on Genesis in *Historia scholastica*, *PL* 198. 1070); namely, that Adam killed a first woman for whom he felt nothing since she was not 'bone of his bone', and (in the *Response* version) a somewhat double-edged deduction that the Fall would therefore never have occurred but for the subse-quent creation of Eve, for whom his love took precedence over obedience to God. The second example is briefly considered below. For the third, Julian's deletion of Eve or rather submergence of her within the figure of a 'servant' who combines male and female, as recently emphasized by Helen Phillips, 'Rewriting the Fall: Julian of Norwich and the *Chevalier des Dames*', in Lesley Smith and Jane H. M.

Books *have* been filled on the final topic of this chapter, the Virgin Mary. Almost always present in the formal defence case, she is presented as the *coup de grace* on women's behalf, clinching victory as in the example of the *Thrush and the Nightingale*, first because in delivering Christ she enables what Eve allegedly lost to be retrieved or transcended, then second because her perfections make her the apogee of ascribed womanhood, and finally because her exaltation confers honour on women by association. Yet while present in one or other, or several, of these capacities in profeminine writing she is often incorporated with a telling brevity. The reasons for restraint are not hard to detect. It is all very well for St Bernard to enthuse that as a result of the Virgin's motherhood 'no longer will man have any reason to accuse woman': but, as we have noted in the case of Mary Magdalene, the 'woman for woman' formula simply headlines the problem of Eve, for if God gave (as Bernard goes on) 'woman for woman: a wise one for a foolish one; a humble one for an arrogant one' and so forth, the case for woman is anchored in systematic rehearsal of ancient guilt, and eternally articulated as a fortunate dropping of charges against her, a heaven-sent acquittal.[88] Writers (like Christine in her *Epistre*) who tried to get away from that bind by focusing on the Virgin Mary simply as Christ's mother, disconnected from Eve, were liable to find themselves circumspectly urging that a women's cause for joy is that they 'resemble' her and have the same 'form' as one who was unequalled in creation except by Jesus.[89]

This is to escape from the clutches of the Eve retrospect on the one hand into the myth of the Virgin's perfections and singularity on the other. 'Singularity' is the operative descriptor, as emphatic in St Anselm's lyrical twelfth-century invocation of her as wondrously singular and singularly wonderful ('O femina mirabiliter singularis et singulariter mirabilis') as it still is in the fourteenth-

Taylor (eds.), *Women, the Book, and the Godly* (Cambridge: D. S. Brewer, 1995), 149–56, see Julian of Norwich, *A Revelation of Love*, ed. M. Glasscoe (Exeter: Exeter University Press, 1976), ch. 51.

[88] *Homiliae in laudibus virginis matris*, II. 3, in *Magnificat: Homilies in Praise of the Blessed Virgin Mary by Bernard of Clairvaux and Amadeus of Lausanne*, tr. Marie-Bernard Saïd and Grace Perigo, Cistercian Fathers ser. 18 (Kalamazoo, Mich.: Cistercian Publications, 1979), 17.

[89] 'Bien estre doit femme joyeuse et cointe | Qui autele comme Celle forme a, | Car oncques Dieux nulle riens ne forma | De dignité semblable, n'aussi bonne, | Fors seulement de Jhesus la personne' (580–4), ed. Fenster and Erler, 62.

century Middle English *Pearl*.[90] Singularity and uniqueness
served encomium of the Virgin better than they served her as a
witness for womanhood. If she was the being described by Alcuin
as 'most glorious in her virginity, with whom none of all the
virgins on earth can be compared',[91] then perhaps comparison
with ordinary women needed to be written off altogether.[92]

I think that the problem was recognized in the formal defence.
The recognition came through from Ambrose, who in one of his
influential discussions of virginity had specifically imagined a
reader protesting against the use of Mary as example, 'as if any
one could be found to imitate the Lord's mother'.[93] It is in that
spirit that Marbod of Rennes passes quickly over the Virgin in the
'De matrona' because her worth 'constitutes something unique'
(*res unica*).[94] A French manual of instruction for girls, the *Book of
the Knight of the Tower* (*c*.1371), seems to continue the same tradition when it discusses Mary's 'laudable' qualities but then leaves
her as one to whom 'none may be lykened ne compared', to move
to more contemporary paragons.[95]

Nevertheless the case is made for the Virgin as superwoman. In
the *Livre des manières* woman, who plucked evil with the apple, is
hailed as having reached through Mary an eminence 'above
man'—in fact above even St Peter, and above the angels.[96] *Le Bien
des fames* offers the elevation of the Virgin above angels as the key
reason for respect for women.[97] The fact that the lustre is being

[90] On Anselm, see Gold, *The Lady and the Virgin*, 70. In *Pearl*, 429–30, the
pearl-maiden says of Mary that 'for synglerty o hyr dousour, | We calle hyr
Fenyx of Arraby'; *The Poems of the Pearl Manuscript*, ed. Malcolm Andrew and
Ronald Waldron (London: Edward Arnold, 1978). See also Bernard's ecstatic 'O
uniquely venerable woman!', Homily 2 on the Virgin, and Amadeus of Lausanne's
'she alone from eternity was worthy to have as son him who was also God',
Magnificat, tr. Saïd and Perigo, 17 and 105. These are commonplaces of Marian
tradition.

[91] *PL* 101. 46–7, cited in Graef, *Mary: A History of Doctrine*, i. 173.

[92] Marina Warner comments that the argument 'that all women resemble the
Virgin Mary . . . is very rare, for every facet of the Virgin had been systematically
developed to diminish, not increase, her likeness to the female condition'; *Alone of
All her Sex: The Myth and Cult of the Virgin Mary* (New York: Alfred Knopf, 1976),
153.

[93] *De virginibus*, II. 3. 21, *PL* 16. 212, *Principal Works of St Ambrose*, tr. de
Romestin, 376.

[94] Leotta, 'De matrona', 78, tr. in Blamires, *Woman Defamed and Woman Defended*,
230.

[95] Caxton's 15th-cent. translation, ed. Offord, ch. cx, p. 148.

[96] Lodge (ed.), 1153–6.

[97] In *Three Medieval Views of Women*, ed. and tr. Fiero *et al.*, 14–18.

conferred on women from, as it were, another planet does not finally matter. Lustre was not so readily available that defenders could afford to disdain the one woman whose unimpeachability was agreed by all Christendom. It did not suit defenders, who needed heroines, to declare the Virgin's ordinary humanity. That was left to devotional literature—and also, tellingly, to theologians who found themselves embarrassed by Mary's wondrousness where it threatened crucial hierarchies. Aquinas, for instance, conducts an elaborate argument defining the Virgin's wisdom and prophetic power as gifts which she could *not* have used in a context of teaching, because that exercise of authority would have been inconsistent with her *condicio* as woman.[98] The Virgin might, it was conceded, be superior to the apostles—even Peter—but it was Peter, not Mary, to whom the keys were given.[99] The Church found itself devalourizing the Virgin, a sure sign that in some ways she was indeed projecting alarming profeminine possibilities.[100]

The Virgin kept her august place in the case for women despite the various limitations opponents or defenders might find in her. Her role gave her the advantage, as it seemed, of hospitable universality within the sisterhood of all women. On that basis a pseudo-Augustinian sermon declares that she 'has passed through all the states of woman in Jesus . . . in order to welcome all women who seek her'.[101] A profeminine narrative which specifically enacts this function and shows Mary responding to a host of diverse women who go seeking her, is Christine de Pizan's *Cité des dames*. (In this respect Christine is a little unusual if—as has been argued—women were not as interested as men

---

[98] *Summa*, III. 27, 5; she did not have all the uses of these gifts, 'sed secundum quod conveniebat conditioni ipsius. . . . Non autem habuit usum sapientiae quantum ad docendum: eo quod hoc non conveniebat sexui muliebri,' quoted by Martin, 'The Ordination of Women and the Theologians in the Middle Ages', 171.

[99] A. J. Minnis, '*De impedimento sexus*: Women's Bodies and Medieval Impediments to Female Ordination', forthcoming in P. Biller and A. J. Minnis (eds.), *Medieval Theology and the Natural Body* (York: York Medieval Press, 1997); Minnis cites also similar views expressed by Thomas Netter. I am extremely grateful for the opportunity to see this article prior to publication.

[100] Albert the Great emphasized that in the process of redemption Mary was 'member' not 'head'; Graef, *Mary: A History of Doctrine*, i. 275. Amadeus of Lausanne ingeniously compromised that she was the 'neck' of the body of the Church, distributing what came from Christ as 'head'; *Magnificat*, tr. Saïd and Perigo, 73–4.

[101] *PL* 39. 1990; cited by Bloch, *Medieval Misogyny*, 67.

were in pursuing the notion of Mary as a model for women.[102])
Book III of the *Cité* begins with Justice inviting 'the assembly of all
women' to beg Mary to dwell as sovereign in their now completed metropolis—in all her humility, virtue, and multifaceted
glory. It is outrageous, Justice suggests, to criticize the female sex
when one contemplates the Virgin's 'dignity'. The Virgin is not
just the recipient of accolades, however, for she addresses the
company confirming that she is happy to dwell among her 'sisters' and proceeds to entitle herself as the eternal 'head of the
feminine sex', an arrangement preordained, she states, by the
Trinity.[103]

Christine's modern translator emphasizes that whatever a
modern reader might think of this as culmination to the text's
construction of a feminine citadel, 'a higher authority for the City
of Ladies than the Virgin Mary was inconceivable for the late
Middle Ages'.[104] The case is actually more powerfully coded than
that implies. Christine has arrestingly redirected patriarchal discourse in two ways. First, she has imagined from *Mary's* (woman's) point of view at the triumphant end of the process the
doctrine that the Incarnation and Mary's elevation over all
women must have been preordained—whereas usually this was
imagined from the point of view of the medieval clerk trying to
mitigate the disaster of Eve.[105] Second and perhaps less obviously,
Christine appropriates for Mary a designation as 'head' which
radically instates her, in relation to women, as Christ is customarily related to the Church and as men are customarily related to
women in patristic and medieval religious tradition.[106] Here is
another instance of that 'mastering of the "master discourse," her
turning it to speak her own words', of which Maureen Quilligan

---

[102] Caroline Walker Bynum, ' ". . . And Woman his Humanity": Female Imagery
in the Religious Writing of the Later Middle Ages', in Caroline Walker Bynum,
Stevan Harrell, and Paula Richman (eds.), *Gender and Religion: On the Complexity of
Symbols* (Boston: Beacon Press, 1986), 257–88 (p. 259).

[103] 'Sy suys et seray a tousjours chief du sexe femenin. Car ceste chose fu des
oncques en la pensee de Dieu le Pere, preparlee et ordenee ou conseil de la Trinité',
Cité, III. 1. 3, ed. Curnow, 977, tr. Richards, 218.

[104] Richards, n. to III. 1, p. 269.

[105] This is precisely Le Fèvre's approach in *Leësce*, 2141–61, asserting God's
foreknowledge of the Fall and its redemption. The *locus classicus* would be the
opening of Augustine's discussion of the Fall in *City of God*, XIV. 11, *PL* 41. 418,
'Now God foreknew everything', tr. Bettenson, 568).

[106] See further Blamires, 'Paradox in the Medieval Gender Doctrine of Head and
Body' (forthcoming). Christine bypasses reservations about ascribing 'headship'
to the Virgin, by making her head of women specifically.

has written.[107] Only in Abelard is the masculinity of 'headship' elsewhere so pointedly queried, as we shall see.

That the Virgin's dutiful 'humility' dogs even her assertion of headship is a mark of her control by masculine ideology. But the Virgin's virtues, like the defences of Eve, and the 'privileges' of women discussed in this chapter, were a significant proportion of what could yet be articulated in defence of women. I have devoted particular attention to the privileges because they have been remarkably underprivileged in modern discussion. Sometimes they are not recognized at all and assumed to be oddities; where they are identified on the other hand, they are often taken to be pallid clichés; or, what is worse, they are taken to be transparent exercises in the rhetoric of paradox—self-mocking attempts to fabricate strengths out of the least defensible parts of the 'weaker' party's case. Maclean invites us to view Renaissance examples in this light, partly on the dubious grounds that as proofs of woman's superiority they 'are clearly inconsistent with the wider context of theology'.[108] It is important to stress that although some medieval proponents like Le Fèvre would not be above suspicion of cultivating paradox, the privileges were certainly taken with utter seriousness by many, including Humbert of Romans, a Master of the Dominican order in the mid-thirteenth-century. Among his sample sermons is one 'For Women in General' (as opposed to nuns, for instance). Almost half of it is devoted to the privileges. They are marshalled under three eras, 'the time of nature' encompassing the familiar advantages of Eve's creation; the 'time of grace' including woman's conception of Christ and first sight of him at the Resurrection; and the 'time of glory' comprising female queenship in heaven, higher than angels and more powerful in God's court than any man.[109]

What would women have thought, hearing such a sermon? Humbert hopes that awareness of such God-given advantages

---

[107] *Allegory of Female Authority*, 204.

[108] *Renaissance Notion of Women*, 91.

[109] 'Sermons for Different Kinds of Audience', XCIV, from the 'Treatise on the Formation of Preachers', in *Early Dominicans: Selected Writings*, tr. Simon Tugwell, OP, Classics of Western Spirituality (Ramsey, NJ: Paulist Press, 1982), 330. Humbert somewhat incongruously incorporates the argument that Eve is created from Adam's *side* as his fellow (which is not a 'privilege' as such), and he is also relatively unusual in envisaging as New Testament privilege the intervention by Pilate's wife on Christ's behalf.

will prompt devotion and good womanly behaviour.[110] That is a glimpse of a hidden agenda, perhaps, intending women to feel *grateful* for privileges, however little use these were, and to want to merit such superiority by conforming with the stereotypical strictures which the subsequent part of the sermon lays upon feminine behaviour. In the formal case the privileges assume a more absolutely aggrandizing purpose. The aggrandizement is essentially a *displaced* phenomenon, of course, since the 'time' to which it applies is never meaningfully the 'time of the present'. Still, aggrandizement of any sort was preferable at an epoch when culture generally gave women a minimal self-concept.

[110] 'All of this ought to encourage women to love the God who gave them all this, and to pursue for love of him all that is good in a woman,' *Early Dominicans*, tr. Tugwell, 330.

5

The Stable Sex

THE Middle Ages inherited opinions alleging feminine weakness, changeability, instability, that had acquired categorical, near-instinctual status over an immense period. These opinions gained cultural authority from the well-honed gibes of antique poetry; especially Virgil's 'woman is always fickle and changeable' (*varium et mutabile semper | femina*), and Ovid's 'girls' promises are lighter than falling leaves' (*verba puellarum, foliis leviora caducis*).[1] Satirists imagined exceptions only as a means of compounding their attack: 'woman is a fragile thing, never constant except in crime', scoffed Bishop Hildebert of Lavardin around 1100.[2] *Mutabilitas, levitas, inconstantia, instabilitas* constituted only part of a copious supply of Latin descriptors to suit, though the two favourites were probably *infirmitas* and *fragilitas*.

Women's reputation for 'weakness' and 'instability' was among the most serious of the impediments to profeminine thinking, and of course it was a negative construction built on exactly the same gender binary of feminine 'softness'/masculine 'hardness' which was used in women's defence.[3] This chapter will consider the defiant revaluations it provoked, but if we are to gauge the horizons of defiance plausibly, the scale of scientific and doctrinal agreement on this attribute of women needs to be emphasized first. Scientifically, the 'softness' of woman's personality was envisaged as one of the symptoms of the 'imbalance' of

---

[1] *Aeneid*, IV. 569–70, where (paradoxically) Mercury is urging Aeneas to abandon Dido; and *Amores*, II. xvi. 45, in *Ovid: Heroides and Amores*, ed. and tr. Grant Showerman, 2nd edn. rev. G. P. Goold (Cambridge, Mass.: Harvard University Press, 1977), 432–3.

[2] 'Femina res fragilis, numquam nisi crimine constans'; Smith, *The Power of Women*, 32.

[3] 'The womanly sex is soft [*mollis*] since it is easily deflected from bad to good or from good to bad', whereas 'the manly sex is harder [*durior*], being not easily turned from bad to good, or recalled from good to bad' (but more often durable in good rather than bad, given the rationality attributed to masculinity), according to a passage quoted from Chrysostom by Wyclif in *Opus evangelicum*, ed. Johann Loserth, 2 vols. (London: Wyclif Society, 1896), vol. ii, bk. III. 11, p. 39.

her constitution towards humidity and wetness (males by contrast having a supposedly more beneficial tendency towards dry-
ness and heat). From her humidity derived her instability,
according to a characteristic formulation by Albertus Magnus
when he is discussing 'Whether men are more inclined to morality than women': 'A woman's *complexio* is more humid than a
man's, but the nature of the humid is to receive easily and retain
badly. Whatever is humid is easily changed, and so women are
inconstant and always seeking new things . . . there is no faith in
woman.'[4] In Albertus and in other medieval physiologists this
general principle was held to govern also specific domains such
as that of intellect. A woman's intellect allegedly could not focus
in a sustained way on a proposition on account of the 'fluxibility'
of her constitution.[5] From a scientific point of view, woman's
'softness' was therefore most often viewed as a failing: hence
Vincent of Beauvais construed softness as inconstancy and contrasted it with perseverance, gendering the one feminine and the
other masculine.[6]

It is not the business of this book to detail how religious doctrine tirelessly reinforced medieval physiology by equating fe-

[4] 'Complexio enim feminae magis humida quam maris sed humidi est enim de
facili recipere et male retinere. Humidum est enim de facili mobile, et ideo
mulieres sunt inconstantes et nova semper petentes . . . nulla fides est in muliere',
Alberti Magni opera omnia, vol. xii: *Quaestiones super De animalibus*, ed. E. Filthaut,
OP (Aschendorff: Monasterii Westfalorum, 1955), XV, qu. 11; cited by J. D.
Burnley, 'Criseyde's Heart and the Weakness of Women: An Essay in Lexical
Interpretation', *Studia Neophilologica*, 54 (1982), 25–38 (p. 35). See also Atkinson,
The Oldest Vocation, 36.

[5] 'As soon as the truth is propounded to a woman, then her intellect inclines to
assent; but if she should ponder very long over that truth, immediately the intellect of women would vary on account of the fluxibility of the phlegmatic material.
Whence comes the varying perturbation of [her] intellect;' 'Quam cito praeponitur
veritas mulieri, tunc intellectus ejus inclinatur ad assentiendum; sed si
consideraret diu de veritate illa, statim intellectus mulierum variatur propter
fluxibilitatem materiae fleumaticae. Unde est varia perturbatio intellectus,' quoted
from the 14th-cent. commentator Johannes Buridanus, *Quaestiones in octo libros
politicorum Aristotelis*, III, qu. 5, in Andrew Galloway, 'Marriage Sermons, Polemical Sermons, and *The Wife of Bath's Prologue*: A Generic Excursus', *Studies in the Age
of Chaucer*, 14 (1992), 3–30 (p. 29).

[6] Softness arises in those who have 'a less constant soul because of weakness
in *complexio*; and in this respect women may be compared to men. . . . And so
those who endure things proper to a woman are called soft, since they have
become like women' ('quia videlicet habent animum minus constantem, propter
fragilitatem complexionis; et hoc modo comparantur foeminae ad masculos. . . . Et
ideo illi qui muliebria patiuntur, molles dicuntur, quasi muliebres effecti'),
Speculum morale, I. xc. 3, quoted by Burnley, 'Criseyde's Heart and the Weakness
of Women', 35–6.

maleness with infirmity in every possible context.[7] Let me mention only the representative case of Gregory's commentary on the Book of Job. Gregory declares it axiomatic that wherever in Scripture the term 'woman' seems not interpretable literally, it may be interpreted metaphorically as 'weakness' (*pro infirmitate*). To exemplify such metaphorical interpretation he suggests that in the notorious fourteenth verse of chapter 42 of Ecclesiasticus, 'Better is the iniquity of a man than a woman doing well', ' "a man" is the term for every strongminded and discreet person, but "a woman" is understood for the weak [*infirma*] and indiscreet mind'.[8] By so reading that ludicrous verse Gregory saves literal women's face only to gall them with the claim that all inadequate persons are 'women'; the misogyny which is too absurd to be literal is reinstated as metaphor.

The tradition that asserted woman's physiological and moral instability was enormous and apparently categorical. Instructional literature maintained that girls have less *estable sens* than boys.[9] In influential poems such as the *Roman de la Rose*, readers found suggestions that a woman is as firm as an eel and that she is never so *estable* that one can stop her being changeable.[10] Encyclopedias proclaimed that women epitomize a changeability found in the female of most species: 'generalliche the femal is of more unstedefast kynde and more chaungyng than the male. And that cometh of feble hete and of strong cold humour that is in more plente in the femel.'[11] It was inevitable that women

---

[7] One of the founding scriptural texts, of course, was 1 Pet. 3: 7: 'Ye husbands, likewise dwelling with them according to knowledge, giving honour to the female as to the weaker vessel'; 'viri similiter cohabitantes secundum scientiam, quasi infirmiori vasculo muliebri impartientes honorem.'

[8] *Moralia in Job*, XI. 49; 'Vir etenim fortis quilibet et discretus vocatur, mulier vero mens infirma vel indiscreta accipitur,' *PL* 75. 982: a reference I owe to Gopa Roy, 'A Virgin Acts Manfully: Ælfric's *Life of St Eugenia* and the Latin Versions', *Leeds Studies in English*, NS 23 (1992), 1–27 (p. 5). Accordingly Gregory frequently terms the changeable mind 'female', while those who serve God unsteadily he calls 'women'; *Moralia in Job*, I. 49 and 78, III. 40, XXVIII. 12; see Ferrante, *Woman as Image*, 20–1. From Gregory, the configuration passed into such vernacular texts as *Ancrene Riwle*; see Blamires, *Woman Defamed and Woman Defended*, 97–8.

[9] Women are at risk in youth because 'ele n'ont mie si estable sens ne si bon porposement come ont li home'; Philippe de Novare (d. 1270), *Des quatre tens d'aage d'ome*, ed. M. de Fréville (Paris: SATF, 1888), cited in Alice A. Hentsch, *De la littérature didactique du Moyen Âge s'addressant spécialement aux femmes* (1903; repr. Geneva: Slatkine, 1975), 85.

[10] Respectively Ami (9903–24), and Genius (16327–8); tr. Horgan, 151–2, 252.

[11] From the entry 'De femina', bk. 18, ch. xlix of John Trevisa's trans. (dated 1398–9) of an encyclopedia first compiled c.1230; *On the Properties of Things: John*

writers—and other women so far as we can judge their views—
internalized the gendering of unsteadfastness as feminine
and perseverance as masculine.[12] What, against this chorus,
could the case for women possibly affirm on behalf of feminine
stability?

Only rarely were the scientific or doctrinal premises used to
defy the usual conclusions, though the very fact that this could be
undertaken is interesting. Thus among the courtship debates of
the *De amore* of Andreas Capellanus, a female speaker's objection
at one point that she has not yet reached sufficient maturity to
achieve constancy in love prompts her suitor to respond that
nature arranges for the constitutional coldness of woman to be
quickly heated (i.e. her puberty and capacity for sexual fidelity is
established earlier) whereas man starts warm and 'heats up'
rather slowly. But this point about women's 'head start' (as it
were) in achieving constancy in relationships is rather surprisingly developed in terms of durability, not just quick efflores-
cence: 'nature works differently with women, for a woman can
love with staunch constancy and unflagging determination from
her twelfth year. . . . The constancy of a woman at the very outset
of womanhood is maintained with more certain strength, *and it
continues unchanging with the utmost dependability*.'[13] Although this
could be seen as partly driven by a wish to legitimize a male right
to sex with barely pubertal spouses (if not driven by downright
irony, or by a wish to out-argue the woman in the dialogue at all
costs), it nevertheless envisages a scientifically demonstrable case

Trevisa's Translation of 'Bartholomaeus Anglicus De proprietatibus rerum', ed. M.
Seymour, 2 vols. (Oxford: Clarendon Press, 1975), ii. 1201.

[12] See Hildegard of Bingen on the 'slack' and 'womanish' clergy of her epoch:
Newman, *Sister of Wisdom*, 3, citing Hildegard's Letters 13, 26, 49. The *Life* of
Christina of Markyate compliments her for resisting sexual feelings 'like a man'
(*viriliter*). One would-be seducer thought her resistance made her 'more like a man
than a woman, though she, with her more masculine qualities, might more justifiably have called him a woman' ('quem virago, virtute virili predita, recte
effeminatum appellare poterat'); *The Life of Christina of Markyate: A Twelfth-Century
Recluse*, ed. and tr. Charles H. Talbot (Oxford: Clarendon Press, 1987), 115. This *Life*
seems to have been written by a monk of St Albans, probably in the 1160s (pp. 5–
10): it is hard to judge how much its writer has edited Christina's views.

[13] 'Secus autem ipsa operante natura dignoscitur in mulieribus evenire; mulier
enim ab anno duodecimo firma potest securitate et invariabili amare tenore.
. . . Nam mulieris constantia inter ipsius pubertatis initia robore solidiore firmatur
et invariabilis certissime perseverat' (my emphasis), *De amore*, I. 8, ed. and tr. Walsh,
174–5. Andreas's rationale is an inventive extension of the physiology of heat:
'what is cold heats quicker when moderate heat is applied to it than if heat is
added to heat.'

for female stability, that is, for the 'wrong' conclusion by medieval tradition.

Andreas's discussion depends on agile manipulation of underlying scientific priciples of heat and cold. Medieval physiologists
were indeed adept at constructing woman to be 'cold' where that
temperature would be demeaning or alternatively as somehow
'hot' (preferably because of her cold!), where that temperature
would be demeaning instead. Matheolus discloses this double
bind in his *Liber lamentationum* when he states that woman is
naturally cold; that what is cold characteristically tightens, a condition of avarice; and that woman is avaricious. Then he confusingly adds that properly speaking, woman will *not* be found
'more cold' (*frigidiorem*) than man.[14] Subsequently he insists that
women are not sexually colder than males—*femina* being
etymologically associated with 'fire'—but that even if their bodies
are cooler, this coolness generates a frantic sexual ardour arising
from the need to 'purge' through coitus humours which they
cannot otherwise disperse.[15] Although Le Fèvre did his best with
these passages when he translated them, it is hardly surprising
that he scoffed at their vacillatory effect when reviewing them in
the *Livre de Leësce*. Le Fèvre is on the verge of an interesting
breakthrough here, rumbling the shiftiness and the doublethink
whereby science and culture sought to demote the female, no
matter whether through heat or through cold:[16] the heroic step
would have been to cast doubt on humoural theory as a credible

[14] 'Frigida cum mulier natura debeat esse, | Et frigus stringat, est quod sit avara
necesse; | Quod sit avara scio. Sed dum bene discutio rem, | Hanc non invenies
maribus fore frigidiorem', *Liber lamentationum* (1121–4), ed. Van Hamel, *Lamentations*, i. 83.

[15] *Liber lamentationum* (1179–99): that is, Matheolus ultimately concurs with a
traditional medieval scientific view that women 'were driven by their craving for
the hottest, most complete being, that is, the male' and the 'excess moisture further
reinforced a woman's condition of perpetual need, for, to commentators such as
Adelard of Bath, humidity in women caused desire'; Elizabeth Robertson, 'Medieval Medical Views of Women and Female Spirituality in the *Ancrene Wisse* and
Julian of Norwich's *Showings*', in Linda Lomperis and Sarah Stanbury (eds.),
Feminist Approaches to the Body in Medieval Literature (Philadelphia: University of
Pennsylvania Press, 1993), 142–67 (p. 147).

[16] In the *Roman de la Rose* Ami recalls Juvenal's caricature of Hiberina, a woman
who 'was of such hot matter that no one man could satisfy her', ed. Poirion, 8291–
2, tr. Horgan, 127: on which Sarah Kay aptly comments, 'This despite the fact that
the "heat" of women is still cooler than the coolest men', 'Women's Body of
Knowledge: Epistemology and Misogyny in the *Romance of the Rose*', in Sarah Kay
and Miri Rubin (eds.), *Framing Medieval Bodies* (Manchester: Manchester University Press, 1994), 211–35, p. 214 and n. 10.

guide to gender matters if it led to such internal inconsistencies. But at this epoch, with an agenda of heat and cold fully in control, Le Fèvre settled for a tamer reflection, that Matheolus must have been dealing in irony.[17]

Nevertheless the case for women could take a stand in defiance of the scientific shibboleths. In the anonymous *Du bounté des femmes*, a thesis about male body hair and facial hair again supports a 'wrong' conclusion. Physiology usually linked hairiness with a 'superior' male capacity to refine and purge superfluities through pores as sweat and hair.[18] However, approaching the topic by way of woman's privileges at creation, and commending her 'naturally' fine and pure body, the writer of *Du bounté* paints a contrasting picture of man not only created of muck but also having to be repeatedly cleansed of the beard which is part of that muck.[19] By identifying a 'finer' (more 'perfect') female body in opposition to this hairy male excrescence which requires repeated removal, the text implicitly counters the physiological preoccupation with women's monthly purgation through menstruation as a sign of her humoural instability; instead it offers evidence of a cyclic male purgation which calls into question *men's* physiological stability and perfection.[20] It is quite salutary to see how gender assumptions could be turned around simply by judging the male beard as a deficit (a lack of unblemished skin) indicative of substandard constituents in the creation of the male. This actually

[17] 'Contre les femmes par injure | Dit que sont de froide nature | Et que toute femme est avere. | Et après, . . . A soy meismes est contraire. | Mais il le dit par yronie, | Par maniere de vilenie. | Des femmes dit, quant il en parle, | Que plus chaudes sont que le masle,' *Leësce*, 2295–304. The relevant parts of *Les Lamentations* are II. 1483–9 and 1663–92 (the latter being tr. in Blamires, *Woman Defamed and Woman Defended*, 192–3).

[18] Joan Cadden, *Meanings of Sex Difference in the Middle Ages: Medicine, Science, and Culture* (Cambridge: Cambridge University Press, 1993), 181–3.

[19] 'Conment purroit estre parfit | Chose fet de purreture? | Ceo serroit encuntre nature; | Dount jeo vous [di] pur jugement | Qu femme est natureument | Blaunche, necte e fin e pure. | E de ceo trés bien moi assure | Qe home fu fet de bowe; | A la barbe e a la jowe | Poez bien veer la matire, | Chescune quinze jour a reire, | De barber e de hoster le ordure' (69–80); *Du bounté des femmes*, ed. Meyer, 'Manuscrits français de Cambridge', 317. Women's freedom from facial hair is noted again by Agrippa, *De nobilitate*, ed. Béné, 59; Newman, 'Renaissance Feminism and Esoteric Theology', 232.

[20] The progression of thought in *On the Properties of Things* links female 'unsteadfastness' with 'cold humour' with (in the next sentence) 'menstrual superfluite'; ed. Seymour, 1201. The progression of thought in *Du bounté des femmes* (81–4) links the suggestion that women are created *fines* with a suggestion that they are sexually more faithful than men; ed. Meyer, 317–18.

seems to situate the male as 'other' for a change, measuring aspects of masculinity from a quasi-feminine subject position.

A more common strategy was to rebut the charge of feminine instability either head-on or by resorting to a compromise theory of feminine 'strength in weakness'. Or, defence frequently became attack, castigating men for operating a double standard whereby they demanded of women a sexual and moral steadfastness which they could not attain themselves: it was especially in these terms that the case for women became a case against men. After investigating these topics, we shall also discover in the next chapter how representation of the 'calumniated' woman in medieval narrative enacted and invigorated the contests about stability.

Since feminine resolve was so often championed in medieval writings in a reactive way against specific or predicted allegations, ownership of moral *stabilitas* assumed the status of something keenly competed for by the sexes. Whence come all these stories about unstable women, protests Deschamps's *Miroir de mariage*, when 'the contrary is true' (9381–91)? 'You claim women are not stable but fickle', protests the speaker in the *Livre de Leësce*. 'God knows, it's the other way round: there's no faith or constancy in males towards women.'[21] In the *Roman de la Rose*, the platitudes about feminine fickleness voiced by the lover's comrade are countered by the Old Woman's conviction that it is men who are unreliable.[22] The earlier Anglo-Norman poem we have just discussed, *Du bounté des femmes*, aims to prove that women show more sexual discipline (are 'de lur cors plus estables', 83) than men by arguing that if a woman laid siege to a man with gifts, visits, and advances as men do women, the man would characteristically lapse into sexual activity more quickly than— *mutatis mutandis*—would the woman (86–103).

Yet so culturally ingrained was the concept of female infirmity inherited by the Middle Ages, that a fiction of strength in weakness was often maintained in order to reconcile received opinion with claims on behalf of female firmness and moral discipline. Deschamps's poem underlines the problem when it proposes that women martyrs have been found a hundred thousand

[21] 'Vous dites femmes mal estables, | Vuides, faulses et decevables. | Mais Dieu scet qu'il est autrement; | Leur amour se tient fermement . . . | Es masles est la faulseté. . . . | Nulle foy ne nulle constance | N'est en masle pour aliance | Tenir et garder vers femelle' (3832–54).
[22] 'Car il ont trop les cuers muables'; 'their hearts are too fickle', ed. Poirion, 13,141–2, tr. Horgan, 202.

times more loyal and constant than men even though, in light of women's reputation for *fragilité*, men ought to be more constant than women.[23] Deschamps has in mind here the patristic and medieval commonplace that women are more 'handicapped' by weakness, have a greater distance to go in achieving fortitude.[24] Their victories were therefore often represented as a peculiar mark of God's mysterious favour. For example, this is instinctively the rationale with which Venantius Fortunatus introduces his *Life* of the sixth-century Frankish queen and abbess Radegund:

Our Redeemer is so richly and abundantly generous that He wins mighty victories through the female sex and, despite their frail physique, He confers glory and greatness on women through strength of mind. By faith, Christ makes them strong who were born weak so that, when those who appeared to be [feeble] are crowned with their merits by Him who made them, they garner praise for their Creator who hid heavenly treasure in earthen vessels.[25]

The theme of female triumph gloriously transcending congenital weakness goes back to Augustine, who makes clear that the 'strength of mind' on which women thus draw is habitually gendered masculine.[26] So, a key flaw in this hypothetically

[23] 'Trueve femmes en leur martire | A voir esté cent mille tans | Plus devotes et plus constans | Assez que les hommes ne furent, | Qui trop plus constans estre durent | Des femmes, veu et recité | D'elles la grant fragilité,' *Miroir de mariage*, 9064–70.

[24] For some discussion, see Newman, 'Flaws in the Golden Bowl', in *From Virile Woman to Woman Christ*, 26; and Bloch, *Medieval Misogyny*, 67–8. Abelard writes that 'inasmuch as the female sex is naturally weaker, so is its virtue more acceptable to God and more worthy of honour' ('Quo naturaliter femineus sexus est infirmior, eo virtus eius est Deo acceptabilior et honore dignior'); *The Authority and Dignity of Nuns*, ed. Muckle, 'Letter of Heloise on Religious Life and Abelard's First Reply', 270, tr. Scott Moncrieff, 158. Boccaccio also gives a classic statement in his chapter about Epicharis, a woman who refused to name names under torture; *De mulieribus claris*, ed. Zaccaria, 378–80, tr. Guarino, 210–11.

[25] 'Redemptoris nostri tantum dives est largitas, ut in sexu muliebri celebret fortes victorias, et corpore fragiliores ipsas reddat feminas virtute mentis inclytae gloriosas. Quas habentes nascendo mollitiem, facit Christus robustas ex fide; ut quae videntur imbecilles, dum coronantur ex meritis, a quo efficiuntur fortes, laudem sui cumulent Creatoris, habendo in vasis fictilibus thesauros coeli reconditos', *Vita S. Radegundis reginae*, PL 88. 497–512 (497); *The Life of the Holy Radegund*, tr. in McNamara *et al.*, *Sainted Women of the Dark Ages*, 70 (but I have substituted 'feeble' as a more accurate rendering of *imbecilles* than 'imbeciles').

[26] In his famous sermon on the female saints Perpetua and Felicity, he writes that 'the crown is all the more glorious when the sex is weaker, and the soul shows itself assuredly more virile in women when they do not succumb to the weight of their fragility'; 'Nam ibi est corona gloriosor, ubi sexus infirmior. Quia profecto virilis animus in feminas majus aliquid fecit, quando sub tanto pondere fragilitas feminea non defecit', Sermon 281, *PL* 38. 1284.

profeminine manœuvre is that whatever strength or stability women are seen or thought to demonstrate is only being devolved to them as a 'manly' virtue: the norm for fortitude remains male.[27] And even when that is not made explicit—as when Peter the Venerable praises Heloise for triumphing over the devil by dedicating herself to the cloister—there is usually a tell-tale note of masculine condescension (in this case, because if the devil 'cannot even sustain a brief conflict with a woman's weakness', his designs on godhead appear truly ridiculous).[28]

Fortunatus in the sixth century and Peter the Venerable in the twelfth doubtless meant to utter genuine profeminine sentiments, by the standards of their times. They projected notably powerful religious women as paradoxes of strength in weakness because that was the construction by which patriarchy sought to make sense of them. It is interesting that Abelard became obsessive about the paradox. Perhaps this was precisely because his involvement with Heloise forced him to confront the disparity between her conspicuous capacities and the weakness supposed to haunt her sex. At various points he echoed the established platitudes. Woman is the weaker sex, he wrote, so her virtue is the more pleasing to God and man.[29] Solitude was yet more essential for nuns in their frailty than for monks, he argued, since men 'are less attacked by the conflicts of carnal tempta-

[27] Widely discussed by medieval scholars, among whom see Cadden, *Meanings of Sex Difference*, 205–6; Margaret Miles, ' "Becoming Male": Women Martyrs and Ascetics', in her *Carnal Knowing: Female Nakedness and Religious Meaning in the Christian West* (Boston: Beacon Press, 1990), 53–77; Roy, 'A Virgin Acts Manfully', 1–27. Eleanor McLaughlin observes that 'in this inheritance of patristic anthropology', to become fully holy is 'to become male', 'Women, Power and the Pursuit of Holiness in Medieval Christianity', in Ruether and McLaughlin (eds.), *Women of Spirit*, 100–29 (pp. 128–9). McLaughlin shows how such thinking continued to affect the ideas—though not necessarily the self-concept—of such a woman as St Catherine of Siena (1347–80), who in one of her letters advised a young follower not to be held back 'by a womanish tenderness for thyself, but be a man, and enter the battlefield manfully' (pp. 119, 121). For a representative 12th-cent. example, see Hrotsvitha's Legend of St Basilius (168–9), in which a courageous girl is projected as one putting aside feminine softness and adopting manly fortitude: 'mollitiem iam deponens muliebrem | Et sumens vires prudenti corde viriles'; cited in A. Daniel Frankforter, 'Hroswitha of Gandersheim and the Destiny of Women', *The Historian*, 41 (1979), 295–314 (p. 302).

[28] Peter the Venerable, Letter 115, to Heloise; in *Letters of Abelard and Heloise*, tr. Radice, 277–84 (pp. 278–9).

[29] 'Quippe quo feminarum sexus est infirmior, . . . earum virtus tam Deo quam hominibus est gratior,' ed. J. T. Muckle, 'Abelard's Letter of Consolation to a Friend (*Historia calamitatum*)', *Mediaeval Studies*, 12 (1950), 163–213 (p. 205); tr. Radice, 97.

tion'.[30] Heloise would appear to have endorsed the stereotype when she wrote to him of the longings of desire which afflicted her the more overwhelmingly in that 'the nature they attack is the weaker'.[31]

Yet these clichés had to coexist in Abelard's mind with memories (or rhetorical reconstructions) of his own uncontrollable desire, and how he fulfilled it on occasion despite Heloise's remonstrations which revealed her to be *fortior continentia*, 'stronger in continence'.[32] Behind his egotistical projection of his own aggressive virility sweeping aside the strong scruples of her continence, Abelard is clearly struggling with a profound sense of Heloise's self-control and his lack of it, and it is in this struggle that we might locate his remarkable commitment to the rationalization of feminine fortitude as a weakness perfected in strength. As much as any other medieval writer, I think, he applied to women the reassurance which, according to St Paul, Christ offered to those who find themselves threatened by bodily temptation: 'My grace is sufficient for thee: for power is made perfect in infirmity.'[33] This doctine was a cornerstone of Abelard's treatise

[30] 'Vestrae vero infirmitati tanto magis est solitudo necessaria, quanto carnalium tentationum bellis minus hic infestamur et minus ad corporalia per sensus evagamur,' T. P. McLaughlin, 'Abelard's Rule for Religious Women', *Mediaeval Studies*, 18 (1956), 241–92 (p. 250); tr. Radice, 196.

[31] 'Hoc autem in me stimulos carnis haec incentiva libidinis ipse iuvenilis fervor aetatis, et iucundissimarum experientia voluptatem accendunt, et tanto amplius sua me impugnatione opprimunt, quanto infirmior est natura quam impugnant', Letter 3 in J. T. Muckle, 'The Personal Letters between Abelard and Heloise', *Mediaeval Studies*, 15 (1953), 47–94 (p. 81); tr. Radice, 133. Heloise referred often to 'the weaker sex'; cf. her question about what rule St Benedict might have laid down for women: 'quid de fragili sexu provideret cuius maxime debilis et infirma natura cognoscitur?', ed. Muckle, 'Letter of Heloise on Religious Life and Abelard's First Reply', 244; 'what would he provide for the weaker sex whose frailty and infirmity is generally known?', tr. Radice, 163.

[32] 'You know the depths of shame to which my unbridled lust had consigned our bodies.... Even when you were unwilling, resisted to the utmost of your power and tried to dissuade me, as yours was the weaker nature I often forced you to consent with threats and blows'; 'Nosti quantis turpitudinibus immoderata mea libido corpora nostra addixerat.... Se et te nolentem et, prout poteras, reluctantem et dissuadentem, quae natura infirmior eras, saepius minis ac flagellis ad consensum trahebam,' 'Personal Letters', ed. Muckle, Letter 4, p. 89; tr. Radice, 147. Some of Abelard's sexual exploits with Heloise have assumed the proportions, in his memory, of near-rape.

[33] 'Sufficit tibi gratia mea; nam virtus in infirmitate perficitur', 2 Cor. 12: 9. Hildegard of Bingen was another 12th-cent. writer who endorsed this paradox; see Barbara Newman, 'Divine Power Made Perfect in Weakness: St Hildegard on the Frail Sex', in John A. Nichols and Lillian Thomas (eds.), *Peace Weavers: Medieval Religious Women*, ii (Kalamazoo, Mich.: Cistercian Publications, 1987), 103–22.

written for Heloise *The Authority and Dignity of Nuns*.[34] He connected it with another Pauline passage which argues that God
particularly honours those parts of the 'body' which seem
'weaker'.[35] He was convinced that grace enabled women's weakness to be perfected as strength, and he pursued with fervent
literalness the idea that feminine weakness and strength were
interlinked.

What is particularly interesting about this is Heloise's own
reference to the formula when at an early stage in their correspondence she is reacting against his confidence in the strength of
her prudence and piety, which had been Abelard's pretext for not
consoling her in writing after their separation. Feeling on the
contrary extremely precarious in faith, she seeks his support but
specifically rejects the Pauline formula; 'I do not want you to
exhort me to virtue and summon me to fight, saying "Power
comes to its full strength in weakness."'[36] In context, this is the
plea of a troubled woman unready to aspire to spiritual triumphs
('I do not seek a crown of victory', she adds). It is nevertheless
tempting to wonder whether it is also a rare glimpse of a woman
unimpressed by contemporary profeminine cliché—a cliché too
complacently abstract to touch a genuine heartfelt conviction of
weakness.

Abelard still founded his profeminine treatise on the strength-
in-weakness paradox, and indeed, variants of this approach remained prominent in the case for women throughout the Middle
Ages. As a commendation of women's resolution (often, of their
sexual discipline) it was of course backhanded: backhanded both
because it implied that feminine *stabilitas* is very surprising, considering the odds;[37] and backhanded because it ascribed women's

Frankforter interprets the same paradox in the 10th-cent. canoness Hrotsvitha;
'Hroswitha of Gandersheim and the Destiny of Women', 303.

[34] Muckle (ed.), 'Letter of Heloise on Religious Life and Abelard's First Reply',
where St Paul's words are quoted on p. 268 and where Abelard goes on to ask:
'who would say that there was so complete a fulfilment by the dispensation of the
divine grace in any as in the very infirmity of the womanly sex?', *Letters of Abelard
and Heloise*, tr. Scott Moncrieff, 155–6.

[35] 1 Cor. 12: 22–4, quoted in *The Authority and Dignity of Nuns*, ed. Muckle,
'Letter of Heloise on Religious Life and Abelard's First Reply', 268, tr. Scott
Moncrieff, 155.

[36] 'Nolo, me ad virtutem exhortans, et ad pugnam provocans, dicas: "Nam
virtus in infirmitate perficitur"'; ed. Muckle, 'Personal Letters', Letter 3, p. 82; tr.
Radice, 135.

[37] Geoffroy de la Tour-Landry's instructional book for girls (*c*.1371) suggests in
ch. cxviii that God praises a woman who is (sexually) 'good' more than a man,

resolve to special grace, not to themselves. As *Dives and Pauper* puts it, man is naturally (biologically) 'more stable' than woman, but experience shows that women are often 'more stable in goodness' through divine grace.[38] However, this text also provides an unexpectedly discerning socio-psychological explanation. It is suggested that whereas men's confidence makes them ready to obey their own inclinations rather than God's, women know their own frailty so are less self-reliant and more dependent on God—more afraid of offending him.[39] We might add, *of course* women in that era (and for centuries after) 'knew their own weakness': they were not allowed to forget it even when they were being praised. But while the text cannot objectify the process of indoctrination (to which it contributes) it does objectively engage the effects of that indoctrination, in terms of a resultant sense of inferiority in women which is construed as producing chaste feminine resolve—because women are reluctant to assert themselves in any way that will transgress religious proprieties.

The 'stability' which most preoccupied laudatory writing about women was sexual stability, or its absence. This emphasis is explicable partly as a function of a patriarchal discourse in which women were defined primarily as sexual beings (virgin, wife, widow, prostitute) whose essence and threat was their sexual relation to men; and it is partly a function of a patriarchal society in which women were not culturally perceived as having many serious opportunities to exercise virtues other than sexual ones. From the fourth century to the twelfth and beyond, one current of opinion insisted that although lust occurs in both men and women, it is more repugnant in women than in men, since the

---

'and by reason she ought to haue more meryte by cause she is of lyghter courage than the man is . . . in so moche that she is more feble than the man is | And yf she resisteth ageynste the temptacions . . . the more she is worthy to haue gretter meryte than the man'; tr. Caxton, *Book of the Knight of the Tower*, ed. Offord, 156–7.

[38] 'how may it ben þat women oftyn kepyn hem mor chast & ben mor stable in goodnesse þan man?' asks Dives, adding that female recluses generally demonstrate more staying-power than male recluses. Pauper answers: 'Man, be weye of kende, is mor stable þan is woman & of mor discrecion, but be grace women oftyn ben mor stable in goodnesse þan ben men' (VI. 13); *Dives and Pauper*, ed. Barnum, vol. i, pt. ii, 92. The whole passage is translated in Blamires, *Woman Defamed and Woman Defended*, 270.

[39] 'men trostyn to mychil in hemself & nout trostyn in God as þei auȝtyn to don. Women knowynge her frelte trostyn nout in hemself but only in God & comendyn hem mor to God þan don men, and þey dredyn mor to offendyn God þan do men,' ed. Barnum, 92–3.

very principle of feminine virtue is in the sexual domain. Public life offers men various paths for the exercise of virtues—but chastity is the singular virtue of women. These sentiments come from John of Salisbury's twelfth-century *Policraticus*, which in turn adapts them from St Jerome's fourth-century *Adversus Iovinianum*.[40]

Nevertheless, modern students and scholars possibly do not realize just how conscious people were in the Middle Ages that society's concern with the singular virtue of women entailed a double standard of sexual morality. Three aspects of medieval discussion about this are relevant to the present chapter. These are: a recognition that feminine sexual mores were exposed to relentless and partisan scrutiny; an allegation that men expected women to sustain a sexual morality far more scrupulous than they imposed upon themselves; and a claim that sexual misconduct was primarily the responsibility of the 'importuning' male.

Instructional literature of the thirteenth century stated quite bluntly that a girl must above all avoid carnal error, or even the appearance of it, because that sort of fault disgraces a woman more than a man.[41] What the instructor portrayed as fact, the profeminine moralist portrayed as outrage. In a digression on women's reliability in a late thirteenth-century English verse text known as *The Southern Passion*, the author indignantly attacks the illogicality whereby society considers a man who resists female seduction a saint, while expecting women to resist pervasive male sexual attentions; and the illogicality whereby a woman committing a single sexual indiscretion is blamed vastly more than a man.[42] Nicole Bozon similarly notes that when a man sins no one fusses about it, whereas a woman's *folie* is quickly notorious in the

---

[40] *Policraticus*, VIII. 11, in *The Frivolities of Courtiers and Footprints of Philosophers*, tr. Joseph B. Pike (London: Oxford University Press, 1938), 363–4; cf. the resounding conclusion to bk. I of *Adv. Iov.* (I. 49), *PL* 23. 281–2, tr. Fremantle, 386.

[41] Hentsch, *De la littérature didactique*, 83–4, citing the section on 'Anfance' in Philippe de Novare, *Des quatre tens d'aage d'ome*.

[42] 'Where wostou so stable mon, þat ʒif a fayr womon come, | Gent and hende, and hym bysouʒt of folye ilome | þat he nolde torne his þouʒt to folye at fyne? | For ʒif he ne dede me wold hym holde worþy to ligge in crine. | And what is þan þe woman worþe, as þe meste del beþ, | þat ne beþ ouercome mid no biddyng, as we ofte iseþ? | ʒhe ne chal be no seint iholde ... | Ac if me ondirʒete of a woman þat ʒhe onys mysgo, | ʒhe worþ more iblamyd þan a man a þousend syþe and mo' (35–44); ed. Pickering, 'The "Defence of Women" from the *Southern Passion*', 154–76 (p. 168); tr. in Blamires, *Woman Defamed and Woman Defended*, 245.

locality.[43] But Bozon also probes rather imaginatively at the social dilemmas forced on women by relentless surveillance. He realizes that they cannot win. If they are quiet or guileless (*symples*) in company, they are written off as aloof or uncouth (82–4). If on the other hand they smile sociably at male guests *par courteysie* they are instantly assumed to be every man's game, so hardly any woman can work out how to avoid being ill thought of (85–96). It is a sharp sympathetic cameo of women as objects of ruthless carping suspicion, and it gives one an idea of the resonances available to (for example) Chaucer when he articulated the social pressures upon the heroine in *Troilus and Criseyde*.[44]

It is a short step from noting the partisan scrutiny of women's behaviour which constantly threatens their reputation for 'stability', to noting the disparity of standards applied to sexual morality. So, *The Southern Passion* makes a vigorous attack on the warped social expectations which cause a 'fallen' woman's marital prospects to collapse, while a thoroughly promiscuous man ('the vilest lecher') finds no difficulty in securing the most virginal wife, especially if he has some wealth.[45] Disgust at such hypocrisy was neither idiosyncratic nor new. It was precedented in the early Church (which indeed had much to contend with in the one-sidedness of late classical sexual mores).[46] Medieval writers

---

[43] 109–14, in Smith and Meyer (eds.), *Contes moralisés de Nicole Bozon*, pp. xxxvi–xxxvii.

[44] As Helen Phillips shows, the concern about surveillance continued to be echoed late in the 15th cent. in the anonymous *Chevalier des dames*: 'Noblesse Feminine protests about the effects of Malebouche on women's lives: if a woman happens to glance at a man people will say she lusts after him; young women dare not laugh, sing, show pleasure or even do good to their fellow-men, for fear of slander', 'Rewriting the Fall', 153. Malebouche (Evil Tongue) in *Le Roman de la Rose*, who found some sort of fault in every woman ('Sor chascun trove quelque herne'), constitutes one *locus classicus* for the topic; ed. Poirion, 3910, tr. Horgan, 51.

[45] Ed. Pickering, 43–54; tr. Blamires, *Woman Defamed and Woman Defended*, 245.

[46] Chrysostom contemplates the legal reinforcement of a double standard in *On Virginity*, lii. 7; tr. Shore, 84–5; his concern for a single sexual standard is displayed in *Homily 5 on 1 Thessalonians*, 2, and in *Homily 19 on 1 Corinthians*, 1, both extracted in Elizabeth A. Clark, *Women in the Early Church* (Wilmington, Del.: Michael Glazier, 1983), 74–6. St Jerome's Letter 77, 'To Oceanus', includes a defence of a single standard; *Select Letters*, tr. Wright, 312–15. See also D. S. Bailey, *Sexual Relation in Christian Thought* (New York: Harper & Row, 1959). The late classical attitudes resisted by the Church Fathers are summarized in Aline Rousselle, *Porneia: On Desire and the Body in Antiquity*, tr. Felicia Pheasant (Oxford: Blackwell, 1988), ch. 5, esp. p. 87: 'the legislation taken as a whole seems to have been designed principally to prevent husbands from allowing their wives a degree of sexual freedom which they themselves enjoyed.'

needed to go no further than the sermons of St Augustine (or to those which borrowed from them) to find caustic repudiations of masculine hypocrisy. In one sermon to married people, Augustine told wives to show no tolerance at all of husbands' infidelities but to condemn them outright: appealing rhetorically for justice, he told men to stop imagining that being male justified their expectation that wives should put up with adulterous behaviour in husbands which husbands would find abhorrent in wives.[47] Similar arguments are presented in another sermon on the Ten Commandments, where he laments that even women have accepted the belief (or rather the 'perversity') that men should be allowed a sexual freedom not granted to themselves.[48] Complacent masculine responses ('it's only a bit of harmless sex with a servant-girl';[49] 'a man's not a man if he gets a reputation for fidelity') are scornfully repudiated, and wives are advised to listen to God, not husbands, in such cases.[50]

Admittedly, the profeminine element in Augustine's position is tightly circumscribed. He takes pains to point out that a woman should comply with all other depredations (for example, if her husband sells off her gold, or her house), since her necessary obedience to the spouse who is doctrinally her 'head' remains unaffected in these other matters.[51] Moreover Augustine's anger at male adultery is prejudicially articulated in terms of a betrayal of manly discipline. If a man's a man, let him overcome libido: how come a wife can be 'stronger' than he?[52] Nevertheless here was an influential voice upholding women's cause against the double standard and encouraging them to speak up against men,

[47] 'Quis ferat uxorem adulteram? Et imperatur feminae ut ferat adulterum virum! O justitia!', Sermon 392, 'Ad conjugatos', PL 39. 1709–13 (1712).

[48] Sermon 9, De decem chordis; CSEL 41 (1961), 105–51 (p. 115).

[49] That little changed between Augustine's time and the Middle Ages in this respect is hinted by the fact that Margherita Datini's husband fathered a number of illegitimate children by household servants in late 14th-cent. Italy; see Women and Writing in Medieval Europe: A Sourcebook, ed. Carolyne Larrington (London: Routledge, 1995), 78, citing I. Origo, The Merchant of Prato (London: Reprint Society, 1959).

[50] De decem chordis (IX. 11–12), 128–31. The question of how a wife might have to go 'over the head' of her husband and collude, as it were, with God against him is negotiated rather carefully: for some reflections, see Blamires, 'Paradox in the Medieval Gender Doctrine of Head and Body' (forthcoming).

[51] Sermon 392, V. 4–5, PL 39. 1712, and De decem chordis, 128–9.

[52] 'Vir es? vince libidinem. Quomodo vir, quia uxor est fortior?', Sermon 392. V. 5, PL 39. 1712; cf. De decem chordis, 130, which adds that women's chastity is the more stringently guarded precisely because of woman's assumed infirmitas, man's greater freedom being granted because he is reckoned stronger (fortior).

and a voice which was widely transmitted by medieval preachers, such as the Dominican Jacobus de Voragine.[53] The protest was therefore not unfamiliar, and was carried further through such texts as *The Southern Passion* and *Dives and Pauper*.[54] And in the latter, the Augustinian observation that fewer men than women are formally charged with adultery provokes a flurry of interesting analytical reflections: that masculine confidence characteristically makes light of sin; that men close ranks to cover their own guilt; and that the male monopoly of the judiciary keeps women's adultery, rather than men's, in the limelight.[55]

The same texts often included an extra defensive point. This centred on the assumption that courtship and sexual activity defines the male as 'active' and the female as 'passive'. The perceived configuration exonerated women on the grounds that men 'pursued' women, while women 'suffered' what men 'did' to them.[56] Hence, the masculine claim to hold women in subjection itself made nonsense of any argument that men were seduced by women, and this was a riposte that circulated through confessional discussion of lechery. 'If a person says he is compelled [to commit fornication] "by a woman", the counterargument is that woman is under man's power and not vice-versa. Therefore, since man rules over woman, he compels her, rather than the other way

[53] His use of Sermon 392 (spliced, perhaps, with another Augustinian sermon) is described in Galloway, 'Marriage Sermons, Polemical Sermons, and *The Wife of Bath's Prologue*', 9–12. The sermons of Jacobus circulated quite widely in late medieval Europe.

[54] *Dives and Pauper*, VI. 5–6, ed. Barnum, vol. i, pt. ii, 67–72, pursues the question whether adultery is a greater sin in man than in woman, drawing extensively on Augustine; tr. in Blamires, *Woman Defamed and Woman Defended*, 261–4. There were, on the other hand, influential statements (e.g. in commentary on canon law, and in Aquinas) which sustained the view that a wife's adultery was much more serious than a husband's: see Jeffrey Richards, *Sex, Dissidence and Damnation* (London: Routledge, 1990), 36–7; also Andreas, *On Love*, II. 6. 15, ed. and tr. P. G. Walsh, 242–3.

[55] *Dives and Pauper*, VI. 5, ed. Barnum, vol. i, pt. ii, 68–9; tr. in Blamires, *Woman Defamed and Woman Defended*, 262. According to Kathryn Gravdal, records of rape trials do tend to suggest that women 'were both sexual and legal victims of male-defined crimes tried by men'; *Ravishing Maidens*, 131 and ch. 5 *passim*.

[56] 'Wheyþer is þenne more to blame þat þe ded deþ so, I Oþer þilke þat ne deþ here nouȝt ac soffreþ þat me here do? I Wel ȝe wete þat þe man hit is þat þe dede deþ' (57–60), ed. Pickering, 'The "Defence of Women" from the *Southern Passion*'; tr. in Blamires, *Woman Defamed and Woman Defended*, 246. Cf. 'Men comounly ben warkeris & begynnerys of lecherie, and þan weþer þe woman assente or nout assente ȝit þe man is gylty', *Dives and Pauper*, VI. 11, ed. Barnum, p. 87, tr. in *Woman Defamed and Woman Defended*, 267. See also Christine de Pizan, *Epistre*, 348–54.

round. Therefore, it follows that a man is led to commit fornica-
tion by the wickedness of his own flesh and not through anyone
else.'[57] It is by this same logic that Le Fèvre dismisses misogynous
tattle about bawds. He insists that men cause women to act as go-
betweens. It is men who tirelessly seek debauchery—the blame
should fall upon the active party, not the passive.[58]

Nevertheless women were blamed and it was a conventional
literary charge that women 'are fickle and inconstant, changeable
and flighty, weak-hearted . . . and lacking all stamina', as
Christine de Pizan puts it in the *Cité des dames*.[59] Droitture (Rectitude) deals with this by adapting the familiar protests. Men, she
says, expect more constancy from women than they themselves
can muster, their own claim to strength being undermined by
grave lapses which they then have the cheek to excuse as 'human
nature'. Illogically they do not allow women, even though they
regard them as congenitally weak, to give in to 'human nature'
too. Instead they judge any lapse in a woman (resulting usually
from a man's importuning) as downright 'inconstancy'.[60] They do
not acknowledge that no law permits men alone to take these
liberties, let alone acknowledge the strength of the women who
put up with their vile exploits.

It is interesting to consider what has changed between Augustine's discussion and Christine's. Gone is the surrounding
patristic vocabulary of masculine 'headship' (still retained, by
contrast, in *Dives and Pauper*); also gone is the androcentric complaint that adulterous men betray the 'strength' that pertains
rightly to men. Replacing those certainties and their coercive
rhetoric is a sceptical rationalism which exposes the shifting
ground of self-serving masculine arguments and queries the underlying construction of gender: *'they claim* women are so fragile.'
The catch, as has sometimes been noted, is that Christine ulti-

---

[57] *Fasciculus morum: A Fourteenth-Century Preacher's Handbook*, ed. and tr.
Siegfried Wenzel (University Park: Pennsylvania State University Press, 1989),
675.
[58] *Leësce*, 2981–4: 'Les hommes ont vertu active | Et les femmes ont la passive.
| L'omme doit assaillir et faire, | La femme doit souffrir et taire.'
[59] 'que variables et inconstans sont, muables et legieres, et de fraille
couraige, . . . ne qu'il n'y a aucune fermeté': II. 47. 1; ed. Curnow, 891, tr. Richards,
164–5.
[60] The observation that when women lapse 'these men themselves, through
their own strivings and their own power, are the cause' seems to indicate that
Christine would distribute blame in accordance with the active/passive binarism
already mentioned; ed. Curnow, 892, tr. Richards, 165.

mately retreats from the implications of such reasoned challenge into quiescence. At the end of the *Cité* she commends patience to women with recalcitrant husbands (III. 19. 1), just as she authorizes women to show humility and toleration to unloving and unfaithful husbands in *The Treasure of the City of Ladies*.[61]

However, what is most notable about Christine's presentation of the stability topos is her decision to address sexual constancy, and men's tarnished record in that, within the wider perspective of rationality and mental equilibrium, and men's tarnished record in those. In effect she runs together what predecessors had considered separately. As we have seen, defenders had protested that men's sexual disloyalty was more evident than women's. Le Fèvre's defence censures masculine doubletalk on the grounds that men consider a casual predatory attitude to women normal, so that husbands habitually betray wives and show no restraint as widowers, while women preserve *estable* loyalty as wives and behave chastely as widows.[62] This passage happens to follow one in which Leësce has pointed out that men have no right to complain about her profeminine selection of examples from history, since promasculine use of history carefully deletes the tyranny and vice characteristic of male figures such as Nero and Herod.[63] This suggestion that the record of men's violence and criminality might far outmatch women's is a separate part of the case for women, repeated elsewhere in *Leësce*[64] and present already in Marbod's 'De matrona' early in the twelfth century.[65]

Now although this type of argument lends itself to witty riposte—'even in wickedness women are inferior', quips Pamela Benson[66]—Christine de Pizan not only takes it seriously but produces, I think, an important initiative in the *Cité des dames* by

[61] *Cité*, ed. Curnow, 1032–3, tr. Richards, 255. Beatrice Gottlieb, while sensing a 'feminist consciousness' in Christine, finds also a conformism and 'quietism' (especially in her ideas about wifely behaviour); 'The Problem of Feminism in the Fifteenth Century', in Julius Kirshner and Suzanne Wemple (eds.), *Women of the Medieval World* (Oxford: Blackwell, 1985), 337–64 (esp. p. 360).

[62] *Leësce*, 3832–73; esp. 'Plus de mil femmes mariées | Fermes, sans estre variées, | Tiennent aux maris foy estable; | ... Qu'après leurs maris trespassés | Se contiennent honnestement | Et saintement et chastement' (3858–67).

[63] *Leësce*, 3794–819.

[64] 1184–96, 3688–91.

[65] Leotta (ed.), 72–6; 'Neither has virtue often been found to be lesser in the inferior sex, nor has wrong-doing been found to be greater: for what woman has been so bad as to outdo the sheer evil of Judas?', tr. in Blamires, *Woman Defamed and Woman Defended*, 230.

[66] *Invention of the Renaissance Woman*, 52.

coalescing it with the topos of sexual stability which had remained separate (though adjacent) in Le Fèvre as indeed in her own earlier work.[67] In the *Cité* Rectitude's discussion of constancy (II. 47. 2) is expressed in carefully unspecific language which implies, but does not confine its reference to, sexual constancy. She then decisively expands the reference (II. 47. 3), demonstrating just how massively irrational and unstable men can be by describing the vicious unpredictability of a whole succession of Roman emperors; Claudius, Tiberius, Nero (especially), Galba, Otho, Vitellius. On this basis Rectitude denies any masculine right to pontificate about steadfastness of any sort (II. 49. 4), and makes the range of her objection clear by defining 'inconstancy or frailty' as any defeat of the rational by the sensual in an individual (II. 49. 5). In these terms frailty encompasses Judas and other notorious figures too: so, men should shut up about constancy, and women should be thankful for what misogyny reckoned a disadvantage—that God 'placed their precious souls in feminine vessels'.[68]

What Christine has done, therefore, is to subsume the narrow traditional question of sexual steadfastness within a much larger category of rational stability. This can be seen as a significant initiative precisely because most attempts to debate sexual stability *per se*, however profeminine in intention, entailed inadvertently accepting the misogynists' implication that a woman's virtue was above all sexually constituted. Although Christine accommodates her profeminine predecessors' repudiation of masculine sexual egotism in the *Cité* she transcends the associated problem by redefining 'frailty' so as to desexualize it, to the extent that it becomes primarily a weakness of *mind* epitomized at its worst by the most infamously deranged of history's tyrannical male rulers.

That said, there was one way in which assertive defence of women's sexual stability had already been linked with a powerfully antimasculine demonstration of male unreliability though one that was biblical not classical, namely, with the defection of the male disciples of Christ at his Crucifixion. The attack on the

---

[67] See Christine's *Epistre au dieu d'amours*, ed. Fenster and Erler, 348–406 and 643–94.

[68] Ed. Curnow, 900, tr. Richards, 170. This is elaborately ironic: as the quotation from Fortunatus earlier in this chapter shows, women's 'frailty' was conventionally stereotyped in the image of a *vas*, a fragile 'vessel'.

sexual double standard in *The Southern Passion* already mentioned is in fact a digression triggered at the point where the writer of this Passion narrative is contemplating the contrast between the male disciples' disappearance and Mary Magdalene's loyalty to Christ, shown by her reluctance to leave his tomb.[69] It seems that the writer instinctively feels that the collapse of male loyalty in the Gospel accounts undermines the androcentric propaganda which holds men and not women sexually reliable.

I am not certain of the history of this connection, but it is interesting to note that its polarities are also present in the twelfth-century *Life of Christina of Markyate*. Here Christina (at this stage named 'Theodora'), having dedicated herself as a virgin to Christ under the tutelage of a canon called Sueno, is trapped into a betrothal by her family. When Sueno learns of the betrothal he interprets it as an instance of womanly inconstancy (*muliebris inconstancie*), and withdraws his support from her. Of course this merely builds irony, since in reality it is Theodora who stands firm, while it is he, her male 'protector', whose loyalty is failing (*puella perseverante vir defecit*). This paradoxical configuration, brought into being by a masculine misperception that a woman has been sexually derailed from the resolution she has made, resolves itself into an echo of the drama of male apostasy at Christ's death: in fact the writer goes on to envisage the heroine not merely as a dedicated follower of Christ but as actually Christ-like, for he derives the change of her name to 'Christina' from this auspicious moment when she was deserted by her special male friend just as Christ was deserted by his special disciple Peter the 'prince of apostles'.[70]

We might easily underestimate just how sharp was the gender contrast in discipleship which the Middle Ages learned to associate with the Passion of Christ. From the Bible's descriptions of Peter's denial that he knew Christ;[71] and from a pointed mention of the women followers standing beside the cross;[72] and from indications of the zeal with which after the disciples went home[73] several named women (especially Mary Magdalene) went on

[69] Ed. Pickering, 'The "Defence of Women" from the *Southern Passion*', 9–26; tr. in Blamires, *Woman Defamed and Woman Defended*, 244–5.

[70] *Life of Christina of Markyate*, ed. and tr. Talbot, 54–7.

[71] John 18: 16–27.

[72] 'Now there stood by the cross of Jesus, his mother, and his mother's sister, Mary of Cleophas, and Mary Magdalene,' John 19: 25.

[73] John 20: 10; Matt. 26: 56, 'Then the disciples all leaving him, fled.'

attending the tomb and tried to convince the men of what they discovered there;[74] and from the fact that eventually all or one of the women saw the resurrected Christ;[75] from all this a lesson in feminine resolution and masculine defection was more or less unavoidable.[76]

The lesson had not been all that welcome to early theologians and they tried to make it avoidable through various kinds of equivocation. Chrysostom construed the women's resolve as a symptom of the unaccountable paradoxes wrought by Christ's death,[77] and their weeping vigil as gendered sentiment.[78] Ambrose noted that when the apostles fled, Mary stood by the cross as befitted the mother of Christ, but he had the cheek to declare of the women's 'diligence' at the tomb, that their coming and going displayed feminine 'lack of constancy' (while yet conceding in the next breath the 'flight' of the men).[79] As for Augustine, when he found himself confronting Luke's account of the disloyal disbelief of the male disciples at the women's report, he sought to neutralize the impression of masculine infidelity by locking it into a rhetorical contrast with the Fall: if women were not to be believed why did Adam believe Eve, and if women were to be trusted why didn't the disciples believe the holy women?[80]

Despite these obfuscations in received commentary, the biblical implication of female perseverance and male retreat at Christ's death asserted itself forcibly in the Middle Ages. One of those who guaranteed this was St Gregory in a remarkable passage of his widely disseminated commentary or *Moralia* (late sixth cen-

[74] Luke 24: 9–11, esp. verse 11, 'And these words seemed to [the male apostles] as idle tales: and they did not believe them.'

[75] Matt. 28: 9; Mark 16: 9; John 20: 14–18.

[76] See Fiorenza, *In Memory of Her*, ch. 8 (esp. pp. 315–34) for a stimulating discussion of the different Gospel accounts of the women disciples.

[77] 'But the women stood by the cross, and the weaker sex then appeared the manlier; so entirely henceforth were all things transformed,' *Homily 85 on St John*, 2, ed. Schaff, 318.

[78] 'Full of feeling somehow is the female sex, and more inclined to pity,' *Homily 86 on St John*, 1, ed. Schaff, 323.

[79] 'Sed nec Maria minor quam matrem Christi decebat fugientibus apostolis ante crucem stabat'; and 'Sollicitae tamen et a monumento posteriores recedunt et ad monumentum priores reuertuntur. Etsi deest constantia, non deest diligentia. Sexus nutat, deuotio calet. Denique resurrectionis tempore praesto sunt et, cum uiri fugarentur, solae tamen ab angelo ne timeant admonentur,' *Expositio evangelii secundum Lucam*, X. 132 and 144–5, ed. Adriaen, 383 and 387.

[80] Sermon 232. 2, *PL* 38. 1108. Augustine overlooks here his own argument (see above, Ch. 4) that Adam could not really have believed Eve.

tury) on the book of Job. Job laments in chapter 19 that his servants, family, all those he loved most, have abandoned him;[81] then
he adds that 'the flesh being consumed, my bone hath cleaved to
my skin'.[82] Gregory uncompromisingly develops this as a figure
for the desertion of Christ (the 'bone') by all but the women
('skin'). 'What is the flesh but the disciples, who tasted weakness
at his passion; and what is the skin—which is exterior to flesh—
but the holy women who generally ministered to the Lord in
exterior things?' The men fled one by one from the cross: the
women 'stuck' to Christ. Neither Peter nor John 'persevered' but
the women were not frightened, did not run away, expressly
stood firm at the tomb.[83] Here, surely, is one of the few occasions
in medieval culture where 'flesh' is gendered masculine. And,
notwithstanding the converse tweak of gendering whereby the
women/skin equation is explained in terms of the women's concern with 'externals',[84] Gregory does not mince words in contrasting the men's fearful flight with the women's staunch loyalty. So
it is not surprising that his influence is felt in subsequent medieval
discourse on women at the Passion. In a sermon in honour of
Mary Magdalene attributed to Odo of Cluny (d. 942), the Job
analogy is recalled in the context of Mary's *constantia* and the
men's lack of it.[85] A twelfth-century *Life* of Mary Magdalene not
only recalls the same analogy but also has the angels in the tomb
exceeding their brief in Mark's Gospel by alluding to the desertion when they instruct the women: 'since he has risen from
death, go and tell his disciples, who, when he was arrested, were
stricken with fear and forsook him, fleeing, all of them.'[86] (The

---

[81] 19: 13–19.   [82] 19: 20.

[83] 'Quid per carnem nisi discipuli, qui passionis ejus tempore infirma
sapuerunt? Per pellem vero, quae exterior carne manet in corpore, quid nisi illae
sanctae feminae figurantur, quae ad preparanda subsidia corporis exterioribus
Domino ministeriis serviebant? . . . Sed cum ad crucis horam ventum est, ejus
discipulos gravis ex persecutione Judaeorum timor invasit: fugerunt singuli,
mulieres adhaeserunt. . . . Mulieres autem non solum non timuisse, neque fugisse,
sed etiam usque ad sepulcrum stetisse memorantur'; *Moralium in Job*, XIV. 49, *PL*
75. 1068.

[84] Gregory is doubtless thinking of a classic summary of the women's service to
Christ in Luke 8: 2–3, concerning Mary Magdalene, Joanna, Susanna, 'and many
others who ministered unto him of their substance'.

[85] 'Quasi enim consumptis carnibus pellis ossi adhaeret, quando, discipulis
fugientibus, beata Maria Magdalena cum Domino perseveravit,' *In veneratione
Sanctae Mariae Magdalenae*, *PL* 133. 713–21 (718).

[86] Cf. Mark 16: 7, 'go, tell his disciples and Peter that he goeth before you into
Galilee'. *Vita beatae Mariae Magdalenae*, xxv, *PL* 112. 1471; *Life of Saint Mary
Magdalene*, tr. Mycoff, 69. The Job analogy is in ch. xx, *PL* 112. 1462, tr. Mycoff, 60.

same biography, incidentally, shows how the weight of prejudicial commentary such as we have seen in Ambrose had to be consciously thrown off. The profeminine author states that the Gospels deliberately mention the women's diverse visits to the tomb 'to show the diligence with which they ran to and fro repeatedly, coming and going, not suffering themselves to be long absent'.[87])

In the same century Abelard, too, drew on Job within his own admiring account of these women's steadfastness in *The Authority and Dignity of Nuns*.[88] He heaps a vocabulary of intrepidity, perseverance, unwaveringness, and constancy upon the women. While the recuperation of the women's role is refreshing, such a mode of narration is not far-reachingly feminist, of course. It is too much governed by the implicit 'infirmity' stereotype which it is reversing, just as Abelard's summary formula 'the rams flee . . . ; the ewes remain unafraid' assumes a readership already certain that women should be ewishly timid.[89] There were other ways of developing the model. The *Meditations on the Life of Christ* famously goes in for emotive narrative embroidery, and it does not fail to orchestrate a scene of pathos in which Peter and the rest shuffle miserably in to visit Christ's mother on the sabbath after Christ's burial, reproaching themselves for abandoning him.[90] But the particular forte of this text is less to harp on the women's resolve than to draw the reader into their emotions as they witness and experience these events (by way of another stereotype of compassionate femininity, of course), to the extent that John, though present in this rendition throughout the Crucifixion and deposition from the cross, is effectively marginalized.

Cleared of patristic equivocation during the Middle Ages, the loyalty of Christ's female disciples provided a profeminine topos of immense power because it carried all the authority of the New Testament. That power could be invoked summarily precisely

[87] *Vita beatae Mariae Magdalenae*, xxiv, PL 112. 1468; tr. Mycoff, 66.

[88] 'Letter of Heloise on Religious Life and Abelard's First Reply', ed. Muckle, 256–7; tr. Scott Moncrieff, 136–7. Paradoxically Abelard also works against the grain of Gregory's interpretation by claiming that 'flesh' ought to be gendered masculine because flesh, nearer bone, has greater strength than skin. This is discussed in my '*Caput a femina, membra a viris*: Gender Polemic in Abelard's Letter "On the Authority and Dignity of the Nun's Profession"' (forthcoming).

[89] 'Fugiunt arietes, immo et pastores Dominici gregis; remanent oves intrepidae'; 'Letter of Heloise on Religious Life and Abelard's First Reply', ed. Muckle, 257; tr. Scott Moncrieff, *Letters*, 138.

[90] *Meditations*, lxxxiv, tr. Ragusa, 348.

because it was familiar through the sermons, the meditations, the *Lives* I have mentioned. This is the reservoir of feminine confidence which Christine de Pizan taps in her *Epistre au dieu d'amours*, where it is argued that the Gospels give no support to misogyny:

instead women are attributed with many a virtue, many an important act, great wisdom, good sense and unwavering constancy, perfect love, unshakeable faith, great charity, a determined will, a strong and steadfast heart eager to serve God: and they gave ample proof of these qualities, for they did not abandon him in life or death. Sweet Jesus, injured, wounded, or dead, was forsaken by everyone except for the women.[91]

For reasons which the present chapter has made clear, 'unshakeability' is necessarily the foundation of my survey of 'many a virtue'; but the reader may be wondering about other virtues asserted in medieval culture on women's behalf. These included prudence, piety, kindness, charity, and sobriety or moderation. It is interesting that prudence and piety were qualities connected with femininity in scientific texts.[92] Women's piety is usually asserted as a matter of experiential proof, against misogyny's lurid speculation that women use attendance at religious functions for sexual adventure.[93] Christine de Pizan makes Lady Reason dismissively point out that churches are full, not of young women dressed to kill but of older women praying in simple clothes.[94] But Reason seems to associate this piety with a broad principle of 'natural' feminine sobriety demonstrated equally by women's readiness to deprive themselves to make up for husbands' wastefulness in taverns. There had been, as it happens, a

[91] 'Mais maint grant bien, mainte haulte besongne, | Grant prudence, grant sens et grant constance, | Parfaicte amour, en foy grant arrestance, | Grant charité, fervante voulenté, | Ferme et entier courage entalenté | De Dieu servir, et grant semblant en firent, | Car mort ne vif oncques ne le guerpirent; | Fors des femmes fu du tout delaissié | Le doulx Jhesus, navré, mort et blecié' (562–70), ed. Fenster and Erler, *Poems of Cupid*, 61; tr. in Blamires, *Woman Defamed and Woman Defended*, 283–4. Cf. 'Wher was ther any wight so ententyf | Abouten him as wommen? perdee noon | Thapostles him forsooken euerichoon | Wommen forsook him noght,' Hoccleve, *Letter of Cupid*, 439–42, ed. Fenster and Erler, 201.

[92] Cadden, *Meanings of Sex Difference*, 205.

[93] *Leësce*, 1777–1804, 3704–9. For examples of the misogynous topos, see *Gawain on Marriage: The 'De coniuge non ducenda'*, ed. and tr. A. G. Rigg (Toronto: Pontifical Institute of Medieval Studies, 1986), L4; Le Fèvre, *Lamentations*, II. 947–1022 and 2145–54; and an antecedent in Juvenal, *Satire* VI. 314–41, in *Juvenal and Persius*, ed. and tr. G. G. Ramsay (London: Heinemann, 1918), 108–9.

[94] *Cité*, I.10.1, ed. Curnow, 656, tr. Richards, 26. Here also Reason notes that it is above all women who perform works of charity among the sick.

'biological' medieval claim, propounded notably by Heloise, that nature had 'protected' women with 'greater sobriety':

> It is well known that women can be sustained on less nourishment and at less cost than men, and medicine teaches that they are not so easily intoxicated. . . . we cannot easily fall victims to gluttony and drunkenness, seeing that our moderation in food protects us from the one and the nature of the female body . . . from the other.[95]

This is not quite the point for Christine, though, whose quiet irony is at its deadliest as she implicitly censures the contemptible masculine self-indulgence which thoughtlessly necessitates the abstemiousness she is praising in women. She contributes personal anecdote to the archetype of masculine excess and feminine forbearance, which was prevalent among moralists and preachers as well as in the formal case for women.[96]

Yet, how far were Christine and others shoring up the oppression of women by agreeing to elevate sobriety, along with constancy, as feminine ideals? On the rebound from allegations of appetitive instability, was there not a risk of capitulating to patriarchy's wish for loyally docile women, self-denying and self-policing on behalf of masculine autonomy? Christine circumvents this problem to some extent, I have suggested, by promoting a transsexual ideal of rationality (while implying that men particularly fail in it); but 'sobriety' is more problematic. Its reflex in Chaucer's writing is the contented—because necessary—frugality of the widow who owns the hens in *The Nun's Priest's Tale*, or the voluntary *mesure* of the ruler's daughter Canacee in *The Squire's*

---

[95] 'ipsa quoque natura providit quae maiore scilicet sobrietatis virtute sexum nostrum praemunivit. Constat quippe multo parciore sumptu et alimonia minore feminas quam viros sustentari posse, nec eas tam leviter inebriari physica protestatur. . . . quarum videlicet corda crapula et ebrietate gravari facile non possunt, cum ab illa nos cibi parcitas, ab ista feminei corporis qualitas . . . protegat'; 'Letter of Heloise on Religious Life and Abelard's First Reply', ed. Muckle, 245–6; tr. Radice, Letter 5, 165–6. Heloise bases her argument on the opinion of Macrobius in *Saturnalia* that female humidity and female purgations disperse the 'fumes' of wine. Abelard, repeating her quotations in his reply, agrees that woman's nature is 'stronger as regards wine' though (he cannot resist adding) 'weaker in itself'; tr. Radice, 234–5.

[96] Christine's anecdote is of a man leaving a tavern whom she overheard commenting that he had spent so much there that his wife would probably volunteer to do without wine for the day; ed. Curnow, 655, tr. Richards, 25–6. Cf. *Leësce* on wives drinking water while men booze in taverns (3767–70). A wife is imagined coping with her disgustingly drunken husband Glotoun in *Piers Plowman*; ed. Schmidt (B. V. 337–65), 54–5: the violent abuse of half-starved wives by such husbands was denounced from the pulpit; e.g. in Jacques de Vitry, *Sermones vulgares*, 66 (see Blamires, *Woman Defamed and Woman Defended*, 145).

Tale who would rather not risk a hangover by late-night carousing at her father's feast.[97] Virginia, in *The Physician's Tale*, is credited with *mesure* among her other disciplined virtues (discretion, chastity, humility, abstinence, 'attemperaunce', 'pacience', decorum, constancy, industry, and sobriety, VI. 41–58). Like Canacee she voluntarily ('of hir owene vertu, unconstreyned', 61) eschews the excesses of party-going: but the moot point here is precisely the claim of unconstraint. The encompassing constraint which Virginia unconstrainedly serves is patriarchy, which wants to police the sexuality of wives and daughters by inculcating such respect for feminine *mesure* that women like Virginia will constrain themselves: so that they will themselves subscribe to that model of a wife's behaviour taught by another of Chaucer's women, the paragon Alceste, in *The Prologue to the Legend of Good Women*, a model based on 'the *boundes* that she oghte kepe'.[98] Such a model of 'bounded' feminine moderation seems to confirm Elaine Hansen's perception that 'females, marked by their gender in ways that males in Western culture consequently seem not to be, are kept within marks, limits and boundaries that define and contain their "individuality"'.[99]

Anne Middleton rightly perceives in Virginia a paradoxically active exercise of passive forbearance and spiritual discipline which had a long history in hagiography.[100] That long history is also in part the long history of the case for women, and if the case for feminine resolve and stability, like the case for sobriety, unwittingly colluded with the patriarchal mentality, it gave men plenty to think about along the way. To harp on the courageous loyalty to Christ of his women disciples (we might argue) was covertly or unwittingly to consolidate an androcentric requirement for women to bond firmly to men. But I rather think that it must also

[97] See *Nun's Priest's Tale*, VII. 2821–46; *The Squire's Tale* states that Canacee 'was ful mesurable, as wommen be; . . . | Hir liste nat appalled for to be, | Ne on the morwe unfeestlich for to se' (V. 362–6), which however colours 'innate' moderation with a nuance of concern lest she look unattractive next day.

[98] F-text, 542–6 (my emphasis); but note that it is her consort the God of Love who describes her teaching in these terms. Other examples in Chaucer of feminine virtue as a matter of 'kepyng the boundes' include *Legend of Good Women* (1673), and *Squire's Tale* (V. 571). Jocelyn Wogan-Browne finds this very vocabulary apt for describing Chaucer's Virginia, 'a model virgin . . . living within the enclosure of her own decorum'; 'The Virgin's Tale', 182.

[99] *Chaucer and the Fictions of Gender* (Berkeley and Los Angeles: University of California Press, 1992), 52.

[100] 'The *Physician's Tale* and Love's Martyrs: "Ensamples mo than ten" as a Method in the *Canterbury Tales*', *Chaucer Review*, 8 (1973–4), 9–32 (pp. 16–17).

have shaken, however momentarily, readers' habitual gendering of strength and instability. Not many writers could imagine a position outside patriarchal culture, a position (for example) which might make rigid binaries such as 'stability/instability' seem irrelevant.[101] Certainly, such a perspective is not to be supposed inconceivable in the Middle Ages. The discourse of Heloise, for example, has recently been described as a 'feminine way of speaking' characterized by a flow of interacting passion and thought which contrasts with Abelard's disdain for unrestrained speech and with his commitment to fixed, oppositionally defined concepts.[102] These were nevertheless remote prospects for most medieval defenders of women: to them it seemed that one of their chief tasks was to enter the traditional debate in order to establish that women constituted the stabler sex.

[101] The existence of an *écriture féminine* antithetical to such binaries has been canvassed in French feminist theory: for some discussion, see Moi, *Sexual/Textual Politics*, 102–63.

[102] Andrea Nye, 'A Woman's Thought or a Man's Discipline? The Letters of Abelard and Heloise', *Hypatia*, 7 (1992), 1–22. The difficulty of achieving consensus on such claims can be seen from the fact that Heloise has conversely been thought to exemplify a woman educated by a masculine system so as to 'use and deploy male styles and arguments'; Larrington (ed.), *Women and Writing in Medieval Europe*, 230.

6

Exemplifying Feminine Stability

WHETHER because ideology everywhere required that men's anxieties about women's loyalty to them be allayed despite preconceptions about feminine instability, or whether because society's guilt about endless criticism of women's instability necessitated frequent acts of cultural atonement, it is a fact that defence of feminine resolve—especially in sexual matters—extended massively beyond formal argument into the shaping of narrative or dramatic episodes throughout medieval literature. Medievalists are used to referring to some of these episodes as belonging to the category of 'the calumniated wife'.[1] It will perhaps be both refreshing and instructive to consider narratives of 'calumniation' in the context of the case for women, for a change, rather than in the context of romance or hagiography of which they are normally discussed as an offshoot.

Of course narratives frequently touch in one way or another upon issues identified in the previous chapter. Thus in the eleventh-century Latin romance *Ruodlieb*, there is a spirited allusion to the double sexual standard when Herilis seeks equal terms in her marriage to Ruodlieb's nephew, demanding 'Why should I be more faithful to you than you to me?'[2] The exemplifications I have in mind, however, are designed more substantially and self-consciously than this to correct misogynous attitudes, above all the allegation of weakness or instability. They occur in an early woman writer's plays, in romances, and in an exemplary narrative by Chaucer, and together they confirm that the concern of the formal case with this question was not a cultural sideshow but a matter of continuing urgency throughout the Middle Ages.

---

[1] A classic study is Margaret Schlauch, *Chaucer's Constance and Accused Queens* (New York: New York University Press, 1927).

[2] 'Cur servare fidem tibi debeo, dic, meliorem, | Quam mihi tu debes?' (XIV. 52–80), Peter Dronke, *Women Writers of the Middle Ages: A Critical Study of Texts from Perpetua to Marguerite Porete* (Cambridge: Cambridge University Press, 1984), 92, citing the edition by F. P. Knapp (Stuttgart, 1977). Dronke speculates that the 'rarity and unusually privileged position of educated young women' at this date contribute to the self-assurance in such projections.

Hrotsvitha of Gandersheim, a canoness who wrote Latin poetry and drama in the tenth century, provides a good starting-point. Punning on the meaning of her native name, she styles herself the 'Strong Voice' (*Clamor validus*) of Gandersheim in her introduction to her six quasi-Terentian plays.[3] What she 'strongly voices' is a reaction against Roman comedy's stereotyping of women as (she suggests) merely 'licentious' beings; she aims to assert instead the power of feminine chastity whereby 'womanly frailty' triumphs and 'virile force' is 'laid low'.[4] In one way, this is an instance of the topos of feminine strength in weakness, celebrated by her powerful personal voice. In another way, I wonder whether Hrotsvitha's project is in fact to argue that women can *share* her 'strength of voice' in rejecting misogynous slurs—for it is especially through their *clamor validus* that the women of the plays transcend their alleged *fragilitas* and subdue predatory masculine force or brawn (*robur*).

This strategy is quietly initiated in the first play *Gallicanus*, where the Emperor's daughter Constance resourcefully holds her vow of Christian virginity against pressure to marry. The only 'change' which occurs is the beneficent change subsequently wrought in her suitor.[5] The strategy grows more conspicuous in the *Passio sanctarum Agapis Chioniae et Hirenae*, a virgin-martyr story concerning imperial efforts to enforce conversion and marriage upon three sisters Agape, Chionia, and Hirena.[6] Their

---

[3] 'Ego, Clamor Validus Gandeshemensis' (where *clamor validus* translates Old Saxon 'Hrothsuith'), Preface to the plays, *Hrotsvithae opera*, ed. Helene Homeyer (Munich: Schöningh, 1970), 233. There is an earlier edition of Hrotsvitha's works in *PL* 137: 941–1168. The plays number six (matching the number of Terence's plays) unless one accepts an argument that concluding verses on the Apocalypse constitute another. See Dronke, *Women Writers*, 70 and 60.

[4] 'praesertim cum feminea fragilitas vinceret et virilis robur confusioni subiaceret', ed. Homeyer, 234. For the preface to the plays I use Dronke's translation, *Women Writers*, 69; but for the plays themselves, *The Plays of Hrotsvit of Gandersheim*, tr. Katharina Wilson (New York: Garland, 1989). There is an earlier translation, *The Plays of Roswitha*, tr. Christopher St John, the pseudonym of Cristabel Marshall (London: Chatto & Windus, 1923).

[5] Constantia: 'Haec mutatio dextrae excelsi!' Gallicanus: 'Si in melius mutatus non essem, tuae promissioni assensum non praeberem', *Gallicanus*, I, sc. xiii, ed. Homeyer, 257 (Constance: 'This change must have come from heaven'. Gallicanus: 'Had I not been changed for the better, I would not have given my consent to your vow', tr. Wilson, 26).

[6] In line with Dronke's suggestion (*Women Writers*, 294 n. 11), I restore Hrotsvitha's own titles instead of the androcentric titles—in this case, *Dulcitius*—which have conventionally replaced them.

clear, firm refusal—their *clamor validus*—makes Emperor Diocletian irrationally accuse them of bacchic madness and dismiss as
'brazen speech' Hirena's criticism of pagan gods.[7] To these misogynous imputations of hysteria and foolish garrulity, the play
then adds those of vanity and sexual availability, when the enrap-
tured Governor Dulcitius imagines that either flattery or force
will bring the sisters into his arms despite their gaolers' perception that they are firm (*stabiles*) in faith.[8] In the event his virility is
grotesquely 'laid low' (to recall the wording in Hrotsvitha's Preface) when he tries to grab the sisters in the dark and finds himself
pawing filthy cooking utensils instead, while his intended victims
watch him with comic disbelief through a crack. Is it not a brilliantly suggestive episode? It simultaneously exposes the blind
egotism, the 'bacchic' madness, and the commodifying degrada-
tion of masculine sexual appetite. It underlines the 'filth' of that
appetite while allowing a reversal of masculine voyeurism
whereby the sisterhood beholds and objectifies the spectacle of
masculine depravity (perhaps implying a more general female
amusement at displays of male 'virility').[9] And it enables the
medieval caricature of woman as 'fragile vessel' to be critiqued

[7] Diocletian says of Chionia, 'ista . . . bachatur', and accuses Hirena of
praesumptio verbositatis ('brazen speech') when she argues that a god who is 'up for
sale' in effigy is 'a slave', *Passio . . . Agapis Chioniae et Hirenae* (*Dulcitius*), sc. i, ed.
Homeyer, 269, tr. Wilson, 38–9.

[8] *Passio . . . Agapis Chioniae et Hirenae* (*Dulcitius*), sc. ii; ed. Homeyer, 270, tr.
Wilson, 40–1. Sexualizing clichés recur in the play in scenes vii and x where
Dulcitius and Sisinnius refer to the sisters as 'wanton' girls (*lascivae puellae*); ed.
Homeyer, 273, tr. Wilson, 43–4.

[9] Hrotsvitha did not, of course, invent all this. The 'rape' of the pans (though not
the sisters' beholding of it) is in her source, the *Acta sanctorum*—rehearsed also in
Aldhelm's *De virginitate*, ch. 50, where Dulcitius is described as 'consumed by
blind passion' so that 'carried away by the fury of his insanity, he began like a
madman or a lunatic to embrace blackened pots and cauldrons'; *Aldhelm: The Prose
Works*, tr. Michael Lapidge and Michael Herren (Ipswich: D. S. Brewer, 1979), 117.
A similar version was disseminated in the later Middle Ages in the *Life* of
Anastasia in Jacobus de Voragine's *Legenda aurea*; ed. J. G. T. Graesse (Osnabrück:
Zeller, 1890; repr. 1969), 47–9; and tr. Ryan in *The Golden Legend*, i. 43–4.
Hrotsvitha's probable invention of the sisters' view of this spectacle enables those
who were intended victims to engage consciously in unexpected triumph; their
commentary magnifies the sense of embarrassment, and situates readers/audi-
ence as members of the women's 'team' contemplating the discomfiture of
Dulcitius. It also appropriates for women the functions of the traditionally masculine 'gaze' (whereby the feminine is usually a spectacle of masculinity), discussed
in Luce Irigaray, *Speculum of the Other Woman*, tr. Gillian C. Gill (Ithaca, NY:
Cornell University Press, 1985).

through the inviolability of the cooking pans which Dulcitius tries to rape.[10]

The strong and deflating voice of women which persists through the martyrdom of these sisters is heard again, paradoxically at the very moment of apparent female powerlessness, in the *Resuscitatio Drusianae et Calimachi*.[11] Drusiana, celibate wife of Andronicus, becomes the object of Calimachus' passion. He misconstructs her as an Ovidian coquette whose sharp resistance to his confident charms is surely only for form's sake:

CAL. The reaction which my love elicited in you could very well make you turn red.
DRUS. I feel no reaction except for disgust.
CAL. But you will change your mind, I trust.
DRUS. *I will never change my mind* on this matter.
CAL. Perhaps you will—and for the better.
DRUS. You insane fool, . . . through what insanity extreme do you believe that I would ever yield?[12]

So Calimachus threatens force, and, fearing her powerlessness, Drusiana uses her voice to pray for death (sc. iv). The result is that just as the stupid ugliness of masculine sexual aggression was revealed as madness by being displaced onto substitute objects in the *Passio Agapis Chioniae et Hirenae*, so here it is opened to devastating scrutiny by being again displaced, this time against Drusiana's 'dead' body, after her appeal to God successfully invokes her own death. Calimachus attempts a macabre rape in her tomb (sc. vii). Through God's agency, her voice has nevertheless

[10] That is, Dulcitius mistakes vessels (*vasa*, sc. ii, Homeyer, 270) for women by association with the biblical description of woman as 'the weaker vessel', 1 Pet. 3: 7. Christine de Pizan appears to make this connection in her version of the story, where Dulcitius is said to embrace each of the pots in turn while thinking he is with the girls ('puis l'un, puis l'autre de ses vaissiaulz; et cuidoit estre avec les pucelles'), *Cité*, III. 4. 1, ed. Curnow, 1020, tr. Richards, 247: cf. her earlier reference to God placing the treasure of women's souls in feminine vessels ('en vaissiaulx femenins'), II. 49. 5, ed. Curnow, 900, tr. Richards, 170. At the same time the utensils may be, as Kathryn Gravdal proposes, 'an ingeniously domestic metaphor of the objectification of women'; *Ravishing Maidens*, 31. Further possibilities are that the worship of material objects satirizes pagan idolatry, or, as suggested by Sandro Sticca, that this locus of moral corruption symbolizes hell; 'Hrotswitha's *Dulcitius* and Christian Symbolism', *Mediaeval Studies*, 32 (1970), 108–27.

[11] Hrotsvitha's title is usually reduced to *Calimachus*.

[12] *Resuscitatio* (*Calimachus*), sc. iii; tr. Wilson, 55 (my emphasis). Calimachus' arrogant certainty of Drusiana's *mutability*, and her denial of it, is the crux: Cal.: 'Credo te hanc sententiam mutatum ire'; Drus.: 'Non mutabo, percerte,' ed. Homeyer, 286.

protected her morally by rendering her soul absent from her
lifeless body,[13] after which divine judgement strikes down both
Calimachus and the cynically corrupt tomb guard who has abetted him. There is a pointed symmetry in the way Drusiana exercises her strong performative voice: she who can utter her death
to sustain chastity subsequently proves equally able to utter the
resurrection of the guard (until he damns himself again) later in
the play.

That women's words are *not* (as Ovid claimed) light as leaves,
but hugely powerful is again demonstrated in the *Conversio
Thaidis meretricis*, which concerns the celebrated prostitute Thaïs.[14]
Here, as Thaïs formally renounces the life she has led (sc. iv), she
dismisses all her clamouring male followers, declaring the termi-
nation of her sinning with them and her severance from them.[15] In
the face of her words (accompanied by a ritual burning of the
profits of her trade) the crowd is left to utter a rhetorical *tour de
force* contrasting the former Thaïs with the present Thaïs.[16] It is the
one change which Hrotsvitha does commend in a woman or
man—a change (like that of the commander Gallicanus earlier) to
embrace continence.

It would be reductive, however, to confine Hrotsvitha's
profeminine inclinations to the presentation of individual female
stabilitas. She clearly has broader objections to dismissive misogynous stereotyping, the mentality which in the final play prompts

[13] There is an interesting connection with something asserted by Hrotsvitha's
Hirena—that where the soul does not consent there can be no guilt; *Passio
sanctarum virginum . . . (Dulcitius)*, sc. xii, ed. Homeyer, 275, tr. Wilson, 46.
Hirena's point draws upon Augustine, *City of God*, I. 16, but Drusiana's more
drastic solution is perhaps intended to obviate Augustine's ignorant (but influential) rider that a raped woman feels shame because the act 'could not have taken
place without some physical pleasure'; tr. Henry Bettenson (Harmondsworth:
Penguin, 1984), 26. Gravdal suggests that the prospective 'rape' of a lifeless
woman implicitly 'refutes the axiomatic notion that it is women who tempt men
and provoke male lust'; *Ravishing Maidens*, 29.
[14] Usual modern title, *Pafnutius*.
[15] 'Dimittite; . . . finis instat peccandi tempusque nostri discidii'; *Conversio
Thaidis (Pafnutius)*, ed. Homeyer, 340, tr. Wilson, 110.
[16] *Conversio Thaidis (Pafnutius)*, sc. iv, ed. Homeyer, 340–1, tr. Wilson, 110–11.
Hrotsvitha has orchestrated the burning scene, which is more briefly recounted in
most versions of the narrative: e.g. *The Golden Legend*, ii, tr. Ryan, 234–5: or in the
13th-cent. Old French *Thais 'B'*, *The Lady as Saint: A Collection of French Hagiographic
Romances of the Thirteenth Century*, tr. Brigitte Cazelles (Philadelphia: University of
Pennsylvania Press, 1991), 302. See further Ruth Mazo Karras, 'Holy Harlots:
Prostitute Saints in Medieval Legend', *Journal of the History of Sexuality*, 1 (1990), 3–
32 (pp. 10–14).

an emperor to question how a handful of Christian women (Sapientia and her three daughters) could 'present a danger for the state', and which prompts his officer's disparaging cliché, 'the female sex's fragility makes it prone to yield to flattery'.[17] The encompassing sense of totalizing patriarchal disdain not only moves Hrotsvitha to champion individual women's resolve and to castigate masculinity for displaying capricious irascibility, manic violence, and uncontrollable bodily urges:[18] it also moves her to adopt a distinctive emphasis on female solidarity. The last play brings to a crescendo the sequence's unusual emphasis on the *communal* 'voice' of women against oppressors.[19] Here the sisterhood of the three girls is explicitly underlined by the last of them to be martyred,[20] but this sisterhood is then itself absorbed into a wider community of women, as an unspecified number of 'Matrons' join Sapientia to mourn the martyred girls (sc. viii–ix).[21] It has been quite persuasively suggested that Hrotsvitha's chief aim is to display female strength in three traditional categories

[17] 'Numquid tantillarum adventus muliercularum aliquid rei publicae adducere poterit detrimentum?'; and 'fragilitas sexus feminei facilius potest blandimentis molliri': *Passio sanctarum virginum Fidei Spei et Karitatis* (usually entitled *Sapientia*), sc. i and iii; ed. Homeyer, 358–9, tr. Wilson, 125 and 128.

[18] The impression of casual male sexual belligerence could be related, as Gravdal has speculated, to the persistence of rapacious practices of pursuit and abduction of women which had been rather characteristic of the 9th cent.; *Ravishing Maidens*, 35. A reservation about the antimasculine stance of Hrotsvitha's plays would be that when they are compared with her preceding series of legends, an intricate patterning can be detected whereby she 'interchanges and carefully balances depictions of different aspects of the moral ideal between male and female protagonists. . . . What constitutes male heroism, Hrotsvit seems to suggest, is what constitutes female heroism as well'; Katharina M. Wilson, *Hrotsvit of Gandersheim: The Ethics of Authorial Stance* (Leiden: Brill, 1988), 26.

[19] Solidarity among women is not a systematic presence in the plays, but it is instigated in Constance's affinity with the two daughters of her suitor in the first, emphasized in the trio of sisters in the second, and paramount in the widened circle of women in the sixth.

[20] Karitas: 'I am born of the same parents as my sisters, imbued by the same sacraments, strengthened by the same firmness of faith. Know, therefore, that we are one and the same in what we want, what we feel and what we think'; *Passio sanctarum virginum Fidei Spei et Karitatis* (*Sapientia*), sc. v, ed. Homeyer, 371, tr. Wilson, 144.

[21] *Passio . . . Fidei Spei et Karitatis* (*Sapientia*), sc. viii and ix. Although Sapientia then dismisses the Matrons to pray alone, she does so partly out of fellow-feeling lest they fatigue themselves further on her account; ed. Homeyer, 374, tr. Wilson, 146–7. The play opens with a complementary suggestion of 'matronly' solidarity in that Antiochus reports that on account of the missionary activities of the women, 'our wives despise us so that they refuse to eat with us, or even more to sleep with us', sc. i, ed. Homeyer, 358, tr. Wilson, 126.

(virgin, wife, prostitute),[22] but I would argue that configurations of female solidarity along with confident assertions of feminine *stabilitas* constitute the major feature of Hrotsvitha's profeminism[23] and perhaps inscribe in the process an ideal of feminine bonding, sceptical of men, appropriate to a female community such as that at Gandersheim.

Hrotsvitha's importance for this chapter is not that she is a woman writer with profeminine instincts, but that her writing explicitly opposes inherited allegations about 'womanly weakness',[24] and therefore participates—not just adventitiously—in the case for women. The same criterion justifies, I believe, a brief look at the central episode in Chrétien de Troyes's romance of *Yvain*, written towards the end of the twelfth century.

Opinion on Chrétien's representation of women in *Yvain* has been nudged (if somewhat equivocally) in a negative direction by the suggestion that the text explores and yet contributes to both the 'mystification' of women's place, and women's underlying status as objects of exchange, in courtly society.[25] While agreeing that the narrator's ambiguity partially 'resists our efforts to . . . assess his degree of "misogyny" or "feminism"',[26] I would like to argue that misogyny is calculatedly set up in *Yvain* (very much as in Hrotsvitha's plays) precisely in order that it may be challenged; the strategy anticipates the comment from *Leësce* already mentioned, 'You claim women are not stable but fickle: God knows, it's the other way round.'

When Yvain kills Esclados, keeper of the fountain of Brocéliande, in a bloody combat then finds himself hiding in his dead opponent's castle, he is suddenly seized with love of Esclados's widow Laudine. In the unfolding of the unlikely 'courtship' which follows, Chrétien teases us with an elaborate smokescreen of misogynous proverbs and reminiscences. For instance, Yvain is catapulted into love by secretly beholding

[22] Frankforter, 'Hroswitha of Gandersheim', 295–314; and id., 'Sexism and the Search for the Thematic Structure of the Plays of Hroswitha of Gandersheim', *International Journal of Women's Studies*, 2 (1979), 221–32.

[23] This *stabilitas* is so serene as to imply, as Frankforter suggests, that lust is 'a characteristically male problem', 'Hroswitha of Gandersheim', 313. Hrotsvitha's profeminism prioritizes female will, not female desire.

[24] Dronke argues brilliantly that conventional references to women's weakness in her prefaces are self-aware and often comically nuanced, 'in such a way as to foil expectations and paradoxically show women's strength'; *Women Writers*, 73.

[25] Krueger, *Women Readers and the Ideology of Gender*, 39 ff.

[26] Ibid. 50.

Laudine at the funeral of her husband. (Ovid had outrageously remarked that funerals were apt occasions for enticing a new husband.[27]) Then, Laudine, crazed with grief, protests vehemently in monologue that the equal of her dead husband cannot be found and curses his killer.[28] (Her extravagant gestures may, if we choose, be interpretable as insincere.) Then, Yvain himself judges that his only hope of gaining her love is that since 'a woman has more than a thousand fancies', Laudine's mood must surely 'change'.[29] Then again, the very idea of a possible relationship developing on the heels of the burial of the corpse positively bristles with recollection of sarcastic medieval anecdotes about the fickleness of widows (especially the tombside sexual indecorum of the 'Widow of Ephesus').[30] Then too, the narrator glibly joins in the growing campaign of suspicion, insinuating that Laudine mounts a stereotypically feminine show of reluctance to accept the plans initiated by Yvain's helper Lunete—plans which she really welcomes—for a remarriage that will provide a new keeper of the fountain.[31] The narrator also gleefully endorses Yvain's hunch about her disposition to 'change'.[32] So, the formal sentimentality of Yvain's untimely love competes with a confusing odour of misogyny, to the extent that when, prompted by Lunete, Laudine argues herself into precipitous marriage with him ('love' making a very late entrance into her own calcu-

---

[27] 'Often a husband is sought for at a husband's funeral; it is becoming to go with dishevelled hair, and to mourn without restraint'; Ars amatoria, III. 431–2, tr. Mozley, 148–9; this allusion is mentioned by Hunt, Chrétien de Troyes: 'Yvain', 81. Chrétien's debt to the Ars is discussed in Jean Frappier, Étude sur 'Yvain' ou 'Le Chevalier au lion' de Chrétien de Troyes (Paris: Société d'Édition d'Enseignement Supérieur, 1969), 72–6.

[28] 1206–42: line numbering and Old French quotations are from The Knight with the Lion, or Yvain, ed. and tr. William W. Kibler (New York: Garland, 1985). But I have preferred the more spirited translation in Chrétien de Troyes: Arthurian Romances, tr. D. D. R. Owen (London: Dent, 1987); here, p. 297.

[29] 'fame a plus de cent corages. | Celui corage qu'ele a ore, | espoir, changera ele ancore' (1440–42); tr. Owen, 300.

[30] For the version of this story (known from the time of Petronius) in Le Fèvre, see Blamires, Woman Defamed and Woman Defended, 185–6; and for the axiom closely following, 'As soon as her husband is in his coffin, a wife's only thought day and night is to catch another husband,' see 187. Hunt notes such reminiscences in Chrétien de Troyes: 'Yvain', 53–7.

[31] Laudine 'had in her an irrational streak that other ladies have and almost all show by . . . rejecting what they really want', tr. Owen, 303; 'mes une folie a en soi | que les autres fames i ont: | . . . et ce qu'eles voelent refusent' (1644–8); a point heavily underlined again at 2111–16.

[32] 'Ez vos ja la dame changiee' (1753); 'See now how the lady has changed already', tr. Owen, 304 (when Laudine begins to agree to an interview with Yvain).

lations at 2143 ff.), the narrator only needs to provide a brusque summary to take what has happened to the very brink of fabliau: 'now my lord Yvain is master, and the dead man is completely forgotten. His slayer is married to his wife, and they sleep together.'[33]

We have been manipulated to think, as Hunt declares, that 'the foundations of this union are shaky',[34] but the rhetoric has had the effect of seeming to problematize Laudine while leaving the strength of Yvain's own commitment largely unquestioned.[35] The 'textual imbalance' noted by Krueger, which disproportionately explores Yvain's amorous feelings but gives little space to Laudine's, is surely explicable primarily as a strategy intended to leave a gap of unknowability about her, into which the misogynous implication can drift.[36]

Interestingly the defined period of leave which Laudine now grants Yvain because he feels obliged to go tourneying with Gawain is described by Hunt as 'a clear testing of the hero's maturity and stability'.[37] *Stabilitas* is in my view precisely the point. We have been inveigled by Chrétien's foxy narration into suspecting *instabilitas* in Laudine, while remaining half-aware that this was an authorial plot against her, and us. But now, when she spells out that her love (which conquered initial hate) will indeed change to hate if Yvain does not return as agreed, we realize that while from his point of view her love has been delivered to him 'on a plate', from her point of view his sincerity remains altogether to be seen. There proves to be no strength in it. Under the influence of masculine camaraderie he drifts thoughtlessly past the deadline once he is away, thus epitomizing the kind of casual disrespect for women which has already contaminated our response (and momentarily his) to the process of her acceptance of him. But instability is now suddenly and crushingly ascribed to the male, and Laudine bitterly repudiates Yvain. Readers sometimes wonder why he has to undergo after this an

---

[33] 'or est mes sire Yvains sire, | et li morz est toz oblïez; | cil qui l'ocist est marïez: | sa famë a et ensanble gisent' (2168–71); tr. Owen, 310.

[34] Hunt, *Chrétien de Troyes: 'Yvain'*, 59.

[35] What we chiefly question in Yvain during the episode is his obsession with acquiring proof of his brutal conquest of Esclados, to satisfy Arthurian society of his success. His replacement of Esclados as husband and hence fountain keeper will, of course, provide unassailable proof.

[36] *Women Readers and the Ideology of Gender*, 45.

[37] Hunt, *Chrétien de Troyes: 'Yvain'*, 62.

interminably long process of rehabilitation, why Laudine's alienation remains so complete. The answer is that logic dictates both, since his own reliability now needs to be demonstrated from scratch, while the lasting certainty of her alienation is crucial in disproving the myth of feminine unreliability ('a woman has more than a thousand fancies') which he himself once frivolously accepted. Chrétien's romance is actually austerely profeminine just where 'romantic' readerly instincts, willing Laudine to soften towards 'her' knight, would destroy the profeminine point. That she can only take Yvain back when Lunete tricks her into committing herself to do so on oath is inexorably the logic of a text which pretends to accept, only to repudiate utterly, traditional gendering of changeability as feminine.[38]

Although there are many other narratives in which calumniated women vindicate themselves, *Yvain* appears to me rather special in the proliferation of its 'planted' generalizing misogynous clichés and in the corresponding impression that Laudine vindicates more than just herself when she disproves them. I would like to argue that, among Middle English romances, *The Erle of Tolous* offers a similarly calculated development of defensive strategies around the calumniation topos. The predictably masculine title of this romance[39] conceals the fact that this narrative tells primarily (as its first stanza states) 'how a lady was greatly wronged, and how she recovered from her misery'.[40] The lady is the Empress of Almayn, commended by the writer for her bodily 'truth' (43-4), whom we first encounter dissociating herself from her husband's unjust and futile warfare against the Earl of Toulouse. The Earl meanwhile becomes enamoured of her upon hearing a lyrical description of her by a captured knight, Trylabas. Trylabas promises to give the Earl a 'sight' of the Empress in

---

[38] Since there is a last-minute reassurance that Yvain is finally 'loved and cherished' by her (6810-1; tr. Owen, 373), one can argue cynically that the trick is a 'face-saving measure' necessary because 'Laudine does love Yvain, but does not wish to be seen to "change" to loving him'; Hunt, *Chrétien de Troyes: 'Yvain'*, 82. On the other hand, the 'trick' obliges Laudine, on oath, to be reconciled with him, so the imperative of *stabilitas* (standing by her word) rather than face-saving should probably be regarded as paramount.

[39] Following the lead of late medieval scribes: cf. the title, 'Here foloweth the Erle of Tolous' in the folio reproduced in *The Breton Lays in Middle English*, ed. Thomas C. Rumble (Detroit: Wayne State University Press, 1965), facing p. 135.

[40] 'How a lady had grete myschefe, | And how sche covyrd of hur grefe' (10-11). All references are to the edition in *Of Love and Chivalry: An Anthology of Middle English Romance*, ed. Jennifer Fellows (London: Dent, 1993), 231-65.

return for his own freedom (205–22), and the Empress dutifully undertakes this obligation despite the risk of compromising herself, when the Earl arrives in her locality disguised as a hermit. Decorously flanked by escorts she 'shows' herself to the Earl (turning round twice for a good inspection) in a chapel (320–60). Does the author select this venue in order to cleanse the encounter of sensual nuance, *or* on the contrary because chapels had a reputation as socializing places, as hotbeds of flirtation even?[41] Uncertainties accumulate. We are told that the Empress stood still and openly showed her face 'for love of that knight' (336)—a Middle English construction tantalizingly equivocal in the circumstances, since it can mean 'because of [her] love of the knight' or 'because of the knight's love [of her]'. Yet more rashly, she rewards the disguised Earl's request for alms with a ring, which he necessarily regards as a latent token of her 'grace' (376–405).

The point of all this, produced entirely by understatement, is surely not to illustrate 'the grave and beautiful dignity' with which she requites the Earl's 'reckless gallantry',[42] but on the contrary to call into question the Empress's reliability. It situates her within an aura of readerly suspicion, perhaps even more insidious than in Laudine's case because unspoken. What is clever about the romance is that it then proceeds to develop the logical *effects* of such suspicion when two knights assigned to protect her hatch a plot to have sex with her one after another.[43] In the face of their pseudo-courtly approaches (accompanied by solemn pleas that she should promise not to 'betray' them) the Empress's marital loyalty as well as her willingness to honour her oath of silence becomes crystal clear; her reaction, 'What woman holdyst thou me?' (648), rebukes the sceptical reader as much as her guards. So by the time the corrupt guards decide to dispose of her by having her tried for alleged adultery with a squire, their misogynous self-justification—'a woman's tongue can't be trusted' (676)—appears as sheer malicious prejudice.

[41] Flirtation within a religious context is intimated in texts as various as Boccaccio, *The Elegy of Lady Fiammetta*, ed. and tr. Mariangela Causa-Steindler and Thomas Mauch (Chicago: University of Chicago Press, 1990), 7–10; Gower, *Confessio Amantis*, ed. Macaulay, V. 7032–90, and *Sir Gawain and the Green Knight*, ed. Andrew and Waldron, *Poems of the Pearl Manuscript*, 930–76.

[42] Laura A. Hibbard, *Mediaeval Romance in England* (Oxford: Oxford University Press, 1924), 42.

[43] The two knights assigned by the emperor are mentioned at 478–83: they appear to be distinct from the two 'earls' who attend her in the chapel at 325.

I think that the text's readers, meanwhile, have been brought through a learning curve from qualms about the Empress to indignation against the misogyny which debases the guards' attitude to her and is thence nearly responsible for her death, but which, in retrospect, has also demeaned our attitude to her during the chapel episode. Thus *The Erle of Tolous* repudiates slick judgements about feminine 'unreliability', yet demonstrates how easily they may arise—even in its audience.[44] And, if there is the degree of self-consciousness about the subject here which I am detecting, then that especially justifies the choice of *The Erle* for the present discussion, as distinct from other English romances which tackle the problem of calumniation.[45] Few other romances, moreover, confirm so intensely the ruthless scrutiny of female behaviour (since we are invited to watch her every move in the chapel) which medieval critics of the double sexual standard observed.

Many other absorbing examples beckon, particularly Jean Renart's thirteenth-century *Roman de la Rose* or *Guillaume de Dole*, which incorporates a 'case for a woman' which is incipiently a case for women. Here, the heroine Liénor resourcefully pursues her own cause in public against a seneschal who falsely claims to have had sex with her.[46] However, narrative writers cultivated most of all a defence of women's reliability which was ostensibly less threatening to masculinity; a defence whereby the allegation of changeability was rebutted through sheer demonstration of feminine steadfastness. I think it may be helpful in concluding this chapter to situate Chaucer's *Clerk's Tale* within the medieval debate about women's *instabilitas*, since commentary on the tale tends to define its focus in terms of patience or obedi-

[44] They have arisen in the Earl, too. That is why he has to undergo a separate education, checking with her confessor that the incriminating ring that she gave him was really an aberration before he will save her from her accusers.

[45] e.g. *Octavian* and *Emaré*, in *Six Middle English Romances*, ed. Maldwyn Mills (London: Dent, 1973), 75–124 and 46–74, and *Syr Tryamowre*, in *Of Love and Chivalry*, ed. Fellows, 147–98.

[46] *Le Roman de la Rose ou de Guillaume de Dole*, ed. Félix Lecoy (Paris: Champion, 1979); Jean Renart, *The Romance of the Rose or Guillaume de Dole*, tr. Patricia Terry and Nancy Vine Durling (Philadelphia: University of Pennsylvania Press, 1993). For misogynous generalization, see 3826–7, where Liénor's nephew comments, 'Femes getent adès dou mains | Por fere honte a lor amis' ('Women will always play fast and loose and dishonor their friends', tr. Terry and Durling, 70). Krueger argues cogently that although there is an exploration of subversive power in Liénor, she is ultimately 'reinscribed as a sign of femininity' by the clerkly narrator, *Women Readers and the Ideology of Gender*, 143–55 (pp. 152–3).

ence,[47] whereas it is against the probability of *change* that the tale's peasant heroine Griselda is chiefly measured.[48] The events of the tale depend crucially upon the oath she takes as the condition of her marriage to Marquis Walter, never willingly to disobey him (IV. 362–4). As a narrative about a woman who refuses to change her mind, and 'repeatedly asserts her commitment to her oath' in the face of huge provocations,[49] the tale is closer to the core of the medieval case for women than some readers might imagine. Just as Laudine's persisting alienation from her husband (which upsets readers of *Yvain*) is necessary to establish that she, a woman, stands staunchly by her formal repudiation of Yvain when he fails her, so Griselda's unshakeability in keeping her vow (even more upsetting in some of its consequences) is necessary to articulate feminine reliability in *The Clerk's Tale*.

One clue to this articulation is the tale's identification of the inadequacies which lead the 'stormy' people of Saluzzo to welcome Marquis Walter's remarriage, after his tests of Griselda have culminated in the strategy of subjecting her to a public ordeal of divorce. The stormy people are chastised by reliable or *sadde* citizens (IV. 1002), in an ostentatious rhetorical catalogue of expressions denoting fickleness, as *unsad, untrewe, chaungynge, delitynge in . . . newe*, without judgement and of poor *constance* (IV. 995–1001). As noted by Derek Brewer, the interest of the word *sad*, which does not mean 'sorrowful', is multiplied by the fact that it

[47] These emphases appear as early as 1875 in remarks by J. W. Hales that 'the patience of Griselda is the one theme of the tale' and that Griselda is 'wifely obedience itself'; quoted in Charlotte C. Morse, 'Critical Approaches to the *Clerk's Tale*', in *Chaucer's Religious Tales*, ed. C. David Benson and Elizabeth Robertson (Cambridge: D. S. Brewer, 1990), 71–83 (p. 73). Barbara Newman describes the Griselda story as 'framed exclusively as a test of female obedience'; ' "Crueel Corage": Child Sacrifice and the Maternal Martyr in Hagiography and Romance', in *From Virile Woman to Woman Christ*, 74–107 (p. 97). Support for patience as the defining theme can be derived from the first line of the tale's *Envoy*, 'Grisilde is deed, and eke hire pacience' (IV. 1177). See also John P. McCall, 'The *Clerk's Tale* and the Theme of Obedience', *Modern Language Quarterly*, 27 (1966), 260–9. More recently 'silence' has been offered as a defining concept: Hansen, *Chaucer and the Fictions of Gender*, ch. 7, 'The Powers of Silence'.

[48] Christine de Pizan also interprets the story precisely in this way, since she gives it pride of place as the first demonstration that women are *not* changeable as men allege: the crux of Christine's version is the *grant fermeté, force et constance* of Gliselidis; *Cité*, II. 50. 3, ed. Curnow, 908, tr. Richards, 175.

[49] Morse, 'Critical Approaches', 78. Mary Carruthers characterizes her as 'true to her word, no matter what the provocation', but defines this virtue as 'integrity', which misses the polemical edge in Griselda's steadfastness; 'The Lady, the Swineherd, and Chaucer's Clerk', *Chaucer Review*, 17 (1983), 221–34 (p. 230).

is one of the first adjectives used to describe Griselda,[50] and even more by the fact that her *sadnesse* is specifically what the Clerk says the Marquis sets out to 'knowe' when he begins to test her after they marry and have a daughter.[51] Brewer is concerned to establish the lateral range of nuance in the concept *sadnesse*, but here is his summary of its meaning:

Chaucer uses *sad* to express *constancy*, of which the sharpest and most interesting kind, for him, is constancy of spirit in adversity, a refusal to be broken down by suffering. It is primarily, and paradoxically, an *anti-expressive* word, or rather, perhaps, an expressive word used to signify the absence of the expression of feeling. . . . The story of Griselda is designed to recommend a heroic Christian stoicism which sacrifices self and personal feelings to steadfast commitment to principle.[52]

Not much of this summary, except 'constancy' and 'steadfast commitment', engages precisely with the priorities which I detect in the word. Walter does not want to *know* Griselda's spirit in adversity exactly, nor her resistance to suffering exactly, nor really her absence of feeling, nor even her steadfast commitment 'to principle'—except in so far as the 'principle' is to sustain steadfastly her oath of obedience.

What Walter wants to know, what he tests, is the unchangeability of Griselda's mind towards him. When he requests her assent to the removal of their first child, she confirms that nothing pleasing to him will displease, and hence *change* her:

> This wyl is in myn herte, and ay shal be;
> No lengthe of tyme or deeth may this deface,
> Ne chaunge my corage to another place. (IV. 509–11)

At the removal of the child Griselda remains 'sad stidefast'. Afterwards, Walter approaches Griselda, all agog to check the result of his experiment—whether by her 'cheere' or by her words he might detect that 'she | Were *chaunged*', but only to find her 'evere in oon ylike sad' (IV. 598–602, where the last expression is a tautology meaning 'constantly constantly constantly constant').

---

[50] 'in the brest of hire virginitee | Ther was enclosed rype and sad corage' (IV. 219–20). See Derek Brewer, 'Some Metonymic Relationships in Chaucer's Poetry' (first published in *Poetica*, 1 (1974), 1–20), reprinted in his *Chaucer: The Poet as Storyteller* (London: Macmillan, 1984), 37–53 (esp. pp. 41–9). There is further subtle analysis of *sadnesse* in Jill Mann, 'Satisfaction and Payment in Middle English Literature', *Studies in the Age of Chaucer*, 5 (1983), 17–48.

[51] 'This markys in his herte longeth so | To tempte his wyf, hir sadnesse for to knowe' (IV. 451–2).

[52] Brewer, 'Metonymic Relationships', 42.

When he proceeds to propose the removal of their second child, it is 'the constance of his wyf' (668) in assenting to his will which strikes Walter, to the extent that he drops his gaze in wonderment (668–70). David Wallace ponders the dropped gaze: 'this sight, something he has seen all along, suddenly becomes unbearable. Perhaps he has seen, in Griselde's "constance", a mystery that he cannot fathom or possess'.[53] The mystery, actually, is the *unexpectedness* of Griselda's unchangedness, baffling to Walter in such circumstances given the tradition of womanly *infirmitas*, yet also, as the next lines reveal, so gratifying to him that if he is to act out the scene, he must not disclose his own mixed emotions by looking her in the eye.[54]

Again, during the period of post-test observation to determine whether Griselda is 'changed of corage' towards him Walter can detect no 'variance' (IV. 709–10), and finds her more rather than less 'trewe' in her love. The ultimate test of divorce follows, its objective being defined as achieving full experiential knowledge about the continuing level of her steadfastness.[55] Steadfastness, in fact, becomes the keyword in the cessation of Walter's campaign, because when he beholds her 'continuynge' in her patient, unresentful, wall-like, 'sad' constancy, he is moved to compassion for her 'wyfly stedfastnesse' (IV. 1044–50). He uses the same word when he announces the successful achievement of his objective (previously identified, we noted, as knowledge of her *sadnesse*): 'Now knowe I, dere wyf, thy stedfastnesse' (IV. 1056).

In isolating the paramount exemplary importance of steadfastness (*firmitas*) in the tale, I think something else that we can resolve is what is meant by a crucial-seeming concluding statement where the Marquis attempts to justify his actions. These actions have been committed, he insists, not out of malice but 'for t'assaye in thee [Griselda] thy wommanheede' (IV. 1075). Womanhood remains unexplained here and seems at first sight peculiar.

[53] ' "Whan She Translated Was": A Chaucerian Critique of the Petrarchan Academy', in Lee Patterson (ed.), *Literary Practice and Social Change in Britain, 1380–1530* (Berkeley and Los Angeles: University of California Press, 1990), 156–215 (p. 203).
[54] 'And forth he goth with drery contenance, | But to his herte it was ful greet plesance' (IV. 671–2). The unchangeability of Griselda's assent has been penetratingly analysed by Linda Georgianna, though in identifying it as a 'suprarational' religious mystery Georgianna departs from the gender implications which I pursue here; 'The Clerk's Tale and the Grammar of Assent', *Speculum*, 70 (1995), 793–821 (pp. 808–9).
[55] 'Fully to han experience and loore | If that she were as stidefast as bifoore' (IV. 788–9).

In conventional Middle English, a test of someone's *manhode* would signify a test of his courage.[56] There was no broadly agreed complementary significance for *wommanheede*. However, from a question asked at 698–9, about what more a stern husband could do 'to preeve hir wyfhod and hir stedefastnesse', it seems that in *The Clerk's Tale* Griselda's 'wifehood' and her 'steadfastness' are symbiotic: one might conjecture that her womanhood and her steadfastness are similarly meant to be symbiotic in this tale. That is to say, in 'assaying' (investigating the quality of) Griselda's womanhood, Walter is investigating the degree of *stabilitas* in her, he is determining the level of unchangeability in her because this was the supreme criterion for assessing women in a culture obsessed with feminine 'weakness'.[57]

The Clerk concludes with an often-quoted disclaimer:

> This storie is seyd nat for that wyves sholde
> Folwen Grisilde as in humylitee,
> For it were inportable, though they wolde,
> But for that every wight, in his degree,
> Sholde be constant in adversitee
> As was Grisilde . . . (VI. 1142–47)

We need to be rather careful about the syntax. It is not quite correct to state that 'Chaucer's moral conclusion literally denies that Griselda is an example for wives while asserting that she is an

---

[56] See Blamires, 'Chaucer's Revaluation of Chivalric Honor', 245–69.

[57] Cf. Hoccleve, 'O yee that seyn wommen be variant, | And can nat sad ben if they been assaillid: | . . . of the soothe foule yee han faillid; | Constance is unto wommanhode entaillid', *Jereslaus's Wife*, 484–8, in *Hoccleve's Works: The Minor Poems*, ed. F. J. Furnivall and I. Gollancz, EETS ES 61, 73 (London: Oxford University Press, 1937 and 1925; repr. as 1 vol. 1970). This reading could also be corroborated by one of the manuscript variants for *Erle of Tolous*, 578 (ed. Fellows): the guard's excuse for having made advances to the Empress runs 'Y dud nothyng but yow to assay'; but one late MS reads, 'It was to prove your woman hode', ed. Rumble, 155 n. 156. Other occurrences of *wommanhede* in Chaucer are often vague; e.g. *Clerk's Tale*, IV. 239; *Legend of Good Women*, 1041; *Troilus and Criseyde*, III. 1302. In *Knight's Tale*, I. 1748–9, Ypolita 'for verray wommanhede | Gan for to wepe', which presumably implies that womanhood ('having the qualities proper to a woman' in the *Riverside* gloss!) here connotes compassion. In *Anelida* (299–300), Anelida envisages *wommanhede* as something (i.e. feminine 'passivity'?) that she would transgress if she were to beg Arcite's love. Chaucer's use of the word can be nuanced according to context as I believe is the case in *The Clerk's Tale*, but is often quite impressionistic. There is interesting discussion of *wommanly* and *wommanysshe*, but not *wommanhede*, in John Fyler, 'Man, Men, and Women in Chaucer's Poetry', in Robert R. Edwards and Stephen Spector (eds.), *The Olde Daunce: Love, Friendship, Sex, and Marriage in the Medieval World* (Albany: State University of New York Press, 1991), 154–76.

example for all men in their relationship to God.'[58] More accurately, wives are not to emulate Griselda *as in her humility*, that is 'so far as her humility is concerned' (because it would be unbearable), but wives, and every person, *are* to emulate her constancy. I do not think there is any doubt that the Clerk is using Griselda to promote the case for women on the basis with which we are now familiar. The level of generalization is paradoxically confirmed just when he begins to climb down from his profeminine perch, in accordance with a game of reversal which Chaucer habitually plays on the 'woman question',[59] speculating that nowadays only two or three women per town would prove under 'assay' to be such pure gold as Griselda, for most are brittle alloy which would break rather than bend. In addition to demonstrating the universalizing intention of the tale,[60] this metaphor clarifies the oxymoronic quality of the steadfastness which defines Griselda's position, which is a *pliable* steadfastness. Paradoxically, she vows to show firmness by resolutely bending to another's will, and this is the provocative heart of the tale's fascination. This is why obedience and patience, which I have mainly elided from my account, are of course also crucial components. The firm pliancy of Griselda's gold is matched by the doublet in lines IV. 936–7 which praises women for truth (firm) and humility (pliant), and again by the doublet in IV. 1053, where Walter pairs Griselda's *feith* with her *benygnytee*. But the overriding factor is surely womanly truth, faith, steadfastness.

And finally, as much as Griselda possesses steadfastness, her husband (in conformity with the antimasculine underside of these profeminine discourses) is, for most of the narrative, a mass of whim and inconsistency. He is convinced of peasant virtue yet cannot believe it. He marries then apparently divorces. His face says one thing, his heart another. As Mary Carruthers has emphasized, he is introduced as a person preoccupied with the gratification of his own will: 'on his lust present was al his thoght' (IV. 80).

---

[58] Morse, 'Critical Approaches', 71.

[59] Discussed further in Ch. 8 below.

[60] Although Anne Laskaya finds here proof that the Clerk 'interprets Griselde as a rare and particular kind of female, not universal', and that 'she is used to slap women in the face' because 'none of them . . . are anything like her', *Chaucer's Approach to Gender in the 'Canterbury Tales'* (Cambridge: D. S. Brewer, 1995), 115–16, I see a universalizing direction consolidated in this passage because it obliges us to consider women as a broad category: besides, the tale's case for feminine stability is arguably assured more than it is damaged by an admission that few women would pursue steadfastness to such lengths as Griselda.

He is a creature of what Chaucer would call 'newefangelnesse' in his sudden tests of his wife, and the yawning gap between his original demeanour and that which he later shows Griselda draws reproach even from her, in words which, as Carruthers puts it, 'sharply contrast Griselda's constancy of spirit with Walter's inconstancy of appearance and behavior'.[61] Carruthers interprets Walter's whims as a 'lack of steadfastness' associable with the degeneracy of the world mentioned in a philosophical poem by Chaucer of that name.[62] I agree very much with her description in terms of lack of steadfastness, but less with the philosophical pedigree proposed, for I believe that in the context of the *Clerk's Tale* personal gratification of will becomes a matter of gender polemic, not of philosophy: it strongly implies what misogyny construed as a feminine yielding to the capricious dictates of the sensual will. The anti-misogynistic stance of the narrative therefore includes a counter-attack which taints Walter with the very shortcomings which he so cruelly seeks to find in his wife.

The *Clerk's Tale* belongs in the present book if, as I have argued, it both prioritizes unchangeability in a woman and polemically claims that quality as essentially feminine. I leave it to readers to test other medieval narratives with which they are familiar against these criteria. Such narratives would in a sense be 'exemplary' profeminine narratives: that is, they would function in medieval terms like *exempla*. So there is overlap between the present chapter and the next, in which profeminine *exempla* commonly offered in the case for women are discussed. But there is a difference. The 'exemplary' element in the narratives, or episodes in narratives, studied in this chapter is generally disclosed during the process of reading. The *exempla* we are about to study are more like pendants to profeminine argument, though as will be shown, these 'pendants' often have an independent existence too, and are not easily secured on behalf of patriarchy.

---

[61] Carruthers, 'The Lady, The Swineherd, and Chaucer's Clerk', 224, 226, 228: cf. 'O goode God! how gentil and how kynde | Ye semed by youre speche and youre visage | The day that maked was oure mariage!' (IV. 852–4).

[62] 'The Lady, The Swineherd, and Chaucer's Clerk', 226, quoting *Lak of Stedfastnesse*, 1–7.

7

Profeminine Role-Models

THE medieval case for women invoked a big cast of foremothers.[1] There was a core of Old Testament favourites (especially Deborah, Judith, Esther). In the New Testament, besides the unimpeachable Virgin Mary, were the women followers of Christ (Mary Magdalene in particular) and others with strong profeminine potential including the Samaritan woman whom Christ met at the well, a Canaanite woman who engaged him sharply in dialogue (but how interesting that both of these are denied a *name* in the Gospels!), and missionary women such as Phoebe, mentioned by St Paul.[2] Classical tradition supplied prophetesses (notably the Sibyls); independent Amazons; an abundance of staunch wives (Penelope, Lucretia, etc.); and the generous, loyal women whom Ovid made famous in his *Heroides* for being let down by unreliable male transients (Phyllis, Medea, Ariadne, Dido, etc.). From sources available to them, patristic writers such as Ambrose and Jerome were already passing on eagerly received lists of virgins, wives, widows, in the fourth century.[3] The rise of Christianity yielded numerous female martyr saints (Thecla, Agnes, Margaret, Catherine of Alexandria, etc.); and campaigns of conversion during the 'Dark' age promoted others whose fame flared more briefly (Leoba, Radegund, etc.).[4]

---

[1] My use of the term 'foremothers' is partly indebted to Barbara Newman, who speaks of heroic women of the Old Testament as 'the great mothers of Israel', *Sister of Wisdom*, 39.

[2] Respectively John 4: 1–42; Matt. 15: 22–8; and Rom. 16: 1.

[3] Jerome has numerous brief catalogues: e.g. Letter 54, to Furia, against remarriage (*Selected Letters*, tr. Wright, 228–65) lists as model widows Anna, the widow of Zarephath, Judith, Deborah, Naomi, the widow with the two mites, and—as a modern instance—Marcella (pp. 258–63); but his most influential, and longer, catalogues of virtuous women are in the *Adversus Iovinianum*, I. 41, I. 43–6, and I. 49 (*PL* 23. 270–82). For an example of a more expansive treatment of foremothers, see Ambrose on the widow of Zarephath, Anna, the widow with the mites, Naomi, Judith, and Deborah, in *De viduis* (*Concerning Widows*), III. 14–VIII. 51, *PL* 16. 239–50, tr. de Romestin, 393–9.

[4] The Old Testament, the New Testament, classical culture, and hagiography naturally supplied a range of *exempla* for purposes of panegyric on specific medi-

Finally there was always the possibility of updating by adding a 'modern instance' or two of impressive women, in line with the nationality or locality of the writer. The number of exemplary women fielded in any one profeminine text obviously varies according to its length, but shorter and longer texts alike frequently allude to examples in a shorthand way, implying that the supporting evidence for this or that woman's exemplary status is too obvious to need spelling out.[5]

Since a history of catalogues of women has recently been written,[6] and since the medieval careers of some of the classical heroines are beginning to be well documented,[7] the approach in the present discussion will be quite selective, identifying foremothers whose legends demonstrate particular profeminine emphases

eval women as well as for the medieval case for women generally. The encomiastic Letter 115 of Peter the Venerable to Heloise (invoking Miriam, Deborah, and Penthesilea) is typical; *Letters of Abelard and Heloise*, tr. Radice, 277–84.

[5] Marbod, 'De matrona', cites eight Old Testament heroines (Sara, Rebecca, Rachel, Esther, Judith, Hannah, Naomi, and Ruth); six martyr saints (Agnes, Fides, Agatha, Lucy, Cecilia, and Thecla); and three women of antiquity (Lucretia, Alcestis, Arria). Abelard, *The Authority and Dignity of Nuns*, comments more capaciously on Old Testament figures (Miriam, Deborah, Hannah, Judith, Esther, the mother of seven sons in 2 Macc.: 7, Jephtha's daughter); on New Testament women (Anna, various named women disciples but esp. Martha and Mary Magdalene, Elizabeth mother of the Baptist, Phoebe, the Samaritan woman (John 4: 7ff.), Pilate's wife, the woman who cried out a blessing (Luke 11: 27)); on figures from antiquity (the Sibyl, Claudia the vestal virgin); and on SS. Agatha, Agnes, Eugenia. Albertanus in the *Liber consolationis* cites Rebecca, Judith, Abigail, and Esther from the Old Testament; and Mary Magdalene from the New. Christine de Pizan in the *Epistre au dieu d'amours* concentrates on polemic more than exemplification, but cites antique heroines (Medea, Dido, Penelope), the women followers of Christ, and—in her conclusion—a list of classical goddesses. The profeminine section in Deschamps, *Miroir de mariage*, cites Judith and Esther as Old Testament exemplars; SS. Catherine, Agatha, Agnes, Margaret, Christine, Barbara, Mary the Egyptian, the 11,000 virgins; and Blanche the mother of St Louis as a modern instance. Le Fèvre's *Leësce* is prolific in citation: Old Testament examples are Judith, Esther, Jephtha's daughter; female saints include Ursula, Catherine, Margaret, Agnes, Lucy, Agatha, Marina, Genevieve; among examples from antique culture are Alithie, Lucretia, Penelope, Medea, Circe, Dido, Virginia, also clusters of examples of courage (Semiramis, Penthesilea, Thamiris, etc.) and of wisdom (Carmentis, the Muses, Medea, the Sibyl, Sappho, etc.); and modern instances including Heloise, Novella of Bologna, and Sr. Jeanne de Neuville.

[6] Mcleod, *Virtue and Venom*.

[7] For example Götz Schmitz, *The Fall of Women in Early English Narrative Verse* (Cambridge: Cambridge University Press, 1990); Ian Donaldson, *The Rapes of Lucretia: A Myth and its Transformations* (Oxford: Clarendon Press, 1982); Mary Louise Lord, 'Dido as an Example of Chastity', *Harvard Library Bulletin*, 17 (1969), 22–44, 216–32; Marilynn Desmond, *Reading Dido: Gender, Textuality, and the Medieval 'Aeneid'* (Minneapolis: University of Minnesota Press, 1994).

and investigating ways in which particular writers constructed these heroines. The investigation will concentrate on female role-models for strength and assertiveness, and for a public function as prophets or preachers. Although an androcentric control of the materials will often be plain to see in the patristic and medieval evidence, I believe it also appears that such control was far from complete. A profeminine energy embarrassing to patriarchy and potentially empowering to women lurked within stubborn details of the legends of many of the role-models, and this energy usually survived the tranquillizing attentions of those who transmitted the medieval Who's Who of history.

It is as well, however, to acknowledge that inherited patriarchal culture did no favours to women in the ways in which it nominated them for honours. Consider the criterion of 'strength'. How 'feminist' was the praise of physically tough and mentally courageous women for taking momentous initiatives in a 'man's world'? There were, certainly, egalitarian implications in the strength shown by (for instance) the prophetess Deborah, identified in the Old Testament as the sole female Israelite 'judge' and one who organized the military strategy necessary to deliver her people from the threat of a Gentile army.[8] Even St Ambrose saw how if a woman could govern, lead armies, and plan war strategy, then logically 'weakness' could not be ascribed to 'nature': what makes someone strong is 'not sex, but valour'.[9] He perceived also how Deborah's story could inspire women with confidence ('the minds of women might be stirred up') and could demonstrate that women do not need men's help.[10] On the other hand, he broached these issues primarily because he wanted to argue that widows must not use the pretext of a 'natural weakness' in their sex to justify remarrying (VIII. 51); so the contextual agenda for his reading of Deborah is actually patriarchy's desire to reserve women's sexual loyalties to one male partner per life-

[8] Judg. 4–5. It is less often noticed that Deborah's conquest of the Gentile commander Sisera is completed by another woman, Jael, whose help he seeks in defeat but who drives a nail into his brain (Judg. 4: 17–22).

[9] 'I think that her judgeship has been narrated, and her deeds described, that women should not be restrained from deeds of valour by the weakness of their sex. A widow, she governs the people; a widow, she leads armies; a widow, she chooses generals; a widow, she determines wars and orders triumphs. So, then, it is not nature which is answerable for the fault or which is liable to weakness. It is not sex, but valour which makes strong'; De viduis, VIII. 44, PL 16. 248, tr. de Romestin, 399.

[10] Respectively, VIII. 50 and VIII. 44 (PL 16. 249 and 248).

time. Anyway he made the 'egalitarian' points against the grain of
an underlying conviction that women *are* weak, that it was aberrant for Deborah to undertake 'the duties of a man', and—em-
broidering the biblical account—that she was 'chosen' by the
Israelites because normal 'manly' strength was temporarily lacking.[11] Ambrose, in short, dabbles with an egalitarian argument not
genuinely to question masculine prerogatives of leadership; but
ultimately, paradoxically, in order to pin widows down to sexual
continence within a gender hierarchy which privileged their dead
husbands.

Yet, the very fact that a profeminine position is glimpsed then
deflected in a process that recuperates Deborah for patriarchy
suggests that the disruptive power of her story is consciously
being headed off. The same thing probably holds true for the
cultural construction of another heroine with whom she is often
twinned, Esther. Esther's story in the Vulgate is part exotic romance and part brilliant psychological novel. An orphan living
among other Israelites under the alien rule of King Ahasuerus,
she is first represented in terms of her utter obedience to her uncle
Mordecai.[12] The narrative foregrounds that obedience by contrasting it with Queen Vashti's transgression, refusing to attend
Ahasuerus at his bidding—a gesture of disdain which is seen to
threaten the whole fabric of the country's masculine household
rule, and which costs her her queenship.[13] Esther is among the
girls trawled to find a replacement, and becomes queen. Soon
there is a crisis because the King's favourite lieutenant, Haman,
promotes an edict to have all the Israelites in the country killed.
Mordecai therefore urges Esther to intercede with her husband,
even though in order to do so she has to resolve to enter the
King's precincts unbidden (a transgression which, ominously,
will inversely recall Vashti's) and thereby run the risk of execu-
tion.[14] Requesting through her uncle Mordecai that all Jews in the
city fast and pray for her, she nevertheless goes before Ahasuerus,
escapes death because the sight of her pleases him, and then
deferentially works up to a moment where she dares ask that the
edict against the Israelites be reversed so that her people have

[11] *De viduis*, VIII. 44, *PL* 16. 248, tr. de Romestin, 398.
[12] 'whatsoever he commanded, Esther observed,' Esther 2: 20.
[13] The King's adviser argues that 'this deed of the queen will go abroad to all
women, so that they will despise their husbands', Esther 1: 17.
[14] 'I will go in to the king, against the law, not being called, and expose myself
to death and to danger,' Esther 4: 16.

permission to slaughter those who would have massacred them. Esther is the preordained saviour of her nation.[15]

The praise-of-women tradition highlighted nearly everything about this drama *except* its essential point. As early as *c*. AD 96, Bishop Clement was already presenting Esther alongside Judith as a role-model of *obedience*, nobility, large-heartedness, and love who, empowered by grace, 'performed deeds worthy of men'.[16] For Marbod of Rennes at the end of the eleventh century Esther, one of the female stars in the Old Testament firmament who 'equalled or surpassed men', was a model of fearlessness in risking her life for her nation.[17] Later, in Deschamps's *Miroir de mariage*, the worth of Esther, 'holy mother' to her people, lies in her 'humility' (contrasted with Vashti's arrogance) and the success with which she pleaded with Ahasuerus after entering his chamber.[18] Her 'humility' is yet more implausibly emphasized in Geoffroy de la Tour-Landry's guide for girls, which assimilates her into the stereotype of a benign wife who privately softens and cajoles an ireful husband.[19]

Yet the obvious nub of Esther's story—the very heart of its network of ironies—is her bold *disobedience*; her premeditated defiance of patriarchal law (albeit the law of an alien nation) when she echoes and inverts Vashti's defiance by attending the court unbidden, just as Vashti refused to attend when bidden. Of the writers mentioned only Marbod gets near the point.[20] What medieval culture mostly respects in Esther is a courage that is linked with her 'obedience' (which in the Vulgate is really only

[15] She is preordained in an elemental dream experienced by Mordecai and originally placed at the beginning of the narrative: it is she who is the little fountain of his dream, which grew into an abundant river and rescued their people from convulsions and darkness, its dawning light turning into the sun. Jerome transferred the account of the dream to ch. 11 (see esp. 11: 5–12) where in the Vulgate it lags improbably behind Mordecai's reference to it at 10: 6.

[16] *First Epistle of Clement*, 54. 1 and 55. 3–6, discussed in Fiorenza, *In Memory of Her*, 292–3.

[17] Leotta (ed.), 'De matrona', 82–4, 89–94, tr. in Blamires, *Woman Defamed and Woman Defended*, 230–1.

[18] *Miroir de mariage*, 9124–49.

[19] Caxton, *Book of the Knight of the Tower*, ed. Offord, ch. lxxxvi, p. 129. Conceivably there is some confusion of identities in this inaccurate account. The disobedience of Vashti is elaborated earlier (ch. lxiiii), and in ch. lxv Esther (inaccurately) 'kneels' to the King to request justice against Haman (pp. 94–6).

[20] In Abelard we see acknowledgement that Esther defies 'even the decree of the law', without any recognition of the gendered context from which this law springs; *The Authority and Dignity of Nuns*, 'Letter of Heloise on Religious Life and Abelard's First Reply', ed. Muckle, 269, tr. Scott Moncrieff, 157.

obedience to her uncle), and, somewhat trickily, her 'humility'.[21] Her defiance is consequently subdued by being relocated within a configuration of familiar 'womanly' virtues to the extent that she can be invoked—as in Chaucer's poetry—as a byword for wifely 'meekness'.[22]

In Esther's reputation, therefore, the element of defiance was close to extinction in the late Middle Ages, and 'meekness' was overtaking courage. But how genuinely profeminine, anyway, was the attribute of courage? Some might argue that because the resolve of women such as Deborah, Judith, and (occasionally) Esther was so often deemed 'outstanding,' or because it was viewed as a kind of emulation of masculinity, or as an embarrassment to masculine self-esteem, the attribution of courage was not productively profeminine. (It has not been sufficiently noticed, I think, that rhetorical tradition specifically held that the use of examples of strong women would be particularly efficacious as a way of exhorting *men* to valour. 'Arguments from unlikes are most useful in exhortation,' claimed Quintilian, and since 'courage is more remarkable in a woman than in a man', men would be inspired by references to female determination.[23]) Moreover, if the courage was so outstanding as to deserve—in Marbod's rhetoric—stellification, then were not ordinary women left stuck with their reputation for 'weakness'?[24] To laud a woman for strength is to confirm that weakness might be the feminine norm and insinuate, as Karma Lochrie has said, 'that a strong woman such as

[21] In *Leësce*, 2122–40, Esther is celebrated for 'humilité', 'obeïssance', and 'debonnaireté': her defiance is being eclipsed by an impressionistic recollection of the strategic circumspection and deferentiality with which she leads up to her plea on behalf of her people (see Esther 5: 4 and 7–8; and 7: 3–4). Doubtless it is in this sense that *The Book of the Knight of the Tower* finds her a model of compliance who got what she wanted by waiting until 'she sawe [Ahasuerus] well attempryd'; ch. xvii, ed. Offord, 35. Christine de Pizan (who is indebted to details in the *Histoire ancienne*) also highlights Esther's strategic humility, completely excluding her act of defiance; *Cité*, II. 32. 1, ed. Curnow, 861–3 and n. (p. 1094), tr. Richards, 145–7.

[22] 'Ester, ley thou thy meknesse al adown', *Prologue to the Legend of Good Women*, 'F' 250; and in *The Merchant's Tale* May's demeanour at her wedding banquet is of such benignity that 'Queene Ester looked nevere with swich an ye | On Assuer, so meke a look hath she' (IV. 1742–45). Emerson Brown Jr. charts ironizing possibilities in the tale's references to biblical wives, without sufficiently registering the processes of cultural accommodation mentioned here; 'Biblical Women in the *Merchant's Tale*: Feminism, Antifeminism, and Beyond', *Viator*, 5 (1974), 389–98.

[23] 'Admirabilior in femina quam in viro virtus'; Quintilian, *Institutio oratoria*, V. xi. 10, ed. and tr. Butler, 276–7.

[24] Cf. Krueger, *Women Readers and the Ideology of Gender*, 6.

Judith therefore approached the male ideals of heroism'.[25] If the commendation is explicitly that courageous women equal or surpass men, women are yet more distinctly being evaluated on their ability to emulate masculine aspirations. Abelard—of conspicuously competitive temperament himself—is rather prone to this type of enthusiasm for women who rival men, suggesting for instance that the virtue of Deborah, Judith, and Esther will surely 'make us blush not a little for the strength of the male sex' and comparing David, who at least had a sling to use against Goliath, with Esther who used 'her word alone' to set free her people, while Judith took nothing at all to battle with Holofernes.[26]

Yet feminist hindsight encourages us to pinpoint flaws in 'profeminine' postures which may have eluded many in that epoch besides Abelard. If we too assiduously chip away the potential for female empowerment in medieval representation of the Old Testament heroines, we may lose contact with reservoirs of invigorating precedent which could 'stir up the minds of women' in the Middle Ages as much as Ambrose thought they could in his time. Who knows what strength some women derived from figures such as Esther, despite the filter of immasculating commendation through which her story was mediated? We are not without hints. A sixth-century *Life* suggests that St Genevieve, missionary in Gaul and especially in Paris, drew inspiration from Old Testament foremothers when the citizens there prepared to flee in panic at the approach of Attila the Hun in 451. Genevieve 'summoned the matrons of the city' and 'as Esther and Judith had done' urged them to fast and pray, to ward off the enemy.[27] Against heated opposition she also persuaded the men not to evacuate their possessions. So far as her biographer is concerned, she 'drove away' the Huns' army and saved the people by her prayers.[28] Although there is no way of proving that the Esther/Judith comparison was not a biographer's embellishment, these

---

[25] 'Gender, Sexual Violence, and the Politics of War in the Old English *Judith*', in Britton J. Harwood and Gillian R. Overing (eds.), *Class and Gender in Early English Literature: Intersections* (Bloomington: Indiana University Press, 1994), 1–20 (p. 18 n. 12).

[26] *The Authority and Dignity of Nuns*, 'Letter of Heloise on Religious Life and Abelard's First Reply', ed. Muckle, 269, tr. Scott Moncrieff, 156–7.

[27] McNamara, *Sainted Women of the Dark Ages*, 23. This *Vita* seems to have been written by a cleric around 520, only two decades after Genevieve's death (p. 18).

[28] Ibid. 24. In modern parlance, the Huns 'changed the route of their march and Paris was spared'; *The Oxford Dictionary of Saints*, ed. David Hugh Farmer (Oxford: Oxford University Press, 1978), 164.

role-models could equally have been potent in Genevieve's own mind—though an interesting variation from them in her case is her preliminary appeal to female solidarity by initiating her plan through a meeting of city 'matrons'.[29]

Another stray hint of the empowering influence of the Old Testament women can be found in Christina of Markyate in the twelfth century. Subjected to a campaign of beatings and terror when she refused to consummate her unwanted espousal with Burthred, she found comfort in nightly visions in which a kindly 'queen' (the Virgin Mary) effortlessly arranged her deliverance. An odd detail of one vision is that when Christina wishes that she could see her benefactor's face more openly, this 'queen' promises to 'bring both you and Judith into my chamber' where she can gaze unhindered.[30] The mention of Judith here is quite unexpected. Retrospectively one can speculate that since in Christina's consolatory fantasy Burthred lies prostrate, unable to touch her and only able to bash his head on the floor in frustrated rage, he has assumed the proportions of Holofernes the would-be despoiler, whom Christina is imagining that she can conquer as a quasi-Judith. The biographer does not orchestrate this analogy as he orchestrates others,[31] so I think it quite possible that the *Life* gives us here an authentic glimpse of the valorizing impact of Judith in a medieval woman's experience. For Christina Judith is, perhaps, an alternative role-model to St Cecilia: in the one role she can destroy the predator, in the other, she can convert him to marital celibacy—as, indeed, according to the biographer she duly invokes Cecilia during an acute crisis when her parents push her spouse into her room at night.[32]

It is not untypical that these examples happen to focus on acts of assertion which (in Genevieve's case) save a people, and (in Christina's) preserve virginity. Medieval culture had a kind of love–hate relationship with the concept of feminine boldness, but

[29] Esther by contrast bids Mordecai summon all the city's Jews to fast and pray, while she and her handmaids in the court pray separately (4: 15–16).

[30] *Life of Christina of Markyate*, chs. 24–5, ed. and tr. Talbot, 74–7 (esp. p. 77).

[31] In ch. 22, Christina escapes from Burthred by loosening her mantle when he tries to hold on to her: a strategy which prompts the writer to a self-conscious comparison with Joseph's escape from the attentions of Potiphar's wife (Gen. 39: 12); ed. Talbot, 72–3.

[32] *Life of Christina of Markyate*, ed. Talbot, 50–1. Christina's implied interest in Judith qualifies, I think, the scepticism sometimes expressed about the empowerment available in this heroine; e.g. Kliman, 'Women in Early English Literature', 36–8.

vows of chastity, and what would now be called considerations of 'national security', constituted two of the areas in which boldness was least uncomfortably tolerated.[33]

The implication that threats to national security (i.e. to national patriarchal stability?) might warrant a woman's public and sometimes military intervention provides a link across the centuries between figures such as Esther or Deborah and Genevieve and the medieval 'modern instance' of Blanche of Castile, Queen of France. Deschamps dwells upon Blanche in the profeminine harangue of the *Miroir de mariage*, in order to demonstrate the 'constancy' (meaning, in this context, the resolve) which women have displayed in national government.[34] He recounts how, faced on her husband's death with a situation of chaotic baronial factionalism which threatens the prospects of the 5-year-old heir Louis, Blanche stakes his future and hers on a showdown with the barons. Placing the boy on a bed in parliament, she melodramatically appeals to their sensibilities by presenting herself as a disconsolate royal widow and committing her little son to their mercies. It works: the nobles are so overtaken by pathos that they unite behind the Queen's governance, and thereafter her active rule and her upbringing of Louis are exemplary. Although Deschamps's account chooses to project Blanche's public intervention through the stereotype of the distressed widow with a vulnerable child,[35] and compliments in her a stereotype of the softening peacemaker,[36] it is her conscious *control* of these stereotypes which emerges from the narrative: her bravery and wis-

[33] There would be some truth in applying to the Middle Ages (though it would be too much of a generalization) Linda Woodbridge's remark that Renaissance defenders of women 'praise martial women only when they act in defense of their country or their children, particularly under siege'; *Women and the English Renaissance*, 21.

[34] *Miroir de mariage*, 9406–661, introduced 'Ou sont les hommes plus constans | Que femmes ont esté tous temps | En gouvernement de pais?' (9403–5). Blanche was the half-English queen of Louis VIII of France. Her husband died in 1226: Blanche assumed the regency during the minority of her son (later Louis IX). Blanche's actions were celebrated in proportion as the life of her sainted son became famous.

[35] See esp. *Miroir de mariage*, 9452–78.

[36] Ibid. 9411–12, 9498–511. In the *Grandes Chroniques de France*, Blanche's peacemaking action is ascribed to Queen Fredegonde of France instead, and Christine de Pizan follows that ascription in *Cité*, I. 13. 1, ed. Curnow, 668–9 and n. 44 (p. 1055), tr. Richards, 33–4. Yet in a 1405 letter to Queen Isabelle urging her to use her influence to bring peace, Christine ascribes the action to Blanche (ed. Curnow, 57), so competing traditions were evidently available.

dom are what finally command attention.[37] Unifying the barons and assuming power by acclamation, she becomes like Deborah an emblem of female capacity to govern. As such she is slotted into the case for women again by Christine de Pizan, who suggests that Blanche governed France 'so nobly and so prudently that it was never better ruled by any man'.[38]

To the extent that Deschamps's narrative inoculates masculine dignity against Blanche's self-assertion by representing power as something *ceded* to her by men (and ceded partly out of compassion for her feminine 'vulnerability' as widow and mother), he epitomizes the problematic, concessionary relation between the prevalent culture and profeminine *exempla* of strong women. This problematic relation is particularly clear in attempts to come to terms with Amazonian women. Boccaccio was evidently excited by the careers of the various Amazons he included in his *De mulieribus claris*; but at the same time he was often tempted to account for their military and governmental success by resorting to the disparaging trope of manly spirits in female bodies.[39] So too, pondering the athletic, hunting, and military skills developed by Camilla the Volscian, which she pursued to the exclusion of any interest in the men who courted her, he tries to accommodate the disconcerting prospect of a powerful, unsocialized, disorderly woman by translating her into a model of decorous continence for the edification of flirtatious women of his time. Let women learn from Camilla modesty, sobriety, and chaste youth so that they 'may attain with maturity to holy matrimony *under the direction of their elders*', he declares.[40] Boccaccio drastically squeezes the dynamic asexual autonomy which his own narrative at first admires

[37] *Miroir de mariage*, 9654–5.

[38] She adds that even after Louis became king, Blanche 'was still the head of his council because of her experience of wise government, nor was anything done without her, and she even followed her son to war'; *Cité*, I. 13. 2, ed. Curnow, 669, tr. Richards, 34.

[39] 'What can we think', he writes, recounting the deeds of Queen Artemisia of Caria, 'except that it was an error of Nature to give female sex to a body which had been endowed by God with a magnificent and virile spirit?', *De mulieribus claris*, ed. Zaccaria, 236, tr. Guarino, 127; and see Benson, *Invention of the Renaissance Woman*, 22. On Amazons, see further Abby Wettan Kleinbaum, *The War against the Amazons* (New York: New Press, McGraw-Hill, 1983).

[40] *De mulieribus claris*, ed. Zaccaria, 160, tr. Guarino, 80 (my emphasis). The perception of Amazons as 'disorderly' women is discussed in Sarah Westphal's article on various masculine strategies for recuperating Camilla employed by Heinrich von Veldeke; 'Camilla: The Amazon Body in Medieval German Literature', *Exemplaria*, 8 (1996), 231–58 (pp. 244–5).

in Camilla, into a lecture on demure premarital behaviour. Pamela Benson's argument that Boccaccio offers young women of his time a liberating practical connection between the freewheeling 'strength' of an ancient woman and the realities of their own socially circumscribed lives surely strains too hard to redeem Boccaccio from his own androcentric anxieties.[41] The autonomous Amazon lifestyle—what Chaucer called 'Femenye'—fuelled anxiety because as Angela Weisl has noted it portended 'a rival state, Cixous' dark and unexplored continent', the autonomy of its women a prospective threat to masculine power structures.[42] Chaucer's *Knight's Tale* follows Boccaccio, rehearsing similar effects of masculine anxiety in that the vestigial Amazonian instincts of the heroine Emelye are reined in under the direction of (male) elders.

By contrast Christine de Pizan sees no need to *account* for Amazon strength, or to try to reconcile Camilla's self-fulfilment with medieval cultural prescription by comparing it with premarital mores. Christine grants that Camilla's capacity for athleticism and boldness was remarkable, but leaves the 'high-mindedness' of her anti-heterosexual stance to speak for itself.[43] Admittedly, Christine's own attitude to assertiveness and physical strength is ambiguous because on the one hand she feels that women generally benefit by lacking the sort of combination of these qualities which perpetrates violent crime; but on the other hand she does not want to deny independence and physical daring to women, since that would deprive her of the Amazonian examples of strength, boldness, and governmental prudence such as Artemisia displays.[44] Therefore on the one hand she defers to tradition by more or less accepting received emphasis on the 'frailty' of female physique—only to hail it as sustaining a moral *advantage* for women: but on the other she does not, like Boccaccio, treat physical strength in authority-wielding women as a cultural affront provoking constant exclamation.

[41] *Invention of the Renaissance Woman*, 23–4.

[42] Angela Jane Weisl, *Conquering the Reign of Femeny: Gender and Genre in Chaucer's Romance* (Cambridge: D. S. Brewer, 1995), 53. I shall qualify this view somewhat in the next chapter, however.

[43] 'Mais tant fu de grant couraige que oncques mari ne daigna prendre, ne se coupler a homme', *Cité*, I. 24. 1, ed. Curnow, 717, tr. Richards, 61. For Christine's version of Boccaccio's Artemisia see I. 21. 1, ed. Curnow, 706–11, tr. Richards, 55–7.

[44] *Cité*, I. 14. 2–3 and I. 21. 1, ed. Curnow, 674–6 and 706–7, tr. Richards, 37–8 and 55.

It is instructive, in fact, to see how much Christine transcends the grudgingness of Boccaccio's presentation of 'famous women' simply by omitting his rhetorical squeaks and concessionary explanations. Boccaccio cannot resist condescending exclamations (where did this girl's strength come from!),[45] and his alacrity with explanations draws attention to the very transgressions which they are meant to explain. A typical example concerns the boldness of public speaking. When he has described the cogent eloquence of Hortensia, an orator's daughter who successfully conducts a formal argument to prevent the triumvirs from levying a huge state tax on women, he feels the need to justify this breach of the convention of female silence in public: the triumvirs 'thought that although silence in public is a praiseworthy quality in a woman, when the occasion requires it a properly prepared speech should be praised'.[46] Christine cuts away the nagging reference to silence; she categorically states the efficacy of Hortensia's case, 'so compelling that she was listened to, no less readily than her father would have been'; and locates the episode within a rational plea for the education of women.[47] Although she is not impervious to the culture's suspicion of public female speech,[48] she has no time for the shut-down of women's capabilities which 'silence' implies.

Of course bold public defiance of masculine authority had been a charismatic feature of women saints from early times. In theory the Church Fathers were committed to an ideal of virginal modesty which (in the words of Ambrose) 'closes the mouth' and eschews socializing lest 'boldness [audacia] breaks forth'.[49] Nevertheless Ambrose himself shows unconcealed admiration for erup-

---

[45] Said of the vestal virgin Claudia, when she rushes forward to push away a tribune who has attacked her father; *De mulieribus claris*, ed. Zaccaria, 252, tr. Guarino, 135.

[46] *De mulieribus claris*, ed. Zaccaria, 334, tr. Guarino, 185. The story is cryptically layered: in praising a woman who 'takes up the cause of women' against masculine authority's proposal of an 'unjust' tax on women, Boccaccio is ambiguously both an exception to the masculine conspiracy against women implied by the fact that 'not a single man' would defend their cause, *and* a confessed supporter in general of the gender conspiracy which would make them silent victims of it.

[47] *Cité*, II. 36. 1–2, ed. Curnow, 873–4, tr. Richards, 153–4.

[48] She intimates a danger of erotic distraction from a woman lecturing in public; and implies a distaste for women's public involvement in pleading 'brazenly' (*baudement*) at law; respectively, *Cité*, II. 36. 3 and I. 11. 1, ed. Curnow, 874–5 and 665, tr. Richards, 154 and 31–2.

[49] Respectively Ambrose, *De virginibus*, III. 3. 13 and 9 (*PL* 16. 222), tr. de Romestin, 382–3.

tions of boldness in women if they are maintaining their own vows of virginity against family or other pressures. He tells of a girl who—in his lifetime—not only took up a stand at the altar in order to assert her choice of Christ as her celestial bridegroom, but also (such was her 'boldness' or *audacia*) destroyed the objection that her father would have insisted on a proper marriage for her if he were alive, by retorting that perhaps he had died precisely to remove such an impediment.[50]

The paradox that the very brusqueness which makes a woman a heroine in pro-Christian and pro-virginity propaganda[51] would simultaneously disgrace her according to the same culture's gendered conventions of conduct is as apparent near the end of the Middle Ages as it is in early Christianity. Karen Winstead wonders at the way Middle English hagiographers of the thirteenth and fourteenth centuries go on allowing women to get away with 'saucy retorts' and with taunting and ridiculing masculine authority so as to 'stand society on its head'.[52] The profeminine implications of this capacity for 'bluntly effective rebuke' are interestingly described by Jocelyn Wogan-Browne as part of a superior eloquence, larger vision, even 'semiotic control'

[50] *De virginibus*, I. 12. 65–6 (*PL* 16. 206–8), tr. de Romestin, 373. Ambrose tries to mitigate the impression by describing the retort, paradoxically, as uttered with 'restrained piety'. See Bloch, *Medieval Misogyny*, 86–8, for a brief contextualization of this example within early Christian sexual and economic politics.

[51] e.g. St Cecilia's intellectual and sexual taunts: 'Almachius again summoned Saint Cecilia and asked her: "What is your status in life?" "I am freeborn and of noble descent," she said. Almachius: "I'm asking about your religion!" Cecilia: "Then your interrogation began badly, because the one question called for two answers." Almachius: "Where do your presumptuous answers come from?' 'From a clear conscience and unfeigned faith!" she retorted. Almachius: "Don't you know where my power comes from?" Cecilia: "Your power is a balloon filled with wind! prick it with a pin and it collapses, and what seemed rigid in it goes limp,"' Jacobus de Voragine, *The Golden Legend*, tr. Ryan, ii. 322. See also the mocking strategies ascribed by hagiographers to St Catherine; Jocelyn Wogan-Browne, 'Saints' Lives and the Female Reader', *Forum for Modern Language Studies*, 27 (1991), 314–32 (pp. 327–8).

[52] 'While the writers of late medieval conduct books admonished women to be demure and to respect the authority of their parents and husbands, fathers, and civil authorities, virgin martyrs defied husbands, fathers, and civil authorities, standing society on its head'; 'Saints, Wives, and Other "Hooly Thynges": Pious Laywomen in Middle English Romance', *Chaucer Yearbook*, 2 (1993), 137–54 (pp. 140–1). On late medieval ideals for women, see Diane Bornstein, *The Lady in the Tower: Medieval Courtesy Literature for Women* (Hamden, Conn.: Archon Books, 1983). A typical example of the ascription of assertive speech exclusively to males is the proposition that a husband 'of right ought to have above his wyf the hyhe talkyng, be it ryght or wrong, and specially in his yre and wrath, and bifore ony folk'; Caxton (tr.), *Book of the Knight of the Tower*, ch. lxiii, ed. Offord, 93.

ascribed to the woman saint, which contributes to our recognition of a source of power in her. Because these texts present a supernaturally insured capacity to 'answer back', they insist 'that when women say no, no is what they mean' and hence offer 'serious encouragement to female readers'.[53]

Hard evidence of such encouragement sometimes appears in practice, notably in the eleventh and twelfth centuries which have been described as a time of 'feminine resistance to the disenfranchisement of women', at least in southern France.[54] (Here Robert d'Arbrissel's community at Fontevrault dating from 1100–1 attracted a surge of women and represented a palpable threat to the 'macho' nobility in that significant numbers of the convertees were apparently escaping from husbands and fathers.[55]) Christina of Markyate's personal allegiance to several female saints from whom she probably derived support for her own defiance a little later in the century seems verifiable.[56] When, therefore, the formal case for women names female saints, there seems no reason to doubt that assertiveness constitutes an important element in what is being invoked. The various ways in which patriarchy reappropriated the women in its narratives of saints (especially, for instance, by redirecting them to a destiny of sublimated sexual obedience in the divine bedchamber, as brides of Christ)[57] do not seem to me to negate this fundamental point. On the contrary medieval doctrine had to resort to a slogan capable of taming the culturally disruptive impulses enmeshed in these narratives—the slogan: 'to be admired, not imitated'.[58]

The case for women made the arbiters of medieval doctrine

---

[53] 'The Virgin's Tale', 179, 181. Acts of defiance are also conspicuous in the *Lives* of early medieval holy women; e.g. Glodesind, Burgundofara, and Rictrude in McNamara, *Sainted Women of the Dark Ages*, 143–4, 158, 206.

[54] Bloch, *Medieval Misogyny*, 178.

[55] Ibid. 180–1 and n. 48, pointing out the complaint of Roscelin that Robert d'Arbrissel would not return resolute wives to husbands who tried to claim them (cited from Jean-Marc Bienvenu, *L'Étonnant Fondateur de Fontevraud Robert d'Arbrissel* (Paris: Nouvelles Éditions Latines, 1981), 89).

[56] Wogan-Browne, 'Saints' Lives and the Female Reader', 316, noting that four of the saints Christina had added to the calendar of her psalter rejected prospective husbands.

[57] See Cazelles, *The Lady as Saint*, 70–1; Wogan-Browne, 'The Virgin's Tale', 169–71, 174.

[58] *Non imitanda sed veneranda*. See Bruce C. Brasington, '*Non imitanda set veneranda*: The Dilemma of Sacred Precedent in Twelfth-Century Canon Law', *Viator*, 23 (1992), 135–52 (pp. 142–8); Winstead, 'Saints, Wives, and Other "Hooly Thynges"', 151–2; and Richard Kieckhefer, *Unquiet Souls: Fourteenth-Century Saints and their Religious Milieu* (Chicago: University of Chicago Press, 1984), 13–14.

more nervous, however, by presuming to use some of the *exempla* already mentioned as part of a justification not just for women to make a stand for their religious beliefs, but also for them to *preach* in public. Here indeed one can speak of a 'case' in a technical sense, because the thirteenth-century scholastics used their customary debate format to lay out the pros and cons of female preaching, as a necessary aspect of the wider theological task of defining the right to preach. But their arguments drew on well-rehearsed positions, and before coming to the role-models that were cited in university debate we should reckon with one position in particular.

The conventional justification for preaching, urging it as a kind of duty for those with appropriate talents, gave a crucial hostage to the aspiring woman evangelist. It so happens that the *De virginibus* (AD 377) by Ambrose, already discussed in this chapter, opens with a classic statement of the *obligation* to spread God's word. If, says Ambrose, we have to account for every idle word, and if we incur blame for hiding in the earth the talents of spiritual grace (*talenta gratiae spiritualis*) entrusted to us so that they may be multiplied, then 'a great necessity [*necessitas maxima*] is laid on him' to 'make increase' of God's sayings entrusted to him.[59] This takes us immediately, uncompromisingly, and with the combined authority of Ambrose and the parable of the talents[60] to the heart of all protestations on behalf of evangelizing: I shall call it 'Justification by Talent'.

This justification is conspicuous in the parts of St Gregory's sixth-century *Liber regulae pastoralis* which urge the shy and the lazy not to shirk pastoral responsibility when they have a talent for it.[61] The greater the gifts which they might exercise for others, the greater the guilt in 'withholding the word' and in 'hiding away the remedies of life from dying souls'. The parable of the talents is lined up with analogous texts, such as 'Wisdom that is hid, and treasure that is unseen, what profit is there in them both?' (Ecclus. 20: 32), 'I will not refrain my lips . . . I have not hid

[59] I. 1 (*PL* 16. 187), tr. de Romestin, 363.

[60] In Matt. 25: 14–30 two servants trade and double the talents given to them by their master while he is away; but a third hides his talent in the earth. The returning lord congratulates the two, but condemns the other as 'wicked and slothful', gives his talent to one of the others, and consigns him (as 'unprofitable servant') to darkness.

[61] Gregory was thinking primarily of those who declined to exercise their pastoral potential, under the pretext of a call to the contemplative life.

thy righteousness within my heart' (Ps. 39: 10–11), and—most theatrically—the angel's command to John, 'Let him that *heareth*, say, "Come"' (Rev. 22: 17).[62] All this was lodged in Gregory's massively disseminated work, the very textbook of the medieval clergy.[63] The persuasions to active evangelism must have seemed very powerful, with disturbing penalty clauses for anyone who felt that her lips were being refrained, that her talents were languishing unused, and that having heard, she should be saying 'Come'.[64]

The other powerful strand in the case for women preachers which had tenacious roots was the appeal to scriptural prophetesses as precedents. Some groups in the earliest history of the Church had insisted on the model public role provided by Old and New Testament prophetesses. Apparently the activities of women leaders in the Montanist and associated movements, of whom Prisca (or Priscilla) and Maximilla were the most famous, were justified in this way. Both Origen in the third century and Epiphanius in the fourth report that Montanists cited as precedents the four daughters of the apostle Philip.[65] (This quartet of Philip of Caesarea's 'four daughters virgins, who did prophesy' is mentioned in Acts 21: 8–9; Eusebius of Caesarea further brought them to attention in his fourth-century *Ecclesiastical History*.[66]) The

---

[62] *Lib. reg. past.* III. 25 (*PL* 77. 96–9), tr. James Barmby, in *Leo the Great, Gregory the Great, Pt. 1,* Select Library of Nicene and Post-Nicene Fathers, 2nd ser. 12 (Oxford: James Parker, 1895), 53–6; and see I. 5, pp. 4–5. Yet another argument that evangelical potential *must* be translated into action came from 1 Pet. 4: 10, 'As every one hath received grace, minister the same to one another, as good stewards of the manifold grace of God.' It was a text much insisted on by those commentators— such as Thomas Aquinas—who wrote extensively on the divine *gratiae*.

[63] A representative example of the ubiquitous dissemination of such views is in St Bernard's Homily 18. 1–2 on the *Song of Songs*, which observes that gifts such as eloquence and prophecy are 'undoubtedly meant to be used for our neighbour's salvation' so it is pernicious to 'smother' them—for the people's curse is on the man who hoards the wheat (Prov. 11: 26, also cited by St Gregory); tr. Walsh, *On the Song of Songs,* 133.

[64] Of course there was usually the stated or implicit rider that the obligation was subject to status. In the *Form of Preaching* (1322), Robert of Basevorn directed the obligation argument at those who were 'preachers by institution'; in *Three Medieval Rhetorical Arts,* ed. James J. Murphy (Berkeley and Los Angeles: University of California Press, 1971), ch. iii, pp. 122–3.

[65] J. Kevin Coyle, 'The Fathers on Women and Women's Ordination', *Église et théologie,* 9 (1978), 51–101 (pp. 73–4, 77).

[66] Eusebius (*a*) quotes an epistle of the Bishop of Ephesus concerning the death of 'luminaries' in Asia including Philip the apostle and 'his two daughters who grew old in virginity, and his other daughter who lived in the Holy Spirit and rests at Ephesus'; (*b*) cites a dialogue in which Proclus locates in 'Hierapolis in Asia four

context for Origen's hostility to the Montanist women is his commentary on the famous Pauline prohibition against women speaking in church.[67] Trying simultaneously to toughen that prohibition and to invalidate heterodox reliance on prophetesses as precedents for a public female role, he runs through biblical women designated as prophetesses—Deborah, Miriam, Huldah, and Anna—controversially claiming that none of them spoke publicly to the people 'in an assembly'.[68] He adds that the Epistle to Titus mentions older women 'teaching', but only teaching good manners, to younger women not men.[69] It is a classic exercise in (from Origen's point of view) damage limitation, but one which has the incidental effect of highlighting the *availability* of profeminine models. Whether Prisca and Maximilla would have claimed all the women in Origen's list as authorizing role-models is not clear,[70] but it would certainly be natural if women of the late second century who were involved in prophesying (whatever form this took in religious assemblies) combed Scripture for the

prophetesses, daughters of Philip. Their tomb is there, and that of their father'; (c) states that Luke in the Acts 'mentions the daughters of Philip as living with their father at Caesarea in Judaea, and as having been accounted worthy of a prophetic gift' (III. 31. 2–4); *The Ecclesiastical History*, tr. Hugh J. Lawlor and John E. L. Oulton, vol. i (New York: SPCK, 1927), 91–2. There is a further mention under Papias in III. 39. 9 (p. 100).

[67] 'Let women keep silence in the churches: for it is not permitted them to speak, but to be subject, as also the law saith. But if they would learn any thing, let them ask their husbands at home. For it is a shame for a woman to speak in the church' (1 Cor. 14: 34–5). Origen's discussion is fragment 74 of *Commentarium in primam epist. ad Corinthios*; ed. C. Jenkins, 'Origen on 1 Corinthians: Pt. iv', *Journal of Theological Studies*, 10 (1908–9), 41–2.

[68] See Judg. 4: 4; Exod. 15: 20–1; 2 Kgs. 22: 14–20; Luke 2: 36; and Coyle, 'The Fathers on Women', 73. It is interesting that two of the prophetesses (Deborah and Huldah) are invoked in an ordination rite for deaconesses in a late 4th-cent. document known as the *Apostolic Canons*: 'Thou shalt lay thy hands upon her in the presence of the Presbyters, the Deacons, and the Deaconesses, saying, "Thou who didst fill Deborah, Hannah and Huldah with the Holy Spirit, thou who in the Temple didst appoint women to keep the holy doors, look upon thy servant chosen for thy ministry (*diakonia*), and give to her the Holy Spirit that she may worthily perform the office committed unto her"'; Jean Daniélou, *The Ministry of Women in the Early Church* (London: Faith Press, 1961), 22. The 85 canons are attributed to the apostles and form the last chapter of the *Apostolic Constitutions*.

[69] Tit. 2: 3–4.

[70] Epiphanius of Salamis later states (c. AD 375) that followers of women sect leaders such as Priscilla and Quintilla cited Miriam or Mary, sister of Aaron (mentioned by Origen), as another precedent; Coyle, 'The Fathers on Women', 77. (In Exod. 15: 20–1 we are told that, after the miraculous crossing of the Red Sea, this 'prophetess' led the Israelite women in a song of praise.) On Montanists and the Pauline prohibitions, see P. de Labriolle, '"Mulieres in ecclesia taceant": Un

names of every woman identified by the epithet 'prophetess'.[71] The list of candidates this yielded was to resurface down the centuries whenever authority for female preaching was sought or challenged.

One instructive instance is the case for lay and female preaching in the heterodox twelfth-century Waldensian movement which sprang up around Valdes of Lyons in the 1170s/1180s. The case is reported by the Premonstratensian abbot Bernard of Fontcaude (who was involved in refuting it) in a treatise *contra Vallenses et contra Arrianos* written probably before 1193.[72] As this tract reveals and as Alain of Lille corroborates, the Waldensians placed much stress on lay preaching using vernacular translations of Scripture, and women as well as men preached at their gatherings.[73]

Two of the propositions ascribed to the sect by Bernard claim our attention. One is 'that everyone including the laity may preach'. Everyone here includes women—not always the case in the period—since the horrified abbot adds: 'without distinction of status or gender'. The umbrella Waldensian argument adopted two justifications by talent, one citing the Epistle of St James, and the other (like Gregory) citing Revelation.[74] However, public

aspect de la lutte anti-Montaniste', *Bulletin d'ancienne littérature et d'archéologie chrétiennes*, 1 (1911), 3–24, 103–22, 291–8; and Elaine C. Huber, *Women and the Authority of Inspiration: The Reexamination of Two Prophetic Movements from a Contemporary Feminist Perspective* (Lanham, Md.: University Press of America, 1985).

[71] For discussion of how the institutional Church gradually distanced itself from the charismatic spirit-based congregational prophecy present in its beginnings, see Fiorenza, *In Memory of Her*, ch. 8. Daniélou, *Ministry of Women in the Early Church*, argues that 'prophecy'—a kind of praying aloud—was a different activity from that objected to by St Paul in 1 Corinthians.

[72] *PL* 204. 793–840: in Migne's edition it is entitled *Adversus Waldensium sectam*. On Bernard, see *Heresies of the High Middle Ages*, ed. Walter L. Wakefield and Austin P. Evans (New York: Columbia University Press, 1969), 210–13; and Libert Verrees, 'Le Traité de l'abbé Bernard de Fontcaude contre les Vaudois et les Ariens', *Analecta Praemonstratensa*, 31 (1955), 5–35. On Waldensian women preaching, see Grado Merlo, 'Sulle "misere donnicciuole" che predicavano', in his *Valdesi e valdismi medievali*, ii: *Identità valdesi nella storia e nella storiografia* (Turin: Claudiana, 1991), 93–112. Bernard was present at a formal debate with the Waldensians at Narbonne in the late 1180s: see Giovanni Gonnet, 'Le Cheminement des Vaudois vers le schisme et l'hérésie', *Cahiers de civilisation médiévale*, 19 (1976), 309–45 (pp. 323–4).

[73] 'mulierculas secum ducunt, et eas in conventu fidelium praedicare faciunt', *Alani de Insulis De fide catholica contra haereticos sui temporis*, II. 1; *PL* 210. 379.

[74] (a) 'To him who knoweth to do good, and doth it not, to him it is sin' (Jas. 4: 17). If we know how to evangelize, and do not, say the Waldensians, shall we not sin gravely? (b) The angel's instruction 'He that heareth, let him say, Come,' is recalled from Revelation.

evangelizing by lay*women* was such an outlandish prospect that it merited, as the sect saw, further justifications all to itself. Hence the other proposition about lay preaching to which Bernard assigned a whole chapter, 'They say that women may preach'.[75]

Amidst Bernard's indignant repudiations, two specific profeminine Waldensian positions emerge. One uses the precedent of the old women whom St Paul urges to teach virtue and obedience to young women (*adulescentulas*).[76] The passage actually—as Origen indicated when he mentioned it—presupposes a domestic and exclusively female context and does not give much of a foothold for public female evangelism. Presumably it was cited despite these shortcomings for its specific vocabulary about women 'teaching'; Vulgate *docentes* and *doceant* furnishing rare New Testament support for women doing that which St Paul did not permit. The second argument used by Waldensians (switching to the realms of Justification by Prophetess) is the biblical example of Anna. St Luke mentions her in the episode known as the Presentation in the Temple when she appears along with Simeon to greet the Christ-child: 'there was one Anna, a prophetess . . . far advanced in years . . . Now she at the same hour coming in, confessed to the Lord [*confitebatur Domino*]; and spoke of him [*et loquebatur de illo*] to all that looked for the redemption of Israel.'[77] In speaking of Christ to all, Anna constituted a significant Gospel authorization for the case for female evangelism, however much the Abbot and his ilk tried to fine-tune a distinction between speaking to everyone, and the act of preaching.[78]

In commentary and debate of the thirteenth century, Justification by Talent and Justification by Prophetess (sometimes with additional reference to appropriate women saints) continued to be a preoccupation of the case for women as preachers. The female luminaries of prophecy were discussed in, for example, the Hugh of St Cher biblical commentary of the 1230s;[79] in a *quaestio* by Aquinas concerning women's possession of the gift (charism) of speech;[80] in another disputation (1263–6) by a Franciscan

---

[75] Ch. 8, *PL* 204. 825–7.   [76] Tit. 2: 3–5.   [77] Luke 2: 36–8.
[78] Bernard claims that preaching and speaking are not the same, and further distinguishes between prophecy and teaching; *PL* 204. 806.
[79] The gloss to St Paul's assertion that women must remain silent in the churches cites Deborah, Huldah, Anna, the daughters of Philip. To these are added the Samaritan woman and SS. Mary Magdalene, and Martha (discussed below); *Postillae* (Basle, 1504), pt. vi, fo. 103[v].
[80] *Summa*, IIa IIae, q. 177, 2, 'Utrum gratia sermonis, sapientiae et scientiae pertineat etiam ad mulieres'; *Summa theologiae*, vol. xlv, tr. Roland Potter (London:

named Eustace of Arras, on whether women merit celestial crowns through preaching and teaching;[81] and in another about women's capacity to be religious teachers by the Parisian master Henry of Ghent.[82] The favoured scholastic way to disempower the prophetesses as models for a public instructional role for women was to harden a distinction which had been slowly growing in the Church, between prophecy and preaching[83] ('teaching' being considered contiguous with preaching), but this strategy had the effect of redoubling the case for women by inviting people to identify *further* models, in the preaching activities ascribed to certain biblical women and female saints. Conspicuous examples arising were Saints Mary Magdalene and Martha, Catherine of Alexandria, Cecilia, and (more rarely) the Samaritan woman.

The amount of preaching activity credited in the Middle Ages to women saints will probably be a surprise to some modern readers.[84] There is a connection, through Mary Magdalene, with the women who accompanied Christ on his preaching tours. St Luke names these women, and the Fathers (for all their reputation for misogyny) took note of them.[85] During the Middle Ages the

Blackfriars, 1963), 132–5 (p. 132): citing Deborah, Huldah, the four daughters of Philip, and the implication of 1 Pet. 4: 10 that a talent must be used.

[81] 'Utrum mulier praedicando et docendo mereatur aureolam'; text in Jean Leclercq, 'Le Magistère du prédicateur au xiiie siècle', *Archives d'histoire doctrinale et littéraire du Moyen Âge*, 21 (1946), 105–47 (pp. 119–20). Eustace cites only Deborah of the prophetesses, but adds SS. Mary Magdalene and Catherine.

[82] 'Utrum mulier possit esse doctor seu doctrix huius scientiae', reprinted Blamires and Marx, 'Woman Not to Preach', 50–5, from *Magistri Henrici Goethals a Gandavo . . . Summa in tres partes*, 3 vols. (Ferrara: F. Succius, 1642–46), i. 193–5. Henry's *Summa quaestionum* is a compilation of lectures dating from 1276–92. He cites Mary (i.e. Miriam), Deborah, Huldah, Anna, Mary Magdalene, and Martha, and the 'obligation' argument from 1 Pet. 4: 10 (p. 50).

[83] Aquinas, 'utrum gratia sermonis . . .', *Ad secundum* (pp. 134–5). The Waldensians had defined prophecy as not only declaration of future events but also revelation of hidden things, including exposition of the mysteries of the divine word; *PL* 204. 808.

[84] Some early medieval descriptions of women preaching (e.g. St Radegund and St Gertrude) were probably safeguarded by the fact that tradition—consolidated by canon law—permitted abbesses to preach to their nuns; McNamara, *Sainted Women of the Dark Ages*, 91–2, 224, 227. But Aldhelm (end of the 7th cent.) appears unembarrassed by the prospect of implicitly public female preaching when he describes Basilissa 'reaping one thousand sheaves of the holy harvest with the scythe of gospel preaching'; *De virginitate*, xxxvi, in *Aldhelm: The Prose Works*, tr. Lapidge and Herren, 100. Christine de Pizan, drawing on Vincent of Beauvais, specifically notes the 'preaching' of several women saints in the *Cité*, including Lucy, Benedicta, Fausta, Justine, Natalia, and Basilissa.

[85] Christ 'travelled . . . preaching and evangelizing the kingdom of God; and the twelve with him. And certain women who had been healed of evil spirits and

women can be found referred to as 'disciplesses', *discipulae*, along-side the male *discipuli*.[86] But because Mary Magdalene seemed conspicuously elevated to an evangelistic role when Christ asked her to inform the apostles of the Resurrection, she above all—and by extension her sister Martha—acquired a reputation for preaching. By the late twelfth century the author of a lyrical *Life* declared: 'It was fitting, then, that just as she had been chosen to be the apostle of Christ's resurrection and the prophet of his ascension, so also she became an evangelist for believers throughout the world.'[87] In the next century, at the same time as the scholastics were worrying about women's eligibility for preaching, Jacobus de Voragine was consolidating in the *Legenda aurea* (*c*.1255–66) a curriculum vitae for Mary which took her to Marseilles with other Christians displaced after Christ's death, and which envisaged her taking a leading role in converting Provence by her preaching.[88] Nor were these details of her career a matter of idle curiosity, for the location of her operations and whereabouts of her bones were fiercely and publicly contested between the authorities at Vézelay and Marseilles during the late thirteenth century. Her preaching exploits had a secure place in her reputation,

infirmities; Mary who is called Magdalen, out of whom seven devils were gone forth, And Joanna the wife of Chusa Herod's steward, and Susanna, and many others who ministered to him of their substance' (Luke 8: 1–3). The women are associated, albeit in a secondary role, with a preaching (Vulg. *praedicans*) campaign. The association was kept in mind by Augustine, *On the Work of Monks* (*De opere monachorum*, PL 40. 552–3).

[86] 'Iesus Christus non solum habuit discipulos sed et discipulas, quae eum sequebantur,' Humbert of Romans, sermon for Franciscan nuns, *De modo prompte cudendi sermones*, pt. i, no. 49; Edward Tracy Brett, *Humbert of Romans: His Life and Views of Thirteenth-Century Society* (Toronto: Pontifical Institute of Medieval Studies, 1984), 68. Elizabeth Clark notes that Chrysostom designates Mary Magdalene as Christ's disciple (Gk. *mathetria*) in *Homily 65 on John*, 2 (*PG* 59. 362); *Jerome, Chrysostom and Friends* (Lewiston, NY: Mellen Press, 1979), 7.

[87] *De vita beatae Mariae Magdalenae*, xxxviii (PL 112. 1495), tr. Mycoff, *The Life of Saint Mary Magdalene*, 96. Hence also one version of the *South English Legendary* simply asserts: 'Crist hire havede aboute isent to sarmoni and to preche' (158); *The Early South-English Legendary or Lives of Saints*, ed. Carl Horstmann, EETS os 87 (London: Oxford University Press, 1887), 466.

[88] The verb *praedicare* is repeatedly used. I have discussed this legend further in 'Women and Preaching in Medieval Orthodoxy, Heresy, and Saints' Lives', *Viator*, 26 (1995), 142–4. See 'De sancta Maria Magdalena', in Jacobus de Voragine, *Legenda aurea*, ed. Graesse, 407–17 (esp. pp. 409–10), and *The South English Legendary*, ed. Charlotte d'Evelyn and Anna J. Mill, 2 vols., EETS os 235–6 (Oxford: Oxford University Press, 1956), i. 304–11; also V. Saxer, *Le Culte de sainte Marie Madeleine en occident des origines à la fin du Moyen Âge*, 2 vols. (Auxerre: Publications de la Société des Fouilles Archéologiques et des Monuments Historiques de l'Yonne; Clavreuil, 1959).

even if it would be wrong to imply that they were paramount: arguably they were more famous in the case of her sister St Martha, because a memorable miracle in the latter's *Life* was the resurrection of a youth who drowned while trying to swim the Rhône to hear her preaching.[89] Mary was more celebrated as the penitent, as the 'special friend' and 'first servant' of Christ;[90] her destiny as personal 'apostle' of the Resurrection transcended her subsequent preaching role and raised her to an epic alignment with John the Baptist: hence the eloquent gender symmetry of her twelfth-century admirer's formulation: 'Among the sons of women, only the King of Heaven is equal to and greater than the Baptist; among the daughters of men, only the Queen of Heaven is equal to and greater than Mary Magdalene.'[91]

A full account of profeminine role-models for preaching would need to address further examples such as St Cecilia, who preached and was buried among popes—to the bemusement of Osbert of Clare in the twelfth century because that was a privilege which 'no woman before her had obtained, nor will any woman after her';[92] and St Catherine of Alexandria, whose intellectual conquest and conversion of a team of pagan philosophers assembled against her by Emperor Maxentius gave her a formidable profile as missionary rhetorician.[93] These women too have a secure niche in the formal literature of the case for women;[94] but let us now move on to consider how justifications of female evange-

---

[89] *The Life of Saint Mary Magdalene*, xlii, tr. Mycoff, 102–4; for other references to Martha's preaching, see xxxix–xl, pp. 97–9.

[90] These expressions are liberally used in the 12th-cent. *Vita*; see Mycoff, 55, 66, 72, 78, 80, 82.

[91] *De vita beatae Mariae Magdalenae*, xxxii (*PL* 112. 1485), tr. Mycoff, 85.

[92] *The Letters of Osbert of Clare*, 42, ed. Williamson, 139; Newman, 'Flaws in the Golden Bowl', in *From Virile Woman to Woman Christ*, 26. Humbert of Romans commended Cecilia ('not only virgin martyr, but also *predicatrix*') and Mary Magdalene for their preaching among several other women saints, in an unpublished section of the *De eruditione praedicatorum* of which Simon Tugwell has kindly let me see his draft edition.

[93] *Legenda aurea*, ed. Graesse, 789–97, tr. Ryan, ii. 334–41; and see Blamires, 'Women and Preaching', 144–5.

[94] Le Fèvre (*Leësce*, 2825–30) highlights St Catherine's wisdom and her skills in rhetoric, theory, and disputation. In Deschamps's *Miroir de mariage* (9071–2) she is referred to as a woman of *doctrine et . . . science*. Fifteenth-cent. developments in the Catherine legend are interestingly discussed in Karen A. Winstead, 'Capgrave's Saint Katherine and the Perils of Gynecocracy', *Viator*, 25 (1994), 361–76. St Cecilia's *Life* imagines her carrying the gospel 'in her bosom'—taken literally, this would have been an interesting model for women with intellectual aspirations which could not always be avowed publicly; *The Golden Legend*, tr. Ryan, ii. 318.

lism entered the self-authorizing strategies of specific religious women who wished to be heard in public.

The biblical prophetesses figure prominently—as demonstrated in Chapter 1—in the self-perceptions of celebrated evangelizing women such as Hildegard of Bingen and Elisabeth of Schönau. God makes women his instruments now, writes Elisabeth, just as in times past 'while men were given to indolence, holy women were filled with the Spirit so that they could prophesy' and govern and conquer: 'I speak of women like Huldah, Deborah, Judith.'[95] Slightly earlier in the twelfth century (c.1143) Heloise found herself compared, as 'leader in the Lord's army', with Penthesilea the Amazon and with Deborah; she was complimented for pouring out the 'hidden sweetness' of Scripture both for her nuns and (whatever this interesting addition implied) 'for all other women', by her 'public instruction'.[96]

But what of Justification by Talent? Awareness of this among scholars lags a little behind awareness of the prophetess dimension, perhaps because it is easily mistaken for a literary modesty-topos. Yet it is surely more than that in (for instance) the case of Hrotsvitha, who states in the Preface to her poems: 'I was eager that the talent given me by heaven should not grow rusty from neglect, and remain silent in my heart from apathy, but under the hammer of assiduous devotion should sound a chord of divine praise.'[97] It is also more than literary modesty in Hildegard, who like the Waldensians claims an *obligation* to speak of salvation in the magnificent opening of *Scivias*, which closely recalls St Gregory's tone of frostiness towards shirkers. She in her frailness is commanded to cry out: 'Let those who see the inner meaning of Scripture, yet do not wish to proclaim or preach it, take instruction . . . Unlock for them the treasury of mysteries, which they, the timid ones, bury in a hidden field without fruit.'[98] What others hide, she who can must bring to light. It was the same with

---

[95] Newman, *Sister of Wisdom*, 39, citing Elisabeth, *Liber visionum*, II. 1.

[96] Peter the Venerable, Letter 115, tr. Radice in *Letters of Abelard and Heloise*, 278, 280. Peter uses a conventional pun on the meaning of Deborah ('bee').

[97] *The Plays of Roswitha*, tr. St John, p. xxxiii. Dronke gives another translation of this passage, *Women Writers*, 65, but his discussion of the 'talents' passage (p. 66) and of a similar allusion in the Preface to the plays (pp. 69, 71) misses the polemical implications they bear in relation to a preaching vocation.

[98] 'quatenus ii erudiantur qui medullam Scripturarum videntes, eam nec dicere, nec praedicare volunt . . . quibus clausuram mysteriorum resera: quam ipsi timidi in abscondito agro sine fructu celant', *Scivias*, I. 1, PL 197. 385; tr. Hart and Bishop, 67.

Elisabeth of Schönau. At first she felt diffident about her visions, but eventually an angel appeared to her, demanding, 'Why do you hide gold in mud?'[99]

Less melodramatic versions of the obligation-not-to-hide argument are found among writing women during and beyond the Middle Ages,[100] but officialdom had a ready response along the lines that what you could unlock, for whom, depended on who— and certainly on which sex—you were. Where women had evangelized, they had done so by special divine dispensation or 'privilege'. This exception clause was a way of reconciling both prophetesses and female preaching saints with dogma,[101] but in concluding this chapter I would like to speculate that the medieval Church was more prepared to tolerate the public role of the scriptural prophetesses than the public preaching associated with some women saints as role-models for women. This preference fostered a situation well described by Bynum, in which throughout the Middle Ages 'the religious authority and significance of holy women for others in the society (both male and female) lay more centrally in their charismatic, especially their prophetic, gifts, whereas male saints often owed their power to ecclesiastical or even secular office'.[102] Since the prophetic gift was (like a seat in the British House of Lords) an object of mingled awe and scepticism, it gave only a pseudo-

---

[99] 'In order that I might avoid arrogance, and that I might not be perceived as the author of novelties, I strove to hide these things as much as possible. Therefore . . . an angel of the Lord stood before me saying "Why do you hide gold in mud?" . . . And he lifted up a scourge over me, which he struck me with most harshly,' Kathryn Kerby-Fulton and Dyan Elliott, 'Self-Image and the Visionary Role in Two Letters from the Correspondence of Elizabeth of Schönau and Hildegard of Bingen', *Vox Benedictina*, 2/3 (1985), 204–23 (p. 215). Rosalynn Voaden categorizes this as 'divine command to write', 'God's Almighty Hand: Women Co-writing the Book', in Lesley Smith and Jane H. M. Taylor (eds.), *Women, the Book and the Godly* (Cambridge: D. S. Brewer, 1995), 55–65 (p. 57).

[100] See the Prologue to the *Lais of Marie de France*, tr. Glyn S. Burgess and Keith Busby (Harmondsworth: Penguin, 1986), 41; and for later examples see Merry E. Wiesner, 'Women's Defense of their Public Role', in Mary Beth Rose (ed.), *Women in the Middle Ages and the Renaissance: Literary and Historical Perspectives* (Syracuse, NY: Syracuse University Press, 1986), 1–27.

[101] Hugh of St Cher's first caveat concerning Deborah, Huldah, Martha, and Philip's four daughters is that in so far as they preached or expounded doctrine, they did so by exceptional privilege; *Postillae* on 1 Cor. 14: 34 (Basle, 1504 edn.), fo. 103[v].

[102] '". . . And Woman his Humanity": Female Imagery in the Religious Writing of the Later Middle Ages', 259–60.

evangelizing power to religious women, pushed them 'upstairs' as it were, leaving male ecclesiastics to continue unimpeded in executive doctrinal roles.[103] Did the prophetic vocation constitute territory politically conceded, so as to divert profeminine energies away from other possible reinforcements for women's religious authority?

What partly inclines me to this view is the surprisingly belated appearance of the Samaritan woman as a role-model. Here, after all, was the New Testament precedent of a woman whose words brought a whole city out to hear Christ after her conversation with him. She is mentioned positively by Abelard in the twelfth century and negatively by Hugh of St Cher in the thirteenth as a possible preaching exemplar but is generally under-represented in the medieval case for women, considering the impact she makes in St John's Gospel, 4: 1–42. There, while the disciples go to buy food Jesus converses with a woman of Samaria at a well about spiritual thirst and, in a cryptic interrogation about her 'husband', shows miraculous insight into her life. She begins to recognize him as Messiah and, going into the city, she then 'speaks' to the people (*dicit illis hominibus*, 4: 28) about her perception of him so that they flock out to hear him (many of them believing through her testimony, some doubting a woman's word at first). Perhaps because she is not called a prophetess or associated with a powerful verb such as *annuntiare*, the momentous, evangelistic nature of her intervention seems to have escaped notice or to have been suppressed in polemic about the status of women until the period of Abelard.

One can talk of 'suppression' advisedly. Some commentators had seen the apostolic dimension of the woman's role.[104] Chrysostom in particular had given an enthusiastic account of her intelligent response to Christ and the wisdom with which she took up an 'apostolic' and 'evangelistic' function, acting as professor

[103] Fiorenza takes a more thoroughly favourable view of the continuing claim by women such as Hildegard and Catherine of Siena to 'mystic-prophetic teaching authority' despite centuries of ecclesiastical erosion of 'women's authority as official prophets and teachers in the church', *In Memory of Her*, 304. But note Hugh of St Cher's second caveat in his gloss on Corinthians, that while prophetesses might give precedent for foretelling the future or uttering praise, they do not give precedent for 'expounding scripture in preaching' (a distinction, in fact, between *praedicere* and *praedicare*).

[104] Origen suggests that Jesus 'uses her as an apostle to the people in the city' but in other ways disparages her, *Commentary on John*, PG 14. 447.

(*magistra*) to the citizens.[105] But it was an Augustinian reading that dominated medieval glosses: in particular, Augustine's demeaning interpretation of Christ's bidding to her to 'call her husband' (when she literally had none) as an allegorical statement of her need to summon up her understanding (her *intellectus*, gendered masculine as 'husband') in order to suppress her incipiently 'carnal' (feminine) response and thence recognize Christ.[106] Fortunately some readers, notably Abelard—who was aware of Chrysostom's work—were prepared to shrug Augustine aside. Abelard lyrically restores respect for the Samaritan's unique colloquy with Christ and communicates the excitement of her mission to the city, where she announced Christ's coming and preached what she had heard—as the very foundress of Christ's work among the Gentiles.[107] By contrast a century later Hugh of St Cher, at a time of reaction to scares about the prominence of women in the Waldensian and Cathar movements, struggles to delete her 'preaching' and rename it 'narration'.[108]

This glimpse of the choppy currents of commentary in which the case for women participated enables us to sense again how equivocal the estimate of a prominent biblical woman as role-model might be. The equivocation could be tracked onwards through the fourteenth century. Take, for example, the cycle of illustrations accompanying an Italian version of the *Meditations on the Life of Christ*, published by Isa Ragusa in 1961: here, in a pictorial narrative extending unexpectedly to eight miniatures across two bifolios, the urgency of the Samaritan woman's appeal to the citizens is palpable (more than in the text of the *Meditations* itself, in fact).[109] The fact that so many miniatures are provided

---

[105] *Homiliae in Johannem*, 31–5, PG 59. 175–200 (esp. 184–5, 193, 198); tr. in Select Library of the Nicene and Post-Nicene Fathers, ed. Philip Schaff, vol. 14 (Grand Rapids, Mich.: Eerdmans, 1969), 106–23 (esp. pp. 112–13, 118, 122).

[106] Augustine, *In Joannis evangelium*, xv. 10–30, PL 35. 1514–21. The reading was disseminated through channels such as the *Glossa ordinaria*; see PL 114. 372. For a fuller account of Augustine's commentary on the Samaritan woman and its contrast with Chrysostom's and Abelard's, see my article ' "*Caput a femina, membra a viris*": Gender Polemic in Abelard's Letter "On the Authority and Dignity of the Nun's Profession" ' (forthcoming).

[107] 'Letter of Heloise on Religious Life and Abelard's First Reply', ed. Muckle, 273; tr. Scott Moncrieff, 163–4.

[108] 'So far as the Samaritan is concerned, one can say that she did not preach (*non praedicauit*); but that she narrated what she heard and saw' (*quod audiuit et vidit hoc narrauit*); *Postillae* on 1 Cor. 14: 34 (Basle, 1504 edn.), fo. 104ʳ.

[109] *Meditations on the Life of Christ*, tr. Ragusa and Green, ch. xxxi, and figs. 169–77, esp. 174, where, in an interesting segregation and sequencing of sexes, the

attests the book designer's high valuation of this episode in a text which addresses itself to a woman. But the fact that the Samaritan's actual gesture to the citizens uses the iconography of supplication, rather than of preaching, serves to curb too radical a view of her as role-model, and complements the text's equivocal nuance of condescension.[110] Moving on to the end of the fourteenth century, the Samaritan is mentioned again by a champion of orthodoxy against the Lollard heresy in England, Thomas Netter (1377–1430). In one passage of his *Doctrinale* Netter aims to refute the defence of lay and female preaching by the Lollard John Purvey.[111] Precedents Netter deals with (raised in Purvey's lost arguments?) include Judith, Mary Magdalene, the Virgin Mary, and the Samaritan woman. Netter offers some standard strategies of refutation (Judith's initiative was at a time of peril, Mary Magdalene's was at a time of extreme staff shortage in the Church's infancy); but he disqualifies all the women in any case—using a Thomistic argument—for their alleged lack of pedagogical authority or *magisterium*.[112]

Not the disqualification, but the perceived need for one, is instructive. This chapter began with prophetesses whose status as role-models for some kind of public role for women gained a measure of conditional assent throughout the Middle Ages. The formal case for women relentlessly cited them. The Samaritan woman is more marginalized—whether or not because she was instinctively feared from as early as the fourth century as ultimately a more serious threat to religious patriarchy, I am not sure. Some of the favourite candidates for encomium and emulation in

Samaritan woman is represented as having already prompted a group of women to action, but is now appealing to a group of men to do likewise (see jacket illustration). She is conspicuous in miniatures 171–4.

[110] The iconography of the gesture was clarified for me by Aline Rousselle. The condescending tone is exemplified in the claim that Christ 'did not disdain her, and said things to her that would have seemed very great if He had said them to many of the wisest men'; tr. Ragusa, 190.

[111] On women and preaching in Lollardy, see Margaret Aston, 'Lollard Women Priests?', *Journal of Ecclesiastical History*, 31 (1980), 441–61, repr. in her *Lollards and Reformers* (London: Hambledon Press, 1984), 49–70; Alcuin Blamires, 'The Wife of Bath and Lollardy', *Medium Aevum*, 58 (1989), 224–42; and Blamires and Marx, 'Woman Not to Preach', 34–9, 44–9, 55–63.

[112] Thomas Netter, *Doctrinale antiquitatum fidei catholicae ecclesiae*, 2 vols. (Venice, 1757–9), i. 639 (II, art. 3, ch. lxxiii, 'Contra quendam Doctorem Wiclevistam [i.e. John Purvey] quod non licet singulis Christianis passim praedicare quiuslibet, sine authoritate antistitis', aimed at Purvey's lost *De compendiis scripturarum*; I owe the reference to Minnis, '*De impedimento sexus*'.

the case for women were no threat to patriarchy at all, as normally constituted, and narrowed rather than widened the options for profeminine assertion. Lucretia for example is a paragon of domesticity, loyally industrious at the hearth in her husband's absence, and liable to take independent action (suicide) after her rape only in defence of a selfhood which is utterly grounded in a masculine belief that she is her husband's sexual property. If this chapter has over-emphasized scriptural role-models, what should be said is that many of these appeared more autonomous than models such as Lucretia; that if they were sometimes less autonomous than Amazons, they were more drilled into people's consciousness (St Mary Magdalene—'perhaps the most popular saint in the Middle Ages after the Virgin Mary'[113]—and St Catherine were probably rivalled in Europe only by St Margaret), and that the model which they supplied of public roles was therefore ever present. The signs are that patriarchy tried to keep the lid on the Samaritan woman's potential for emulation; but she did not go away either. With its right hand the Church wanted to acknowledge something of the public efficacy of its received heroines; to women who responded to that, the Church's left hand must have seemed at least awkward in seeking to curb the consequences.

[113] Karras, 'Holy Harlots', 17; Saxer, *Le Culte de sainte Marie Madeleine en occident*, *passim*.

8

The Formal Case in Abelard, Chaucer, Christine de Pizan

THIS book has already made many incidental references to the three writers who are the subject of this chapter. However, the challenge of coming to terms with the medieval case for women would seem poorly met if no concerted attempt were made to focus the relevant works of these well-known authors in the context of the traditions I have discussed. Each produced a version of the formal case. Abelard did so adventitiously, in that a case for the supreme importance of women in religious history was what actually transpired when he set out to analyse the origins of and authority for the nun's vocation. Chaucer produced in *The Legend of Good Women* a version of the case so opaque in its inflatory and deflatory impulses that people will argue for ever whether it is a sort of hoax. Christine de Pizan, after her reconnaissance of the subject in the *Epistre au dieu d'amours*, went on to construct a whole literary fortress for women in the *Cité des dames*, whose comprehensiveness as a profeminine statement was not really exceeded in my opinion until the humanist debates of the sixteenth century.[1]

The correspondence between Heloise and Abelard is traditionally dated to the 1130s,[2] some fifteen years after their intense relationship had foundered when he was castrated by Heloise's guardian, and had hurried her into taking vows at the convent of Argenteuil before himself retreating into the abbey of St Denis.[3] In

---

[1] Subsequent 15th-cent. defences sometimes sprawled more expansively, without being more comprehensive: e.g. Martin le Franc, *Le Champion des dames*, ed. Arthur Piaget, Mémoires et documents publiés par la Société d'Histoire de la Suisse Romande, 3rd ser. 8 (Lausanne: Payot, 1968).

[2] See the chronology in Constant Mews, 'On Dating the Works of Peter Abelard', *Archives d'histoire doctrinale et littérature du Moyen Âge*, 51 (1985), 73–134 (pp. 130–2), which dates the correspondence tentatively to 1132–7.

[3] Earlier scholars' doubts about the authenticity of the correspondence have been systematically removed by: Peter Dronke, 'Abelard and Heloise in Medieval Testimonies', originally published as a lecture by Glasgow University Press (1976) and now repr. in his *Intellectuals and Poets in Medieval Europe*, Storia e Letteratura, Raccolta di Studi e Testi 183 (Rome: Edizioni di Storia e Letteratura, 1992), 248–94;

the intervening period Abelard briefly explored an independent form of monasticism by setting up his rural oratory of the Paraclete beside the river Ardusson (1123). Then, installed as unpopular abbot in a Brittany monastery, he made tongues wag by resuming contact with Heloise, to help her nuns re-establish themselves at the now deserted Paraclete when they lost possession of Argenteuil.

What is significant from the present point of view about the period leading up to their letters[4] is that Abelard seems to have been attempting (probably most successfully when he founded the Paraclete) to identify and validate a suitably august role for a self which was becoming professionally alienated and rootless: he was keen to define monkhood in such a way that he could insert himself, as autonomous 'philosopher-monk', into an ancient tradition of the ascetic Christian intellectual.[5] He found authority for this vision of himself in St Jerome's several reflections on the philosopher life, which connected it both with 'Pythagorean' solitude and with a passage in the Old Testament which showed, according to Jerome, that the drop-out followers of Elisha—the 'sons of prophets' who left society to build a hut community by the Jordan—were 'monks'.[6] But while Abelard ostentatiously

David Luscombe, 'From Paris to the Paraclete: The Correspondence of Abelard and Heloise', *Proceedings of the British Academy*, 74 (1989), 247–83; and Barbara Newman, 'Authority, Authenticity, and the Repression of Heloise', *Journal of Medieval and Renaissance Studies*, 22 (1992), 121–57 (repr. in her *From Virile Woman to Woman Christ*, 46–75).

[4] The correspondence is edited by J. T. Muckle in: 'Abelard's Letter of Consolation to a Friend (*Historia calamitatum*)' *Mediaeval Studies*, 12 (1950), 161–213; 'The Personal Letters between Abelard and Heloise', *Mediaeval Studies*, 15 (1953), 47–94; and 'The Letter of Heloise on Religious Life and Abelard's First Reply', *Mediaeval Studies*, 17 (1955), 240–81; and by T. P. McLaughlin, 'Abelard's Rule for Religious Women', *Mediaeval Studies*, 18 (1956), 241–92. The numbering of the letters is a nightmare, because some scholars number the *Historia calamitatum* as the first, while others number Heloise's response to the *Historia* as the first. So, the letter I am concerned with below is numbered 6 in *The Letters of Abelard and Heloise*, tr. Radice, and 7 in *The Letters of Abelard and Heloise*, tr. Scott Moncrieff.

[5] See further my paper '*Caput a femina, membra a viris*: Gender Polemic in Abelard's Letter "On the Authority and Dignity of the Nun's Profession"' (forthcoming); also Mary McLaughlin, 'Abelard as Autobiographer: The Motives and Meaning of his "Story of Calamities"', *Speculum*, 42 (1967), 463–89 (pp. 477–80).

[6] Muckle, 'Abelard's Letter of Consolation', 187 and 199–200, tr. Radice, 72 and 88–90; cf. 'For us, the leaders [*principes*] of our calling should be the Pauls, Antonies, Hilaries and Macharius and, to return to the Scriptures [i.e. 2 Sam. 6: 4], let our leaders [*noster princeps*] be Elijah and Elisha, the chief of the prophets, who lived in fields and the wilderness and made themselves huts by the river Jordan', McLaughlin, 'Abelard's Rule' (quoting Jerome, Letter 58. 5), 248, tr. Radice, 192.

traced his new life to classical and scriptural founders (*principes*), Heloise found herself at his bidding a nun without a clear sense of vocation, and subsequently a prioress who felt (I believe) that the ex-husband who could dignify his monkhood with such a history owed it to her to dignify her nunhood with a comparable history. This explains why, when Abelard stonewalled the appeals she made for personal consolation in her first two letters, she shifted ground and asked him in her third to communicate to her both the origins of female monasticism—the *auctoritas* of her profession[7]—and also a rule properly designed for nuns. There is less of a break from the previous 'personal' letters than is usually assumed (as well as more connection between these two requests) because Heloise is still challenging Abelard to respond to her personally, only now by asking him to supply her with foundations—with 'authority', in the medieval sense—commensurate with her identity, just as he has done for himself.[8]

Because Abelard's first reply, sometimes entitled 'On the Origin of Nuns', so wholeheartedly accepts that challenge, scholars ought to insist on its implicit title 'The Authority and Dignity of the Nun's Profession';[9] they ought to remedy the obscurity to which this letter has been consigned by its neglect in

[7] 'unde sanctimonialium ordo coeperit, et quae nostrae sit professionis auctoritas'; Muckle, 'Letter of Heloise on Religious Life and Abelard's First Reply', 242.

[8] Other important explanations of Heloise's requests are offered by Mary McLaughlin—notably, that they articulated widespread anxieties (felt by the fledgeling community of the Paraclete in particular) about the status of nuns at a time when there was a great surge of women's interest in the monastic and 'apostolic' vocation; and that they provided an opportunity for Abelard to dignify a community which regarded him as its founder (and through advising which he could accomplish some of the dreams unrealized in his own career); 'Peter Abelard and the Dignity of Women: Twelfth Century "Feminism" in Theory and Practice', in *Pierre Abelard—Pierre le Vénérable: Les Courants philosophiques*, Actes, Colloque International, Cluny, 1972 (Paris: Centre National de la Recherche Scientifique, 1975), 287–333, an outstanding discussion to which I am deeply indebted.

[9] Scott Moncrieff's translation uses the quaint title 'Touching the Origin of Nuns', *Letters of Abelard and Heloise*, 129. When first describing the manuscripts, Muckle used the designation *De origine sanctimonialium*; 'Abelard's Letter of Consolation', 164, 165. When he came to edit the letter, he adopted a manuscript title, 'Rescriptum ad ipsam de auctoritate vel dignitate ordinis sanctimonialium'. This *De auctoritate* ... format is followed by Barbara Newman, 'Flaws in the Golden Bowl', in *From Virile Woman to Woman Christ*, 255 n. 38 and implicitly by Mary McLaughlin who designates the letter 'On the Authority and Dignity of the Order of Nuns', in 'Peter Abelard and the Dignity of Women', 291. This title is justified not by the letter's opening (which echoes Heloise's request by undertaking to discuss 'whence the religion of nuns began') but by its conclusion, which ex-

translation;[10] and they ought to root out the old prejudice that Abelard's extraordinary investigation here into the foundations of female religion is some sort of rigmarole which 'must have cost him much dreary toil'.[11]

On the contrary it is a zealously pugnacious piece, exuding energy and a sense of discovery. In urging female 'authority' of any sort Abelard is on unusual ground for the Middle Ages, since *auctoritas* was not in general a concept associated with women.[12] All the more striking, therefore, is the extent to which he is prepared to go not just in digging out evidence about women in early Christianity appropriate to an essay on origins, but in actually ascribing both 'priority' and 'prerogative' to women (reinforcing their authority) in many aspects of religion. Examples of this in successive stages of his argument are, that it was a woman who exercised the prerogative of consecrating Christ; that women took precedence over men in announcing the Resurrection; that the *auctoritas* for women singing divine office goes back furthest—to Miriam in the Book of Exodus who sang while Moses did not; that Anna preached the new-born Christ, but her colleague Simeon did not; that special feast days are set aside for the consecration of virgin women; that woman but not man was created in paradise; that Eve was 'restored' in Mary before Adam was restored in Christ; that Anna and Mary provided a model for female sanctity before a model of monasticism was disclosed to men in John the Baptist or the apostles; that Elizabeth took precedence over the Baptist because she prophesied about Christ before his birth not after; that the Sibyl's prophecies of Christ exceeded even Isaiah's; that the Samaritan woman initiated Christ's preaching to the Gentiles; that prostitutes are said to 'precede' men into heaven; that forms of sacred female chastity already existed in pagan religion; and that St Jerome prioritized his women correspondents over Augustine.

presses the hope that he has given sufficient reply concerning the authority of Heloise's order and also commendation of the dignity belonging to that order ('de auctoritate . . . ordinis vestri, et insuper de commendatione propriae dignitatis'); 'Letter of Heloise on Religious Life and Abelard's First Reply', ed. Muckle, 253, 281.

[10] Radice's Penguin translation of the letters omits *The Authority and Dignity of Nuns*, giving only a three-page summary of what she terms this 'prolix' piece, 180–2.

[11] R. W. Southern, 'The Letters of Abelard and Heloise', in his *Medieval Humanism and Other Essays* (Oxford: Blackwell, 1970), 101.

[12] Except, nebulously, through literary personifications such as Philosophia or Iustitia.

Of course such an abstract does little justice to the coherent structure which these examples support. Careful reading would show how they configure a discussion under five heads: (a) the key role of holy women in the time of Christ; (b) the conjunction of female with male religion in the Old Testament and early Church; (c) proof that the divine grace of strength has persistently been showered upon women in religious history; (d) the ancient roots of the *institutio* of religious chastity for women; and (e) the Church Fathers' privileging of devout women in their teaching. To a modern reader's possible objection that trivia seem to jostle with weightier evidence, specific replies can usually be given in each instance, as well as an overarching reply. For instance, that Jerome wrote so often to Paula and other women but left a request by Augustine unanswered was no trivial matter to Abelard because Jerome was his self-appointed intellectual mentor; the more special in having—like himself—provoked notoriety for an association with women, and special again in that this very letter to Heloise emulates (but also distinguishes itself from) the consolatory epistles written by Jerome for his women friends.[13]

In any case, the overarching reply is that it would be illogical to protest against Abelard's use of every scrap, however small, of historical evidence of women's dignity when one considers the enormous empire of masculine *auctoritas* which he was confronting. Nor was he alone in adducing some of the flimsiest-looking scraps, such as the fact that St John places women before a man in his verse, 'Now Jesus loved Martha, and her sister, and Lazarus', as though (says Abelard) 'believing [the women] to come first' in Christ's affections.[14] The prefix *prae-* in verbs which describe women taking precedence over men, found here in *praeposuit* and *praecellere*, crops up frequently in the letter along with adjectives

---

[13] Abelard's debts to St Jerome are ubiquitous; some are discussed in McLaughlin, 'Peter Abelard and the Dignity of Women', 309–11. I develop elsewhere the argument that the conclusion of the *The Authority and Dignity of Nuns* nevertheless pointedly dissociates itself from the encomiastic excesses which he noticed in Jerome's epistles to women; '*Caput a femina, membra a viris*; Gender Polemic in Abelard's Letter' (forthcoming).

[14] See John 11: 5. Abelard states that John, himself privileged as the 'beloved of the Lord', 'has distinguished the women with that same privilege. ... In which honour, moreover, if he associated their brother with them, yet he placed them before him, believing them to come first in love'; 'Letter of Heloise on Religious Life and Abelard's First Reply', ed. Muckle, 274, tr. Scott Moncrieff, 165. The 12th-cent. *Life* of Mary Magdalene quotes the verse twice, and comments, 'rarely in Scripture do we find mentioned by name any believer whom the Lord particularly loved', tr. Mycoff, 47 (also p. 27); and *Vita beatae Mariae Magdalenae*, xiii, (PL 112. 1449) and prologue (PL 112. 1431).

and adverbs of 'priority'. Chronological precedence was not generally a major element in the formal medieval case for women
except in the emphasis on the resurrected Christ's appearance
first to women, and on the first announcement of the Resurrection
by women. Abelard, however, even though far from feminist in
his underlying assumptions about women's 'weakness' as shown
earlier, perceived a proto-feminist way to construct a fresh reading of Scripture by identifying and emphasizing—as if from a
female subject position—priority of female rather than male
achievement. He saw what I think few profeminine writers after
him saw until Christine de Pizan—that the case for women had to
be built on claims for their *foundational* importance. Women had
to be seen to have initiated, to have got there first, in order to
attain *auctoritas*. That is why Abelard is so relentless on the subject. That is why he brings a seemingly mad pedantry to bear,
observing for example that there is no mention of Moses when
Miriam and other women chant in sequence after the crossing of
the Red Sea, and that no men play timbrels on that occasion
either. It is an odd-looking point. But if the orderly chant and the
timbrels are figures for 'the spiritual song in monastic congregations' as Abelard maintains,[15] then the omission of men from the
Exodus account is indeed a significant coup for female authority,
and an erosion of male authority, in liturgical matters.

Abelard's vigilant eye enables him to rebalance women's history so as to produce fascinating results, both in instances where
one can find parallels in the formal case and where not. Take
Anna, who is already familiar to us as a contested model of
prophetess/preacher. To Abelard she is categorically a public
preacher[16] but also more than that; an originary prototype of
assiduous feminine monasticism, to be juxtaposed in his first
paragraph with those 'sons of prophets' from whom he believes
monkhood to descend; and she is on equal terms with Simeon in
the temple.[17] When he analyses her role a second time, her 'equal-

---

[15] 'Letter of Heloise on Religious Life and Abelard's First Reply', ed. Muckle,
261, tr. Scott Moncrieff, 144. See Exod. 15: 20–1: 'So Mary [Miriam] the prophetess
the sister of Aaron, took a timbrel in her hand: and all the women went forth after
her with timbrels and with dances: And she began the song [*praecinebat*] to them,'
where *praecinere* is taken by Abelard to indicate organized quasi-liturgical song.

[16] He says that St Luke has described Anna's *publicam . . . praedicationem*; 'Letter
of Heloise on Religious Life and Abelard's First Reply', ed. Muckle, 263, tr. Scott
Moncrieff, 147.

[17] Ibid., ed. Muckle, 253, tr. Scott Moncrieff, 131.

ity' even acquires an edge, in light of St Luke's failure to attribute
to Simeon either conscientious temple attendance or chastity, let
alone prophecy and preaching, on a par with Anna's.[18] The same
tendency to enlarge equality into superiority is conspicuous in
two further areas of the treatise which I would also like to mention, first to underline Abelard's interest in women's prophetic
and intellectual potential, and then to identify his distinctive thesis that Jesus was conducted through his most important *rite de
passage* by a woman.

So far as the traditional prophetesses are concerned, Abelard
typically manages to outstrip conventional encomium by pursuing comparisons to the detriment of famous men, as readers may
already have noticed in the case of Elizabeth's alleged superiority
over John the Baptist.[19] (The persistent contrastive mechanism
bespeaks Abelard's confrontational style and his dialectical instincts.[20] If the method might now be suspect because liable to
perpetuate gender friction and an obsession with seniority, we
should also recognize that the confrontational mentality is actually what drives Abelard to discover how the Bible could be made
to yield valencies in women like Elizabeth.) But the hunt for
'authority' takes him further. It prompts him to combine his
knowledge of Augustine, Lactantius, and Virgil to present the
Sibyl's prophecies of Christ as the most comprehensive ever
made.[21] The 'accuracy' of the prophecies is not actually surprising
to modern scholars since, unbeknown to Abelard, most of those
he quotes were early forgeries.[22] But from his point of view the
Sibyl (whether Erythraean or Cumaean; he mentions both) clearly

[18] Ibid., ed. Muckle, 263, tr. Scott Moncrieff, 147–8. According to Muckle's notes,
three late affiliated MSS of the *Letters* omit this entire segment on Anna: whether
accidentally, or to exclude claims about Anna's role which someone found unpal-
atable, needs investigating.

[19] This extends even to the suggestion that Elizabeth should be called
prophetarum propheta, 'prophet of the prophets' (as Mary Magdalene is called
'apostle of the apostles'); ibid., ed. Muckle, 271, tr. Scott Moncrieff, 160.

[20] On the 'disputational dynamic' in Abelard, see Solterer, *The Master and
Minerva*, 28–9.

[21] 'If we compare [with the Sibyl] all the prophets, Isaiah himself even, . . . we
shall see that in this grace also the woman far excels the men' (*in hac quoque gratia
feminam viris longe praestare*); 'Letter of Heloise on Religious Life and Abelard's
First Reply', ed. Muckle, 271, tr. Scott Moncrieff, 160.

[22] The subject is explored in Bernard McGinn, '*Teste David cum Sibylla*: The
Significance of the Sibylline Tradition in the Middle Ages', in Julius Kirshner and
Suzanne F. Wemple (eds.), *Women of the Medieval World: Essays in Honor of John H.
Mundy* (Oxford: Blackwell, 1985), 7–35; and Peter Dronke, 'Hermes and the Sibyls:
Continuations and Creations', in *Intellectuals and Poets in Medieval Europe*, 219–41.

provides another formidable instance of female *auctoritas*. And although he cannot furnish a 'philosophical' pre-Christian ancestry for nuns to match the stunning vatic Christianity of pagan Sibyls, he produces from Eusebius' history of the dawn of Christianity a quotation from Philo about women who eschewed marriage for love of philosophy (*propter amorem philosophiae*), committing themselves to wisdom and sharing a proto-monastic life with men.[23] Yet, female monastic philosophy and Sibylline chastity were closely linked in Abelard's mind. His *Theologia Christiana*, written *c.*1124, deduces from Jerome a 'power of continence . . . in those women who have been outstanding in their philosophical and literary endowment'; an endowment exemplified in the Sibylline gift of prophecy.[24]

Yet the most daring point in Abelard's case, in fact the rock on which it is founded, is his claim that a woman consecrated Christ. It seems that meditation on the traditional topic of the loyalty of Christ's women followers led Abelard to discover radical sacramental possibilities within the episodes where Christ's feet and his head are anointed by women. The trigger is a connection with a prophecy in the Book of Daniel (9: 24) of a time when sin will end and 'the saint of saints may be anointed'. Abelard notes that men (here equality is glimpsed) anointed Christ's dead body: but only women (transcending equality) anointed him when alive. Since 'Christ' *means* 'the anointed', the logic of the anointing action is that it was a woman who therefore effectively named him, designated him Christ. Add to this that the two anointings parallel the sacraments of unction performed subsequently by men through history when instituting priests and kings, and we have a dramatic case for female instrumentality at a critical ritual moment in Christ's life, in consecrating the 'head' of the Church as mystical king and priest in actions which would

[23] 'Letter of Heloise on Religious Life and Abelard's First Reply', ed. Muckle, 260, tr. Scott Moncrieff, 142. The evidence here comes from quotations by the historian Eusebius from Philo's *De vita contemplativa* about a community of *therapeutae* and *therapeutrides*; *Ecclesiastical History*, II. 17, tr. Lawlor and Oulton, i. 48–52 (esp. p. 51). In that Philo actually claimed them as *pre*-Christian, they supported Abelard's argument for the *auctoritas* of female monasticism even better than he realized.
[24] 'Sed nec ista continentiae virtus, aut pudicitiae amor, feminis ipsis philosophiae et litterarum abundantia insignitis defuisse cognoscitur. . . . Unde Hieronymus in eodem contra Jovinianum libro: "Quid referam, inquit, Sibyllam Erythream atque Cumanam et octo reliquas,"' *PL* 178. 1201–2: a point noted by Peter Dronke, 'Peter Abelard: *Planctus* and Satire', 147–8.

subsequently be used by men to consecrate only the Church's 'members'.[25] Of the various unique challenges to gender paradigms which are thus discovered in what Abelard calls this *dignitas* of women, it is (as I elaborate elsewhere) the affiliation between woman and 'head' which is most explosive.[26] Small wonder that Abelard launches the *De auctoritate* with this argument. It casts woman in an authoritative relation to Christ: no greater authority for the religious vocation of women could easily be imagined.[27]

Abelard had to square such profeminine claims with the period's understanding of women's supposed inadequacies by embracing—as I showed earlier—an ultimately misogynous view of women's 'strength in weakness'. With all due allowances made for that and for inconsistencies of standpoint in his writings as a whole, his achievement is probably too damply acknowledged in the suggestion that 'no one went further in the ritual praise of women' than he.[28] In extending familiar profeminine topoi he got beyond ritual and charged them with a new surge of electricity. He was ahead of his time in his sweeping historical vision, in his characteristically defiant interpretative moves, and above all in championing feminine *auctoritas*.

Although as will be seen shortly Abelard's closest successor in this respect was Christine de Pizan, I should like first to juxtapose Chaucer across the gap of 260 years with Abelard, because this will clarify the temperamental and cultural difficulties which muddled the response of the English poet (who has sometimes been considered quasi-feminist) to profeminine tradition. An interesting symptom of the differences which emerge from this juxtaposition would be the two writers' responses to Jerome. Both were deeply indebted to Jerome's anti-matrimonial treatise *Adversus Iovinianum*, Abelard the more emotionally in that he took to heart Jerome's model of the ascetic *philosophus*, and in that he and Heloise hotly debated whether or not they should marry

[25] 'Letter of Heloise on Religious Life and Abelard's First Reply', ed. Muckle, 254–5, tr. Scott Moncrieff, 133–5.
[26] 'Paradox in the Medieval Gender Doctrine of Head and Body', and '*Caput a femina, membra a viris*: Gender Polemic in Abelard's Letter "On the Authority and Dignity of the Nun's Profession"' (forthcoming).
[27] This seems further to consolidate McLaughlin's emphasis on the 'Christ-centred force' of the argument in the *De auctoritate*; 'Peter Abelard and the Dignity of Women', 303.
[28] Newman, 'Flaws in the Golden Bowl', 27, in the course of what is nevertheless a cogent summary of Abelard's views.

when their love affair was becoming public. Chaucer by contrast viewed the treatise as a text for critical play, creative manipulation: it drew out his own skills in both using, and disclosing the usability of, 'authoritative' texts on gender matters. The fact that Abelard represented Heloise, rather than himself, as having quoted Jerome's misogamous arguments bears interestingly (as Jill Mann has suggested) on Chaucer's decision to make a woman—the Wife of Bath—voice those same arguments.[29] While I agree that this decision suggests Chaucer's fascination with ironies of subjectivity and voicing attendant upon gender controversy, in other words his fascination with the way speakers' circumstances, agendas, and assumed audiences undermine the hypothetical 'authority' of whatever statements about gender they make, I think we should also notice that Chaucer thereby disqualifies himself from producing anything like the kind of uncluttered, positive view of feminine *auctoritas* reached by Abelard. Abelard discovers that history inscribes women's authority and dignity no less than men's when it is read afresh. Chaucer, too, reads history afresh in the sense that he is prepared to retrieve the viewpoint of a Criseyde or a Dido against the grain of their common negative representation, but this is not a matter of giving women serious *auctoritas*.

Is Chaucer too conservative to make that kind of Abelardian commitment, or is it just that his agenda is different? When direct profeminine assertions are made in Chaucer's poetry, they are often so entangled in ironizing complications that they become intellectual juggling acts. Before discussing *The Legend of Good Women*, Chaucer's most formally profeminine text, I should like to glance at the effect of ironizing contextualizations on traditional profeminine topoi in *The Merchant's Tale*.

This bleak tale about the sordid old egotist January, his pragmatic young bride May, and the panting youth Damien whom she satisfies in a tree, sets out to sour many sentiments. At its close the tale dwells upon the old question of masculine versus feminine sexual instability. It does so in such a way as to suggest that a profeminine strategy which merely returns misogyny's fire by indignantly redefining instability as a masculine stereotype

---

[29] Abelard quotes *Adv. Iov.* at length in *Historia calamitatum* (*The Story of his Misfortunes*), ed. Muckle, 199–200, tr. Radice, 89; and ascribes the *Historia*'s antimatrimonial arguments to Heloise; ed. Muckle, 186–9, tr. Radice, 71–3. Mann's suggestion is in her *Geoffrey Chaucer*, 52–5.

would be pointless. Refreshing though such redefinition might appear, it is seen to lead only to loggerheads, a juvenile impasse of the 'you are/no, we're not' variety. Chaucer expresses the problem within an ironizing matrix of gender psychology and individual subjectivity. The impasse itself is formally presented as a verbal collision between two domesticated mythological figures who preside over the tale's denouement, Pluto and Proserpina. For Pluto the impending adultery of May with squire Damien exemplifies feminine 'untrouthe and brotilnesse', the 'tresons whiche that wommen doon to man' (IV. 2339–41); whereas Queen Proserpina asserts abundant evidence of 'wommen ful trewe' (IV. 2281) against Pluto's misogynous authority Solomon, whom she condemns as a mere lecher (IV. 2298).[30] The 'vileynye' of men's writings against women and against their so-called wrangling necessitates, she declares, a wrangling feminine retaliation (IV. 2303–4).

The cue for this contretemps, productive of a stalemate in which each speaker declares sex solidarity in defiance of the other, is May's provocative response to January's whining plea for her wifely fidelity (which she is about to breach). May protests,

> 'Why speke ye thus? But men been evere untrewe,
> And wommen have repreve of yow ay newe.
> Ye han noon oother contenance, I leeve,
> But speke to us of untrust and repreeve.' (IV. 2203–6)

It is quite clear that Chaucer means to mock the dispute over men's and women's 'untrouthe' for its unwinnability. Pluto eventually gives up, on the pretext that Proserpina is threatening to deluge him with protest (IV. 2312), but not before she has shown that any claim on one side can be echoed on the other side. It is equally clear that Chaucer means to underline the subjective conditionality of these claims.[31] Pluto adopts the type of absolutist disdain of women that might be expected of the legendary rapist

---

[30] 'The unresolvable nature of the dispute is best expressed through the figure of Solomon, who is "fulfild of sapience" (IV. 2243) or a "lechour and an ydolastre" (IV. 2298), depending on which gender is mustering him to its cause'; A. S. G. Edwards, 'The Merchant's Tale and Moral Chaucer', Modern Language Quarterly, 51 (1990), 409–26 (p. 423).

[31] This would be in accord with Laskaya's view that the tale 'suggests that we often give credence to particular definitions of "men" and "women" . . . because those interpretations happen to complement our own fantasies', Chaucer's Approach to Gender, 98.

of Proserpina.[32] Proserpina argues as she does because 'I am a womman' (IV. 2305); she notes the interpretability of Solomon's utterance, and its subjectivity as the opinion both of a lecher and of one who personally happened to find 'no good womman'.[33] Judged in the same light of personal motivation, May's protest on behalf of women stands exposed as expedient rhetoric designed to put her husband at a psychological disadvantage prior to cuckolding him.[34] But there are further layers to her protestation. First, readerly indignation is of course tempered by recognizing that January's personal premarital career of egotistical promiscuity (IV. 1249–50) would warrant precisely the judgement she cynically offers. Second, for all its audacious subjectivity, May's protest involves a striking psychological speculation, that men's hostility to women is actually a front (a *contenance*, IV. 2205) disguising characteristic male infidelity.[35] The text seems on the verge of an essentializing claim that misogyny, particularly the allegation that women lack constancy, is inseparable from male guilt—a claim, however, altogether confused by the fact that it is being uttered by a woman covering the guilt of her impending adultery.

[32] That his association with rape disqualifies him as an authority on women's morals has increasingly been emphasized: e.g. Elizabeth Simmons-O'Neill, 'Love in Hell: The Role of Pluto and Proserpine in Chaucer's *Merchant's Tale*', *Modern Language Quarterly*, 51 (1990), 389–407 (p. 394); Edwards, 'The Merchant's Tale and Moral Chaucer', 422; Mann, *Geoffrey Chaucer*, 65.

[33] She also suggests (echoing Prudence in *Tale of Melibee*, VII. 1077–9) that Solomon's words are open to the alternative interpretation that no sovereignly good *person* (woman or man) could be found except God. Lawrence Besserman notes that this critique of the Ecclesiastes verse originates in biblical commentary (*Glossa ordinaria*, PL 113. 1124); 'Glosynge is a Glorious Thyng: Chaucer's Biblical Exegesis', in David Lyle Jeffrey (ed.), *Chaucer and Scriptural Tradition* (Ottawa: University of Ottawa Press, 1984), 65–73 (pp. 66–7).

[34] Chaucer is fully aware, however, that the relation between subjective experience and generalization is complex. He demonstrates through the Host's opinion in the tale's epilogue that masculine subjectivity can hold (or self-flatteringly want to believe) that a wife is 'trewe as any steel' while simultaneously asserting that women generally are deceivers (IV. 2421–7). The flat disjunction between May's speech and her intentions needs considering in light of this paradox, though Edwards dwells interestingly on that disjunction as a facet of the tale's 'moral vacuum' which reduces conduct to 'commodity, not morality'; 'The Merchant's Tale and Moral Chaucer', 421, 425.

[35] May connects male reproof of women with male untruth (2203–4), then adds that men have 'noon oother contenance' but to speak to women of their distrust [of women]. The Riverside editors gloss *contenance* vaguely as 'manner of behaviour', but the point is surely that men's own guilt is hidden under a guise or outward expression of misogyny (cf. Pandarus who assumed the demeanour—*fond his contenaunce*—of one looking at a romance in *Troilus and Criseyde*, III. 979–80).

Chaucer therefore develops in the reader of this text a perception of the clichéd and contingent and *usable* nature of the 'stability' topos. Inheriting an obsession with it in misogynous and anti-misogynous tradition, he finds it partly a smokescreen behind which people can get on with their ulterior purposes and partly a self-conscious focus for target practice between the sexes. Misogynous and profeminine assertion alike are undermined by the same processes: blown up by misapplication, distorted by speakers' motives.[36]

There are positive ways of describing this sort of game in Chaucer. It used to be thought harmless literary raillery. More ambitiously one can deduce that he disdains essentializing statements about gender, and juggles mockingly with them in order to undermine gender stereotypes.[37] But a less attractive consequence of a see-saw gender discourse emerges if it can be defined, as Helen Solterer defines the posture of Le Fèvre, as 'sycophantic'. Solterer points out that the sycophantic persona adopts different positions so as to curry favour; reviles or exaggeratedly supports as the climate dictates. Such a persona 'conveys a two-timing discourse: neither of its positions is convincing—neither condemnation nor adulation of women'.[38] The obvious exoneration of Chaucer in this regard is that he does not aim at 'convincing positions' in either direction: rather, at a conspicuous alternation which creatively disrupts the polarity itself.[39] Yet there is quite a fine line between a genuinely productive mock-two-timing cajolery, and an oscillation of postures which panders for wit's sake to each sex in turn. In an optimistic reading, Chauntecleer's famous mistranslation of woman from man's *confusio* to his 'bliss' may be reckoned to mock 'the male stereotyping which fails to confront its own contradictory attitudes, preferring to keep them

---

[36] See further the narrator's comment, 'Heere may ye se how excellent franchise I In wommen is' (IV. 1987–8) when May makes a prompt decision to reciprocate Damien's desire, in a context which intimates that, for May's excellent generosity, we are to read 'indecent haste'. A statement about women's *franchise* becomes the victim of a sarcastic narrator's vindictive irony.

[37] Alastair Minnis points out that 'for Chaucer the thought that if certain women were bad then so were certain men, was something of a reflex action'; Minnis *et al.*, *Shorter Poems*, 439. I have explored some further aspects of this in 'Questions of Gender in Chaucer, from *Anelida* to *Troilus*', 83–110.

[38] *The Master and Minerva*, 146–8. Solterer's charge against Le Fèvre is that his 'conversion' from a misogynous to a profeminine posture is unconvincing.

[39] Hence Mann's remark, 'changeability, as Chaucer shows it to us, is not specifically female but is simply a human condition', *Geoffrey Chaucer*, 30.

both in play'.[40] Less optimistically it is bound to strike some readers as gratuitous equivocation. Chaucer is perhaps not always clear of sycophancy in this respect.

Two of his writings which incorporate explicitly profeminine positions are the *Tale of Melibee* and *Legend of Good Women*. The first is a close prose rendering of the treatise by Albertanus of Brescia discussed in Chapter 1, and I have shown elsewhere that Chaucer was committed to its critique of masculine honour.[41] But its *raison d'être* is not profeminine polemic: the *Legend* is the single Chaucer text which looks most like a formal case for women.[42]

The narrator (an oblique version of Chaucer the poet) represents himself in this poem's Prologue as being whimsically torn between devotion to the 'truths' of books and devotion to the daisy flower as a sort of feminine principle.[43] This flower is subsequently revealed as 'truth' in another form since it is the emblem of Queen Alceste, the poem's exemplar of feminine loyalty who chose to die that her husband might live (and was 'rescued' from 'hell' to 'bliss' by Hercules in recompense; F-text, 513–16).[44] The genesis of the poem is carefully located in May, time of the literal 'resurrection' of this flower (F 110) amidst the recovery of all nature from winter (F 125–7). It is also a time, the narrator specifies, when birds celebrate their escape from the nets of the fowler, described punningly as the *foule cherl*, who sought to betray them with his *sophistrye*. They sing: ' "The foweler we deffye, | And al his craft" ' (F 130–9). The poetry enacts rhythms of reprieve, renewal, and defiant exultation over eluded predators. I do not doubt that we are meant to speculate that the birds here figure women, and that the 'craft' and sophistry of the bird-catcher figures the artfulness of untrustworthy men who prey treacher-

[40] Mann, *Geoffrey Chaucer*, 191.

[41] 'Chaucer's Revaluation of Chivalric Honor', 245–69.

[42] The *Legend* cannot be dated with precision, but is usually assigned to the early or mid-1380s. The poem's Prologue is extant in two versions: my discussion confines itself to the 'F' text, though the 'G' text does not differ on details pertinent to my argument.

[43] For discussion of this dilemma see Alcuin Blamires, 'A Chaucer Manifesto', *Chaucer Review*, 34 (1989), 29–44.

[44] Some idea of the elusive significance of the daisy in the Prologue can be gained from Sheila Delany's definition of it as 'at once flower, object of erotic devotion, female poetic muse, poetic topic, linguistic equivalent to (Saint) Margaret, and "remembraunce" (F 530) of Alceste'; *The Naked Text: Chaucer's 'Legend of Good Women'* (Berkeley and Los Angeles: University of California Press, 1994), 86.

ously on them.[45] After all, the first rule of seduction enunciated by Ovid is that 'all women can be caught; spread but your nets and you will catch them'.[46]

Within bird society itself, the text goes on to note, there are betrayals too, but only such as can happily be resolved when (male) remorse complements (female) 'pitee' and forgiveness (F 153–68). The prospect of defiance is therefore here suspended, indeed feminine pity and compassion take over the Prologue and become unexpectedly crucial to the safety of the poet/narrator. In a dream, he is repudiated by Cupid as unworthy to approach the daisy on the grounds that his writings have defamed Love's followers and (in the case of *Troilus and Criseyde*) damaged men's trust in women.[47] Against Cupid's wrath, which seems provoked by a shallow and unbalanced misreading of Chaucer,[48] the God's consort Alceste assumes the classic role of feminine intercessor— 'the paradigmatic position of women in patriarchal social structure', as Dinshaw calls it.[49] A situation has here been brilliantly engineered in which a defence of women begins with a man being defended by a woman against slurs emanating (the woman goes on to suggest) from court tittle-tattle; from the very sort of malicious talk, in fact, which Christine de Pizan sees as a catalyst of misogyny.

Since as devotee of the daisy the poet/narrator is actually a champion of women's truth-in-love, it is a fine irony that as the

[45] Such a parallel is noted by Delany in the course of a *tour de force* of meditations on the 'fowler' passage; ibid. 75–82 (p. 77).

[46] *Ars amatoria*, I. 269–70, tr. Mozley, 31. In the *Roman de la Rose*, deceivers who make sham promises to women are said to operate just like 'the fowler hidden in the woods', spreading nets to take the bird captive: 'the foolish bird approaches, unable to reply to the sophism which has deceived him' and leaps into the net; ed. Poirion, 21475–513, tr. Horgan, 331. The 'sophymes' of the 'art' of a duplicitous lover are referred to in *The Squire's Tale* (V. 554); a duplicitous lover in *Anelida and Arcite* is 'subtil in that craft [of love]' (88). 'Craft' is also used negatively in this way in *Legend of Good Women*, 1286, 1607, 2528, and 2546, though there can be a positive craft, such as that of *fyn lovynge* exemplified by Alceste (F-Prologue, 544). A predatory male 'bird-catcher' would be a *cherl* on the same basis that a rapist knight loses the claim to *gentillesse* in *The Wife of Bath's Tale*, since 'vileyns synful dedes make a cherl' (III. 1158).

[47] Defamation is what is indicated in the charges of 'mis-speaking' (F 323) and 'speaking wilfully' (F 332).

[48] Cupid has been supposed to epitomize the reductive reading of stories for simplistic exemplary function alone; see Carol Meale, 'Legends of Good Women in the European Middle Ages', *Archiv*, 144 (1992), 55–70 (p. 58). But the poem actually suggests that Chaucer's poetry has been *misreported* to the God.

[49] *Chaucer's Sexual Poetics*, 70; and see Minnis *et al.*, *Shorter Poems*, 379–80.

victim both of slander and of the unstable peremptoriness of the Love-God,[50] he is made to experience at first hand the distress which (as the whole *Legend* insists) women frequently endure in their 'trouthe'. That is, he himself endures the distress of sudden, unjust, and near-catastrophic repudiation by the very Love to which he considered himself true.[51] Momentarily, he is like a Dido devastated by Aeneas' lordly repudiation of her loyal affection. (Criticism has deduced various manifestations of 'feminized masculinity' in the *Legend* without, it seems to me, adequately emphasizing the special quasi-feminine role into which the poet/narrator is inserted here.[52]) His advantage over women victimized by men, however, is that a powerful woman (Alceste) is available to him, to temper the ruthlessness of male 'tyranny'.[53] Thanks to her, the attack on this particular victim ends in forgiveness, subject to penitentiary community service.

The penance is that, year on year, the poet/narrator must write a glorious 'legende' or martyrology of 'wommen trewe in lovyng', and of the false men who betrayed them (F 484–6). Hypothetically there is the prospect of a significant contribution to the case for women: but in practice the contribution has been thought at best unformidable and at worst a travesty. In order to see why, it will help if we invoke the bird-netting discourse of the Prologue and ask how the stories 'sing defiance' of masculine 'craft'.

The bereaved or betrayed women of the legends do not defy; for the most part they merely suffer and lament. In the background is the pull of Ovid's *Heroides*, the ancestral narrative of

[50] Instability is a defect implicitly attributed to Cupid when Alceste observes that 'A god ne sholde nat thus be agreved, | But of hys deitee he shal be stable' (F 344–5).
[51] When he attempts to speak in his own defence, he declares 'yt was myn entente | To forthren trouthe in love and yt cheryce' (F 471–2).
[52] Mann argues that the *Legend* aims overall to feminize the reader through an immersion in 'the womanly ethos of pity', and that the God of Love in accepting Alceste's plea for pity projects a model of feminized masculinity; *Geoffrey Chaucer*, 41, 43. Hansen argues that heterosexual love presents a threat to the masculine identity of the males in the individual legends because it involves them in feminizing postures of submission and vulnerability. She also finds the poet/narrator feminized, by the intervention of Alceste which silences him, and (more tenuously I think) because he is 'not recognized as a man by the male ruler', and is 'blocked from proving his manhood either by loving an actual female or by ignoring the subject of women altogether'; *Chaucer and the Fictions of Gender*, 1–10 (p. 9).
[53] Alceste advises Cupid to adopt the proper response of a 'ryghtwis lord' to this case, 'And nat be lyk tirauntz of Lumbardye' (F 373–4).

feminine lament:[54] and it is worth recalling that within the *Heroides* is voiced an influential essentializing assumption that while men can 'do' things to channel or disperse emotion, women are allegedly for ever bound to inertia, to a stasis which heaps up and locks in melancholic emotion through protracted and passive meditation. Ovid's Hero writes to Leander that whereas 'you men' are busy with a whole variety of matters—trade, keeping fit, riding, fishing, drinking—

for me who am denied these things, even were I less fiercely aflame, there is nothing left to do but love. What there is left, I do; and you, O sole delight of mine, I love with even greater love than could be returned to me! Either with my aged nurse I whisper of you, and marvel what can keep you from your way; or, looking forth upon the sea, I chide the billows stirred by the hateful wind, in words almost your own; or, when the heavy wave has a little laid aside its fierce mood, I complain that you indeed could come, but will not; and while I complain tears course from the eyes that love you, and the ancient dame who shares my secret dries them with tremulous hand.[55]

Other than looking for Leander's footprints on the shore and asking whether anyone is going to his town, Ovid's Hero can find no relief but to spin thread with her nurse: 'with woman's art we beguile the slow hours of waiting' (XIX. 38). Although it is a vision of emotional frustration which obviously makes historically selective assumptions about the class, occupations, and patriarchal cultural formation of the women it inscribes, it rings so true with Boccaccio centuries later that he incorporates it nearly verbatim in the 'Proemio' to the *Decameron*.[56] For Chaucer again, it is apparently a recognizable part of the construction of femininity, for he invests it in Criseyde when she reflects on the possible adversities of love: 'Therto we wrecched wommen nothing konne, | Whan us is wo, but wepe and sitte and thinke.'[57]

---

[54] The *Heroides* have been described as 'arguably the most influential of Chaucer's sources in the *Legend*'; Meale, 'Legends of Good Women', 67. The *Heroides* contribute, to a varying extent, to the accounts of Dido, Hypsipyle and Medea, Ariadne, Phyllis, and Hypermnestra.

[55] *Heroides*, XIX. 9–26, tr. Showerman, 261.

[56] Ed. Cesare Segre (Milan: Mursia, 1966), 26; tr. G. H. McWilliam (Harmondsworth: Penguin, 1972), 46–7. The Heroidean *dolorosa* (a woman 'who has thought passionately about the loss of one she loved' in Dronke's definition, *Poetic Individuality*, 141) is a model for laments—sometimes female-authored— throughout the Middle Ages: cf. Dronke, *Women Writers*, 85–90.

[57] *Troilus and Criseyde*, II. 782–3 (where Chaucer has developed the vaguer fear of love's torments expressed by the Boccaccian Criseida (*Il Filostrato* 2. 75) into a more decisive generalization about women).

Undertaking to write the stability and 'trouthe' which women have sustained under duress of abandonment, bereavement, or rape, Chaucer does not, therefore, imagine them taking defiant initiatives. In the first story Cleopatra fulfils her promise to share Antony's every feeling, by quietly committing suicide after his death. It is left to the narrator to exclaim defiantly against the contrasting emptiness of men's oaths about dying for love.[58] Carolyn Dinshaw complains that because the *Legend*'s women are 'nothing but steadfast', they merely rehearse a caricature of passivity, a formula which enables the narrator to 'enervate' and even 'immobilize' women. The women ought to be more 'aggressive, passionate, even dangerous'.[59] It is interesting to note that according to Alceste, Chaucer had translated the homily *De Maria Magdalena*,[60] for that homily's heroine, in the depth and emotion of her loyalty to Christ, would be at home among the women of the *Legend*, as has been pointed out.[61] Yet the centre of the homily also envisages the daring, the *audacia* of Mary in the fearlessness of her faith, as well as the profundity of her love.[62] The *Legend*'s heroines show little *audacia*, let alone dangerousness.[63] I think that Chaucer has cut out their dangerousness (acts of revenge by Medea and Progne, for instance) not only

[58] 'But herkeneth, . . . I Ye men that falsly sweren many an oth I That ye wol deye, if that youre love be wroth, I Here may ye sen of wemen which a trouthe!' (F 665–8). The emptiness of men's talk of 'dying' for love is emphasized again in Jason's case (*Hypsipyle and Medea*, 1378–80) but is perhaps in any case a commonplace in the 14th cent.: cf. *Book of the Knight of the Tower*, ed. Offord, ch. cxxiii, p. 166.

[59] *Chaucer's Sexual Poetics*, 70–2. Similar strictures are offered by John Fyler, 'The heroines lose their diversity and individuality in order to suffer martyrdom passively . . . the preconceived pattern of sanctity defeats its own intent by enervating female heroism'; *Chaucer and Ovid* (New Haven: Yale University Press, 1979), 107. See also Delany, 'once we introduce "false men" into the structure of female goodness, the "good" woman will almost inevitably be an abused woman, faithful despite the atrocities done to her'. Such women 'wind up affirming the model of masculine power and feminine weakness all over again'; *The Naked Text*, 108.

[60] 'He made also . . . Origenes upon the Maudeleyne' (F 428); i.e. a version of the 12th/13th-cent. pseudo-Origen homily *De Maria Magdalena*.

[61] John P. McCall, 'Chaucer and the Pseudo Origen *De Maria Magdalena*: A Preliminary Study', *Speculum*, 46 (1971), 491–509 (p. 504).

[62] The homilist contrasts the *audacia* of Mary, who was prepared to take Christ's dead body away, with the failure of St Peter's nerve: 'O Mary, if the body of Jesus had, by chance, been laid in the courtyard of the Chief Priest where the Chief Apostle warmed himself by the fire—What would you have done? "I will take Him away." O, the boldness of this wonderful woman! O woman, no woman!' (*O mirabilis mulieris audacia. O Mulier non mulier*). Translation and text from McCall, 'Chaucer and the Pseudo Origen', 500.

[63] The chief exception is Thisbe, proving by her suicide that whatever a man's strength in love, 'A woman dar and can as wel as he' (923).

because the plan is to expound unqualified feminine steadfastness, but also because even more than Ovid in the *Heroides*
his chief understanding of how to represent unswerving
feminine loyalty is by maximizing the pathos of emotional
entrapment.[64]

There is therefore no one to produce 'defiance' except the narrator. He obliges, liberally: but with an element of jaunty bluster
and self-conscious posturing that has baffled critics. The problem
is conspicuous in the case of an attack on Jason, who shrinks from
sinister 'devourere' of women (1369) to local fox flushed out of
English bushes by the narrator's blustering rhetoric; 'Have at
thee, Jason! now thyn horn is blowe!' (1382).[65] By the sixth *Legend*,
villainous masculinity has become a matter for jocular public
mockery when the narrator heckles the next victim: 'Now cometh
thy lot, now comestow on the ryng' (1887).

Chaucer seems to be compounding a disadvantage already
structured into his plan. The disadvantage is that if the gestures of
defiance are to be offered *for* betrayed women *by* a (male) narrator, this renders the women unnecessarily defenceless—voice-
less—in support of their own innocence.[66] Isn't that disadvantage
compounded, if their male 'champion' does not take their enemies totally seriously, cannot help indulging touches of bur-
lesque as he deals with them? The fact that the poem campaigns
stridently against masculine treachery is not itself the problem,
for I agree with Jill Mann and Alastair Minnis that conspicuous
indictment of men could make an educative contribution against
misogyny (though the *Legend* is by no means novel in this respect,
as preceding discussion has shown).[67] What is a problem is the
equivocal tonality of the narrator's campaign, most notoriously at

[64] Hence the detailed changes such as Chaucer's reduction of the passionate
hostility felt by Ovid's Hypsipyle to Medea, who has supplanted her in Jason's
affections; Minnis *et al.*, *Shorter Poems*, 368–9.

[65] The figuration is confusingly lavish. Jason is both wily fox (preying on
women as on 'tendre capoun' (1389)) and also falconer (bringing women in like
falcons to his 'lures' (1371–2)): but note that both metaphors confirm the reading
offered above of the Prologue's 'fowler' passage.

[66] They can only, in this view, *pray* desperately that God will 'kepe' them from
such deceivers as Demophon (2400–1).

[67] Mann argues that the poem deliberately adopts 'a single-mindedness and
refusal of compromise' which mirrors the 'intransigence' of misogyny, *Geoffrey
Chaucer*, 32; Minnis likewise (but with an exaggerated assumption of its novelty)
suggests that 'reduction is being used to problematize reduction; an action of
"new" stereotyping relating to men challenges the traditional stereotyping which
relates to women', *Shorter Poems*, 435.

the end of the *Legend of Phyllis* in his warning to women to beware
of 'youre subtyl fo . . . And trusteth, as in love, no man but me'
(2559–61). Whether we take this as parodic seduction ploy, or as
wry admission that he is trapped by his own indictments of his
sex, or as the bravura of a would-be Ovidian legislator on love,[68]
it produces a jarring, disconcerting note. Although such notes are
only occasional in the *Legend*, they may lead us to wonder
whether the poet who elsewhere so sharply demonstrates the
pragmatic usability of partisan gender assertions, when he tries to
explore in this poem the challenge of *becoming* a partisan, cannot
manage the role without flickers of mirth.[69]

What is missing from Chaucer's structure really, and without
which he is left high and dry with these problems, is a grounding
of the 'trouthe' argument in more substantial profeminine polemic. Where we have seen feminine loyalty and masculine promiscuity asserted in other texts—even by Augustine, and
certainly by polemicists such as the writer of *The Southern Passion*,
or Jean Le Fèvre—it has been in the context of hard-hitting commentary on society's sexual double standard, extending even to
commentary on the legislative structures whereby misogyny was
bolstered. While I agree with Mann that Chaucer conjoins his
inscription of feminine 'trouthe' with pointed demonstrations of a
quality of 'pite' in women unreciprocated by men,[70] he does not
conjoin it with much else. Hardly any ancillary topoi of the formal
case for women are included. The exception which proves the
rule is a reference to Christ's praise of the solidity of the Canaanite
woman's faith:

> For wel I wot that Crist himselve telleth
> That in Israel, as wyd as is the lond,

[68] Minnis sees an Ovidian posture here, *Shorter Poems*, 358, and then connects
the comic irony of the passage with a 'festive' quality in the poem's profeminism
(pp. 440–1): he also writes interestingly of the 'self-reference . . . imbued with
elaborate self-irony' in the poem's narratorial role—of the way that the speaker's
'awareness of himself as male' includes awareness of his own 'anomalous, perhaps even slightly ridiculous, role as scapegoat' (p. 430).

[69] The flickers do not in my view amount to wholesale ironic intent. I therefore
disagree with Delany, who declares that 'for Chaucer, to write in unambiguous
praise of women would be to reduce the natural complexity of reality: it is to be set
right again, rendered complex again, by irony', *The Naked Text*, 99 (a view which
complements that of Lisa Kiser in *Telling Classical Tales: Chaucer and the 'Legend of
Good Women'* (Ithaca, NY: Cornell University Press, 1983), 89, and of John Fyler,
Chaucer and Ovid, 114–15).

[70] *Geoffrey Chaucer*, 39.

> That so gret feyth in al that he ne fond
> As in a woman. (1879–82)[71]

In the absence of efforts to build a profeminine case in any direction other than those of compassion and truth, the poem's appetite for a polemical engagement with misogyny (as opposed to a stand-off with masculine fickleness) seems unnecessarily attenuated.

So, whereas the *Prologue to the Legend* offers unusual profeminine perspectives, the *Legend* still as a whole, despite the best efforts of its advocates, leaves the reader with double misgivings. The first misgiving is simply that its profeminine impulse lacks a suitably broad infrastructure. The second arises from the ambivalence of tone—'so subtle that critics still can't decide whether the poet is making fun, or saints, of all those women'.[72] Chaucer has often been thought a non-committal poet. Just as *The Wife of Bath's Prologue* strikes many readers as hugely equivocal—voicing resistance to misogyny in such a way as to reinforce certain misogynous allegations—so perhaps the speaker of the *Legend*, who pointedly refuses to 'take sides' in the fashionable courtly contest of flower versus leaf,[73] is temperamentally unable to fashion an unambivalent profeminine discourse.

Some twenty years after the *Legend*, Christine de Pizan fashioned in her *Cité des dames* the most powerful profeminine work of the Middle Ages. She constructed it to be a monument to women's capacities, and it should have been epoch-making. Her book's relation to the procedures and topoi of the existing case for women will particularly concern us here, but what first challenges attention is Christine's determination to correct misogyny by es-

[71] Christ actually says to her, 'O woman, great is thy faith' (Matt. 15: 28), and it is to a centurion that he says 'I have not found so great faith in Israel' (Matt. 8: 10). To the defence of Chaucer's 'inaccuracy' offered by Minnis (*Shorter Poems*, 407–8) it needs to be added that Chaucer was probably using or remembering an amalgamated Gospel narrative, and that (possibly for the same reason) exactly the same 'inaccuracy' recurs in Christine de Pizan, *Cité*, I. 10. 5, ed. Curnow, 662, tr. Richards, 29. The woman of Canaan is not prominent in extant earlier profeminine literature, but Christ's commendation of her faith is picked out in the *Meditations on the Life of Christ*, tr. Ragusa and Green (p. 220), and doubtless there were precedents for Chaucer's and Christine's use of her.

[72] Arlyn Diamond, 'Chaucer's Women and Women's Chaucer', in Arlyn Diamond and Lee R. Edwards (eds.), *The Authority of Experience: Essays in Feminist Criticism* (Amherst: University of Massachusetts Press, 1977), 65.

[73] 'But natheles, ne wene nat that I make | In preysing of the flour agayn the leef . . . | For, as to me, nys lever noon ne lother' (F 188–92).

tablishing feminine authority on the basis both of women's foundational significance in history (which struck Abelard too, as we saw) and of rational feminine self-knowledge.

The book itself is structured through a metaphor of founda-tion—the construction of a city of ladies under the guidance of Reason, Rectitude, and Justice—which brilliantly conjoins several functions as noted before in critical commentary, especially the function of re-securing the citadel of feminine virtue presumed so rickety in the *Romance of the Rose*.[74] Less often noted are the antecedents for this citadel-building in virginity literature, for instance Ambrose's imagery of the resolute virgin as one who 'builds towers so that, encircled with the precious battlements of the saints, she may not only render fruitless the attacks of the enemy, but also erect the safe defences of holy merits'.[75] Yet another resonance is the civilizing connotation of the city. Christine follows Boccaccio in detailing women's contributions (through agricultural and technological improvements) to the civilizing process, but whereas he qualifies these with nostalgia for a pre-civilized golden age, she sees the urbanizing process as an indispensable evolution of society. The *Cité* is therefore in part a monument to women's power to benefit humanity 'by leading wandering and savage men, living in the woods like cruel beasts . . . to reside in cities and towns'.[76]

---

[74] Christine's fortified city provides women with a defence against detractors; it rectifies the misogynous presentation in the *Roman de la Rose* of women's sexuality as an easily penetrated tower; and it claims for Christine's work something of the moral and religious authority of Augustine's *City of God*, to which a concluding reference is made in the quotation, 'Gloriosa dicta sunt de te, civitas Dei'; III. 18. 9, ed. Curnow, 1031, tr. Richards, 254. For further discussion see Glenda McLeod, 'Poetics and Antimisogynist Polemics in Christine de Pizan's *Le Livre de la cité des dames*', in Richards *et al.*, *Reinterpreting Christine de Pizan*, 37–47 (p. 44); Christine Reno, 'Virginity as an Ideal in Christine de Pizan's *Cité des dames*', in Bornstein, *Ideals for Women in the Works of Christine de Pizan*, 69–90 (p. 81).

[75] *De virginibus*, II. vi. 43 (*PL* 16. 219–20), tr. de Romestin, 380, drawing on the language of the Song of Songs (e.g. Cant. 8: 9). Peter the Venerable likewise writes to Heloise of nuns 'building high walls of virtue in the foundation of their inno-cence, and raising the summit of their blessed edifice to the very threshold of heaven'; *Letters of Abelard and Heloise*, tr. Radice, 281.

[76] I. 38. 1, ed. Curnow, 749, tr. Richards, 79; and *De mulieribus claris*, ed. Zaccaria, 44–6, tr. Guarino, 12–13. See Rosalind Brown-Grant, 'Des hommes et des femmes illustres: Modalités narratives et transformations génériques chez Pétrarque, Boccace et Christine de Pizan', in Dulac and Ribémont, *Une femme de lettres*, 469–80 (p. 475), and id., 'Décadence ou progrès? Christine de Pizan, Boccace et la question de l' "âge d'or"', *Revue des langues romanes*, 92 (1988), 295–306.

The *literal* resonance of city-foundation is nevertheless also worth emphasizing. One only has to remember the sonorous opening of the English poem *Sir Gawain and the Green Knight*, invoking Aeneas as ancestor of western nations, and 'Romulus', 'Tirius', 'Langaberde', and 'Brutus' as city-state founders,[77] to realize the culture's reverence for foundational impulses of this kind that were normatively gendered masculine. Christine aims not only to found a city, but one which inaugurates a 'New Kingdom of Femininity', permanent unlike Troy (whose destruction is recalled in the first two lines of *Sir Gawain*) and unlike even the 800-year Amazonian state whose longevity Christine herself emphasizes.[78] Christine's *nouvel royaume de Femenie* is in one sense of course her book, a permanent realm of female achievement, still in circulation: in another sense it is the new reign of values which she believes should inform the *polis* or commonwealth of men and women together since, as Solterer has explained, in contrast to defamatory writing Christine 'offers a socially responsible discourse' which 'speaks responsibly for the polis as a whole'.[79]

Above all, she is situating herself as the foundress of a feminist history of the world which shows women to be the initiators of major political and cultural institutions of all kinds. Along with various other foundational acts such as the establishment of Carthage by Dido, the origins and early security of Rome itself are conspicuously presented as gynocentric developments. The key figure is a princess called Carmentis, an emigrant from Greece who sailed to Italy, landed by the Tiber, named the Palatine hill where Rome (she prophesied) would be founded, and built a fortress 'in order to be the first to lay a stone there'. Her pioneering spirit was accompanied by cultural colonialism, for in this barbaric region she 'was the first to institute laws', whence the mighty influence of Roman law would flow. Intuiting the future grandeur of Rome, she employed her formidable intellect in the

---

[77] 'Hit watz Ennias þe athel, and his highe kynde, | þat . . . patrounes bicome | Welne3e of al þe wele in þe west iles. | Fro riche Romulus to Rome ricchis hym swythe, | With gret bobbaunce þat burghe he biges vpon fyrst . . . | Ticius to Tuskan and teldes bigynnes, | Langaberde in Lumbardie lyftes vp homes,' etc. (5–15); ed. Andrew and Waldron, *Poems of the Pearl Manuscript*, 207.

[78] The 'nouvel royaume de femenie' is announced in II. 12. 1, ed. Curnow, 815, tr. Richards, 117.

[79] Solterer, *The Master and Minerva*, ch. 6, pp. 172, 175; Solterer is discussing the ethical basis of the *Chemin de long estude*, but her arguments apply with equal force to the *Cité*.

task of inventing the Latin alphabet and grammar.[80] That Romulus and Remus 'founded' Rome seems a purely technical supplement to this comprehensive originary activity of Carmentis, and indeed in another story in the *Cité*, all the good sense and nerve of women (the Sabine women) is required to prevent Romulus' men and the Sabine men from destroying each other and ruining that foundation.[81] Once Rome is established, the Sibyl Almathea foresees and provides counsel for its entire future: 'all the affairs of the empire' are circumscribed in one woman's writing (which, however, a sceptical and parsimonious emperor nearly fails to acquire).[82] But the network of female priority extends ever outwards. Does Mantua seem famous as the birthplace of the Roman epic poet Virgil? Mantua is itself named after a Theban woman called Manto who died there: behind Virgil's own city is the *auctorité* of a woman, expert in the arts of divination.[83]

Christine's policy is to promote the originary powers of women in every area of life. Adapting materials from Boccaccio's *De mulieribus claris*,[84] she identifies women as inventors not only of the Latin language but also of numeracy, cloth-making, body armour, literary forms, agriculture, nets, and silk, to name but a few. In the process she naturally conducts various negotiations with the Boccaccian position. The one I should like to mention concerns the 'Heroidean' assumption that women are emotionally and mentally constricted or immobilized by their privatization within domestic space. While Boccaccio took this to be the norm, he used his narratives of female achievement to suggest, amidst a good deal of backhanded condescension and sarcasm, that women could nevertheless galvanize themselves out of the

[80] I. 33. 2, ed. Curnow, 735–8 and 798, tr. Richards, 71–3 and 106.

[81] Ed. Curnow, 865–8, tr. Richards, 148–50.

[82] II. 3. 1, ed. Curnow, 792–4, tr. Richards, 102–4. Christine envisaged the same Sibyl as personal guide in her Dantesque journey, the *Chemin de long estude*; Curnow, 1080, and Solterer, *The Master and Minerva*, 166–7.

[83] I. 31. 1, ed. Curnow, 731–2, tr. Richards, 68–9.

[84] Christine probably used the 1401 French translation *De cleres et nobles femmes* by Laurent de Premierfait (Curnow, *Cité*, 138–47). On the revisionary nature of Christine's adaptations, see esp. Patricia A. Phillippy, 'Establishing Authority: Boccaccio's *De claris mulieribus* and Christine de Pizan's *Le Livre de la cité des dames*', *Romanic Review*, 77 (1986), 167–93; and Anna Slerca, 'Dante, Boccace, et le *Livre de la cité des dames* de Christine de Pizan', in Dulac and Ribémont, *Une femme de lettres*, 221–30.

alleged 'sluggishness' of domesticity, childcare, and gossip to which their 'sloth' and diffidence confined them, if they would develop the mental talents which they have in common with men.[85]

Women's disconsolate assumption that their only talents are procreative and domestic is quoted from Boccaccio in the *Cité* at one point (minus the vocabulary of sluggishness), but Christine then makes it clear that such women in fact internalized a masculine prejudice; it is men who convince them of their inadequacy.[86] She therefore raises important questions about female privatization, uncovering a basis in gender prejudice and going on to pinpoint lack of informal education (by more exposure to life outside the home) and also of formal education as key factors[87]—yet rather than pressing home these findings she has to sustain a compromise position because she nevertheless holds that there are sensible divisions of labour whereby society properly assigns some public functions broadly to men.[88] The point remains that she has not only penetrated the disempowerment built into the masculine 'Heroidean' construction of the privatized heroine, but has also articulated something which as we saw earlier Abelard seemed to perceive, that only by demonstrable intellectual *auctoritas*—by *l'auttorité de son savoir*—could a woman ultimately make headway against misogyny in that culture.[89]

A further notable dimension of Christine's case is that 'experience' is assimilated into, rather than—as in the case of Chaucer's

---

[85] *De mulieribus claris*, ed. Zaccaria, 338 and 394–6, tr. Guarino, 188, 220; see Ch. 3 above.

[86] Boccaccio is quoted by Reason at I. 28. 1, ed. Curnow, 724–5, tr. Richards, 65. But at I. 37. 1, Christine points out that *men* 'usually say that women's knowledge is worthless . . . the typical opinions and comments of men claim that women have been and are useful in the world only for bearing children and sewing'; ed. Curnow, 746, tr. Richards, 77.

[87] For the former, see I. 27. 1, where Reason posits that women 'know less' than men 'because they are not involved in many different things, but stay at home', whereas 'there is nothing which so instructs a reasonable creature as the exercise and experience of many different things', ed. Curnow, 722, tr. Richards, 63.

[88] I. 11. 1, summarized again in I. 27. 1; ed. Curnow, 664–5 and 722, tr. Richards, 31–2 and 63–4. Quilligan suggests that Christine's stance on division of labour is not 'conservative' but 'authorizes a peculiarly female set of potencies that provide for reciprocity with men', *Allegory of Female Authority*, 66.

[89] The 'authority of knowledge' is a phrase found in the section on Ceres at I. 35. 1, ed. Curnow, 744, tr. Richards, 76.

Wife of Bath—imagined to conflict with, the traditional concept of *auctoritas*.[90] Experience in Christine's definition is both self-knowledge, the clear understanding of herself that a woman achieves by using Reason's mirror to consider her nature rationally and hence authoritatively, and is also women's collective knowledge of their 'natural behaviour and character' (*les naturelz meurs et condicions femenines*) which enables them to state with confidence (authoritatively) that certain allegations are lies.[91] Where Chaucer produces a rich cocktail out of the fact that the Wife of Bath's 'experiential' arguments are actually largely derived from the *auctoritee* (Jerome) which she would like to rip up, Christine's cogent project is to show how individual and collective feminine experience and the literary record of feminine authority might mutually reinforce the rebuttal of misogyny.

These, then, are some of the innovative strategies in the *Cité*. There is no diminution of that innovation, I think, in realizing that Christine actually develops much of her profeminine structure and thought from the inherited case for women. In fact, the city-building structure has been cleverly superimposed upon a substructure which is rather familiar. In the substructure are the key lineaments of the formal case, that is, dismissal of misogyny by critiquing the reliability and motives of detractors; objections against generalized slander; assertions of the 'natural' love which men should feel for women (who are their mothers) and which they should demonstrate by defending them; the privileges of women's creation; the positive projection of Mary Magdalene, the Samaritan, and other women in the Gospels; and analysis of various feminine 'virtues'—with appropriate *exempla*—which refute alleged failings.

Christine develops new possibilities in many of these topoi

---

[90] Christine offers 'a complicated amalgam of compilator's written practice and author's responsibility to both a lived experience and an oral tradition of communal female speakers', writes Quilligan, *Allegory of Female Authority*, 37, in the context of an interesting comparison of Chaucer's *Wife of Bath's Prologue* with the *Cité*.

[91] The 'mirror of Reason' is explained to Christine in I. 3. 2, ed. Curnow, 627, tr. Richards, 9. As Meale points out, women are asked to look within themselves to discover their authority by applying rational principles; 'Legends of Good Women', 65. Christine contrasts misogynous discourse with women's collective sense of their own behaviour in I. 1. 1, ed. Curnow, 618–19, tr. Richards, 4; and the power of this collective experiential knowledge to expose lies is exemplified at I. 9. 2, ed. Curnow, 650, tr. Richards, 22.

even as she takes them over. In the critique of detractors she finds
an opportunity to dispute the infallibility of 'authorities' as famous as Aristotle and to conduct a systematic inquiry into possible motives for misogyny such as: jealousy of women's potential,
or of other men's sexual conquests; old age and impotence (in
Ovid's case, castration); and the sheer temptation of literary imi-
tation. To the usual objection against slander that it merely dam-
ages the slanderer and that blanket statements are irrational, she
adds a scathing ethical critique of the fallacy of claiming that
partisan attack can be in any way socially beneficial.[92] Christine's
position on this strictly requires her to avoid generalized commendation of women or aspersions against men, or indeed perhaps to avoid any demotion of the masculine while she promotes
the feminine. In practice she is quite careful,[93] but reserves a right
(as we shall see) to question men's 'stability', and does not altogether resist the temptation to exercise discreet levels of reproof
and disparagement, which no equitable reader will begrudge.
Like Abelard, only less stridently, she employs a rhetoric of dis-
placement. 'Many' women have 'better minds' than 'most men',
women have 'freer and sharper minds'.[94] Unlike all male rulers of
her time, Zenobia always travelled on horseback and never in-
dulged herself with a litter for transport.[95] The painter Marcia
'excelled all men', and the Sibyls (as Abelard had averred) outdid
the prophets in their foreknowledge of Christ's coming.[96] Can one
name a single man who equalled the momentous achievements of
Carmentis, or who surpassed Ceres in beneficial initiative?[97] To
match these examples of calibration there is also, if I am not
mistaken, a certain amused satisfaction in reporting inadequacies
of Great Men: Alexander was a small ugly person, Hercules and
Theseus were unhorsed by Amazons (though no doubt the horses
were to blame).[98] Gauging the humour in such details is a delicate
matter, however. Christine's great city is built with due gravity.
As we saw earlier, she finds blasphemy, not wit, in the misogynist

---

[92] I. 8. 3, II. 53. 2–II. 54. 1, ed. Curnow, 641–2 and 925–9, tr. Richards, 17–18 and
185–8.
[93] For instance, II. 13. 1 posits plenty of 'good' husbands and 'some unreason-
able women', ed. Curnow, 818–19, tr. Richards, 119–20.
[94] I. 13. 7 and I. 27. 1, ed. Curnow, 672 and 721, tr. Richards, 35 and 63.
[95] I. 20. 1, ed. Curnow, 704, tr. Richards, 53–4.
[96] I. 41. 3 and II. 1. 3, ed. Curnow, 759 and 787–8, tr. Richards, 85 and 100.
[97] I. 33. 3 and I. 38. 1, ed. Curnow, 738 and 749, tr. Richards, 73 and 79.
[98] I. 14. 2 and I. 18. 4, ed. Curnow, 674 and 691, tr. Richards, 36–7 and 46.

'joke' that Christ revealed his Resurrection to a woman first in order for the news to be spread more quickly.[99] To concede humour in misogyny would have been to pretend that nothing was really at stake, that misogyny had no connection with women's exclusion from education, or with wife-beating.

Masculine 'obligation' to women is another topos purposefully expanded by Christine. She begins with standard remarks about the 'natural' love which should subsist between man and woman, together with the 'ingratitude' of masculine indifference to the mother sex, and to all the other good things women do for men.[100] When these good things effected for men by women later turn out to include the very language in which the professional cleric and misogynist assumes cultural loftiness, the very agriculture which has brought men from 'caverns of ignorance' to 'heights of contemplation', and even the very armour in which masculinity asserts its superior strength, the force of the old argument against ingratitude is exponentially magnified.[101]

In almost every sector of the existing case for women, Christine explores arguments either with renewed cogency or in some revealing juxtaposition. The latter is seen in the formulaic privileges of woman's creation, which she reproduces quite traditionally (privilege of place of creation, substance, and symbolism of rib), though she adds an interesting polemical warning against androcentric interpretation of the biblical statement that God made man in his image. What is more exciting here, though, is the context she supplies, having picked up from Boccaccio a useful moment of self-correction. Boccaccio catches himself accusing Nature of 'erring' by giving women 'souls' which were intended for men: he then concedes that this criticism cannot be right because souls come from God not Nature and must all be intrinsically perfect.[102] And this thought is precisely what Christine uses in order to transform the traditional privileges from isolated

[99] I. 10. 5, ed. Curnow, 660–1, tr. Richards, 28–9.

[100] I. 8. 3, I. 8. 9, and I. 38. 4, ed. Curnow, 640–1, 646, and 751, tr. Richards, 16–17, 20, and 80. The 'caring' role of women is given a new twist by Christine's sharp comments about sons who swan around the country while daughters (as in her own case, apparently) look after parents; II. 7. 1, ed. Curnow, 808, tr. Richards, 112–13.

[101] The relevant discussion runs from I. 37. 1 (men are 'like people who live off the goods of others without knowing their source and without thanking anyone') to I. 38. 5, ed. Curnow, 747–52, tr. Richards, 77–81.

[102] *De mulieribus claris*, ed. Zaccaria, 378, tr. Guarino, 210–11.

topos merely asserting that God did not disparage woman, into a direct refutation of the persistent physiological belief that the female body is an 'imperfect' creation in nature. Since God out-ranks Nature as creator of the human form, argues Reason—and moreover since he gave such tokens of woman's nobility in crea-tion—there cannot be defect in the 'form' of woman any more than in that of man.[103]

In the *Livre de Leësce*, Le Fèvre had followed a bipartite plan. First he produced *ad hoc* responses to allegations in Matheolus' *Lamentations* (covering such topics as exclusion from law, marital loyalty, piety, generosity, and courage). Then he instituted a section exemplifying women's achievements under several major headings: prowess, learning, sexual constancy. As Christine's 'building' takes shape, so she increasingly adopts the second of those strategies, using the same sequence of head-ings, though she continues to trigger each phase by referring to misogynous insinuation. Again it is the investigative rigour she brings to each discussion that enhances the positive case.

Thus, although she demonstrates that Amazonian and other women *have* possessed physical power, she also uses a familiar suggestion that courage is not related to strength ('build doesn't make bold')[104] in order to develop a hypothesis that there are checks and balances in Nature whereby paucity of one quality is compensated in a person by abundance of another—for instance, paucity of physical strength by abundance of moral inclination. In fact she converts the old strength-in-weakness trope into an argument that women's slighter force is an 'agreeable defect' which saves them from perpetrating violent crimes.[105] Really it amounts to a complete inversion: men's strength is men's defect, a disagreeable advantage as it were. The compensation theory also drives her conviction that women have particularly sharp

---

[103] I. 9. 2, ed. Curnow, 650–2, tr. Richards, 23–4. Curnow points out that Christine is referring rather vaguely to the *Secreta mulierum* tradition, while think-ing probably of Aristotelian ideas mentioned in the *Lamentations* of Matheolus (pp. 1048–9). On the physiology see further Blamires, *Woman Defamed and Woman Defended*, 39–42, 91–3.

[104] My translation of Reason's epigram in I. 14. 2, 'le grant et fort corpsage ne fait mie le vertueulx poyssant couraige' (ed. Curnow, 674), whose *corpsage/couraige* antithesis is attenuated in Richards, 'a large and strong body never makes a strong and virtuous heart' (p. 37).

[105] I. 14. 1–3, ed. Curnow, 673–6, tr. Richards, 36–8.

intellects,[106] even while, as we have noted, she recognizes that prevailing ideology constricts their opportunities to apply them.

A profound sociological, moral, and psychological acumen underpins Christine's ability to probe misogynous tradition. The virulence of attacks on women's 'avarice' is not just countered with *exempla* of female generosity, it is exposed as a concomitant of socio-economic pressures. Women, it is suggested, have to be thrifty in running households since they rarely have personal access to money: their consequent tendency to jib at free-spending husbands must be what tends to produce a myth of feminine stinginess.[107] No one had brought such observant rationality to the case for women before, and it is felt most powerfully at the very flashpoint of gender debate, the 'stability' question. For Christine, sexual loyalty (the major focus of *The Legend of Good Women*) is not to be severed from the wider issue of stability, which in turn is to be interpreted (as we saw in Chapter 5) as a matter of self-control, the discipline of reason over appetite. If I have been censorious about a 'lack of intellectual infrastructure' in the *Legend*, it is because the maturity of such a perspective is present only very elusively there—in Alceste's warning to Cupid to be 'stable' and not to deal tyrannically with the poet/narrator. What the *Legend* thus glimpses, Christine rigorously examines.[108] She exposes the hypocrisy of the masculine gendering of 'instability' as female, a hypocrisy which can be sustained, she shows, only by overlooking the manifest tyrannical instability demonstrated through history by men in positions of power. Here indeed she lets rip, in a scathing review of the mindless depravities of Emperor Nero and the rest. Masculine talk of women's 'childish inconstancy' becomes laughable in the context of the macabre whims of Roman emperors.[109] The cue for an attack on male

---

[106] 'Just as women have more delicate bodies than men, weaker and less able to perform many tasks, so do they have minds that are freer and sharper whenever they apply themselves'; I. 27. 1, ed. Curnow, 721, tr. Richards, 63.

[107] II. 66. 1, ed. Curnow, 962–3, tr. Richards, 209–10.

[108] II. 47. 1–2, and II. 49. 5, ed. Curnow, 891–3 and 899, tr. Richards, 164–6 and 169–70.

[109] Droitture marvels that men are not ashamed to talk of women's inconstancy, since 'their own actions, not those of women, show so little constancy and steadfastness that their behavior appears childish'; II. 49. 4, ed. Curnow, 898–9, tr. Richards, 169. A story of a 'drunken monarch gone out of control' who is challenged by a woman in the *Chemin de long estude* bears out the seriousness with which Christine regarded this issue; Solterer, *The Master and Minerva*, 172.

criminality comes from Le Fèvre;[110] the imperial examples come from Boccaccio's *De casibus virorum illustrium*; but the cool moral logic of the whole is classic Christine, and the reader comes away feeling that a major intervention has been made in the 'stability' debate in the *Cité des dames*.[111]

Christine de Pizan set this book up as a monument. She equipped it with extraordinary self-authorizing allusions, which include the representation of herself at the beginning as a kind of Virgin Annunciate, blessed with a unique mission by a trinity of ladies.[112] She shares with her namesake St Christine—whose story is told in the third book—the ambition not to be shut up: just as St Christine speaks on even when her tongue is torn out, Christine means her city, her book, to go on speaking out to posterity from the space which she has strenuously cleared for it in the canon.[113] She is to have, like a St Peter, the keys to the city. Her trinitarian guides declare that this work will actually vanquish women's belief in misogynous myth, and that the time is now fulfilled for Christine (as if a predestined saviour of women) to challenge the 'uncontradicted' accusations endured for so long by women.[114] So, it is dispiriting to discover that copying of the book dried up in the mid-fifteenth century when it was superseded by a complete French version of *De mulieribus claris*,[115] and it is a major irony of literary history that the text has taken agonizingly long to

[110] *Leësce*, 3811–19; though suggestions that male criminality far exceeds female go back at least to Marbod of Rennes, for whom Judas's evil far exceeds any woman's ('De matrona', ed. Leotta, 76, tr. in Blamires, *Woman Defamed and Woman Defended*, 230). Christine's survey of male 'perversity' concludes with Judas in II. 49. 5, ed. Curnow, 899, tr. Richards, 170.

[111] Christine's sense of the importance of the topic is confirmed by the fact that towards the end of the third book she is still fielding examples 'to support the contention that women are constant'; III. 12. 1, ed. Curnow, 1012, tr. Richards, 241.

[112] On the Annunciation allusions, see Quilligan, *Allegory of Female Authority*, 54–5, and V. A. Kolve, 'The Annunciation to Christine: Authorial Empowerment in *The Book of the City of Ladies*', in Brendan Cassidy (ed.), *Iconography at the Crossroads*, Index of Christian Art, Occasional Papers II (Princeton: Department of Art and Archaeology, Princeton University, 1993), 171–96.

[113] III. 10. 1, ed. Curnow, 1008–9, tr. Richards, 239. See Quilligan on the severed tongue as 'an apt image of the voice that refuses to be silenced, and therefore a wonderful image of the power of female authority', *Allegory of Female Authority*, 221; also Kevin Brownlee, 'Martyrdom and the Female Voice: Saint Christine in the *Cité des dames*', in Renate Blumenfeld-Kosinski and Timea Szell (eds.), *Images of Sainthood in Medieval Europe* (Ithaca, NY: Cornell University Press, 1991), 115–35.

[114] I. 3. 3 and II. 53. 1, ed. Curnow, 629–30 and 924–5, tr. Richards, 10–11 and 185.

[115] Phillippy, 'Establishing Authority', 174; *Cité*, tr. Richards, 267.

regain a place in 'the field of letters' in a modern edition. In the conclusion to this study we shall need to ask, among other things, how the case for women could reach such epic proportions—could seem, as I said earlier, epoch-making—and yet not make much difference.

Conclusion

WE have discovered that a vigorous case for women was available by the late Middle Ages. How might we evaluate the strengths of the case, and why did it not have a greater cultural and social impact on the underlying or 'structural' misogyny of the period? Addressing these questions in the conclusion to this book, I would like to begin by considering briefly what profeminine writers had in mind when they thought about the possibility of women undertaking concerted action. When they projected women making a stand on their own behalf, how radical might the possibilities be?

Female solidarity seems to have been envisaged characteristically as an *ad hoc* reaction, its objectives being limited to defending the Christian faith; averting defeat by military enemies in emergencies; intervening on behalf of individual men *in extremis*; challenging male victimization of a particular woman; or taking vengeance against male outrage.

So far as defence of faith is concerned, we have seen Hrotsvitha suggestively enhancing the sense of sisterhood among her female characters, who assert their united faith in the face of coercive pagan authorities and who are even willing to operate through connubial insurgency, since converted wives are reported during one play to be withdrawing sexual co-operation from husbands.[1] A more familiar medieval expression of female solidarity in face of aggression against the Church would be that of nuns uniting in prayer—a form of passive resistance—against oppression.[2]

In an earlier chapter we mentioned an example of women's corporate action against invasion: St Genevieve convened matrons in Paris to use the force of joint prayer against Attila's advancing army.[3] On reflection this is really an act of deliverance, allied to the feminine 'peacemaking' function, differing only in

---

[1] *Passio . . . Fidei Spei et Karitatis (Sapientia)*, sc. i, where Antiochus reports to Hadrian that wives are refusing to eat or sleep with unconverted husbands; ed. Homeyer, 358, tr. Wilson, 126.

[2] See the *Life* of St Anstrude (7th cent.); McNamara, *Sainted Women of the Dark Ages*, 297.

[3] See Ch. 7 above.

degree from the role of the women who plead in *The Knight's Tale*
for the deliverance of Arcite and Palamon from Theseus' wrath,
or who plead in *The Wife of Bath's Tale* for the chance to deliver a
condemned rapist knight into an educative form of justice.
Moreover there is no thought of women gaining anything *for*
women in such instances—a permanent council of civic mothers,
for example, or permanent female jurisdiction over rapists.[4]
The closest approximation to achievement of institutional change
that I have noticed in these contexts concerns Veturia in the *De
mulieribus claris* and merely serves to confirm that the culture
cannot easily conceive of rights that women might corporately
claim.[5] Veturia is Coriolanus' mother, and, together with his
wife and numerous other women, she angrily and successfully
pleads with Coriolanus not to attack Rome. Duly grateful, the
Roman Senate institutes a special women's temple and passes
liberating decrees, of which the most far-reaching enables women
to inherit property freely, 'something which previously had
not been allowed'.[6] A key socio-economic change for women is
represented as an unexpected reward, given spontaneously by
men to women out of gratitude for the city's deliverance. The
change is in effect a piece of magnanimous masculine courtesy—
indeed, Boccaccio claims that this was when certain formal
courtesies to women officially began. There is no hint that 'something which previously had not been allowed' *would* have been
allowed had women agitated specifically for it under normal
circumstances. Moreover, so far is Boccaccio from sensing positive implications in the changes that he bemoans the haughtiness
and prodigality which he considers women to have acquired with
these prerogatives.[7]

Women join forces on behalf of women in medieval narrative
chiefly to defend them from torture[8] or to deal with unsatisfactory

---

[4] In the *Wife of Bath's Tale* something more subtle is perhaps gained, in so far as
the women's action produces genuine reflection about male coercion; but the only
specific consequence the tale inscribes is moral change in an individual male.

[5] The case of Hortensia, negotiating on women's behalf against tax burdens,
was discussed in Ch. 7 above: it is an important witness to an individual woman's
rhetorical power, but not to corporate action.

[6] *De mulieribus claris*, ed. Zaccaria, 218–26 (p. 224), tr. Guarino, 118–21 (p. 120).

[7] Christine de Pizan adopted the Veturia narrative in *Cité*, I. 34. 1, ed. Curnow,
868–9, tr. Richards, 150–1, but perhaps put off by Boccaccio's negative commentary she omitted the resultant 'prerogatives'.

[8] Women mob one of the torturers of St Christine in the version of her legend in
the *Cité des dames*; ed. Curnow, 1085, tr. Richards, 237.

partners. In Chrétien de Troyes's *Cligés* a great crowd of women suddenly saves Fénice from physicians who are trying to force her to confess that she is not dead. While ostensibly the women are avenging the physicians' brutalization of a defenceless female body, unwittingly they are assisting in a plot to remedy Fénice's allocation to the 'wrong' male partner in the romance.[9] A more premeditated unity of purpose is shown by the trio Queen Isolde, Princess Isolde, and Brangane in Gottfried von Strassburg's *Tristan*, enabling them to eliminate the unwanted attentions of an arrogant and misogynous steward who claims Isolde's hand.[10] Yet the hints which these episodes deliver of consolidated female protest at society's oppression of women tend to be swallowed up within a focus on personal vengeance. It is therefore noteworthy that the chief antecedent for mass female intervention also involves personal vengeance; namely, that of the Ciconian women in Ovid's *Metamorphoses* who kill and dismember Orpheus when he rejects women after Eurydice's death and turns his affections to boys. Deschamps recalls this in the *Miroir de mariage* when Folie suggests that if women knew the extent of Repertoire de Science's misogyny and could catch him in the open, they would justifiably stone and destroy him like Orpheus.[11] This, of course, reductively insinuates that what most antagonizes women about misogyny is its imputed affiliation with homosexuality (or, for that matter, with impotencies or frustrations of heterosexuality such as were increasingly alleged to motivate misogynists in the late Middle Ages).[12]

The 'Ciconian' model of women's personal revenge for sexual deprivation even extends to medieval understanding of the origin of the Amazon kingdom. According to Boccaccio, large numbers of women who had been widowed by invaders in the Scythian

---

[9] Ed. Luttrell and Gregory, 5966–6031, tr. Owen, *Arthurian Romances*, 173–4.

[10] Ed. de Gruyter (esp. 9898–928), tr. Hatto, ch. 12 (esp. pp. 170–2). Blumstein emphasizes what an enlightened and cogent rebuttal of the steward's misogyny is produced here; *Misogyny and Idealization*, 155–9.

[11] *Miroir*, 9874–90; *Metamorphoses*, X. 1–67, tr. Innes, 246–7. As Minnis points out (*Shorter Poems*, 446), the ladies in Castiglione's *Il cortegiano*, bk. II, also recall this episode when they make a mock attack on Gaspare for uttering misogynous remarks; *The Book of the Courtier*, tr. Sir Thomas Hoby (London: Dent, 1974), 181–2.

[12] And in the early modern period: for in *The Book of the Courtier* Signora Emilia makes light of Gaspare's misogyny, caused 'more because he could never finde woman that was willing to looke upon him, than for any want that is in women', tr. Hoby, 158.

region took up arms as an act of revenge for losing their husbands: then, rather than find themselves placed in subjection by
becoming wives to foreigners, they resolved to set up a dominion
of women from which all men would be banished.[13] A separate
women's state could not, it seems, be envisaged brought into
being as a purely constructive enterprise resulting from female
collaboration; but only as women's indignant reaction to the
loss of sexual partners (though Christine de Pizan succeeds in
modifying this impression a little).[14] And, having described the
establishment of the Amazon state together with its system for
sustaining a female population by using men in nearby lands
for occasional procreation[15] and by raising only girl children,
medieval accounts do not elaborate any further ideas about
the women's collaboration. Instead, attention is focused on the
'virile' military and territorial exploits of individual Amazons
who compete in the big league of masculine soldiership; Thamiris,
Hippolyta, Penthesilea.[16]

    What all this demonstrates is that the medieval notion of corpo-
rate female action, including that of the Amazons, is filtered to us
through the *structural* misogyny of the period. I borrow the term
from Alastair Minnis. He uses the expression 'structural anti-
feminism' to encompass the entirety of traditional medieval
concepts about gender difference, as opposed to 'phobic anti-
feminism', in which moral failings are predicated on the structural assumptions and used to direct criticism at women.[17] Of
course, what we read as structural misogyny, most medieval
writers articulated as the 'natural' condition of woman. A typical
example would be Boccaccio's assertion that 'in general Nature
has given men proud and high spirits, while it has made women
humble in character and submissive, more apt for delicate things

---

[13] *De mulieribus claris*, ed. Zaccaria, 62–4, tr. Guarino, 23–4.

[14] In *Cité*, I. 16. 1, ed. Curnow, 681–3, tr. Richards, 40–2, the women's decision
appears more constructive than it is in Boccaccio: Christine attenuates, but does
not delete, the revenge motive.

[15] A classic instance of the inversive procedures of medieval gender discourse:
men are here reduced to the status of wives, used as sexual staging-posts by
Amazon partners who occasionally return to them to conceive when not out on
military business.

[16] See Le Fèvre, *Leësce*, 3558 ff., in a section on female *prouesce*, giving accounts
of Penthesilea and Thamiris and naming several other Amazons.

[17] *Shorter Poems*, 427. The broad distinction appears useful to me even though,
I suspect, the boundary between 'structural' and 'phobic' would elude precise
definition.

than for ruling'.[18] Hypothetically, a phenomenon such as the Amazon narrative could nevertheless have challenged the horizons of the 'natural'. Boccaccio himself does incipiently recognize this challenge when he says of Amazon warriors that 'custom had changed their nature' (*usus in naturam vertatur alteram*), and indeed that by raising girls in athletic skills rather than in 'womanly tasks', they 'hardened' them in 'the aptitudes and strength of a man' (*durabant in aptitudinem et virile robur*).[19] As Benson points out, such passages acknowledge in effect 'that the qualities of "masculine" and "feminine" that are conventionally tied to biological gender are actually socially induced'.[20] It is perhaps surprising to discover that a similar acknowledgement can even be found way back in the fourth century. There Chrysostom, in order to urge congregations against spiritual debility, finds himself needing to argue that 'softness' is not tied to female gender but is the outcome of a person's lifestyle and upbringing. Is it biological sex that makes women 'soft', he asks?

Not at all. Softness arises from manner of living and from upbringing. Sheltered upbringing, leisure, baths, lotions, numerous perfumes and soft couches make women so. . . . And the proof of this is that women who are nourished out in the fields are stronger than men who live in cities, and would be able to overthrow most such men in a wrestling match.[21]

For a moment, Chrysostom proves that patristic writing could grasp the constructedness of dominant ideas about women— though, as Elizabeth Clark shows, this was extremely unusual.[22]

[18] 'cum illos ferventis animi, ut plurimum, natura produxerit; has vero mitis ingenii et remisse virtutis, lautitiis potius quam imperiis aptas, produxit'; *De mulieribus claris*, ed. Zaccaria, 78–80, tr. Guarino, 32.

[19] Ibid., ed. Zaccaria, 136 and 64, tr. Guarino, 66 and 24.

[20] *Invention of the Renaissance Woman*, 23.

[21] 'Num unde nisi ex hoc putatis mulieres esse adeo molles, dic quaeso? num ex solo sexu? Nequaquam, sed ex vivendi ratione et educatione: nam in umbra educatio, otium, lavacra, unguenta, multitudo aromatum, cubilis mollities eas tales efficit. . . . Quod autem hoc sit verum, mulieres quae aluntur in agris, sunt fortiores viris qui in urbibus habitant, et multos ejusmodi illae in lucta prostraverint'; *Homily 29 on Heb.* 3, *PG* 63. 206 (my tr.). The passage is prompted by Matt. 11: 8, 'they that are clothed in soft garments, are in the houses of kings', to which Chrysostom adds, 'and those who are not in soft garments, are in heaven'. In this context it becomes advisable for him to unpack the wholesale attribution of softness to women. (I owe this reference to Clark, 'Ideology, History, and the Construction of "Woman"', 181.)

[22] 'Ideology, History, and the Construction of "Woman"', 182. However, one challenging argument ascribed by St Augustine to an opponent, Julian of Eclanum, was that severe labour pains were not universal since some barbarian

It took a Christine de Pizan to probe that constructedness further, for instance by declaring that women would show all sorts of aptitudes not normally associated with them if they were educated equally with men and given more exposure to experience beyond the home. It is instructive to check her case for women against summaries of structural misogyny, such as the following by Caroline Walker Bynum: '*Male* and *female* were contrasted and asymmetrically valued as intellect/body, active/passive, rational/irrational, reason/emotion, self-control/lust, judgment/ mercy, and order/disorder.'[23] Preceding chapters have shown, I think, that there is hardly one of these asymmetries in which Christine did not seek to intervene. Yet her power to transcend what was *structured* in her culture was, by definition, constrained. If misogyny pervaded scholarly writing then the very attempt to write, positively, of women, necessarily embroiled the writer in numerous paradoxes with which feminism is still struggling. Some of these paradoxes (as usefully picked out by Karen Sullivan) are, that in beginning to write from a woman's point of view, 'one is already within the realm of a masculine idiom'; that the inspiration of a feminist critique originating 'outside the given framework' is difficult to recuperate from scholarly discourse; and that a feminism which strives to speak about woman risks repeating 'the very prejudice of misogynist authors who look upon her as a fixed object of study separate from him who studies'.[24]

I do not want to dwell on the negatives because that is not the point of this book. But it is only sensible to admit that the medieval case for women had very little room in which to manœuvre. Structural misogyny monopolized written authority. It suppressed what it deemed inconvenient for women to ponder (the biblical Samaritan woman as a model of public action and evangelism, for instance, or the calculated disobedience of the biblical

nomad women 'accustomed to physical exertion, give birth in the course of their travels with such facility that, without stopping, they . . . continue on their way, transferring the burden of their womb to their shoulders'; *Opus imperfectum contra Julianum* (VI. 29), tr. in Pagels, *Adam, Eve, and the Serpent*, 136. It is interesting that this questioning of the constructedness of 'biological' woman is uttered by a thinker marginalized by Augustine.

[23] '". . . And Woman his Humanity": Female Imagery in the Religious Writing of the Later Middle Ages', 257. In my view, however, an important omission in Bynum's list is 'stability/instability'.

[24] Karen Sullivan, 'At the Limit of Feminist Theory: An Architectonics of the *Querelle de la Rose*', *Exemplaria*, 3 (1991), 435–66.

Esther). It manipulated its androcentric science wherever that science threatened gender asymmetry. (We noted some juggling with formulae of heat and cold in Chapter 5. Another blatant instance of juggling would be the way science got around gender implications of the Aristotelian principle that intellectual subtlety depended on physiological sensitivity and softness of skin: the logical deduction that woman's intellect ought therefore to be superior was averted by declaring woman's softness to be a 'humid' sort which promoted not intellectual vision but only *astutia*, 'a condition of worldly knowingness'.[25]) Everywhere structural misogyny consolidated asymmetry with the utmost deviousness, consciously or not. St Bernard could write that Thomas's desire to touch Christ's wounds manifested greatness of soul, and that Mary Magdalene's desire to touch Christ manifested her purely carnal mentality, without registering any inconsistency. Even where the case for women raised the prospect of an alternative Amazonian empire of women, strategies of masculine reappropriation insinuated that, were women to launch out on their own, they would spend all their time impersonating men: doing 'masculine' things, even to the extent of withering one breast in order to wield military equipment like men.

Does this mean that the medieval case for women has to be viewed as no more than a licensed zone of ideological deviance,[26] little more than a palliative whereby structural misogyny released the guilt of its monopoly in a safely controlled way and provided women with a 'feelgood factor'? Certainly, as we have frequently had occasion to observe, many of the defence arguments could be interpreted as misogyny in disguise. By urging men to respect women for their maternity and their 'softening' influence, the defence fixes women in reproductive, domestic, and mediatory functions without relaxing masculine prerogatives of toughness and judicial control. By locating women's 'privileges' in relation to Adam and Christ, the defence reinforces maleness as the standard of value, gives women 'honour' which is no practical use, and

[25] This solution is worked out by Albertus Magnus and other commentators on Aristotle, as clarified by David Burnley, 'Criseyde's Heart and the Weakness of Women', 33–5; and see Atkinson, *The Oldest Vocation*, 37 ff. Atkinson also explains the scientific juggling to which Albertus resorted in order to reconcile the 'natural' tendency of men to live longer than women, with his own perception of women's apparently greater longevity (pp. 35–6, and see Cadden, *Meanings of Sex Difference*, 175–6).
[26] Angenot, *Champions des femmes*, 160.

risks exacerbating Eve's infamy by efforts to mitigate it. By engaging in a contest over stability, the defence yields to structural misogyny's determination that women's loyalty to men is their *raison d'être*. In any case, there is always the danger that praise of such qualities as constancy, compassion, or generosity (in Solterer's words) 'functions as a way to legislate a woman's speech and conduct'.[27]

This is a defeatist view of defence-of-women discourse, and it should not foreclose study of this rich and tenacious tradition. A more positive view might start even at the weakest-looking point, that is, the defence's attempt to use structural misogyny's own asymmetries to deliver profeminine (or at least, anti-misogynist) conclusions. The logic here was to accept as a premiss a disparaging epithet for women, such as 'passive', 'gullible', or 'weak', and deduce the consequences for moral analysis of both sexes. The underlying proposition is that if women are deemed 'naturally' handicapped, then it is illogical to criticize them for not performing on a par with men. Thus if women are 'weaker', then whatever strength they conspicuously display shows to greater advantage than men's. Or if women are considered relatively more 'passive', then (as preachers as well as profeminine writers were keen to assert) it is illogical to suggest that they rather than men are the instigators of sexual immorality. And if women are passive, weak, and gullible, Eve was the less equipped to deal with temptation, and would have seen no harm in offering Adam the apple, whereas he far more seriously underachieved in accepting it so unthinkingly.

It is a mistake to dismiss such moves as facetious chop-logic. Sometimes, it is true, they are not above suspicion: Le Fèvre has a rather rambling discussion of women's alleged 'disobedience', in which he seems to suggest—with what gravity I do not know—that since God has given woman less reason and more will (*voulenté*) she therefore must have more freedom.[28] But mostly these arguments aim seriously to embarrass misogyny by articulating the antimasculine consequences of the logical application of misogynous lore in moral and scriptural contexts. They refuse to let misogyny get away with a view of woman as a being of congenital un-responsibility on the one hand who is simultane-

---

[27] *The Master and Minerva*, 55.

[28] *Leësce*, 2019–70, esp. 2063–5: 'Car Dieu a es femmes planté | Mains raison et plus voulenté; | Si doit avoir plus de franchise.'

ously, on the other hand, held profoundly responsible for sin. And such argument is able to draw on formidable authority: did not Augustine himself argue that Adam would have seen straight through the temptation, to which Eve's limited understanding left her exposed?[29]

Characteristically, this debate about what could be *expected* of women focused on moral responsibility, for that was very much the perceived crux of the case for women. As was noted quite early in the development of gender studies, 'the quarrel of pro- and anti-feminism does not revolve about woman as a sociological entity, but rather about her moral existence'.[30] Most hotly contested in the moral domain was woman's constancy, her resolution, whether in terms of sustaining faith or sexual loyalty. Behind the unedifying Punch-and-Judy show of claim and counter-claim on behalf of feminine or masculine stability, productive reflection went on. People could not reconcile traditional dogma on 'womanly infirmity' with various sorts of evidence, hagiographical (all those tenacious women saints), legendary (redoubtable heroines of antiquity), scriptural (the female disciples' courageous loyalty to Christ), or indeed experiential. Devices invented to explain the inconsistency, such as the theory of women's 'strength in weakness', really only underlined the problem. It was therefore in this area that the hypocrisy and condescension of misogyny was most rigorously critiqued, with the help of influential theological ammunition on the defection of Christ's male disciples and with the help of pastoral disgust over the sexual double standard. It was not just that the case for women retaliated by persuasively emphasizing an unstable masculine capacity for disloyalty, promiscuity, and violence. Concentrating on these moral issues, defenders began to be able to speculate about psychological and social causation. Some writers, we have seen, began to ask whether men were trying to offload guilt about their own moral inadequacies onto women, just as Adam tried to blame Eve. We have also seen that it was clear to several observers that society's scrutiny of women's moral behaviour was such, and men's solidarity and control of the judiciary was such, that women's misdemeanours always received disproportionate attention, with the result that there was no parity in the moral

[29] See above, Ch. 4 n. 64, for this argument in *De Genesi ad litteram*.
[30] Jacob Ornstein, 'Misogyny and Pro-feminism in Early Castilian Literature', *Modern Language Quarterly*, 3 (1942), 221–34 (p. 233).

evaluation of men and women. Here were the lineaments of important questions about relationships between power and constructions of the feminine.

Far less enlightened to modern eyes at first sight would be all that incessant concern with women's so-called 'privileges'—with various kinds of priority in creation and in Christian history. While there would be some truth in suspecting that the rehearsal of these suited medieval masculine ideology, in the sense that the privileges amounted only to harmless anti-depressants for women, I have made clear that I do not think that we should ever underestimate the sheer importance of priority as an authorizing and valorizing mechanism in the Middle Ages. This is the thread of continuity between the desire to find elements of priority for woman in creation, the desire to find woman assuming priority in announcing the Resurrection, and the desire to find women founding cities or leading the way in cultural and technological innovation: and Christine de Pizan and Peter Abelard are no less susceptible to the concern with priority, I have suggested, than the merest hack profeminine polemicist.

By the same token the commendation of female role-models who demonstrated women's excellence or even priority in 'masculine' activity was crucial, too, though this would not now be considered a promising strategy from one feminist point of view: 'the straightforward proof that women can achieve in male fields of endeavour reinforces the conventional valuing of the masculine and suggests that women are valuable only insofar as they can compete with men.'[31] Yet at a period when almost all socially prestigious and culturally dominant 'fields of endeavour' were totally monopolized by men, such an objection would perhaps have seemed peculiar. Among the models which profeminine discourse favoured—Deborah, Mary Magdalene, Dido, Semiramis, St Catherine, and others—the demonstrations that a woman could 'compete' with men in governing, preaching, founding a city, or disputing with philosophers amounted to sites of resistance against patriarchy, despite all the neutralizing efforts of patristic and other commentary. A protestation that women could compete at all in such fields involved an element of cultural rebellion, whatever endorsement of masculine values it contained.

[31] Benson, *Invention of the Renaissance Woman*, 57.

There was even an advantage in the one category of public intervention that *was* conceded to women as an extension of their culturally inscribed 'softness' and compassion,[32] namely peace-making, for it could easily throw into relief a contrasting mascu-line indulgence in irascibility. That was perhaps a price the dominant culture did not mind paying while men benefited from a system which gendered finer feelings feminine. Recent criticism has rightly begun to wonder whether, in attributing 'civilizing' and 'ennobling' functions to woman whereby she 'incarnates the cultural standards of her society', medieval writing both made women key agents in sustaining rigid class barriers, and obliter-ated women's own desire.[33] I have some sympathy for this con-spiracy theory, but at the same time I suppose that we should not pour too much retrospective cynicism upon those constructive roles which the conspiracy allowed women to play. Peacemaking was such a role. The Paston women late in the fifteenth century, and Christine de Pizan early in it, concurred in finding a challenge and identity for women in the peacemaking function.[34]

The last aspect of the case for women which I would flag in this conclusion is that it was a prime instrument for demystifying literary authority and for penetrating the subjectivity of dis-course. Since defenders denounced misogynists as slanderers, they were necessarily drawn into analysis of who uttered slander, and for what motives. This was not just a matter of cultivating suspicions about the sexual status and moral reliability of misogy-nous 'authorities' such as Ovid, and it was not even just a matter of questioning the truth-value of lurid stories, such as that of Pasiphaë, which had been used to attack women. It extended on the one hand (most notably in Chaucer's writing) into an insight that gender statements as often articulate a speaker's personal agenda as they contribute to gender debate itself. It extended on the other hand (rather widely in the later Middle Ages) into a more pervasive demystifying of literary authority. Christine de Pizan could clear a place for her 'city' only by insisting that even the great philosophers might be wrong. Notorious slurs such as that of Solomon, that the misdeed of a man is better than the

[32] For the *naturalis compassio* of women, see e.g. Abelard, *The Authority and Dignity of Nuns*, 'Letter of Heloise on Religious Life and Abelard's First Reply', ed. Muckle, 274, tr. Scott Moncrieff, 165.

[33] Toril Moi, 'Desire in Language', in David Aers (ed.), *Medieval Literature* (Brighton: Harvester, 1986), 22.

[34] See Ch. 3 above.

good deed of a woman, were increasingly opened to quizzical analysis.[35]

The investigative process was even beginning to chip at the cornerstone of the disqualification of women from public life—St Paul's prohibitions against women teaching and speaking in the congregation.[36] Some thirteenth-century academic theologians were prepared to accept that St Paul was really referring to married women (thereby allowing for the teaching roles of selected holy women such as Mary Magdalene or St Catherine).[37] The formal case for women does not appear to have had the nerve to pursue this during the Middle Ages. It would be interesting to know how often the Pauline doctrine was queried between the thirteenth century and the sixteenth, when John Aylmer complained that the injunction to women to 'keep silence' was used as a 'Hercules clubbe that beateth all downe before it'.[38] He protested that no one thought to consider whether St Paul had actually aimed his restrictions at the unruliness of a particular congregation. Here was 'a way of reading Scripture', as Constance Jordan observes, which 'prohibits an interpretation of its prescriptions as absolute'.[39] Medieval literature defending women played a part in the gradual process of dissolving such 'absolutes'. It encouraged an attitude of scepticism about the motives and vested interests of propagandists. It nourished the possibility of re-representing women in received stories about women, and as both Chaucer

[35] Ecclus. 42: 14. See Christine's reply to Pierre Col in the *Querelle de la Rose*; ed. Hicks, 165, tr. in Blamires, *Woman Defamed and Woman Defended*, 289. She wonders whether Solomon meant that anything would have been better for him than the 'goodness' in the mistresses for whom his infatuation made him worship idols; or that the 'misdeed' of Judas would ultimately benefit humanity more than the great deeds of Judith or other heroines.

[36] 1 Tim. 2: 12; 1 Cor. 14: 34–5.

[37] I have analysed a discussion by Eustace of Arras, who suggested that St Paul meant married women, not others who might be specially privileged, in 'Women and Preaching', 148: and see pp. 136–7 for rehearsal of a similar reservation by the English Lollard Walter Brut in 1391–3, during his trial. For a patristic contrast, see Origen's commentary on 1 Cor. 14: 35, arguing that virgins and widows are included in the prohibition; Coyle, 'The Fathers on Women', 74.

[38] Constance Jordan, *Renaissance Feminism*, 129, quoting from John Aylmer, *An Harborowe for Faithfull and Trewe Subjectes agaynst the Late Blowne Blaste, Concerninge the Gouernment of Wemen* (Strasbourg, 1559). In a full analysis we would need to consider Aylmer's own agenda in this pro-Elizabeth piece (see Benson, *Invention of Renaissance Woman*, 235–45).

[39] Jordan, *Renaissance Feminism*, 129. Further refutation of the absoluteness of the prescriptions can be found in the writing of Margaret Fell Fox in the 17th cent.; Aughterson, *Renaissance Woman*, 39–40.

and Christine de Pizan realized, it pointed to the probability that if women themselves were to write the stories, men might find themselves—let alone women—represented in a drastically different light.[40]

Experiential evidence also dealt sharp blows of scepticism, the more powerfully so where a writing woman vouched for her own experience, as could Christine. Her insistence early in the *Cité* that the characters of women of her own acquaintance are definitively at odds with the nightmare constructs offered by misogyny[41] is compelling and fresh: indeed, so far as one can tell, this confident rebuke had never before been uttered in writing by a woman. But the appeal to empirical experience was a double-edged instrument. Drawing discussion towards the observable patterns of existing social phenomena, it risked plunging back into structural misogyny. Thus when Christine wants to explode the myth that wives are rancorous creatures who terrorize husbands, she suggests that if 'a new book in accordance with the truth' were written to replace the Theophrastan perspective on marriage, what it would actually reveal would be the sufferings and humiliations of abused wives. Droitture asks Christine where, among her neighbours, can all those hypothetical tyrannical wives be seen? The fact is that 'men are masters over their wives' and would 'never allow their wives to have such authority'.[42] This shows how experience can be cited to overturn Theophrastan fantasy, but only by appealing to the practical 'truth' of a social structure in which masculine authority appears impenetrable.

As I believe this book has shown, however, the medieval case for women did contrive to strike out against the complacency of masculine authority. Scholars have sometimes been uncomfortable with the materials of the case, mainly because the difficulty of accessing those materials and uncertainties about their tonality have interfered with sympathetic appraisal. There has been a temptation to disparage them: Helen Solterer refers dismissively to the 'theorems' of the 'standard gynocentric repertory' of the later Middle Ages.[43] Her point, which I respect, is that one must be ready to distinguish writings in which the theorems merely confirm 'existing symbolic domination of women' from those that

---

[40] *Wife of Bath's Prologue*, III. 688–96; Christine de Pizan, *Epistre*, 407–19.
[41] *Cité*, I. 1. 1, ed. Curnow, 618, tr. Richards, 4.
[42] Ibid. II. 13. 1, ed. Curnow, 817–19, tr. Richards, 118–19.
[43] *The Master and Minerva*, 146.

'envisage some change'.[44] But it has also seemed necessary to me to restore to our understanding the premedieval and medieval resonance of the elements of the defence discourse. There is a premedieval resonance because, whether or not the theory of a single origin in the apocryphal Esdras is accepted, it is clear that important cues came from patristic writings (which were not always, as some might assume, the kiss of death for profeminine thinking). We can speak of a medieval resonance in the sense that, as I have tried to show, there was a productive interface between defence-of-women literature and other medieval discourses, such as the confessional manual, romances, hagiography, and theological disputation. The medieval case for women was something to reckon with, and it should be better known. Although the impact of the Herculean club of misogyny was to last for centuries, women had the capacity to unhorse Hercules and force a truce, as Christine thought.[45] The development of medieval profeminine literature was not irrelevant to such an outcome.

---

[44] *The Master and Minerva*, 147.
[45] *Cité*, I. 18. 4–6, ed. Curnow, 691–3, tr. Richards, 46–7.

Bibliography

PRIMARY SOURCES

ABELARD, PETER, 'Abelard's Letter of Consolation to a Friend (*Historia calamitatum*)', ed. J. T. Muckle, *Mediaeval Studies*, 12 (1950), 161–213.
—— 'The Personal Letters between Abelard and Heloise', ed. J. T. Muckle, *Mediaeval Studies*, 15 (1953), 47–94.
—— *De auctoritate vel dignitate ordinis sanctimonialium* (*The Authority and Dignity of Nuns*); ed. J. T. Muckle, 'The Letter of Heloise on Religious Life and Abelard's First Reply', *Mediaeval Studies*, 17 (1955), 240–81 (pp. 253–81).
—— 'Abelard's Rule for Religious Women', ed. T. P. McLaughlin, *Mediaeval Studies*, 18 (1956), 241–92.
—— *Sermones*, PL 178. 379–610.
—— *The Letters of Abelard and Heloise*, tr. Betty Radice (Harmondsworth: Penguin, 1974).
—— *The Letters of Abelard and Heloise*, tr. C. K. Scott Moncrieff (New York: Cooper Square, Inc., 1974).
Acta sanctorum; J. Bollandus and G. Henschenius, *Acta sanctorum: Editio novissima*, ed. J. Carnandet *et al.* (Paris: Palmé, 1863).
AGRIPPA VON NETTESHEIM, HEINRICH CORNELIUS, *De nobilitate et praecellentia foeminei sexus*, ed. C. Béné, with French tr. by O. Sauvage (Geneva: Droz, 1990).
—— *A Treatise of the Nobilitie and excellencye of woman kynde*, tr. David Clapham (London, 1542).
ALBERTANUS of Brescia, *Albertani Brixiensis Liber consolationis et consilii*, ed. Thor Sundby, Chaucer Society, 2nd ser. viii (London: Trubner, 1873).
ALBERTUS MAGNUS, *Quaestiones super De animalibus*; *Alberti Magni opera omnia*, vol. xii, ed. E. Filthaut, OP (Aschendorff: Monasterii Westfalorum, 1955).
ALDHELM, *De virginitate*, in *Aldhelm: The Prose Works*, tr. Michael Lapidge and Michael Herren (Ipswich: D. S. Brewer, 1979).
ALEXIS, GUILLAUME, *Le Debat de l'omme et de la femme*, in *Guillaume Alexis: Œuvres poétiques*, ed. Arthur Piaget and Emile Picot, 3 vols. (Paris: Firmin Didot, 1896–1908), i. 121–44; and English tr. *An Interlocucyon with an Argument betwyxt Man and Woman*, i. 145–55.
AMADEUS of Lausanne, *Homiliae octo de laudibus beatae Mariae*, PL 188. 1303–46; and see under Bernard of Clairvaux.
AMBROSE, St, *De Paradiso*, PL 14. 275–314.
—— *De viduis*, PL 16. 247–75.
—— *De virginibus*, PL 16. 187–232.
—— *Expositio evangelii secundum Lucam*, ed. M. Adriaen, CCSL xiv (Turnhout: Brepols, 1957).

AMBROSE, St, *Hexameron, Paradise, and Cain and Abel*, tr. J. J. Savage, Fathers of the Church 42 (New York: Fathers of the Church, Inc., 1961).

——*The Principal Works of St Ambrose*, tr. H. de Romestin, Select Library of Nicene and Post-Nicene Fathers, 2nd ser. 10 (Oxford: James Parker, 1896).

AMT, EMILIE (ed.), *Women's Lives in Medieval Europe* (London: Routledge, 1993).

ANDREAS CAPELLANUS, *De amore; Andreas Capellanus on Love*, ed. and tr. P. G. Walsh (London: Duckworth, 1982).

AQUINAS, St THOMAS, *Summa theologiae*, gen. ed. Thomas Gilby, OP, 60 vols. (London: Blackfriars, in conjunction with Eyre & Spottiswoode; and New York: McGraw-Hill, 1963–).

AUGHTERSON, KATE (ed.), *Renaissance Woman. A Sourcebook: Constructions of Femininity in England* (London: Routledge, 1995).

AUGUSTINE, St, *De civitate Dei*, PL 41. 13–804.

——*City of God*, tr. Henry Bettenson (Harmondsworth: Penguin, 1984).

——*De Genesi ad litteram*, PL 34. 220–486.

——*The Literal Meaning of Genesis*, tr. J. H. Taylor, Ancient Christian Writers, nos. 41–2 (New York: Newman Press, 1982).

——*In Joannis evangelium*, PL 35. 1379–976.

——*Homilies on the Gospel of John*, tr. John Gibb and James Innes, in Philip Schaff (ed.), A Select Library of the Nicene and Post-Nicene Fathers 7 (Grand Rapids, Mich.: Eerdmans, 1956).

——*De decem chordis*, in CSEL 41 (1961), 105–51.

——*Sermones*, PL 38. 23–1484; 39. 1493–736; 46. 817–1004; 47. 1189–248.

BAIRD, JOSEPH L., and KANE, JOHN R. (trs.), *La Querelle de la Rose: Letters and Documents* (Chapel Hill: University of North Carolina Press, 1978).

BARRATT, ALEXANDRA (ed.), *Women's Writing in Middle English* (London: Longman, 1992).

BEDE, *Bede's Ecclesiastical History of the English People*, ed. Bertram Colgrave and R. A. B. Mynors (Oxford: Clarendon Press, 1969).

Beowulf, ed. C. L. Wrenn, rev. W. F. Bolton (London: Harrap, 1973).

BERCHER, WILLIAM, *The Nobility of Women*, ed. R. Warwick Bond (London: Roxburghe Club, 1904).

BERNARD of Clairvaux, *Magnificat: Homilies in Praise of the Blessed Virgin Mary by Bernard of Clairvaux and Amadeus of Lausanne*, tr. Marie-Bernard Saïd and Grace Perigo, Cistercian Fathers series 18 (Kalamazoo, Mich.: Cistercian Publications, 1979).

——tr. Kilian Walsh, *On the Song of Songs*, 2 vols., *The Works of Bernard of Clairvaux*, vols. ii–iii, Cistercian Fathers series 4 and 7 (Kalamazoo, Mich.: Cistercian Publications, 1976).

BERNARD of Fontcaude, *Contra Vallenses et contra Arrianos*, PL 204. 793–840.

Bible, Vulgate: *Biblia Sacra iuxta Vulgatam Clementinam*, ed. Alberto Colunga, OP, and Laurentio Turrado, 8th edn. (Madrid: Biblioteca de Autores Cristianos, 1985).

——*The Holy Bible Translated from the Latin Vulgate* (Douai, 1609, and Rheims, 1582; rev. edn. Belfast: Robert & Daniel Read, 1852).

Biblia breves in eadem annotationes . . . (Paris: Robertus Stephanus, 1532).

Le Bien des fames, see Fiero, Gloria K., *et al.*

BLAMIRES, ALCUIN, with PRATT, KAREN, and MARX, C. W. (eds.), *Woman Defamed and Woman Defended: An Anthology of Medieval Texts* (Oxford: Clarendon Press, 1992).

BOCCACCIO, GIOVANNI, *Decameron*, ed. Cesare Segre (Milan: Mursia, 1966).

——*The Decameron*, tr. G. H. McWilliam (Harmondsworth: Penguin, 1972).

——*De mulieribus claris*, ed. Vittorio Zaccaria, in *Tutte le opere*, vol. x (Verona: Mondadori, 1970).

——*Concerning Famous Women*, tr. Guido A. Guarino (New Brunswick, NJ: Rutgers University Press, 1963).

——*The Elegy of Lady Fiammetta*, tr. Mariangela Causa-Steindler and Thomas Mauch (Chicago: University of Chicago Press, 1990).

BONAVENTURE, St, *Opera omnia*, 10 vols. (Quaracchi: Collegium S. Bonaventurae, 1882–1902).

The Book of the Knight of the Tower, see Caxton, William.

BOZON, NICOLE, *De la bonté des femmes*, ed. Lucy Toulmin Smith and Paul Meyer, in *Les Contes moralisés de Nicole Bozon*, SATF (Paris: Firmin Didot, 1889), pp. xxxii–xli.

CAPES, W. W. (ed.), *Registrum Johannis Trefnant* (London: Canterbury and York Society, 1916).

CASTIGLIONE, BALDASSARE, *The Book of the Courtier*, tr. Sir Thomas Hoby (London: Dent, 1974).

CAXTON, WILLIAM (tr.), *The Book of the Knight of the Tower*, ed. M. Y. Offord, EETS ss 2 (London: Oxford University Press, 1971).

CAZELLES, BRIGITTE (ed.), *The Lady as Saint: A Collection of French Hagiographic Romances of the Thirteenth Century* (Philadelphia: University of Pennsylvania Press, 1991).

CHARLES, R. H. (ed.), *The Apocrypha and Pseudepigraphia of the Old Testament in English*, 2 vols., i: *Apocrypha* (Oxford: Clarendon Press, 1913).

CHARTIER, ALAIN, *Excusacioun aux dames*, ed. J. C. Laidlaw in *The Poetical Works of Alain Chartier* (Cambridge: Cambridge University Press, 1974).

CHAUCER, GEOFFREY, *The Riverside Chaucer*, ed. Larry D. Benson (Boston, Mass.: Houghton Mifflin, 1987).

Le Chevalier des dames du dolant fortuné: Allégorie en vers de la fin du xve siècle, ed. J. Miquet (Ottawa: University of Ottawa Press, 1990).

CHRÉTIEN DE TROYES, *Cligés*, ed. Claude Luttrell and Stewart Gregory (Cambridge: D. S. Brewer, 1993).

——*The Knight with the Lion, or Yvain*, ed. and tr. William W. Kibler (New York: Garland, 1985).

——*Arthurian Romances*, tr. D. D. R. Owen (London: Dent, 1987).

CHRISTINA of Markyate, *The Life of Christina of Markyate: A Twelfth-Century Recluse*, tr. Charles H. Talbot (Oxford: Clarendon Press, 1987).

CHRISTINE DE PIZAN, *Œuvres poétiques*, ed. Maurice Roy, 3 vols. (Paris: Firmin Didot, 1886–96).

——*L'Avision Christine*, ed. Sr. Mary Louise Towner (Washington: Catholic University of America Press, 1932).

CHRISTINE DE PIZAN, *Le Livre de la cité des dames*: Maureen Curnow (ed.), 'The *Livre de la cité des dames* of Christine de Pisan: A Critical Edition', Ph.D. dissertation, Vanderbilt University (1975): Xerox University Microfilms (Ann Arbor).
—— *The Book of the City of Ladies*, tr. Earl Jeffrey Richards (New York: Persea Books, 1982).
—— *Epistre au dieu d'amours*, ed. and tr. Thelma S. Fenster and Mary Carpenter Erler, in *Poems of Cupid, God of Love* (Leiden: E. J. Brill, 1990).
—— *Le Livre des trois vertus*, ed. Charity Cannon Willard and Eric Hicks (Paris: Champion, 1989).
—— *The Treasure of the City of Ladies, or The Book of the Three Virtues*, tr. Sarah Lawson (Harmondsworth: Penguin, 1985).
CHRYSOSTOM, see John Chrysostom, St.
CICERO, MARCUS TULLIUS (attrib.), *Rhetorica ad Herennium*, tr. Harry Caplan (London: Heinemann, 1954).
CLARK, ELIZABETH (ed.), *Women in the Early Church* (Wilmington, Del.: Michael Glazier, 1983).
CONLEE, J. W. (ed.), *Middle English Debate Poetry: A Critical Anthology* (East Lansing, Mich.: Colleagues Press, 1991).
Cursor Mundi: Four Versions, ed. Richard Morris, pt. iii, EETS os 62 (London: Oxford University Press, 1876).
DESCHAMPS, EUSTACHE, *Le Miroir de mariage*, in *Œuvres complètes*, vol. ix, ed. Gaston Raynaud, SATF (Paris: Firmin-Didot, 1894).
DICKINS, BRUCE, and WILSON, R. M. (eds.), *Early Middle English Texts* (London: Bowes & Bowes, 1951).
Dives and Pauper, ed. Priscilla H. Barnum, vol. i, pt. ii, EETS os 280 (Oxford: Oxford University Press, 1980).
Du bounté des femmes, ed. Paul Meyer in 'Les Manuscrits français de Cambridge, ii: Bibliothèque de l'Université', *Romania*, 15 (1886), 236–357 (pp. 315–20).
The Early South-English Legendary or Lives of Saints, ed. Carl Horstmann, EETS os 87 (London: Oxford University Press, 1887).
Esdras, Book of, see Charles, R. H.
ÉTIENNE DE FOUGÈRES, *Le Livre des manières*, ed. R. Anthony Lodge (Geneva: Droz, 1979).
EUSEBIUS, *The Ecclesiastical History*, tr. Hugh J. Lawlor and John E. Oulton, 2 vols. (New York: SPCK, 1927).
Fasciculus morum: A Fourteenth-Century Preacher's Handbook, ed. and tr. Siegfried Wenzel (University Park: Pennsylvania State University Press, 1989).
FELLOWS, JENNIFER (ed.), *Of Love and Chivalry: An Anthology of Middle English Romance* (London: Dent, 1993).
FENSTER, THELMA S., and ERLER, MARY CARPENTER (eds.), *Poems of Cupid, God of Love* (Leiden: E. J. Brill, 1990).
FIERO, GLORIA K., PFEFFER, WENDY, and ALLAIN, MATHÉ (eds. and trs.), *Three Medieval Views of Women* (New Haven: Yale University Press, 1989).
FRANCESCO DA BARBERINO, *Reggimento e costumi di donna*, ed. Giuseppe E. Sansone (Turin: Loescher-Chiantore, 1957).

GOTTFRIED VON STRASSBURG, *Tristan*, ed. Karl Morold and Werner Schröder (Berlin: de Gruyter, 1969).

——*Tristan*, tr. A. T. Hatto (Harmondsworth: Penguin, 1960).

GOWER, JOHN, *The English Works of John Gower*, ed. G. C. Macaulay, 2 vols., EETS ES 81–2 (London: Oxford University Press, 1900–1).

——*Mirour de l'omme*, tr. William Burton Wilson (East Lansing, Mich.: Colleagues Press, 1992).

GREGORY the Great, *Liber regulae pastoralis*, in *Leo the Great, Gregory the Great, Pt. 1*, tr. James Barmby, Select Library of Nicene and Post-Nicene Fathers, 2nd ser. 12 (Oxford: James Parker, 1895).

——*Moralia in Job*, PL 75–8.

GREGORY of Nyssa, *Grégoire de Nysse: Traité de la virginité*, ed. Michel Aubineau (Paris: Éditions du Cerf, 1966).

——*On Virginity*, in *Ascetical Works*, tr. Virginia Callahan (Washington: Catholic University of America Press, 1967).

GRIGSBY, J. L. (ed.), *'Miroir des bonnes femmes'*, pt. i, *Romania*, 82 (1961), 458–81; pt. ii, 83 (1962), 30–51.

GUILLAUME DE LORRIS, and JEAN DE MEUN, *Le Roman de la Rose*, ed. Daniel Poirion (Paris: Garnier-Flammarion, 1974).

——*The Romance of the Rose*, tr. Frances Horgan (Oxford: Oxford University Press, 1994).

Hali Meiðhad, ed. Bella Millett, EETS OS 284 (Oxford: Oxford University Press, 1982).

HELOISE, 'The Personal Letters between Abelard and Heloise', ed. J. T. Muckle, *Mediaeval Studies*, 15 (1953), 47–94.

——'The Letter of Heloise on Religious Life and Abelard's First Reply', ed. J. T. Muckle, *Mediaeval Studies*, 17 (1955), 240–81 (pp. 241–53).

——*The Letters of Abelard and Heloise*, tr. Betty Radice (Harmondsworth: Penguin, 1974).

HENRY of Ghent, *Magistri Henrici Goethals a Gandavo ... Summa in tres partes*, 3 vols. (Ferrara: F. Succius, 1642–6).

HICKS, ERIC (ed.), *Le Débat sur le 'Roman de la Rose'* (Paris: Champion, 1977).

HILDEGARD of Bingen, *Opera omnia*, PL 197.

——*Scivias*, tr. Mother Columba Hart and Jane Bishop (New York: Paulist Press, 1990).

HOCCLEVE, THOMAS, *Letter of Cupid*, see Fenster, Thelma, and Erler, Mary.

——*Hoccleve's Works: The Minor Poems*, ed. F. J. Furnivall and I. Gollancz, EETS ES 61 and 73 (London: Oxford University Press, 1925 and 1937; repr. as 1 vol. 1970).

——*The Regement of Princes*, ed. F. J. Furnivall, EETS ES 72 (London: Oxford University Press, 1897).

HONORIUS AUGUSTODUNENSIS, *De Maria Magdalena*, PL 172. 979–82.

HROTSVITHA of Gandersheim, *Hrotsvithae opera*, ed. Helene Homeyer (Munich: Schöningh, 1970); also PL 137. 941–1168.

——*The Plays of Roswitha*, tr. Christopher St John (London: Chatto & Windus, 1923).

——*The Plays of Hrotsvit of Gandersheim*, tr. Katharina M. Wilson (New York: Garland, 1989).

HUGH of St Cher, *Postillae domini Hugonis cardinalis*, 6 parts (Basle, 1503–4).

HUMBERT of Romans, *Treatise on Preaching*, tr. the Dominican Students, Province of St Joseph (London: Blackfriars, 1955).

ISIDORE of Seville, *Etymologiarum sive originum libri xx*, ed. W. M. Lindsay, 2 vols. (Oxford: Oxford University Press, 1911).

JACOBUS DE VORAGINE, *Legenda aurea*, ed. Theodor Graesse, 2nd edn. (Leipzig, 1850; repr. Osnabrück: Zeller, 1969).

——*The Golden Legend: Readings on the Saints*, tr. William Granger Ryan, 2 vols. (Princeton: Princeton University Press, 1993).

JAMES, MONTAGUE RHODES (ed.), *The Apocryphal New Testament* (Oxford: Clarendon Press, 1924).

JEHAN LE FÈVRE, *Les Lamentations de Matheolus et le Livre de Leesce de Jehan le Fèvre, de Ressons*, ed. A.-G. Van Hamel, 2 vols. (Paris: Émile Bouillon, 1892, 1905).

JEROME, St, *Adversus Iovinianum*, PL 23. 221–352.

——*Selected Letters of St Jerome*, ed. and tr. F. A. Wright (Cambridge, Mass.: Harvard University Press, 1963).

——*The Principal Works of St Jerome*, tr. W. H. Fremantle, Select Library of Nicene and Post-Nicene Fathers, 2nd ser. 6 (Oxford: James Parker, 1893).

JOHN CHRYSOSTOM, St, *Homiliae in Johannem*, PG 59. 1–482.

——*Homilies on St John*, tr. in Select Library of Nicene and Post-Nicene Fathers, ed. Philip Schaff, vol. 14 (Grand Rapids, Mich.: Eerdmans, 1969).

——*Homiliae in Genesim*, PG 53.

——*On Virginity, against Remarriage*, tr. Sally Rieger Shore (Lewiston, NY: Edwin Mellen Press, 1983).

JOHN of Salisbury, *Policraticus* (selections); *The Frivolities of Courtiers and Footprints of Philosophers*, tr. J. B. Pike (London: Oxford University Press, 1938).

JOSEPHUS, FLAVIUS, *Jewish Antiquities*, in *Josephus*, ed. and tr. H. St J. Thackeray and Ralph Marcus, vol. vi (London: Heinemann 1937).

JULIAN of Norwich, *A Revelation of Love*, ed. Marion Glasscoe (Exeter: Exeter University Press, 1976).

LANGLAND, WILLIAM, *The Vision of Piers Plowman*, ed. A. V. C. Schmidt (London: Dent, 1978).

LARRINGTON, CAROLYNE (ed.), *Women and Writing in Medieval Europe: A Sourcebook* (London: Routledge, 1995).

Legenda aurea, see Jacobus de Voragine.

LYDGATE, JOHN, *The Fall of Princes*, ed. Henry Bergen, EETS ES 121–4 (London: Oxford University Press, 1924–7).

MCNAMARA, JO ANN, and HALBORG, JOHN E., with WHATLEY, E. GORDON (eds.), *Sainted Women of the Dark Ages* (Durham, NC: Duke University Press, 1992).

MAIDSTONE, RICHARD, *Concordia: Facta inter Regem Riccardum II et civitatem Londinie*, ed. Charles Roger Smith (Ann Arbor: University Microfilms, 1972).

MARBOD of Rennes, 'De matrona', in *Liber decem capitulorum*, ed. Rosario Leotta (Rome: Herder, 1984).
MARIE DE FRANCE, *Lais*, ed. Jean Rychner (Paris: Champion, 1983).
——*The Lais of Marie de France*, tr. Glyn S. Burgess and Keith Busby (Harmondsworth: Penguin, 1986).
MARTIN LE FRANC, *Le Champion des dames*, ed. Arthur Piaget (Lausanne: Payot, 1968).
Mary Magdalene, Life of, see Mycoff, David; and *Vita beatae Mariae Magdalenae*.
Meditations on the Life of Christ, tr. Isa Ragusa and ed. Rosalie B. Green (Princeton: Princeton University Press, 1961).
MILLETT, BELLA, and WOGAN-BROWNE, JOCELYN (eds. and trs.), *Medieval English Prose for Women from the Katherine Group and 'Ancrene Wisse'* (Oxford: Clarendon Press, 1992).
MILLS, MALDWYN, *Six Middle English Romances* (London: Dent, 1973).
Miroir des bonnes femmes, see Grigsby, J. L.
MURPHY, JAMES J. (ed.), *Three Medieval Rhetorical Arts* (Berkeley and Los Angeles: University of California Press, 1971).
MYCOFF, DAVID (tr.), *The Life of Saint Mary Magdalene and of her Sister Saint Martha: A Medieval Biography*, Cistercian Studies series 108 (Kalamazoo, Mich.: Cistercian Publications, 1989).
NETTER, THOMAS, *Doctrinale antiquitatum fidei catholicae ecclesiae*, 2 vols. (Venice, 1757–9).
ODO of Cluny, *In veneratione Sanctae Mariae Magdalenae*, PL 133. 713–21.
OSBERT of Clare, *The Letters of Osbert of Clare*, ed. E. W. Williamson (London: Oxford University Press, 1929).
OVID, *The Art of Love and Other Poems*, ed. and tr. J. H. Mozley (Cambridge, Mass.: Harvard University Press, 1957); 2nd edn. rev. G. P. Goold (1979).
——*Heroides and Amores*, ed. and tr. Grant Showerman, 2nd edn. rev. G. P. Goold (Cambridge, Mass.: Harvard University Press, 1977).
——*Metamorphoses*, tr. Mary M. Innes (Harmondsworth: Penguin, 1955).
The Paston Letters and Papers of the Fifteenth Century, ed. Norman Davis, 2 vols. (Oxford: Clarendon Press, 1971, 1976).
Pearl, ed. Malcolm Andrew and Ronald Waldron, in *The Poems of the Pearl Manuscript* (London: Edward Arnold, 1978).
PETER LOMBARD, *Magistri Petri Lombardi Sententiae in IV libris distinctae*, 3rd edn. (Rome: Editiones Collegii S. Bonaventurae ad Claras Aquas, 1971).
PETER the Venerable, *The Letters of Peter the Venerable*, ed. G. Constable, 2 vols. (Cambridge, Mass.: Harvard Unversity Press, 1967).
PFEFFER, WENDY, 'La Louange des femmes: "Oez seignor, je n'otroi pas" (Berne, Bibliothèque de la Bourgeoisie no. 354)', *Neuphilologische Mitteilungen*, 93 (1992), 221–34.
PHILO, *Philo*, tr. Ralph Marcus (London: Heinemann, 1953).
PICKERING, O. S., 'The "Defence of Women" from the *Southern Passion*: A New Edition', in Klaus P. Jankovsky (ed.), *The South English Legendary: A New Assessment* (Tübingen: Stauffenburg, 1992), 154–76.
POWER, EILEEN (tr.), *The Goodman of Paris* (London, 1928).

Quintilian, *Institutio oratoria*, tr. H. E. Butler, 4 vols. (London: Heinemann, 1960).

Renart, Jean, *Le Roman de la Rose ou de Guillaume de Dole*, ed. Félix Lecoy, Classiques Français du Moyen Âge (Paris: Champion, 1979).

——*The Romance of the Rose or Guillaume de Dole*, tr. Patricia Terry and Nancy Vine Durling (Philadelphia: University of Pennsylvania Press, 1993).

Richard de Fournival, *Master Richard's Bestiary of Love and Response*, tr. Jeanette Beer (Berkeley and Los Angeles: University of California Press, 1986).

Robert de Blois, *Robert von Blois, Sämtliche Werke*, ed. Jacob Ulrich, 3 vols. (Berlin: Mayer & Muller, 1889–90; repr. Geneva: Slatkine, 1978).

Rumble, Thomas (ed.), *The Breton Lays in Middle English* (Detroit: Wayne State University Press, 1965).

Serlo of Bayeux, 'Ad Muriel sanctimonialem', ed. Thomas Wright, in *The Anglo-Latin Satirical Poets and Epigrammatists of the Twelfth Century*, vol. ii, Rolls Ser. (London: Longman, 1872).

Sir Gawain and the Green Knight, ed. Malcolm Andrew and Ronald Waldron, in *The Poems of the Pearl Manuscript* (London: Edward Arnold, 1978).

Smith, Harold (tr.), *Ante-Nicene Exegesis of the Gospels*, 6 vols. (London: SPCK, 1926).

The South English Legendary, ed. Charlotte d'Evelyn and Anna J. Mill, 2 vols., EETS os 235–6 (Oxford: Oxford University Press, 1956).

The Southern Passion, ed. Beatrice Brown, EETS os 169 (London: Oxford University Press, 1929); see also Pickering, O. S.

Trevisa, John, *On the Properties of Things: John Trevisa's Translation of 'Bartholomaeus Anglicus De proprietatibus rerum'*, ed. M. C. Seymour, 2 vols. (Oxford: Clarendon Press, 1975).

Tugwell, Simon, OP (ed.), *Early Dominicans: Selected Writings* (Ramsey, NJ: Paulist Press, 1982).

Vita beatae Mariae Magdalenae, PL 112. 1431–508.

Wyclif, John, *Sermones*, ed. Johann Loserth, 4 vols. (London: Wyclif Society, 1888).

——*Opus evangelicum*, ed. Johann Loserth, 2 vols. (London: Wyclif Society, 1896).

Zimmermann, Rudolf (ed.), 'Li Houneurs et li vertus des dames par Jehan Petit d'Arras', *Archiv für das Studium der Neueren Sprachen und Literaturen*, 108 (1902), 380–8.

SECONDARY SOURCES

Abels, R., and Harrison, E., 'The Participation of Women in Languedocian Catharism', *Mediaeval Studies*, 41 (1979), 215–51.

Aers, David, *Chaucer* (Brighton: Harvester, 1986).

——*Community, Gender, and Individual Identity: English Writing 1360–1430* (London: Routledge, 1988).

ALLEN, PETER, 'Reading Chaucer's Good Women', *Chaucer Review*, 21 (1987), 419–34.

ALLEN, Sr. PRUDENCE, RSM, *The Concept of Woman: The Aristotelian Revolution 750 BC–AD 1250* (Montreal: Eden Press, 1985).

AMES, RUTH M., 'The Feminist Connections in Chaucer's *Legend of Good Women*', in Julian Wasserman and R. J. Blanch (eds.), *Chaucer in the Eighties* (Syracuse, NY: Syracuse University Press, 1986), 57–74.

ANGENOT, MARC, *Les Champions des femmes: Examen du discours sur la supériorité des femmes, 1400–1800* (Montreal: Les Presses de l'Université de Québec, 1977).

ANSON, JOHN, 'The Female Transvestite in Early Monasticism: The Origin and Development of a Motif', *Viator*, 5 (1974), 1–32.

ARJAVA, ANTTI, 'Jerome and Women', *Arctos: Acta philologica Fennica*, 23 (1989), 5–18.

ARMSTRONG, GRACE, 'Women of Power: Chrétien de Troyes's Female Clerks', *Stanford French and Italian Studies*, 58 (1988), 29–46.

ASTON, MARGARET, 'Lollard Women Priests?', in her *Lollards and Reformers* (London: Hambledon Press, 1984), 49–70.

ATKINSON, CLARISSA, '"Precious Balsam in a Fragile Glass": The Ideology of Virginity in the Later Middle Ages', *Journal of Family History*, 8 (1983), 131–43.

——*The Oldest Vocation: Christian Motherhood in the Middle Ages* (Ithaca, NY: Cornell University Press, 1991).

BAILEY, DERRICK S., *Sexual Relation in Christian Thought* (New York: Harper & Row, 1959).

BAIRD, JOSEPH L., and KANE, JOHN R., '*La Querelle de la Rose*: In Defense of the Opponents', *French Review*, 48 (1974–5), 298–307.

BAKER, DEREK (ed.), *Medieval Women*, Studies in Church History Subsidia 1 (Oxford: Blackwell, 1978).

BAL, MIEKE, *Lethal Love: Feminist Literary Readings of Biblical Love Stories* (Bloomington: Indiana University Press, 1987).

BARBEY, LÉON, *Martin Le Franc* (Fribourg: Éditions Universitaires, 1985).

BAUMGARTNER, EMMANUÈLE, 'De Lucrèce à Héloïse: Remarques sur deux exemples du *Roman de la Rose* de Jean de Meun', *Romania*, 95 (1974), 433–42.

BEER, FRANCES, *Women and Mystical Experience in the Middle Ages* (Woodbridge: Boydell & Brewer, 1992).

BEER, JEANETTE, 'Richard de Fournival's Anonymous Lady: The Character of the Response to the *Bestiaire d'amour*', *Romance Philology*, 42 (1988), 267–73.

BELL, SUSAN GROAG, 'Christine de Pizan (1364–1430): Humanism and the Problem of the Studious Woman', *Feminist Studies*, 3 (1976), 173–84.

BENNETT, JUDITH M., 'Medievalism and Feminism', *Speculum*, 68 (1993), 309–31.

BENSON, C. DAVID, and ROBERTSON, ELIZABETH (eds.), *Chaucer's Religious Tales* (Cambridge: D. S. Brewer, 1990).

BENSON, PAMELA JOSEPH, *The Invention of the Renaissance Woman: The Challenge of Female Independence in the Literature and Thought of Italy and England* (Philadelphia: Pennsylvania State University Press, 1992).

BESSERMAN, LAWRENCE, 'Glosynge is a glorious thyng: Chaucer's Biblical Exegesis', in David Lyle Jeffrey (ed.), Chaucer and Scriptural Tradition (Ottawa: University of Ottawa Press, 1984), 65–73.

BIENVENU, JEAN-MARC, L'Étonnant Fondateur de Fontevraud Robert d'Arbrissel (Paris: Nouvelles Éditions Latines, 1981).

BILLER, P., and MINNIS, A. J. (eds.), Medieval Theology and the Natural Body (York: York Medieval Texts, 1997).

BLAMIRES, ALCUIN, 'Chaucer's Revaluation of Chivalric Honor', Mediaevalia, 5 (1979), 245–69.

——'A Chaucer Manifesto', Chaucer Review, 34 (1989), 29–44.

——'The Wife of Bath and Lollardy', Medium Aevum, 58 (1989), 224–42.

——'Questions of Gender in Chaucer, from Anelida to Troilus', Leeds Studies in English, NS 25 (1994), 83–110.

——'Women and Preaching in Medieval Orthodoxy, Heresy, and Saints' Lives', Viator, 26 (1995), 135–52.

——'Paradox in the Medieval Gender Doctrine of Head and Body', forthcoming in P. Biller and A. J. Minnis (eds.), Medieval Theology and the Natural Body (York: York Medieval Texts, 1997).

——and MARX, C. W., 'Woman Not to Preach: A Disputation in British Library MS Harley 31', Journal of Medieval Latin, 3 (1993), 34–63.

BLOCH, R. HOWARD, 'Medieval Misogyny', Representations, 20 (1987), 1–14.

——Medieval Misogyny and the Invention of Western Romantic Love (Chicago: University of Chicago Press, 1991).

BLUMENFELD-KOSINSKI, RENATE, 'Christine de Pizan and the Misogynistic Tradition', Romanic Review, 81 (1990), 279–92.

——'Jean le Fèvre's Livre de Leësce: Praise or Blame of Women?', Speculum, 69 (1994), 705–25.

——and SZELL, TIMEA (eds.), Images of Sainthood in Medieval Europe (Ithaca, NY: Cornell University Press, 1991).

BLUMSTEIN, ANDRÉE K., Misogyny and Idealization in the Courtly Romance (Bonn: Bouvier, 1977).

BOLTON, BRENDA M., 'Mulieres sanctae', in Susan Mosher Stuard (ed.), Women in Medieval Society (Philadelphia: University of Pennsylvania Press, 1976), 141–58.

——'Vitae matrum: A Further Aspect of the Frauenfrage', in Derek Baker (ed.), Medieval Women (Oxford: Blackwell, 1978), 253–73.

BORNSTEIN, DIANE (ed.), Ideals for Women in the Works of Christine de Pizan (Detroit: Michigan Consortium for Medieval and Early Modern Studies, 1981).

——The Lady in the Tower: Medieval Courtesy Literature for Women (Hamden, Conn.: Archon Books, 1983).

——'Anti-Feminism in Thomas Hoccleve's Translation of Christine de Pizan's Epistre au dieu d'amours', English Language Notes, 19 (1981), 7–14.

BOSSY, MICHEL ANDRÉ, 'Woman's Plain Talk in Le Débat de l'omme et de la femme by Guillaume Alexis', Fifteenth Century Studies, 16 (1990), 23–41.

BOURASSA, FRANÇOIS, 'Excellence de la virginité: Arguments patristiques', Science ecclésiastique, 5 (1953), 29–41.

Brasington, Bruce C., 'Non imitanda set veneranda: The Dilemma of Sacred Precedent in Twelfth-Century Canon Law', Viator, 23 (1992), 135–52.

Brett, Edward Tracy, Humbert of Romans: His Life and Views of Thirteenth-Century Society (Toronto: Pontifical Institute of Medieval Studies, 1984).

Brewer, Derek, 'Some Metonymic Relationships in Chaucer's Poetry', in his Chaucer: The Poet as Storyteller (London: Macmillan, 1984), 37–53.

Brown, Emerson, Jr., 'Biblical Women in the Merchant's Tale: Feminism, Antifeminism, and Beyond', Viator, 5 (1974), 389–98.

Brown, Peter, The Body and Society: Men, Women and Sexual Renunciation in Early Christianity (London: Faber, 1989).

Brown-Grant, Rosalind, 'Décadence ou progrès? Christine de Pizan, Boccace et la question de l' "âge d'or"', Revue des langues romanes, 92 (1988), 295–306.

——'Des hommes et des femmes illustres: Modalités narratives et transformations génériques chez Pétrarque, Boccace et Christine de Pizan', in Liliane Dulac and Bernard Ribémont (eds.), Une femme de lettres au Moyen Âge (Orléans: Paradigme, 1995), 469–80.

Brownlee, Kevin, 'Discourses of the Self: Christine de Pizan and the Rose', Romanic Review, 78 (1988), 199–221.

——'Martyrdom and the Female Voice: Saint Christine in the Cité des dames', in Renate Blumenfeld-Kosinski and Timea Szell (eds.), Images of Sainthood in Medieval Europe (Ithaca, NY: Cornell University Press, 1991), 115–35.

Bullough, Vern L., Shelton, Brenda, and Slavin, Sarah, The Subordinated Sex: A History of Attitudes toward Women, rev. edn. (Athens, Ga.: University of Georgia Press, 1988).

Burchmore, Susan, 'Traditional Exegesis and the Question of Guilt in the Old English Genesis "B"', Traditio, 41 (1985), 117–44.

Burnley, J. D., 'Criseyde's Heart and the Weakness of Women: An Essay in Lexical Interpretation', Studia neophilologica, 54 (1982), 1–14.

Burns, E. Jane, Bodytalk: When Women Speak in Old French Literature (Philadelphia: University of Pennsylvania Press, 1993).

Butler, Judith, Gender Trouble: Feminism and the Subversion of Identity (London: Routledge, 1990).

Bynum, Caroline Walker, 'Jesus as Mother and Abbot as Mother: Some Themes in Twelfth-Century Cistercian Writing', in her Jesus as Mother: Studies in the Spirituality of the High Middle Ages (Berkeley and Los Angeles: University of California Press, 1982), 110–69.

——'". . . And Woman his Humanity": Female Imagery in the Religious Writing of the Later Middle Ages', in Caroline Walker Bynum, Stevan Harrell, and Paula Richman (eds.), Gender and Religion: On the Complexity of Symbols (Boston: Beacon Press, 1986), 257–88.

——Holy Feast and Holy Fast: The Religious Significance of Food to Medieval Women (Berkeley and Los Angeles: University of California Press, 1987).

Cadden, Joan, Meanings of Sex Difference in the Middle Ages: Medicine, Science, and Culture (Cambridge: Cambridge University Press, 1993).

CARRUTHERS, MARY, 'The Lady, the Swineherd, and Chaucer's Clerk', *Chaucer Review*, 17 (1983), 221–34.

CASTELLI, E., 'Virginity and its Meaning for Women's Sexuality in Early Christianity', *Journal of Feminist Studies in Religion*, 2 (1982), 61–88.

CHANCE, JANE, *Woman as Hero in Old English Literature* (Syracuse, NY: Syracuse University Press, 1986).

CIXOUS, HÉLÈNE, 'The Laugh of the Medusa', in Elaine Marks and Isabelle de Courtivron (eds.), *New French Feminisms* (Hemel Hempstead: Harvester, 1981), 245–64.

CLARK, ELIZABETH A., *Jerome, Chrysostom and Friends* (Lewiston, NY: Edwin Mellen Press, 1979).

——'Ideology, History, and the Construction of "Woman" in Late Ancient Christianity', *Journal of Early Christian Studies*, 2 (1994), 155–84.

CLAYTON, MARY, *The Cult of the Virgin Mary in Anglo-Saxon England* (Cambridge: Cambridge University Press, 1990).

COOPER, HELEN, *Oxford Guides to Chaucer: The Canterbury Tales* (Oxford: Clarendon Press, 1989).

COWEN, JANET, 'Chaucer's *Legend of Good Women*: Structure and Tone', *Studies in Philology*, 82 (1985), 416–36.

——'Women as Exempla in Fifteenth-Century Verse of the Chaucerian Tradition', in Julia Boffey and Janet Cowen (eds.), *Chaucer and Fifteenth-Century Poetry* (London: King's College, Centre for Late Antique and Medieval Studies, 1991), 51–65.

COYLE, J. KEVIN, 'The Fathers on Women and Women's Ordination', *Église et théologie*, 9 (1978), 51–101.

CRANE, SUSAN, *Gender and Romance in Chaucer's 'Canterbury Tales'* (Princeton: Princeton University Press, 1994).

CURNOW, MAUREEN CHENEY, ' "La Pioche d'inquisicion": Legal-Judicial Content and Style in Christine de Pizan's *Livre de la cité des dames*', in Earl Jeffrey Richards *et al.* (eds.), *Reinterpreting Christine de Pizan* (Athens, Ga.: University of Georgia Press, 1992), 157–72.

DAILEADER, CELIA R., 'The *Thopas-Melibee* Sequence and the Defeat of Antifeminism', *Chaucer Review*, 29 (1994), 26–39.

DALARUN, JACQUES, *L'Impossible Sainteté: La Vie retrouvée de Robert d'Arbrissel (v. 1045–1116)* (Paris: Éditions du Cerf, 1985).

DANIÉLOU, JEAN, *The Ministry of Women in the Early Church*, tr. G. Simon (London: Faith Press, 1961).

DAVIES, STEVAN L., *The Revolt of the Widows: The Social World of the Apocryphal Acts* (Carbondale: Southern Illinois State Press, 1980).

DAVIS, NATALIE, 'Women on Top', in her *Society and Culture in Early Modern France* (Stanford, Calif.: Stanford University Press, 1975).

DE LABRIOLLE, P., ' "Mulieres in ecclesia taceant": Un aspect de la lutte anti-Montaniste', *Bulletin d'ancienne littérature et d'archéologie chrétiennes*, 1 (1911), 3–24, 103–22, 291–8.

DELANY, SHEILA, *Medieval Literary Politics: Shapes of Ideology* (Manchester: Manchester University Press, 1990).

——*The Naked Text: Chaucer's 'Legend of Good Women'* (Berkeley and Los Angeles: University of California Press, 1994).

DE LOOZE, LAURENCE, 'The Gender of Fiction: Womanly Poetics in Jean Renart's *Guillaume de Dole*', *French Review*, 64 (1991), 797–819.

DESMOND, MARILYNN, *Reading Dido: Gender, Textuality, and the Medieval 'Aeneid'* (Minneapolis: University of Minnesota Press, 1994).

DIAMOND, ARLYN, 'Chaucer's Women and Women's Chaucer', in Arlyn Diamond and Lee R. Edwards (eds.), *The Authority of Experience: Essays in Feminist Criticism* (Amherst: University of Massachusetts Press, 1977), 60–83.

—— 'Troilus and Criseyde: The Politics of Love', in Julian Wasserman and Robert J. Blanch (eds.), *Chaucer in the Eighties* (Syracuse, NY: Syracuse University Press, 1986), 93–103.

DICKSON, LYNNE, 'Deflection in the Mirror: Feminine Discourse in *The Wife of Bath's Prologue* and *Tale*', *Studies in the Age of Chaucer*, 15 (1993), 61–90.

DINSHAW, CAROLYN, *Chaucer's Sexual Poetics* (Madison: University of Wisconsin Press, 1989).

DONALDSON, IAN, *The Rapes of Lucretia: A Myth and its Transformations* (Oxford: Clarendon Press, 1982).

DOW, BLANCHE, *The Varying Attitude toward Women in French Literature of the Fifteenth Century: The Opening Years* (New York: Institute of French Studies, 1936).

DRONKE, PETER, *Poetic Individuality in the Middle Ages* (Oxford: Clarendon Press, 1970).

—— 'Peter Abelard: *Planctus* and Satire', in his *Poetic Individuality in the Middle Ages* (Oxford: Clarendon Press, 1970), 114–49.

—— *Abelard and Heloise in Medieval Testimonies* (Glasgow: University of Glasgow Press, 1976).

—— *Women Writers of the Middle Ages: A Critical Study of Texts from Perpetua to Marguerite Porete* (Cambridge: Cambridge University Press, 1984).

—— *Intellectuals and Poets in Medieval Europe*, Storia e Letteratura: Raccolta di Studi e Testi 183 (Rome: Edizioni di Storia e Letteratura, 1992).

—— 'Hermes and the Sibyls: Continuations and Creations', in his *Intellectuals and Poets in Medieval Europe* (Rome: Edizioni di Storia e Letteratura, 1992), 219–41.

DULAC, LILIANE, and RIBÉMONT, BERNARD (eds.), *Une femme de lettres au Moyen Âge: Études autour de Christine de Pizan* (Orléans: Paradigme, 1995).

EDWARDS, A. S. G., 'The Merchant's Tale and Moral Chaucer', *Modern Language Quarterly*, 51 (1990), 409–26.

EDWARDS, MARY CAROL, 'A Study of Six Characters in Chaucer's *Legend of Good Women* with Reference to Medieval Scholia in Ovid's *Heroides*', unpublished B.Litt. thesis (University of Oxford, 1970).

ELLIOTT, DYAN, *Spiritual Marriage: Sexual Abstinence in Medieval Wedlock* (Princeton: Princeton University Press, 1993).

ELLIS, ROGER, 'Chaucer, Christine de Pisan, and Hoccleve: The "Letter of Cupid"', in C. Batt (ed.), *Essays on Thomas Hoccleve*, Westfield Publications in Medieval Studies 10 (London: Centre for Medieval and Renaissance Studies, Queen Mary and Westfield College, 1996), 29–54.

ENGEL, MONIQUE, 'Le *Miroir de mariage* d'Eustache Deschamps', in Franco Simone *et al.* (eds.), *Seconda miscellanea di studi e ricerche sul quattrocento francese* (Chambéry: Centre d'Études Franco-Italien, 1981), 145–67.

ERLER, M., and KOWALESKI, M. (eds.), *Women and Power in the Middle Ages* (Athens, Ga.: University of Georgia Press, 1988).

EVANS, RUTH, and JOHNSON, LESLEY (eds.), *Feminist Readings in Middle English Literature: The Wife of Bath and All her Sect* (London: Routledge, 1994).

FAHY, CONOR, 'Three Early Renaissance Treatises on Women', *Italian Studies*, 11 (1956), 30–55.

FARMER, DAVID HUGH, *The Oxford Dictionary of Saints* (Oxford: Oxford University Press, 1978).

FARMER, SHARON, 'Persuasive Voices: Clerical Images of Medieval Wives', *Speculum*, 61 (1986), 517–43.

—— 'Softening the Hearts of Men: Women, Embodiment, and Persuasion in the Thirteenth Century', in Paula Cooley, Sharon Farmer, and Mary Ellen Ross (eds.), *Embodied Love: Sensuality and Relationship as Feminist Values* (New York: Harper & Row, 1987), 115–33.

FENSTER, THELMA, '*Simplece* et *sagesse*: Christine de Pizan et Isotta Nogarola sur la culpabilité d'Eve', in Liliane Dulac and Bernard Ribémont (eds.), *Une femme de lettres au Moyen Âge: Études autour de Christine de Pizan* (Orléans: Paradigme, 1995), 481–93.

FERRANTE, JOAN M., *Woman as Image in Medieval Literature from the Twelfth Century to Dante* (New York: Columbia University Press, 1975).

—— 'The Education of Women in the Middle Ages in Theory, Fact, and Fantasy', in Patricia H. Labalme (ed.), *Beyond Their Sex: Learned Women of the European Past* (New York: New York University Press, 1984), 9–42.

—— 'Male Fantasy and Female Reality in Courtly Literature', *Women's Studies*, 11 (1984), 67–97.

—— 'Public Postures and Private Maneuvers: The Roles Medieval Women Play', in Mary Erler and M. Kowaleski (eds.), *Women and Power in the Middle Ages* (Athens, Ga.: University of Georgia Press, 1988), 213–29.

—— 'Notes toward the Study of a Female Rhetoric in the Trobairitz', in William D. Paden (ed.), *The Voice of the Trobairitz* (Philadelphia: University of Pennsylvania Press, 1989), 63–72.

FIORENZA, ELIZABETH, *In Memory of Her: A Feminist Reconstruction of Christian Origins* (New York: Crossroad, 1983).

FRANK, ROBERT W., *Chaucer and the 'Legend of Good Women'* (Cambridge, Mass.: Harvard University Press, 1972).

FRANKFORTER, A. D., 'Hroswitha of Gandersheim and the Destiny of Women', *The Historian*, 41 (1979), 295–314.

—— 'Sexism and the Search for the Thematic Structure of the Plays of Hroswitha of Gandersheim', *International Journal of Women's Studies*, 2 (1979), 221–32.

FRAPPIER, JEAN, Étude sur 'Yvain' ou 'Le Chevalier au lion' de Chrétien de Troyes (Paris: Société d'Édition d'Enseignement Supérieur, 1969).

FUSS, DIANA, Essentially Speaking: Feminism, Nature, and Difference (London: Routledge, 1989).

FYLER, JOHN, Chaucer and Ovid (New Haven: Yale University Press, 1979).

——'St Augustine, Genesis, and the Origin of Language', in Edward B. King and Jacqueline T. Schaefer (eds.), Saint Augustine and his Influence in the Middle Ages (Sewanee, Tenn.: Press of the University of the South, 1988), 69–78.

——'Man, Men, and Women in Chaucer's Poetry', in Robert R. Edwards and Stephen Spector (eds.), The Olde Daunce: Love, Friendship, Sex, and Marriage in the Medieval World (Albany: State University of New York Press, 1991), 154–76.

GALLOWAY, ANDREW, 'Marriage Sermons, Polemical Sermons, and The Wife of Bath's Prologue: A Generic Excursus', Studies in the Age of Chaucer, 14 (1992), 3–30.

GARTH, HELEN, Saint Mary Magdalen in Mediaeval Literature (Baltimore: Johns Hopkins University Press, 1950).

GEORGIANNA, LINDA, 'Any Corner of Heaven: Heloise's Critique of Monasticism', Medieval Studies, 49 (1987), 221–53.

——'The Clerk's Tale and the Grammar of Assent', Speculum, 70 (1995), 793–821.

GHISALBERTI, F., 'Mediaeval Biographies of Ovid', Journal of the Warburg and Courtauld Institute, 9 (1946), 10–59.

GOLD, PENNY SCHINE, The Lady and the Virgin: Image, Attitude, and Experience in Twelfth-Century France (Chicago: University of Chicago Press, 1985).

GONNET, GIOVANNI, 'Le Cheminement des Vaudois vers le schisme et l'hérésie', Cahiers de civilisation médiévale, 19 (1976), 309–45.

GOTTLIEB, BEATRICE, 'The Problem of Feminism in the Fifteenth Century', in Julius Kirshner and Suzanne Wemple (eds.), Women of the Medieval World (Oxford: Blackwell, 1985), 337–64.

GRAEF, HILDA, Mary: A History of Doctrine and Devotion, 2 vols., i: From the Beginning to the Eve of the Reformation (New York: Sheed & Ward, 1963).

GRAVDAL, KATHRYN, Ravishing Maidens: Writing Rape in Medieval French Literature and Law (Philadelphia: University of Pennsylvania Press, 1991).

GUTHRIE, JERI S., 'La Femme dans Le Livre des manières: Surplus économique, surplus érotique', Romanic Review, 79 (1988), 251–61.

HAIGHT, ANNE L., Hrotswitha of Gandersheim: Her Life, Times and Works and a Comprehensive Bibliography (Charlottesville: University Press of Virginia, 1978; repr. 1988).

HANNA, RALPH, 'The Difficulty of Ricardian Prose Translation: The Case of the Lollards', Modern Language Quarterly, 51 (1990), 319–40.

HANSEN, ELAINE TUTTLE, Chaucer and the Fictions of Gender (Berkeley and Los Angeles: University of California Press, 1992).

HASKINS, SUSAN, Mary Magdalene: Myth and Metaphor (London: Harper Collins, 1993).

HEFFERNAN, THOMAS J., *Sacred Biography: Saints and their Biographies in the Middle Ages* (Oxford: Oxford University Press, 1989).

HENTSCH, ALICE A., *De la littérature didactique du Moyen Âge s'addressant spécialement aux femmes* (1903; repr. Geneva: Slatkine, 1975).

HIBBARD, LAURA A., *Mediaeval Romance in England* (Oxford: Oxford University Press, 1924).

HUBER, ELAINE C., *Women and the Authority of Inspiration: The Reexamination of Two Prophetic Movements from a Contemporary Feminist Perspective* (Lanham, Md.: University Press of America, 1985).

HUNT, TONY, *Chrétien de Troyes: 'Yvain' ('Le Chevalier au lion')* (London: Grant & Cutler, 1986).

HUOT, SYLVIA, 'Seduction and Sublimation: Christine de Pizan, Jean de Meun, and Dante', *Romance Notes*, 25 (1985), 361–73.

IRIGARAY, LUCE, *Speculum of the Other Woman*, tr. Gillian C. Gill (Ithaca, NY: Cornell University Press, 1985).

JEANROY, ALFRED, 'Boccace et Christine de Pisan, le *De claris mulieribus*, principale source du *Livre de la cité des dames*', *Romania*, 48 (1922), 92–105.

JENKINS, C., 'Origen on 1 Corinthians: Pt. iv', *Journal of Theological Studies*, 10 (1908–9), 29–51.

JOHNSON, PENELOPE D., *Equal in Monastic Profession: Religious Women in Medieval France* (Chicago: University of Chicago Press, 1991).

JORDAN, CONSTANCE, *Renaissance Feminism: Literary Texts and Political Models* (Ithaca, NY: Cornell University Press, 1990).

KAMUF, PEGGY, *Fictions of Feminine Desire: Disclosures of Heloise* (Lincoln, Nebr.: University of Nebraska Press, 1982).

KARRAS, RUTH MAZO, 'Holy Harlots: Prostitute Saints in Medieval Legend', *Journal of the History of Sexuality*, 1 (1990), 3–32.

KAY, SARAH, 'Women's Body of Knowledge: Epistemology and Misogyny in the *Romance of the Rose*', in Sarah Kay and Miri Rubin (eds.), *Framing Medieval Bodies* (Manchester: Manchester University Press, 1994), 211–35.

KELLY, DOUGLAS F., 'Reflections on the Role of Christine de Pizan as a Feminist Writer', *sub-stance*, 2 (1972), 63–71.

KELLY, JOAN, 'Early Feminist Theory and the *Querelle des femmes*, 1400–1789', *Signs*, 8 (1982), 4–28.

KELSO, RUTH, *Doctrine for the Lady of the Renaissance* (Urbana: University of Illinois Press, 1956).

KERBY-FULTON, KATHRYN, and ELLIOTT, DYAN, 'Self-Image and the Visionary Role in Two Letters from the Correspondence of Elizabeth of Schönau and Hildegard of Bingen', *Vox Benedictina*, 2/3 (1985), 204–23.

KIECKHEFER, RICHARD, *Unquiet Souls: Fourteenth-Century Saints and their Religious Milieu* (Chicago: University of Chicago Press, 1984).

KIRSHNER, JULIUS, and WEMPLE, SUZANNE (eds.), *Women of the Medieval World: Essays in Honor of John H. Mundy* (Oxford: Blackwell, 1985).

KISER, LISA, *Telling Classical Tales: Chaucer and the 'Legend of Good Women'* (Ithaca, NY: Cornell University Press, 1983).

KLEINBAUM, ABBY WETTAN, *The War against the Amazons* (New York: New Press, McGraw-Hill, 1983).

KLIMAN, BERNICE W., 'Women in Early English Literature, *Beowulf* to the *Ancrene Wisse'*, *Nottingham Medieval Studies*, 21 (1977), 32–49.

KOLVE, V. A., 'The Annunciation to Christine: Authorial Empowerment in *The Book of the City of Ladies'*, in Brendan Cassidy (ed.), *Iconography at the Crossroads*, Index of Christian Art, Occasional Papers, II (Princeton: Index of Christian Art, Department of Art and Archaeology, Princeton University, 1993), 171–96.

KRISTELLER, PAUL O., 'Learned Women of Early Modern Italy: Humanists and University Scholars', in Patricia H. Labalme (ed.), *Beyond their Sex: Learned Women of the European Past* (New York: New York University Press, 1984), 102–14.

KRUEGER, ROBERTA L., 'Love, Honor, and the Exchange of Women in *Yvain*: Some Remarks on the Female Reader', *Romance Notes*, 25 (1985), 302–17.

—— 'Constructing Sexual Identities in the High Middle Ages: The Didactic Poetry of Robert de Blois', *Paragraph*, 13 (1990), 105–31.

—— *Women Readers and the Ideology of Gender in Old French Verse Romance* (Cambridge: Cambridge University Press, 1993).

LABALME, PATRICIA H. (ed.), *Beyond their Sex: Learned Women of the European Past* (New York: New York University Press, 1984).

LASKAYA, ANNE, *Chaucer's Approach to Gender in the 'Canterbury Tales'* (Cambridge: D. S. Brewer, 1995).

LECLERCQ, JEAN, 'Le Magistère du prédicateur au xiiie siècle', *Archives d'histoire doctrinale et littéraire du Moyen Âge*, 21 (1946), 105–47.

—— *Monks on Marriage: A Twelfth-Century View* (New York: The Seabury Press, 1982).

LOCHRIE, KARMA, 'Gender, Sexual Violence, and the Politics of War in the Old English *Judith*', in Britton J. Harwood and Gillian R. Overing (eds.), *Class and Gender in Early English Literature: Intersections* (Bloomington: Indiana University Press, 1994), 1–20.

LOMPERIS, LINDA, and STANBURY, SARAH (eds.), *Feminist Approaches to the Body in Medieval Literature* (Philadelphia: University of Pennsylvania Press, 1993).

LORCIN, MARIE-THÉRÈSE, 'Mère nature et le devoir social: La Mère et l'enfant dans l'œuvre de Christine de Pizan', *Revue historique*, 282 (1989), 29–44.

LORD, MARY LOUISE, 'Dido as an Example of Chastity', *Harvard Library Bulletin*, 17 (1969), 22–44, 216–32.

LOWES, JOHN L., 'Is Chaucer's *Legend of Good Women* a Travesty?', *Journal of English and Germanic Philology*, 8 (1909), 513–69.

LUCAS, PETER J., '*Judith* and the Woman Hero', *Yearbook of English Studies*, 22 (1992), 17–27.

LUSCOMBE, DAVID, 'From Paris to the Paraclete: The Correspondence of Abelard and Heloise', *Proceedings of the British Academy*, 74, for 1988 (1989), 247–83.

MCCALL, JOHN P., 'Chaucer and the Pseudo Origen *De Maria Magdalena*: A Preliminary Study', *Speculum*, 46 (1971), 491–509.

—— 'The *Clerk's Tale* and the Theme of Obedience', *Modern Language Quarterly*, 27 (1966), 260–9.

McGINN, BERNARD, 'Teste David cum Sibylla: The Significance of the Sibylline Tradition in the Middle Ages', in Julius Kirshner and Suzanne F. Wemple (eds.), Women of the Medieval World: Essays in Honor of John H. Mundy (Oxford: Blackwell, 1985), 7–35.

McLAUGHLIN, ELEANOR C., 'Women, Power, and the Pursuit of Holiness in Medieval Christianity', in Rosemary Ruether and Eleanor McLaughlin (eds.), Women of Spirit: Female Leadership in the Jewish and Christian Traditions (New York: Simon & Schuster, 1979), 100–30.

McLAUGHLIN, MARY M., 'Abelard as Autobiographer: The Motives and Meaning of his "Story of Calamities"', Speculum, 42 (1967), 463–89.

—— 'Peter Abelard and the Dignity of Women: Twelfth Century "Feminism" in Theory and Practice', in Pierre Abelard–Pierre le Vénérable, Colloques internationaux du CNRS, Cluny, 1972 (Paris: CNRS, 1975), 287–334.

MACLEAN, IAN, The Renaissance Notion of Woman: A Study in the Fortunes of Scholasticism and Medical Science in European Intellectual Life (Cambridge: Cambridge University Press, 1980).

McLEOD, GLENDA, Virtue and Venom: Catalogs of Women from Antiquity to the Renaissance (Ann Arbor: University of Michigan Press, 1991).

—— 'Poetics and Antimisogynist Polemics in Christine de Pizan's Le Livre de la cité des dames', in Earl J. Richards et al. (eds.), Reinterpreting Christine de Pizan (Athens, Ga.: University of Georgia Press, 1992), 37–47.

McNAMARA, JO ANN, 'The Herrenfrage: The Restructuring of the Gender System, 1050–1150', in Clare A. Lees, with Thelma Fenster and Jo Ann McNamara (eds.), Medieval Masculinities: Regarding Men in the Middle Ages (Minneapolis: University of Minnesota Press, 1994), 3–29.

MALVERN, MARJORIE, Venus in Sackcloth. The Magdalen's Origins and Metamorphoses (Carbondale: Southern Illinois University Press, 1975).

MANN, JILL, 'Satisfaction and Payment in Middle English Literature', Studies in the Age of Chaucer, 5 (1983), 17–48.

—— Apologies to Women (Cambridge: Cambridge University Press, 1990).

—— Geoffrey Chaucer, Feminist Readings series (Hemel Hempstead: Harvester Wheatsheaf, 1991).

MARCHELLO-NIZIA, CHRISTIANE, 'Amour courtois, société masculine, et figures du pouvoir', Annales ESC 36 (1981), 969–82.

MARGOLIS, NADIA, 'Elegant Closures: The Use of the Diminutive in Christine de Pizan and Jean de Meun', in Earl J. Richards et al. (eds.), Reinterpreting Christine de Pizan (Athens, Ga.: University of Georgia Press, 1992), 111–25.

MARTIN, JOHN HILARY, 'The Ordination of Women and the Theologians in the Middle Ages', Escritos del Vedat, 16 (1986), 115–77.

MARTIN, PRISCILLA, Chaucer's Women: Nuns, Wives and Amazons (Basingstoke: Macmillan, 1990).

MEALE, CAROL M., 'Legends of Good Women in the European Middle Ages', Archiv, 144 (1992), 55–70.

—— (ed.), Women and Literature in Britain, 1150–1500 (Cambridge: Cambridge University Press, 1993).

MERLO, GRADO, 'Sulle "misere donnicciuole" che predicavano', in his *Valdesi e valdismi medievali*, ii: *Identità valdesi nella storia e nella storiografia* (Turin: Claudiana, 1991), 93–112.

MEWS, CONSTANT, 'On Dating the Works of Peter Abelard', *Archives d'histoire doctrinale et littéraire du Moyen Âge*, 51 (1985), 73–134.

MEYER, PAUL, 'Mélanges de poésie française, iv: Plaidoyer en faveur des femmes', *Romania*, 6 (1877), 499–503.

—— 'Les Manuscrits français de Cambridge, ii: Bibliothèque de l'Université', *Romania*, 15 (1886), 236–357.

MIDDLETON, ANNE, 'The *Physician's Tale* and Love's Martyrs: "Ensamples mo than ten" as a Method in the *Canterbury Tales*', *Chaucer Review*, 8 (1973), 9–32.

MILES, MARGARET, '"Becoming Male": Women Martyrs and Ascetics', in her *Carnal Knowing: Female Nakedness and Religious Meaning in the Christian West* (Boston: Beacon Press, 1990), 53–77.

MILLETT, KATE, *Sexual Politics* (New York: Doubleday, 1970).

MINNIS, A. J., *Chaucer and Pagan Antiquity* (Cambridge: D. S. Brewer, 1982).

—— '*De impedimento sexus*: Women's Bodies and Medieval Impediments to Female Ordination', forthcoming in P. Biller and A. J. Minnis (eds.), *Medieval Theology and the Natural Body* (York: York Medieval Texts, 1997).

—— with SCATTERGOOD, V. J., and SMITH, J. J., *Oxford Guides to Chaucer: The Shorter Poems* (Oxford: Clarendon Press, 1995).

MOI, TORIL, *Sexual/Textual Politics: Feminist Literary Theory* (New York: Methuen, 1985).

—— 'Desire in Language: Andreas Capellanus and the Controversy of Courtly Love', in David Aers (ed.), *Medieval Literature: Criticism, History, Ideology* (Brighton: Harvester, 1986), 11–33.

MORSE, CHARLOTTE, 'The Exemplary Griselda', *Studies in the Age of Chaucer*, 7 (1985), 51–86.

—— 'Critical Approaches to the *Clerk's Tale*', in C. David Benson and Elizabeth Robertson (eds.), *Chaucer's Religious Tales* (Cambridge: D. S. Brewer, 1990), 71–83.

NEWMAN, BARBARA, 'Divine Power Made Perfect in Weakness: St Hildegard on the Frail Sex', in John A. Nichols and Lillian Thomas Shank (eds.), *Peace Weavers: Medieval Religious Women*, ii (Kalamazoo, Mich.: Cistercian Publications, 1987), 103–22.

—— *Sister of Wisdom: St Hildegard's Theology of the Feminine* (Berkeley and Los Angeles: University of California Press, 1987).

—— *From Virile Woman to Woman Christ: Studies in Medieval Religion and Literature* (Philadelphia: University of Pennsylvania Press, 1995).

NYE, ANDREA, 'A Woman's Thought or a Man's Discipline? The Letters of Abelard and Heloise', *Hypatia*, 7 (1992), 1–22.

OLSSON, KURT, *John Gower and the Structures of Conversion: A Reading of the 'Confessio Amantis'* (Woodbridge: Boydell & Brewer, 1992).

ORNSTEIN, JACOB, 'Misogyny and Pro-feminism in Early Castilian Literature', *Modern Language Quarterly*, 3 (1942), 221–34.

OVERBECK, PAT T., 'Chaucer's Good Women', *Chaucer Review*, 2 (1967), 75–94.

PADEN, WILLIAM D. (ed.), *The Voice of the Trobairitz: Perspectives on the Women Troubadours* (Philadelphia: University of Pennsylvania Press, 1989).

PAGELS, ELAINE H., *Adam, Eve, and the Serpent* (Harmondsworth: Penguin, 1990).

PEARSALL, DEREK, *Old English and Middle English Poetry* (London: Routledge, 1977).

PECK, RUSSELL, *Kingship and Common Profit in Gower's 'Confessio Amantis'* (Carbondale: Southern Illinois University Press, 1978).

PHILLIPPY, PATRICIA A., 'Establishing Authority: Boccaccio's *De claris mulieribus* and Christine de Pizan's *Le Livre de la cité des dames*', *Romanic Review*, 77 (1986), 167–93.

PHILLIPS, HELEN, 'Rewriting the Fall: Julian of Norwich and the *Chevalier des dames*', in Lesley Smith and Jane H. M. Taylor (eds.), *Women, the Book, and the Godly* (Cambridge: D. S. Brewer, 1995), 149–56.

PHILLIPS, JOHN A., *Eve: The History of an Idea* (New York: Harper & Row, 1984).

POWELL, JAMES M., *Albertanus of Brescia: The Pursuit of Happiness in the Early Thirteenth Century* (Philadelphia: University of Pennsylvania Press, 1992).

PRATT, KAREN, 'Analogy or Logic; Authority or Experience? Rhetorical Strategies for and against Women', in Donald Maddox and Sara Sturm-Maddox (eds.), *Literary Aspects of Courtly Culture: Selected Papers from the Seventh Triennial Congress of the International Courtly Literature Society* (Cambridge: D. S. Brewer, 1994), 57–66.

QUILLIGAN, MAUREEN, *The Allegory of Female Authority: Christine de Pizan's 'Cité des dames'* (Ithaca, NY: Cornell University Press, 1991).

RENO, CHRISTINE, 'Virginity as an Ideal in Christine de Pizan's *Cité des dames*', in Diane Bornstein (ed.), *Ideals for Women in the Works of Christine de Pizan* (Detroit: Michigan Consortium for Medieval and Early Modern Studies, 1981), 69–90.

RICHARDS, EARL JEFFREY, 'Christine de Pizan and the Question of Feminist Rhetoric', *Teaching Language through Literature*, 22 (1983), 15–24.

——with WILLIAMSON, JOAN, MARGOLIS, NADIA, and RENO, CHRISTINE (eds.), *Reinterpreting Christine de Pizan* (Athens, Ga.: University of Georgia Press, 1992).

——'In Search of a Feminist Patrology: Christine de Pizan and "Les Glorieux Dotteurs"', in Liliane Dulac and Bernard Ribémont (eds.), *Une femme de lettres au Moyen Âge: Études autour de Christine de Pizan* (Orléans: Paradigme, 1995), 281–95.

RICHARDS, JEFFREY, *Sex, Dissidence and Damnation: Minority Groups in the Middle Ages* (London: Routledge, 1990).

RICHARDSON, LULA MCDOWELL, *Forerunners of Feminism in French Literature of the Renaissance from Christine de Pisan to Marie de Gournay* (Baltimore: Johns Hopkins University Press, 1929).

RIDDY, FELICITY, ' "Women talking about the things of God": A Late Medieval Sub-culture', in Carol Meale (ed.), *Women and Literature in Britain, 1150–1500* (Cambridge: Cambridge University Press, 1993), 104–27.

—— 'Engendering Pity in the *Franklin's Tale*', in Ruth Evans and Lesley Johnson (eds.), *Feminist Readings in Middle English Literature* (London: Routledge, 1994), 54–71.

ROBERTSON, ELIZABETH, 'Medieval Medical Views of Women and Female Spirituality in the *Ancrene Wisse* and Julian of Norwich's *Showings*', in Linda Lomperis and Sarah Stanbury (eds.), *Feminist Approaches to the Body in Medieval Literature* (Philadelphia: University of Pennsylvania Press, 1993), 142–67.

ROSE, MARY BETH (ed.), *Women in the Middle Ages and the Renaissance* (Syracuse, NY: Syracuse University Press, 1986).

ROUSSELLE, ALINE, *Porneia: On Desire and the Body in Antiquity*, tr. Felicia Pheasant (Oxford: Blackwell, 1988).

ROY, GOPA, 'A Virgin Acts Manfully: Ælfric's *Life of St Eugenia* and the Latin Versions', *Leeds Studies in English*, NS 23 (1992), 1–27.

RUBIN, GAYLE, 'The Traffic in Women: Notes on the "Political Economy" of Sex', in Rayna Reita (ed.), *Toward an Anthropology of Women* (New York: Monthly Review Press, 1975), 157–210.

RUETHER, ROSEMARY, and MCLAUGHLIN, ELEANOR C. (eds.), *Women of Spirit: Female Leadership in the Jewish and Christian Traditions* (New York: Simon & Schuster, 1979).

SAMUEL, IRENE, 'Semiramis in the Middle Ages: The History of a Legend', *Mediaevalia et humanistica*, 2 (1943), 32–44.

SANKOVITCH, TILDE, 'Lombarda's Reluctant Mirror', in William D. Paden (ed.), *The Voice of the Trobairitz* (Philadelphia: University of Pennsylvania Press, 1989), 183–93.

SAXER, VICTOR, 'La "Vie de sainte Marie Madeleine" attribuée au pseudo-Raban Maur, œuvre claravallienne du xiiᵉ siècle', in *Mélanges Saint-Bernard*, XXIVᵉ Congrès de l'Association Bourgignonne dans Sociétés Savantes, Dijon, 1953 (Dijon, 1954), 408–21.

—— *La Culte de sainte Marie Madeleine en occident des origines à la fin du Moyen Âge*, 2 vols. (Auxerre: Publications de la Société des Fouilles Archéologiques et des Monuments Historiques de l'Yonne; Clavreuil; 1959).

SCHLAUCH, MARGARET, *Chaucer's Constance and Accused Queens* (New York: New York University Press, 1927).

SCHMITZ, GÖTZ, *The Fall of Women in Early English Narrative Verse* (Cambridge: Cambridge University Press, 1990).

SCHULENBURG, JANE TIBBETTS, 'Sexism and the Celestial Gynaeceum from 500 to 1200', *Journal of Medieval History*, 4 (1978), 117–33.

SIMMONS-O'NEILL, ELIZABETH, 'Love in Hell: The Role of Pluto and Proserpine in Chaucer's *Merchant's Tale*', *Modern Language Quarterly*, 51 (1990), 389–407.

SKLUTE, LARRY H., 'Freothuwebbe in Old English Poetry', *Neuphilologische Mitteilungen*, 71 (1970), 534–41.

SLERCA, ANNA, 'Dante, Boccace, et le *Livre de la cité des dames* de Christine de Pizan', in Liliane Dulac and Bernard Ribémont (eds.), *Une femme de lettres au Moyen Âge: Études autour de Christine de Pizan* (Orléans: Paradigme, 1995), 221–30.

SMITH, SUSAN L., *The Power of Women: A Topos in Medieval Art and Literature* (Philadelphia: University of Pennsylvania Press, 1995).

SOLTERER, HELEN, *The Master and Minerva: Disputing Women in French Medieval Culture* (Berkeley and Los Angeles: University of California Press, 1995).

SOUTHERN, R. W., *Medieval Humanism and Other Essays* (Oxford: Blackwell, 1970).

SPISAK, JAMES, 'Anti-Feminism Bridled', *Neuphilologische Mitteilungen*, 81 (1980), 150–60.

STICCA, SANDRO, 'Hrotswitha's *Dulcitius* and Christian Symbolism', *Mediaeval Studies*, 32 (1970), 108–27.

STROHM, PAUL, *Hochon's Arrow: The Social Imagination of Fourteenth-Century Texts* (Princeton: Princeton University Press, 1992).

SULLIVAN, KAREN, 'At the Limit of Feminist Theory: An Architectonics of the *Querelle de la Rose*', *Exemplaria*, 3 (1991), 435–66.

TRIBLE, PHYLLIS, 'Depatriarchalizing in Biblical Interpretation', in Elizabeth Koltun (ed.), *The Jewish Woman: New Perspectives* (New York: Schocken, 1976), 217–40.

VERDUCCI, FLORENCE, *Ovid's Toyshop of the Heart* (Princeton: Princeton University Press, 1984).

VERREES, LIBERT, 'Le Traitié de l'abbé Bernard de Fontcaude contre les Vaudois et les Ariens', *Analecta Praemonstratensa*, 31 (1955), 5–35.

VOADEN, ROSALYNN, 'God's Almighty Hand: Women Co-writing the Book', in Lesley Smith and Jane H. M. Taylor (eds.), *Women, the Book, and the Godly* (Cambridge: D. S. Brewer, 1995), 55–65.

WALLACE, DAVID, '"Whan She Translated Was": A Chaucerian Critique of the Petrarchan Academy', in Lee Patterson (ed.), *Literary Practice and Social Change in Britain, 1380–1530* (Berkeley and Los Angeles: University of California Press, 1990), 156–215.

WALTERS, L., 'The Woman Writer and Literary History: Christine de Pizan's Redefinition of the Poetic *Translatio* in the *Epistre au dieu d'amours*', *French Literature Series*, 16 (1989), 1–16.

WARNER, MARINA, *Alone of All her Sex: The Myth and Cult of the Virgin Mary* (New York: Alfred Knopf, 1976).

WASSERMAN, JULIAN, and BLANCH, ROBERT J. (eds.), *Chaucer in the Eighties* (Syracuse, NY: Syracuse University Press, 1986).

WEISL, ANGELA J., *Conquering the Reign of Femeny: Gender and Genre in Chaucer's Romance* (Cambridge: D. S. Brewer, 1995).

WEISSMAN, HOPE PHYLLIS, 'Antifeminism in Chaucer's Characterization of Women', in George. D. Economou (ed.), *Geoffrey Chaucer: A Collection of Original Articles* (New York: McGraw-Hill, 1975), 93–110.

WEMPLE, SUZANNE, *Women in Frankish Society: Marriage and the Cloister, 500 to 900* (Philadelphia: University of Pennsylvania Press, 1981).

WESTPHAL, SARAH, 'Camilla: The Amazon Body in Medieval German Literature', *Exemplaria*, 8 (1996), 231–58.

WIESNER, MERRY E., 'Women's Defense of their Public Role', in Mary Beth Rose (ed.), *Women in the Middle Ages and the Renaissance: Literary and Historical Perspectives* (Syracuse, NY: Syracuse University Press, 1986), 1–27.

WILLARD, CHARITY C., 'A New Look at Christine de Pizan's *Epistre au dieu d'amours*', in Franco Simone *et al.* (eds.), *Seconda miscellanea di studi e ricerche sul quattrocento francese* (Chambéry: Centre d'Études Franco-Italien, 1981), 74–91.

——*Christine de Pizan: Her Life and Works* (New York: Persea Books, 1984).

WILSON, KATHARINA M., *Hrotsvit of Gandersheim: The Ethics of Authorial Stance* (Leiden: Brill, 1988).

——and MAKOWSKI, ELIZABETH M., *Wykked Wyves and The Woes of Marriage* (New York: State University of New York Press, 1990).

WINSTEAD, KAREN A., 'Saints, Wives, and Other "Hooly Thynges": Pious Laywomen in Middle English Romance', *Chaucer Yearbook*, 2 (1993), 137–54.

——'Capgrave's Saint Katherine and the Perils of Gynecocracy', *Viator*, 25 (1994), 361–76.

WOGAN-BROWNE, JOCELYN, 'Saints' Lives and the Female Reader', *Forum for Modern Language Studies*, 27 (1991), 314–32.

——'The Virgin's Tale', in Ruth Evans and Lesley Johnson (eds.), *Feminist Readings in Middle English Literature: The Wife of Bath and All her Sect* (London: Routledge, 1994), 165–94.

WOLFZETTEL, FRIEDRICH (ed.), *Arthurian Romance and Gender*, Selected Proceedings of the XVIIth International Arthurian Congress (Amsterdam: Rodopi, 1995).

WOODBRIDGE, LINDA, *Women and the English Renaissance: Literature and the Nature of Womankind 1540–1620* (Urbana: University of Illinois Press, 1984).

Index

Aalais 75
Abelard, Peter 17–18, 20, 30, 95, 104, 107, 133, 134–6, 148, 150, 152, 172, 175, 177, 195–6, 199–207, 223, 240
Abigail 25, 29, 172
Acta sanctorum 155
activity, as masculine attribute, *see* gender
Adam 3, 28, 32, 48, 72, 83, 96–125, 146, 202, 237, 238–9
Adams, Thomas 107
advice, of women 13, 25–6
Aeneas 48, 214, 221
Aers, David 32, 93–4
Agatha, St 35, 172
Agnes, St 171–2
Agrippa von Nettesheim, Cornelius 50, 97, 105, 108, 112, 117, 119, 131
Alain of Lille 188
Albertanus of Brescia 14, 22–6, 28, 86, 106, 108, 172, 212
Albertus Magnus 122, 127, 237
Alcestis 20, 56–7, 172, 212–14, 216, 228
Alcuin 121
Aldhelm 155, 190
Alexander 22, 225
Alithie 43, 172
Allain, Mathé 21
Amadeus of Lausanne 121–2
Amazons 9, 19, 94, 171, 180–1, 193, 198, 221, 225, 227, 233–4, 237
Ambrose, St 8, 67, 76–7, 101, 104, 109, 119, 121, 146, 171, 173–4, 182–3, 185
Amt, Emilie 2
Andrea, Giovanni 39
Andreas Capellanus 115–16, 129–30, 141
androgyny 45
Angenot, Marc 3, 10, 63, 65, 97, 112, 237
anger, *see* irascibility
Anna 66, 171–2, 187, 189–90, 202, 204–5
Anne of Bohemia, Queen 88–9
Anselm, St 120

Anstrude 231
Apame 53, 56, 87
apocrypha, *see* Bible
Apostolic Constitutions, The 187
apostles, women as 110–12, 191–2
Aquinas, St Thomas 99, 114, 122, 189–90, 197
Ariadne 171, 215
Aristotle 92, 97, 225, 227, 237
Arjava, Antti 92
Arria, 20, 172
Artemisia of Caria 180–1
assertion, *see* boldness
Aston, Margaret 197
Astralabe 94
Atkinson, Clarissa 81, 127, 237
Attila 177, 231
Aubineau, Michel 76
Augustine, pseudo 122
Augustine, St 30, 98, 114, 202
     De civitate Dei 113, 117, 123, 157, 220
     De Genesi ad litteram 100, 113, 239
     In Joannis evangelium 99–100, 109–10, 196
     Opus imperfectum 81, 235–6
     Sermons 106–7, 110, 113, 133, 140–2, 146
authority:
     of female precedent 8, 112, 193, 229
     of men 45, 46, 84, 195, 243
     of women 20, 27, 52–3, 67–8, 92, 122, 179, 194–5, 201–5, 220
autonomy, women's 5, 180–1
Aylmer, John 242

Bailleul, Chevalier de 68
Bailey, D. S. 139
Barbara, St 172
Basilissa 190
Bathsheba 35, 38
beards, as defects in men 131–2
Bede, pseudo 113
Bede, *Ecclesiastical History* 114
Beer, Jeanette 4
Benedicta, St 190

Benson, Pamela Joseph 3, 5, 8, 11, 50, 63–4, 117, 143, 180–1, 235, 240, 242

Beowulf 86–7

Bercher, William 20

Bernard of Fontcaude 188–9

Bernard, St 34, 75, 110, 112, 120, 121, 186, 237

Besserman, Lawrence 210

Bible, the, women in 9–10, 29–30, 42–3
  Acts 286
  Canticles 220
  Corinthians 34, 52, 135–6, 187, 188, 195, 242
  Ecclesiastes 14, 24–5, 106, 210
  Ecclesiasticus 71, 128, 185, 241–2
  Esdras 50–60, 71, 244
  Esther 174–6
  Exodus 29, 187, 204
  Genesis 58, 72, 81, 96, 98, 105–6
  James 188
  Job 128, 147
  John 118, 145, 146, 172, 195–6, 203
  Judges 173–4, 187
  Kings 187
  Luke 30, 146, 172, 187, 190–1, 204
  Maccabees 172
  Mark 146, 147
  Matthew 118, 145, 146, 185, 219, 235
  Peter 85, 128, 156, 186, 190
  Proverbs 71, 186
  Revelation 186, 188
  Timothy 113, 242
  Tobit 72

Le Bien des fames 21, 58–9, 71, 87, 94, 108, 121

Blamires, Alcuin 3, 8, 13, 30, 35, 40, 95, 123, 168, 190, 191, 196, 197, 200, 203, 207, 212

Blanche of Castile 36, 86, 172, 179–80

Bloch, R. Howard 10, 12–13, 33, 122, 133, 183, 184

Blumenfeld-Kosinski, Renate 3, 37, 46, 68, 95

Blumstein, Andrée Kahn 4, 10, 11, 233

Boccaccio, Giovanni 3, 163, 215, 229
  De mulieribus claris 4, 70, 92, 133, 180–2, 220, 222–3, 226, 229, 232, 233–5

body, woman as 30, 113–14, 140, 196, 237

boldness, in women 178–9, 182–4, 216

Bonaventure, St 83, 99

Bond, R. Warwick 20

The Book of the Knight of the Tower 89–90, 121, 136–7, 175–6, 183, 216

books, male monopoly of 2, 47

Bornstein, Diane 10, 40, 74, 183

Du Bounté des femmes 4, 21, 28, 72–3, 98, 107, 116, 131–2

Bozon, Nicole 4, 37, 47, 48, 54–5, 118
  De la Bonté des femmes 15, 31–3, 59, 90, 116–17, 138–9

Brasington, Bruce C. 184

Brett, Edward Tracy 191

Brewer, Derek 165–6

Brown, Emerson, Jr. 176

Brown, Peter 67, 80

Brown-Grant, Rosalind 220

Brownlee, Kevin 45, 229

Brut, Walter 242

Burchmore, Susan 113–14

Burgundofara 184

Burnley, J. D. 127, 237

Bynum, Caroline Walker 12, 75, 123, 194, 236

Cadden, Joan 131, 134, 149, 237

Calphurnia 39–40

calumniation, of women 10, 64, 132, 153–70

Camilla 180–1

Canaanite woman, the 171, 218–19

caring, *see* compassion; nurturing

Carmentis 42, 66, 172, 221–2, 225

Carruthers, Mary 165, 169–70

Cassandra 42

Castelli, Elizabeth 76

Castiglione, Baldassare 50, 233

castration 41–2, 199, 225

Cathars 196

Catherine of Alexandria, St 35, 67, 171–2, 190, 192, 198, 240, 242

Catherine of Siena, St 134, 195

Cazelles, Brigitte 157, 184

Cecilia, St 172, 178, 183, 190, 192

Ceres 225

Charles, R. H. 51, 54

chastity, as feminine virtue 37, 42, 137–8, 143, 151

Chaucer, Geoffrey 3, 16, 17, 25, 33, 44, 153, 181, 207, 241
  Anelida and Arcite 168, 213
  Book of the Duchess 44, 118
  Clerk's Tale 10, 90, 164–70
  Franklin's Tale 11
  Knight's Tale 85–6, 88, 168, 181, 232

Legend of Good Women 31, 151, 168, 176, 199, 212–19, 228
Tale of Melibee 14, 23–6, 210, 212
Merchant's Tale 82–3, 92, 176, 208–11
Monk's Tale 66
Nun's Priest's Tale 12–13, 16, 25, 150, 211
Parson's Tale 102
Physician's Tale 151
Squire's Tale 17, 150–1, 213
Troilus and Criseyde 32, 93–4, 139, 168, 215
Wife of Bath's Prologue and Tale 9, 34–5, 36, 46, 47, 73, 77, 88, 115, 118, 208, 213, 219, 224, 232, 242
Le Chevalier des dames 139
childbearing 6, 9, 18, 21, 61, 70–82, 234, 235–6, 237
Chrétien de Troyes 17
Cligés 87, 233
Yvain 10, 159–62, 165
Christ:
anointed by women 20, 29, 206–7
appearance first to women after Resurrection 27, 97, 104, 106, 108–10, 124, 146, 204
choice of woman to announce Resurrection 24, 61, 65, 109–12, 191–2, 202, 204, 226
incarnation an honour to women 24, 27, 28, 72, 97, 98, 104, 106–8, 124
loyalty of women to 20, 29, 48, 109, 110, 144–9, 151–2, 206, 216, 239
see also Samaritan woman
Christina of Markyate 129, 145, 178, 184
Christine de Pizan 3, 5, 8, 22, 25, 36, 40, 213, 240, 241
L'Epistre au dieu d'amours 15–16, 18, 44–9, 74, 84, 87, 99, 105, 106, 108, 117–19, 120, 141, 144, 149, 172, 243
Le Livre de la cité des dames 39–40, 41, 43, 47, 49, 62, 91, 95, 103, 105, 106, 109, 122–3, 142–4, 149–50, 156, 165, 176, 179–82, 190, 199, 219–30, 232, 234, 236
Le Livre des trois vertus 89–91
Christine, St 172, 229, 232
Chrysostom, *see* St John Chrysostom
Cicero 62–3
Ciconian women, the 36, 233

civilization, women as agents of 21, 94, 220, 241
see also transformation
Cixous, Hélène 95, 181
Clark, Elizabeth 68, 107, 191, 235
Claudia, the vestal virgin 172, 182
Claudius, Emperor 144
Clement, Bishop 175
Cleopatra 216
clothes, women as producers of 21, 52, 54, 58–60
Clothild, Queen 86
coldness, as feminine attribute 129–31, 237
commodification, of women 11, 57, 76–7, 155
compassion, as feminine attribute 16, 168, 213, 218–19, 241
complexion, *see* coldness, heat, humidity, physiology
constancy, of women 16, 56, 61, 109, 110–11, 151, 179, 228–9, 239
sexual 10, 28, 32, 38, 48, 129–30, 132, 137–45, 156, 163–4, 212–19, 227
see also Christ
Cooper, Helen 34
Coriolanus 232
Cornificia 70
courage, of women 37, 176–7, 179
see also strength; valour
courtesy:
caused by women 94
of women 13–14, 22, 139
to women 21, 27, 41, 45, 59, 73, 75, 232
courtly love 10, 27
Coyle, J. Kevin 186–7, 242
Crane, Susan 11
creation, of humankind 17, 19, 65, 83
rib symbolism in 3, 28, 38, 48, 83, 96, 98–103, 119, 131, 226
sequence in 97, 105
of woman as helper 6
of woman inside paradise 27, 48, 96–7, 98, 103–5, 202, 226
credulity, as feminine attribute 113–18
see also guilelessness
crime, as masculine phenomenon 49, 61, 143–4, 227–8
Curnow, Maureen Cheney 39, 62, 179, 222, 227
Cursor mundi 111

Daileader, Celia R. 23
Daniélou, Jean 187–8
Darius 51–60
Datini, Margherita 140
David 35, 38, 177
Deborah 8, 29, 66, 171–4, 176, 177,
    179–80, 187, 189–90, 193, 194, 240
deceit:
    of men 48, 164
    of women 117, 118, 164
defiance, by women 175–6, 183–4,
    212–14, 216–17
de Labriolle, P. 187
Delany, Sheila 212–13, 216, 218
Delilah 29
Denis of Sicily 49
Deschamps, Eustache 33, 47, 66
    Le Miroir de mariage 9, 33–6, 38, 43,
        73, 86, 92, 115, 132–3, 172, 175,
        179–80, 192, 233
desire, female 13, 130, 241
Desmond, Marilynn 172
determination, in women, see
    constancy, stability
detraction, see slander
diaconate, female 20, 187
Diamond, Arlyn 219
Dickson, Lynne 88
Dido 48, 68, 171–2, 214, 215, 221, 240
Dinshaw, Carolyn 14, 213, 216
disciples of Christ:
    defection of 145–9
    women as 10, 30, 146, 190–1
    see also Christ, loyalty of women to
disobedience, see defiance
Dives and Pauper 30, 71, 99, 102–3,
    107–8, 118–19, 137, 141–2
Donaldson, Ian 172
double standard, see sexuality
Dow, Blanche 3, 73, 96
Dronke, Peter 104, 153, 154, 159, 193,
    205–6, 215
drunkenness, of men 6, 149–50

écriture féminine 152
education, and women 40, 47, 50, 182,
    223, 226, 236
Edward III 86
Edwards, A. S. G. 209, 210
effeminacy 4, 7–8
Elisabeth of Schönau 8, 100–1, 193–4
Elizabeth (mother of John the Baptist)
    172, 202, 205
Elliott, Dyan 17, 194

Ellis, Roger 118
eloquence, of women, see speech
encomium on women 19
Engelbert of Admont 108
Epiphanius 186–7
equality of sexes:
    circumscribed by patriarchy 5, 236,
        239–40
    in creation 20, 59–60, 101–3
    in attainment 70, 95, 173
    in marital fidelity 139–41, 153
Erigena, John Scotus 113
The Erle of Tolous 162–4, 168
Erler, Mary Carpenter 96
Ermengard 85
essentialism 11, 13, 16, 44, 82, 210–11
    see also generalization; stereotypes
Esther 25, 29, 171–2, 174–7, 179, 236–7
Étienne de Fougères 4, 115
    Le Livre des manières 20–1, 67, 121
etymology, and women 82–3, 87
Eugenia, St 172
Eurydice 42, 233
Eusebius of Caesarea 109, 186, 206
Eustace of Arras 189–90, 242
Eve 25, 29, 58, 59, 61, 109, 146
    as companion of Adam 101–3
    as complement to Virgin Mary 13,
        60, 112, 123, 202
    exoneration of 9, 17, 28, 32, 48, 60,
        83, 96–7, 107, 112–19, 238
    as helpmate to Adam 6, 25, 72
    see also creation
exempla 15, 25, 28–31, 36, 38–9, 42–4,
    61, 65–9, 143, 170, 171–98, 224
    modern 21, 36, 42, 66–8, 172, 179–80
experience, women's, as defence 223–
    4, 236, 239, 243

fable 36, 42–3, 46, 66–8
facetiousness, in profeminine discourse
    5–7, 34, 36–7, 44, 106, 109, 124,
    217–19, 226
Facetus 73
Fall, the 32, 59, 81, 96, 112–19, 146
    see also Adam, Eve
fantasy, masculine 5–6
Farmer, David Hugh 177
Farmer, Sharon 84–5, 94
Fasciculus morum 141–2
Fausta, St 190
feminism, and profeminine discourse
    10, 11–12, 18, 64–5, 93, 176–7, 236
feminization, of men 214

Fenster, Thelma S. 96, 117–18
Ferrante, Joan M. 83, 102, 114, 128
Ficino, Marsilio 50
fidelity, *see* constancy, stability
Fides, St 172
Fiero, Gloria 21, 50
Fiorenza, Elizabeth S. 112, 146, 175, 188, 195
Fontevrault 35, 184
Fortunatus, Venantius 86, 133–4
foundation, women as agents of, *see* innovation
Fox, Margaret Fell 242
Francesco da Barberino 103
Frankforter, A. Daniel 134, 159
Frappier, Jean 160
Fredegonde, Queen 179
Freud 41
Froissart, Jean 86
Furia 66
Fuss, Diana 13
Fyler, John 97, 168, 216, 218

Galba, Emperor 144
Galloway, Andrew 127, 141
Gawain, Sir 14
generalization, in gender polemic 1, 9, 12–17, 24–6, 31–2, 38, 44, 45, 61, 164, 224–5
generosity, as feminine attribute 32, 37, 211, 227, 228
gender, constructions of 12, 57, 74, 94, 146, 151, 162, 168, 176, 183, 234–6
binaries in 236; active/passive 48, 138, 141–2, 215, 216, 236, 238; body/intellect 196; hard/soft 82–6, 126–7; stable/unstable 126–34, 147, 152, 162, 168, 170
binaries in, challenged 38, 211, 221, 228–9
see also nature; stereotypes
Genevieve, St 172, 177–9, 231–2
gentleness, as feminine attribute 16, 49, 84, 90
Georgianna, Linda 167
Gerontius 81
Gertrude, St 190
Glodesind 72, 184
Glossa ordinaria 196, 210
Goggio, Bartolomeo 117
Gold, Penny Schine 75, 121
Gonnet, Giovanni 188
Good Wife Taught her Daughter, The 85

Gosynhyll, Edward 81
Gottfried von Strassburg 85, 233
Gottlieb, Beatrice 143
government, by women 8, 36, 57–8, 92, 173, 179–80, 234, 235, 240
Gower, John 55–7, 87, 103, 163
Graef, Hilda 107, 108, 121, 122
Grandes chroniques de France, Les 179
Gravdal, Kathryn 2, 141, 156–7, 158
Green, Rosalie B. 196–7
Gregory of Nyssa 76, 78
Gregory, St 60, 113–14, 128, 146–7, 185–6, 193
Grigsby, J. L. 28–31, 43, 105
guilelessness, of women 16, 113, 115–19, 238
Guillaume de Lorris, see *Roman de la Rose*
Guillaume de Machaut 31
Guthrie, Jeri S. 21

hair, facial 131–2
Hales, J. W. 165
Hali Meiðhad 78–80
Hannah 29, 172
Hansen, Elaine Tuttle 151, 165, 214
hardness, as masculine attribute 83–5, 88, 90, 126–8
Hasenohr-Esnos, Geneviève 6
head:
man as 114, 117, 140, 142
woman as 122–4, 207
healing, as feminine skill 22, 26, 61, 91, 93–4
heat, as masculine attribute 127, 129–31
Heloise:
encomium to 172, 193, 220
intellectual reputation 39
and motherhood 94–5
on misogamy 207–8
mode of writing 152
quest for authority 20, 199–201
on women's sobriety 149–50
strength of 134–6
helper, woman as, *see* Eve
Henry of Ghent 8, 190
Hentsch, Alice A. 128, 138
Hercules 36, 212, 225, 244
Hereford, Countess of 21, 67
Hero 215
Herod 72, 143
Hibbard, Laura 163
Hildebert of Lavardin 78, 126

Hildegard of Bingen 3, 7–8, 81, 101, 112, 115, 129, 135, 193, 195
Hippolyta 234
Hippolytus 110
Hoccleve, Thomas 103, 168
  Letter of Cupid 74, 87, 118, 149
Holofernes 177–8
home-making, *see* household
Homer 42, 43
homosexuality 29, 233
Honorius Augustodunensis 110
Hortensia 182, 232
household, women and 6, 35, 54, 61, 76, 82, 91–3, 198, 223, 228
Hrotsvitha of Gandersheim 4, 8, 10, 17, 154–9, 193, 231
Huber, Elaine C. 188
Hugh of St Cher 189, 194, 195–6
Hugh of St Victor 102
Huldah 187, 189–90, 193, 194
Humbert of Romans 124–5, 191, 192
humidity, as feminine attribute 127, 237
humility, as feminine virtue 32, 37, 67, 90, 124, 143, 151, 175–6, 234
Hunt, Tony 10, 160–2
Hutin de Vermeille 45
Hypermnestra 215
Hypsipyle 215, 217

impotence, and misogyny 41, 46, 225
inconstancy:
  of men 28, 132, 161, 169–70, 214, 225, 239
  of women 22, 48, 126–9, 132, 142, 145–6, 160, 163–4, 209
infidelity, of men 33, 38, 90–1, 140–3
  see also inconstancy; promiscuity
inheritance, by women 232
innocence, of women 115, 117
  see also guilelessness
innovation, by women 203–4, 220–2, 240
intelligence, of women:
  asserted 39–40, 223, 225, 227–8
  denied 5, 113–14, 127, 236, 237, 239
  exemplified 39, 192, 206, 221–2
  liberated by Eve 117
intercession, *see* peacemaking
intercourse, sexual, refusal of 231
irascibility, as masculine attribute 23, 56, 85–9, 158, 175, 241
Irigaray, Luce 155

Isabelle, Queen 179
Isidore of Seville 30, 82, 97
Isolde 233

Jacobus de Voragine 43, 141
  The Golden Legend 67, 155, 157, 183, 191–2
Jacques de Vitry 98, 104, 150
Jason 48, 217
Jean de Meun, see *Roman de la Rose*
Jean Le Fèvre 3, 45, 47, 66, 124, 211, 218
  Livre de Leësce 5–7, 15, 36–44, 48, 55, 64, 65–6, 67–8, 73, 83, 92–3, 101, 103–4, 130–1, 132, 142, 149, 172, 176, 192, 229, 234, 238
Jeanne de Neuville 42, 67–8, 172
Jehan Petit d'Arras 83
Jenkins, C. 187
Jephtha's daughter 42, 172
Jerome, St 51, 92
  Adversus Iovinianum 9, 28, 50, 71, 73, 138, 171, 207–8, 224
  Letters 43, 66–7, 75, 76, 139, 171, 200, 202–3
Joanna, wife of Herod's steward 30, 147, 191
John the Baptist 192, 202, 205
John Chrysostom, St 126, 235
  Homilies on Genesis 113, 114
  Homilies on John 146, 191, 195–6
  On Virginity 76–9, 81, 89–90, 91–2, 139
John of Salisbury 138
John, St 148, 203
Jordan, Constance 3, 242
Josephus, *Jewish Antiquities* 54–5, 58–9
Judas 49, 144, 229, 242
judicial rhetoric, *see* rhetoric
judiciary, *see* law
Judith 25, 29, 66, 171–2, 175, 176–8, 193, 197, 242
Julian the Apostate 49
Julian of Eclanum 81, 235–6
Julian of Norwich 119–20
Justine, St 190
Juvenal 42, 149

Karras, Ruth Mazo 157, 198
Kay, Sarah 130
Kelso, Ruth 3
Kerby-Fulton, Kathryn 194
Kiser, Lisa 218
Kleinbaum, Abby Wettan 180

Kliman, Bernice 87–8, 178
knowledge, women's 37, 42
Kolve, V. A. 229
Kristeller, Paul O. 39
Krueger, Roberta L. 11, 27, 32, 159,
 161, 164, 176

La Calabre 6
Langland, William 109, 150
Laskaya, Anne 169, 209
Laurent de Premierfait 222
law:
 defending women 1–2
 women's exclusion from 39–40,
  141, 227, 237, 239–40
 women's skill in 39, 62
Leah 29
Leander 215
Leclercq, Jean 86, 110, 190
Leoba, St 171
Liber Iamentationum Matheoluli, see
 Matheolus
Lochrie, Karma 176–7
Lollardy 197
Lord, Mary Louise 172
Lot's wife 29, 39
Louis, St 36, 86
loyalty, of women, *see* constancy
Lucretia 42, 68, 171–2, 198
Lucy, St 172, 190
Luscombe, David 200
Lydgate, John 7, 117
lyric, courtly 10–11

Maccabees, mother in 29, 172
McCall, John P. 165, 216
McGinn, Bernard 205
McLaughlin, Eleanor 134
McLaughlin, Mary 200, 201, 203, 207
Maclean, Ian 92, 96, 102–3, 106, 124
McLeod, Glenda 3, 12, 50, 62–3, 172,
 220
McNamara, Jo Ann 18, 88
Macrobius 150
Maidstone, Richard 89
Makowski, Elizabeth M. 17
Malvern, Marjorie 112
Mann, Jill 3, 13, 31, 33, 36, 117, 166,
 208, 210, 211–12, 214, 217, 218
Manto 222
Map, Walter 9
Marbod of Rennes 4, 6, 17–18, 19–20,
 59–60, 72, 79–80, 82, 84, 91–2, 121,
 143, 172, 175–6, 229

Marcella 67
Marchello-Nizia, Christiane 11
Marcia, the painter 225
Margaret, St 21, 171, 198
Margolis, Nadia 48
Marie de France 194
Marina, St 172
marriage 33, 34, 37, 70, 89–91, 153,
 160–1, 180, 184
 troubles (*molestiae*) of 71–2, 75–82
Martha, St 29, 68, 172, 189–92, 194,
 203
Martin Le Franc 199
Martin, John Hilary 83, 122
Martin, Priscilla 13
Marx, C. W. 3, 8, 40, 190, 197
Mary the Egyptian, St 172
Mary Magdalene, St 29, 198, 224
 anointing Christ 206–7
 assisting Christ's ministry 30, 171
 loyalty at Christ's tomb 145, 147–8,
  216
 first to see risen Christ 65, 106, 108–
  12, 237
 first to report Resurrection 61, 65,
  109–12, 192
 as preacher 189–91, 197, 240, 242
Mary, the Virgin 120–4
 as Christ's mother 27, 97, 111, 146,
  148
 exemplar of feminine honour 21,
  28, 48, 58, 97, 107
 singularity, as profeminine witness
  22, 108, 120–1, 192, 197, 229
 succour to women 122–3, 178
 see also Eve
Matheolus 6, 39, 49, 64, 130–1, 227
matriarchy 92, 233–4
Maximilla 186–7
Meale, Carol 213, 215, 224
Medea 42, 48, 66, 171–2, 215, 216,
 217
Meditations on the Life of Christ 111,
 148, 196–7, 219
Melania, the Younger 81
menstruation 131
Merlo, Grado 188
Mews, Constant 199
Meyer, Paul 4, 21, 28, 50, 96
Michal 29
Middleton, Anne 151
Miles, Margaret 134
Millett, Bella 78, 80
Millett, Kate 5, 96

Minnis, Alastair 12, 43–4, 122, 197, 211, 213, 217, 218, 219, 233, 234
Miriam 172, 187, 190, 202, 204
Le Miroir des bonnes femmes 28–31, 43, 105
misogamy 34, 73, 78–80, 208, 211
misogyny 1, 16, 239
  clichés of 57, 62, 71, 72, 80, 83, 106, 109, 115, 128, 154–5, 157–8, 159–62, 163, 228
  internalization of 81, 229
  motivation for 9, 40–6, 210, 213, 225, 233, 239
  subjectivity of 33, 40–2, 47, 49, 208–11, 241–2
  structural 231, 234, 236–8
  see also slander; stereotype
moderation, *see* sobriety
Moi, Toril 12, 152, 241
molestiae nuptiarum, see marriage
Montanists 186–8
morality, superior in women 9, 28, 32, 48, 61, 92–3, 107, 135, 143–4, 170, 216, 239
Morse, Charlotte C. 165, 169
motherhood 108, 179–80
  as impediment to aspirations 94–5
  as reason for honouring women 9, 18, 19, 21, 27, 28, 32, 36, 38, 45, 49, 52, 55, 58, 60–1, 70–6, 78–82, 226, 237
Muckle, J. T. 200, 201
Muses, the 66, 172
Mycoff, David 110

Naomi 66, 171–2
Natalia, St 190
nature, and feminine disposition 15, 17, 142, 173, 224, 226–7, 235
  alien to crime 16, 49
  lacking authority 122
  compassionate 16
  constant 129
  deceitful 117
  resistant to intoxication 149–50
  submissive 234
  trusting 16, 115–16
  unstable 137; *see also* gender
Nero, Emperor 143–4, 228
Newman, Barbara 7–8, 32, 77, 78, 81, 84, 97, 100–1, 105, 108, 112, 115, 117, 129, 133, 135, 165, 171, 193, 200, 201, 207
Netter, Thomas 122, 197

Niobe 70
Norfolk, Duchess of 85
Novella of Bologna 39–40, 42, 172
nuns:
  consecrated by bishops 21
  instructed by abbess 193
  uniting against aggressors 231
nurturing, as feminine skill 4, 17, 32, 60, 70–1, 74–5, 82, 91, 94–5
Nye, Andrea 152

obedience, as feminine attribute 26, 29, 30, 98, 102, 140, 141, 164–5, 174–6, 234, 238
Odo of Cluny 110, 147
'Oez seignor, je n'otroi pas' 5, 13–14, 21, 115
Olsson, Kurt 56–7
ordination of women 2, 187
organs, sexual 6, 41, 107
Origen 186–7, 195, 242
Origen, pseudo, *De Maria Magdalena* 216
Ornstein, Jacob 239
Orpheus 36, 233
Orwell, George 1
Osbert of Clare 78, 192
Otho, Emperor 144
Oton de Grandson 45
Ovid 41–4, 47, 218, 225, 241
  Amores 126
  Ars amatoria 14, 160, 213
  Heroides 118, 171, 214–15, 217, 222–3
  Metamorphoses 36, 233
  Remedia amoris 23, 46
Ovide moralisé 44

Pagels, Elaine 81, 117
Pasiphaë 42, 241
passivity, *see* gender
The Paston Letters 85–6, 241
patience, as feminine virtue 35, 89–91, 143, 164–5
Paul, St 67, 113, 135–6, 187, 189, 242
Paula 203
peacemaking, as feminine skill 17, 22, 23–5, 27, 56, 82, 85–9, 175, 179, 213, 222, 231–2, 241
Pearl 121
Pearsall, Derek 22
Peck, Russell 57
Penelope 42, 48, 68, 171–2
Penninah 29

Penthesilea 42, 172, 193, 234
perseverance, *see* constancy, stability
Peter, St 145, 147–8, 216, 229
Peter of Blois 78
Peter Comestor 97, 113, 119
Peter Lombard 97, 102
Peter the Venerable 134, 172, 193, 220
Pfeffer, Wendy 5, 10, 21
Pharaoh's daughter 29
Philip, four daughters of 186–7, 189–90, 194
Philippa, Queen 86
Philippe de Novare 128, 138
Phillippy, Patricia A. 222, 229
Phillips, John A. 105, 114
Phillips, Helen 119, 139
Philo 113–14, 206
Phoebe 171–2
Phyllis 171, 215
physiology 126–32, 227, 237
   see also coldness; heat; humidity
Pickering, O. S. 15
piety, as feminine virtue 61, 67, 149, 227
Pilate's wife 172
Plato 50
pornography 6
Potiphar's wife 29
Powell, James M. 22–3
Pratt, Karen 3, 5, 7, 37, 44
preaching, by women 2, 7–8, 29–30, 84, 110, 185–97, 202, 204–5, 240, 242
predatoriness, as masculine attribute 38, 48, 141–3, 155, 156, 178, 212–13, 217
pregnancy, *see* childbearing
Prisca (or Priscilla) 186–7
privatization, of women 91–3, 151, 214–15, 223
   see also public roles
privileges, of women 4, 9, 17, 38, 48, 60, 96–112, 124–5, 226, 237, 240
   see also creation, Christ
procreation, *see* childbearing
Progne 216
promiscuity:
   of men 38, 139–41, 210, 217–18, 239
   of women 14
   see also constancy; stability
prophecy, as feminine role 8, 20, 61, 186–90, 193, 194–5, 197, 202, 204–6
prostitutes 38, 137, 157, 159, 202
Pseustis 43

public roles, for women 39–40, 91, 223, 242
   as lecturers 39–40
   in litigation 164, 182
   organizing city defence 177–8
   as rulers 8, 173, 179
   see also preaching; prophecy

Querelle de la Rose 46, 242
Quilligan, Maureen 11, 21, 223, 224, 229
Quintilian 63, 65–6, 176
Quintilla 187

Rachel 29, 172
Radegund, St 86, 133, 171, 190
Radice, Betty 20, 202
Ragusa, Isa 196–7
Rahab 29
Raoul de Cambrai 74–5
rape 1–2, 135, 141, 155–7, 209–10, 216, 232
rationality, and women 143–4, 150
Raynaud, G. 34
Rebecca 25, 29, 68, 172
reliability, of women, *see* constancy, stability
Renart, Jean 164
Reno, Christine 220
Renaud de Louens 23, 25
responsibility:
   for fall of great men 22, 28, 35, 38, 57
   for sin 38, 48, 238–9
rhetoric:
   epideictic 63
   judicial 1, 9, 50, 62–4
Richard II 88–9
Richard de Fournival, *Response* to the *Bestiaire d'amour* 4, 98, 105, 119
Richards, Earl Jeffrey 3, 48, 102
Richards, Jeffrey 141
Rictrude 184
Riddy, Felicity 11, 85–6
Robert d'Arbrissel 184
Robert of Basevorn 186
Robert de Blois, *L'Honneur des dames* 26–8, 36, 73–4, 104, 107, 108
Robertson, Elizabeth 130
Roman de la Rose, Le 6, 18, 21, 36, 41, 45, 47–8, 128, 132, 139, 213, 220
Rousselle, Aline 139, 197
Roy, Gopa 128, 134
Rubin, Gayle 32

Ruether, Rosemary 81
Rumble, Thomas C. 162
Ruodlieb 153
Ruth 29, 172
Rychner, Jean 34

Sabine women, the 222
Samaritan woman, the 20, 99, 171–2,
    189–90, 195–8, 202, 224, 236
Samson 22
Sankovitch, Tilde 10
Sappho 42, 66, 172
Sarah 29, 68, 172
Saxer, V. 191, 198
Schlauch, Margaret 153
Schmitz, Götz 172
Semiramis 42, 172, 240
Seneca 24–5
Serlo of Bayeux 79, 92
sexuality:
    double standard in 32, 91, 132, 137–
        43, 153, 163, 218, 239
    frustration in 19, 41, 233
Sibyls, the 42, 171–2, 202, 205–6, 222,
    225
Simmons-O'Neill, Elizabeth 210
Sir Gawain and the Green Knight 163,
    221
Sklute, Larry H. 87
slander 15–16, 22, 40, 45–6, 48, 60,
    119, 213–14, 224, 225, 241
Slerca, Anna 222
Smith, Susan L. 14, 126
sobriety, as feminine virtue 149–51,
    180
softness, as feminine attribute 4, 82–7,
    90, 113, 126–8, 235, 237, 241
solidarity, women's 36, 122–3, 158,
    178, 209, 224, 231–4
Solomon 28, 209–10, 241
Solterer, Helen 20, 44, 74, 205, 211,
    221, 222, 228, 238, 243
The South English Legendary 191
The Southern Passion 14–15, 111, 138–
    41, 145, 218
Southern R. W. 202
speech, of women 24–5, 26, 39, 85–6,
    109, 152, 155–7, 163, 182, 189,
    195–6, 229
stability, of women 17, 32, 35, 36, 37,
    38, 126–70, 208–14, 216, 228–9
stereotypes, of femininity 5, 13, 16,
    38, 57, 70, 82–5, 125, 148, 154,
    157–8, 160, 211, 217

see also gender, nature
Sticca, Sandro 156
strength, of women 51–6, 67, 99–100,
    140, 173, 176–7, 180–2, 203, 227,
    235
    in weakness 132–7, 154, 207, 227,
    239
    see also valour
Strohm, Paul 88–9
Strozzi, Agostino 50
subject, woman as 26, 33, 35, 76, 132,
    155, 204
Sullivan, Karen 236
surveillance, of women's behaviour
    32, 138–9, 164, 239–40
Susanna 29, 147, 191
sweetness, as feminine attribute 83–6,
    89

teaching, women and 122
    see also preaching
Tertullian 110
Thamiris 42, 172, 234
Thecla, St 21, 67, 171–2
Theophrastus 33, 34, 50, 59, 76–7, 243
Theseus 225
Thomas, St 110, 237
Thomas of Chobham 84–5
The Thrush and the Nightingale 14, 21–
    2, 87, 91, 120
Thisbe 216
Tobias's wife 29
transformation, of men by women 21,
    27, 53, 55, 58–9, 60
Trevisa, John 128–9, 131
Trible, Phyllis 98, 105
Troy 36, 48
trustingness, in women, *see*
    guilelessness
Truth, Sojourner 107
Tugwell, Simon 192

Ulysses 48
Ursula, St 67, 172

valour:
    of women 37, 173, 175, 181
    women as stimulus to 27, 53, 58–9
value, ascribed to women 13, 20, 21–
    2, 26, 32–3, 52, 58, 59–60
Van Hamel, A.-G. 6, 42, 67
Vashti, Queen 174–5
Verrees, Libert 188
Vespasiano da Bisticci 117

vessel, woman as 72, 156
Veturia 232
Vincent of Beauvais 127, 190
violence, ascribed to men 23, 35, 79–
    80, 89–90, 143–4, 150, 158, 181,
    226, 227, 233, 239
    see also crime
Virgil 126, 205, 222
Virginia 42, 172
virginity, as feminine virtue 10, 20,
    28, 45, 61, 73, 78, 80, 137, 139, 154,
    156, 159, 171, 178–9, 183, 202, 203,
    206, 220
virility, as model for women 7–8,
    175–7, 234, 237, 240
Vita beatae Mariae Magdalenae 111–12,
    147–8, 191–2, 203
Vitellius, Emperor 144
Voaden, Rosalynn 194

Waldensians 188–9, 190, 193, 196
Wallace, David 167
Walters, Lori 18, 45
Warner, Marina 121
weakness, and women 61, 70, 100,
    113–14, 126–8, 134–7, 153, 159,
    168, 173–4, 176, 181, 204, 238–9
Weisl, Angela 181
Weissman, Hope Phyllis 12–13
Westphal, Sarah 180
widows 8, 10, 66, 91, 137, 159–60, 171,
    173–4, 179–80
Wiesner, Marry E. 194
Willard, Charity Cannon 46, 89
Wilson, Katharina M. 17, 158
Winstead, Karen 183–4, 192
wisdom, and women 21, 61, 192, 195
Wogan-Browne, Jocelyn 80, 151,
    183–4
Woodbridge, Linda 3, 9, 10, 20, 63–5,
    81–2, 119, 179
writers, women 2, 4, 7–8, 47, 95, 98,
    128–9, 136, 152, 159, 193–4, 222,
    243
Wyclif, John 72, 126

Zarephath, widow of 66, 171
Zenobia 225
Zorobabel 52–9, 61, 87